Economics of Social Issues

Economics of Social Issues

Ansel M. Sharp
Frank W. Wilson Professor of Political Economy
The University of the South

Charles A. Register
Kent State University

Richard H. Leftwich
Leftwich Associates

1988 Eighth Edition

BUSINESS PUBLICATIONS, INC.
Plano, Texas 75075

© BUSINESS PUBLICATIONS, INC., 1974, 1976, 1978, 1980, 1982, 1984, 1986, and 1988

This book was set in Palatino by The Clarinda Company.
The editors were Michael W. Junior, Janette S. Stecki, Ann Cassady, and Jean Roberts.
The production manager was Bette Ittersagen.
The drawings were done by Jay Bensen/Artforce.
Arcata Graphics/Kingsport was the printer and binder.

ISBN 0-256-06173-4

Library of Congress Catalog Card No. 87-71674

Printed in the United States of America

1 2 3 4 5 6 7 8 9 0 K 5 4 3 2 1 0 9 8

PREFACE

The objectives and the orientation of the eighth edition of *Economics of Social Issues* remain the same as in previous editions. Our objectives are to (1) create student interest in the study of economics and (2) provide a framework of basic analytical tools useful in the analysis of social problems. To reach these objectives, we first introduce and discuss an issue. Next, we develop the economic concepts and principles germane to the issue. Then we apply the principles to the issue to discover if there are ways in which they can help us resolve it. The arrangement of the issues in the book is planned to provide a logical development of basic economic concepts and to reinforce understanding of those concepts through repeated use and application. As always, we are concerned about the timeliness of our issues and their usefulness in helping students learn the important basic principles of economics.

NEW FEATURES

There are no new chapters in this edition of our book; however, there are many new features. One of the most important is that Charles A. Register has joined Sharp and Leftwich as a coauthor. In general, there is more emphasis on empiricism and the use of graphic presentation. More specifically, the changes and additions are (1) empirical evidence of the impact of the minimum wage on teenage employment in Chapter 2; (2) a new section in Chapter 7 on concentration ratios and their use as a measure of the degree of potential monopoly power, including empirical estimates; (3) two new sections in Chapter 7 including a discussion of the dead weight loss due to monopoly and empirical estimates of this loss; (4) a new discussion of the costs and benefits of free trade in Chapter 9, emphasizing the net loss to the U.S. economy due to Japan's limits on auto exports to the U.S.; (5) a rewrite of the section on the factors explaining the rapid growth in health care costs in Chapter 10; (6) a reorganization of the section on government attempts to alleviate poverty in Chapter 11, including two new parts—government programs for the poor and the real growth and relative importance of low-income programs; (7) a new section in Chapter 12 on comparable worth pay systems; (8) a rewrite of the section on supply policies and the economy in the 1980s; (9) new sections with charts on the rate of inflation and historical data on the growth of the money supply; (10) a new section on the Tax Reform Act of 1986; and (11) a new discussion and section on the federal debt as a percent of total credit market debt.

We are grateful to the users of the book who have been good enough to send us comments and suggestions for this edition. We will welcome your help as we prepare the ninth edition. We especially want to thank the following persons who have reviewed the book in the past, giving us much guidance and help for the revision:

John Altazen, *University of New Orleans;* Michael W. Babcock, *Kansas State University;* Walter Baumgartner, *SUNY–Oneonta State College;* David Blanchard, *University of Wisconsin-Oshkosh;* Basil Cooil, *Tompkins Cortland Community College;* Harry L. Cook, *Southern Oregon State College;* Edward J. Deak, *Fairfield University;* James H. Dukes, *University of West Florida;* Allen Early, *West Texas State College;* James Gapinski, *Florida State University;* David E. R. Gay, *University of Arkansas;* George H. Hand, *Southern Illinois University;* Sydney Hicks, *Interfirst Bank of Dallas;* Doug Hodo, *University of Texas–San Antonio;* Willard W. Howard, *Phoenix College;* John Jambura, *Eastern Oregon State College;* Barry Krissoff, *Western Michigan University;* Howard D. Leftwich, *Oklahoma Christian College;* E. Victor Maafo, *North Carolina Central University;* Thomas McCann, *Northeastern Louisiana University;* James McLain, *University of New Orleans;* Douglas McNeil, *McNeese State University;* Jim Mangum, *Louisiana Tech University;* James Marsden, *University of Kentucky;* Charles Meyerding, *Inver Hills Community College;* Jeff Moore, *University of Houston;* Clair E. Morris, *United States Naval Academy;* Roland Mullins, *Arkansas State University;* Dave Nagao, *Sacramento City College;* John Neal, *Lake-Sumter Community College;* Thomas Parsons, *Massachusetts Bay Community College;* Michael Sattinger, *SUNY at Albany;* Harold M. Seeberger, *Heidelbert College;* Robert Smith, *Louisiana State University;* Gary L. Stone, *Winthrop College;* Philip F. Warnken, *University of Missouri;* and Shiu-fang Yu, *Texas Tech University.*

We gratefully acknowledge Charles Smith of *California State University—Fresno* and Steven J. Weiss of the *University of Toledo* for their help with this edition.

We would like to thank two graduate students, Cynthia Rogers and Timothy Walters, for their valuable assistance in the collection of data. We would also like to thank Malinda Sutherland for her editorial advice and assistance. We, however, are responsible for errors of fact and theory.

Ansel M. Sharp
Charles A. Register
Richard H. Leftwich

Contents

Introduction

1. **Human Misery**   3
    The World Poverty Problem, **4**   *Factors generating concern.*
    Population aspects of poverty. World Poverty and Economics, **6**
    Our insatiable wants. Our limited means. The capacity of the
    economy to produce. Living standards. Causes of Poverty and the
    Requisites of Economic Growth, **12**   *Quality of the labor force.*
    Stock of capital and capital accumulation. Technology. Efficiency.
    Population. Can Governments Help? **17**   *Governments of LDCs.*
    Governments of DCs. Summary, **20**

Part One
Resource Allocation

2. **Government Control**   25
    Why Do Governments Control Prices? **26**   *Price floors. Price*
    ceilings. Some Useful Economic Concepts, **28**   *Market*
    structure. Demand. Supply. Competitive market price determination.
    Price elasticity of demand. Economic Analysis of Price Floors,
    37   *Agricultural markets. Labor markets.* Economic Analysis of
    Price Ceilings, **48**   *Housing markets. Natural gas markets.*
    Summary and Evaluation, **60**

3. **Economics of Higher Education**   63
    Problems in Higher Education, **64**   *What kinds of services? How*
    much service? What institutional structure? Who should pay? The
    economic basis of the problems. The "Product" of Higher

Education, **66** *Investment in human capital. Direct consumption. Social spillovers. The incidence of the benefits.* Economic Concept of Cost, **68** *The Alternative cost principle revisited. Explicit and implicit costs.* The Costs of Higher Educational Services, **72** *The explicit costs. The implicit costs. Sources of support. The incidence of the costs.* Economic Evaluation of the Problems, **77** *What kinds of services? How much service? Who should pay? An alternative institutional structure.* Summary, **89**

4. **Energy Problems**   93
The Problems Perceived by the Public, **95** The Economics of Energy, **96** *Demand. Supply.* How to Create Energy Problems, **104** *Price controls. Allocations of crude oil. Conservation and other measures.* Toward Alleviating the Problems, **111** *The adequacy of petroleum supplies. Alternative energy sources. The efficiency of the price mechanism. The role of the government.* Summary, **118**

5. **Economics of Crime and Its Prevention**   123
What Is Crime? **124** *Immorality? Illegality? Classification of criminal acts. Causes of crime.* The Costs of Crime, **127** Individually and Collectively Consumed Goods, **128** *Individually consumed goods. Collectively consumed goods. Semicollectively consumed goods. The "free rider" problem. Government production of collectively consumed items.* The Economics of Crime Prevention Activities, **131** *The "correct" level. Allocation of the crime prevention budget.* The Economics of Legalizing Illegal Activities, **137** Summary, **139**

6. **Pollution Problems**   143
What Is Pollution? **144** *The environment and its services. Recycling of wastes and the concept of pollution. Common forms of pollution.* Economics of Pollution, **149** *Why polluters pollute. Pollution and resource use. The costs of controlling pollution. The benefits of controlling pollution. The appropriate level of pollution control.* What Can Be Done about Pollution? **159** *Direct control. Indirect controls. Private property rights.* Summary, **164**

7. **The Economics of Bigness**   167
The Public View of Big Businesses, **168** The Economics of Monopoly Power, **168** *What is monopoly power? Outputs and prices. Entry restrictions. Nonprice competition.* Should We Fear Bigness? **183** *Bigness and monopoly power. Outputs and prices. Entry restrictions and resource allocation. Nonprice competition. Income distribution.* Summary, **187**

8. **Consumerism**   191
    The Consumer's Problems, **192**   *Shady business practices. Why
    the practices occur. Consequences of the practices.* The Nature of
    Consumerism, **196**   *Description. Private consumer adovcates. The
    role of the government.* The Economics of Consumerism, **198**
    The economic benefits. The economic costs. Evaluation, **202**   *The
    provision of information. The prevention of spillover costs. Protection
    from business manipulation.* Summary, **204**

9. **Protectionism versus Free Trade**   209
    The Controversy over International Trade, **210**   *The
    protectionist viewpoint. The free-trade viewpoint.* The Economics of
    International Trade, **212**   *How trade takes place. Production
    possibilities. The principle of comparative advantage. How
    international trade is financed.* Analysis of the Controversy,
    221   *Protection from cheap foreign goods. Payments problem.
    Protection of key industries.* Summary, **225**

10. **Health Issues**   229
    Growth and Nature of Health Services, **230**   *Health care
    dollars—where they came from and where they went. Factors
    explaining the growth in expenditures for personal health services.
    Special characteristics of health services.* Health Care Problems,
    237   *The public view. The economist's view.* Analysis of demand
    for health services, **238**   *Elasticity of demand. Factors changing
    the demand for health services.* Analysis of Supply of Health
    Services, **242**   *Supply characteristics: Physicians. Supply
    characteristics: Hospitals. Factors affecting the supply of hospital
    services.* Evaluation of the U.S. Health Care System, **245**
    Reducing entry barriers. Increasing efficiency. National Health
    Insurance, **250**   *Basic issues. Alternative proposals to national
    health insurance.* A Final Look at Rising Health Care Costs,
    254   *Supply approach. Demand approach. Reform approach.*
    Summary, **259**

Part Two
Distribution of Income

11. **Poverty Problems**   265
    Poverty in Terms of Absolute Income Levels, **266**   *What is
    poverty? Who are the poor? The upward struggle of the poor.*
    Poverty in Terms of Income Distribution, **270**   *Income equality.
    Income inequality.* The Economic Causes of Poverty, **273**
    Determinants of resource prices and employment. Determination of

*individual or family income. Determinants of income distribution.
Causes of differences in labor resource ownership. Causes of
differences in capital resource ownership. Summary of the causes of
poverty.* Government Attempts to Alleviate Poverty, **277**
*Government programs primarily for the poor. Real growth and
relative importance of low-income programs. Evaluation of low-
income programs.* Negative Income Tax Proposals, **282** *The
negative income tax. Evaluation of the negative income tax scheme.*
Summary, **284**

12. **Discrimination**   289
What Is Discrimination? **290** *The public view. A working
definition.* Economic Analysis of Discrimination, **290** *Sources
of market discrimination. Kinds of market discrimination. Economic
costs of discrimination.* Nonmarket Discrimination, **297** *Social
discrimination. Educational discrimination.* What Can be Done
about Discrimination? **298** *Reduce tastes for discrimination.
Reduce market imperfections. Reduce discrimination in development
of human capital. Reduce occupational segregation.* The
Comparable Worth Controversy, **302** *Proponents. Opponents.
Comparable worth: A definitive conclusion?* Summary, **304**

**Part 3
Stabilization**

13. **Unemployment Issues**   309
Some Effects of Unemployment, **309** *Effects on GNP. Effects
on social relations.* What Is Unemployment? **311** *General
definition. Involuntary unemployment.* Analysis of the
Unemployment Problem, **312** *Types of unemployment. Further
dimensions of the unemployment problem.* What Causes People to
Lose Their Jobs? **316** *Circular flow of economic activity.
Aggregate demand. Aggregate supply. Aggregate demand and
supply. Reasons for deficient aggregate demand. Reasons for weak
aggregate supply.* Combating Unemployment, **325** *Aggregate
demand policies. Aggregate supply policies and the economy in the
1980s.* Summary, **328**

14. **Inflation**   333
Meaning and Measurement of Inflation, **334** *Inflation defined.
Further aspects of inflation. Measurement of inflation. Rate of
inflation.* Economic Effects of Inflation, **338** *Equity effects.
Efficiency effects. Output effects.* What Is Money? **340** *Functions
of money. The basic money supply (M1). Other money measures.*
The Process of Creating Money, **343** *Commercial banks. Other*

depository institutions. Balance sheet of a bank. The fractional reserve banking system. Demand deposit creation. The Issue of Control, **348** *The Federal Reserve System. Federal Reserve controls. Federal Reserve targets.* Inflationary Causes and Cures, **351** *Quantity theory of money. Demand-pull inflation. Cures for demand-pull inflation. Cost-push inflation. Demand-pull and then cost-push inflation. Is there a cure for cost-push inflation?* Summary, **358**

Part Four
The Public Sector

15. **Government Expenditure and Tax Issues**   363
What Are People Afraid of? **363** *Size of government. Tax inequities.* The Problem of Size, **365** *Government expenditures. Government receipts.* Economic Analysis of the Problem of Size, **368** *An efficient level of government expenditures. Collective goods and services. External benefits and costs. Income distribution. Summary.* Tax Principles and Analysis, **374** *Tax equity. Tax efficiency. Principles of shifting and incidence.* Who Really Pays Taxes? **378** *Federal, state, and local tax distribution in 1980. Federal tax incidence versus state and local tax incidence. Tax rates by type of tax.* Policy Reforms, **381** *The problem of size. Income tax reform: A dream come true.* Summary, **387**

16. **The Big National Debt**   391
The Course of the National Debt, **391** The Relative Growth in the National Debt, **392** *Gross federal debt as a percent of GNP. Federal debt held by the public as a percent of total credit market debt.* What Is the National Debt? **395** *Types of federal securities. Who owns the national debt?* Problems with a Large National Debt, **397** *The views of the public. The concern of economists. Summary in regard to national debt problems.* Economic Analysis of National Debt Financing, **400** *Methods of finance. Economic effects of government debt financing. Differing effects of tax and debt financing.* Managing a Large National Debt, **405** *Debt management policy. Debt management principles.* When Should the Government Borrow? **406** *Public investments. Economic instability. Is government debt accumulation necessary during wartime? A budget proposal.* Summary, **410**

Glossary   413

Index   423

INTRODUCTION

HUMAN MISERY

Introduction
The world poverty problem
  Factors generating concern
  Population aspects of poverty
World poverty and economics
  Our insatiable wants
  Our limited means
  The capacity of the economy to
    produce
  Living standards
**Causes of poverty and the requisites of
economic growth**
  Quality of the labor force
  Stock of capital and capital
    accumulation
  Technology
  Efficiency
  Population
Can governments help?
  Governments of LDCs
  Governments of DCs
Summary

**Checklist of
Economic Concepts**

Malthusian theory
Wants
Labor resources
Capital resources
Technology
Production
Alternative costs
Gross national product, current
  dollar
Gross national product, real
Gross national product, per
  capita
Production possibilities curve
Living standards
Price index numbers
Efficiency
Lesser developed countries
Developed countries
Social overhead capital

1

Human Misery

The biggest issue of them all

A poor man in a least developed country—and his number runs into millions—suffers from poor nutrition. He is vulnerable to diseases. His average life span is short. He lives in huts where squalor perpetually surrounds him. He is illiterate both in letter and skills. He does not get his meals regularly, but when he does, he is haunted with the fear of where his next meal will come from. He is clad in rags, if at all. He walks without a pair of shoes. Lack of hygiene, minimal food, or contagious diseases have inflicted some scars on his body. He lives mostly in villages—remote and inaccessible to the rest of the world—or in slums or shanty towns. The water he drinks is neither safe nor clean. He is either unemployed or underemployed. But when he is employed he is overworked and underpaid.

He suffers from apathy and ignominy. From birth to death he remains a destitute. Usually he dies an infant, but if he does survive, dearth and want haunt him to his end. Flood, famine, drought, and other natural disasters continually plague him. If he is a villager, he may be landless; if he is a town-dweller, he rarely has a roof over his head. When the price goes up, the quality and quantity of his food goes down, because his income can no longer buy him the food he needs. His wife if she is pregnant can only have a worse fate.

He cannot buy books for his children nor pay fees for the school, let alone the tool-box he would love to buy for them to make their ends meet. When he falls ill, he cannot pay fees to a doctor, nor can he buy the medicine for himself let alone getting better amenities of life on these crises. He can neither read nor afford to buy a newspaper. A radio-transistor is a luxury to him. Many of his kin never see a bicycle. Starvation and death stare him at his face as in medieval times. Indeed, for him, times have not changed since the Dark Ages. And as though these afflictions were not enough, it is he—and this is the greatest

3

irony of all—who gives birth to the largest number of children, thus spreading and multiplying misery to a dark universe of destitution. When death comes to him finally, he seems to be happier than those he has left behind him.

I speak of a destitute at such length not merely because this occasion places on me the special obligation to speak for him, but even more, because his story is perpetrated on a scale and dimension that indeed is tragic in view of what man can do for man and yet is not done. . . .

Let us resolve to work together, to work with the people and governments of the less-developed world, to help the poor man out of his poverty.[1]

THE WORLD POVERTY PROBLEM

Some two thirds of the world's population go to sleep hungry at night. Famine occurs periodically in parts of Asia and Africa, the latest example being mass starvation in Ethiopia. Most of the hungry have no protection from the summer's heat or the winter's cold. They receive little or no medical care and live in unsanitary surroundings. Infant mortality is high and life expectancy is low. They are unable to read or write. Although poverty is as old as the human race itself, the concern that most of us feel for its victims is of fairly recent origin, dating roughly from World War II.

Factors generating concern

Never before in the history of the world were so many people transported to so many different countries and exposed to so many different cultures as during World War II. Military personnel from advanced countries stationed in some of the Pacific Islands, Asia, and Africa saw first hand, and for the first time, the grinding subhuman poverty that engulfs a large part of the world's population. Similarly, soldiers from lesser developed areas found themselves in countries where living standards exceeded their wildest dreams. Civilian populations of poverty areas were exposed to "lavish" spending habits of troops from advanced countries. Out of the exchange, knowledge of the economic conditions of the rest of the world received great forward impetus.

More recently, growing awareness of poverty problems has been nurtured by peacetime travel and by advancing technology in trans-

---

[1]Keynote address of Nepal's King Birendra Bir Bikram to the Least Developed Countries Conference, Paris, France, September 1981.

portation and communications networks. Travel abroad has become commonplace. Firms from advanced countries have made an increasing number of commitments abroad, inducing a flow of technical personnel and their families to countries where the commitments are made. Aid programs, along with student and teacher exchanges among countries, have grown steadily. All of these have been facilitated by the availability of jet aircraft. Radio and television technology have made all parts of the world more aware of what is happening in the rest of the world.

The dismantling of colonial empires since World War II and the creation of new independent countries have generated growing interest in world poverty problems and economic development. Rivalry between the United States and the Soviet Union for the allegiance of new and usually very poor countries of Asia and Africa has sparked much concern over the economic well-being of the latter. Revolutions, counter revolutions, and dissipation of resources in civil wars in Asia, Africa, and Latin America may leave us wondering if there is any chance for impoverished miserable people to better their lots.

Population aspects of poverty

It is commonly believed that world poverty is rooted in high rates of population growth and/or population densities. High birth rates of such countries as Mexico, Kenya, and Thailand are thought to be a major economic problem in those countries, holding their living standards down. High population densities in such countries as India, Korea, and the Philippines are believed to impede their economic growth. Much concern over population growth has been evidenced in recent years,[2] but the classic statement of that concern was made in the late 1700s by British clergyman-sociologist-economist Thomas Robert Malthus.[3] He presented the issues logically and systematically, and his analysis is well known today as the Malthusian theory.

Malthus believed that the world's population tends to increase faster than its food supply, keeping the bulk of the population at the verge of starvation or subsistence. He argued that an unrestrained population tends to increase in *geometric* progression, that is, in the series 2–4–8–16–32. . . . The food supply increases in *arithmetic*

---

[2] See Paul R. Ehrlich, *The Population Bomb*, rev. ed. (New York: Ballantine Books, 1978).

[3] Thomas Robert Malthus, *On Population*, ed. Gertrude Himmelfarb (New York: Modern Library, 1960). Originally published in 1778.

progression: 2–4–6–8–10. . . . This being the case, living standards can never rise far above subsistence levels because of constant population pressure on the food supply.

Malthus pointed to two sets of checks or restraints that operate on the total population. The first consists of *positive* checks—starvation, disease or pestilence, and war. All of these are the natural outgrowth of population pressure on the food supply and serve to limit the size of the total population. The second is made up of *preventive* restraints that humans can use to limit population growth. Chief among them are celibacy, late marriage, and birth control. Do these ideas have a familiar, modern ring?

WORLD POVERTY AND ECONOMICS

Recognition that the misery of poverty is the lot of the largest part of the world's population leads us to ask the questions: Why is it so? What are the causes? How can it be alleviated? This in turn leads us directly into the province of economics. An assessment and analysis of poverty problems requires an explicit understanding of the very foundations of economic activity. In this section, we sketch out its fundamental aspects.

Our insatiable wants

Economic activity springs from human wants and desires. Human beings want the things necessary to keep them alive—food and protection from the elements of nature. We usually want a great many other things, too, and the fulfillment of these wants and desires is the end toward which economic activity is directed.

As nearly as we can tell, human wants in the aggregate are unlimited or insatiable. This is true because once our basic needs are met, we desire variety in the way they are met—variety in foods, in housing, in clothing, and in entertainment. Additionally, as we look around, we see other people enjoying things that we do not have (videocassette recorders and home computers, for example), and we think that our level of well-being would be higher if we had those things, too. But most important, want-satisfying activity itself generates new wants. A new house generates wants for new furnishings—the old ones look shabby in the new setting. A college or university education opens the doors to wants that would never have existed if we had stayed on the farm or in the machine shop. To be sure, any one of us can saturate ourselves—temporarily, at least—with any one kind of good or service (like ice cream or beer), but almost all of us would like to have more of almost everything than we now have and higher qualities of purchases than we now can obtain.

Our limited means

The fundamental economic problem is that the means available for satisfying wants are *scarce* or limited relative to the extent of the wants. The amounts and qualities of goods and services per year that an economic system can produce are limited because (1) the resources available to produce them cannot be increased by any great amount in any given year and (2) the technology available for production is subject to a limited degree of annual improvement.

An economy's *resources* are the ingredients that go into the making of goods (like automobiles) and services (like physical examinations). Production is similar to cooking. Resources (ingredients) are brought together; technology is used to process these resources in certain ways (stir and cook them), and finally a good or service results (a cake, perhaps). Some outputs of production processes are used directly to satisfy wants. Others become inputs for additional production processes. The resources available in an economy are usually divided into two broad classifications: (1) labor and (2) capital.

Labor resources consist of all the efforts of mind and muscle that can be used in production processes. The ditch digger's output along with that of the heart surgeon and the university professor is included. There are many kinds and grades of labor resources; their main common characteristic is that they are human.

Capital resources consist of all the nonhuman ingredients that go into the production of goods and services. They include land that provides space for production facilities, elements that enable it to grow crops, and many useful mineral deposits. They also include buildings and equipment that have been built up over time, along with the economy's stock of tools. In addition, all of the raw and semifinished materials that exist in the economy at any given time and that are available for use in production are capital resources. Sheets of steel and grocery store inventories are examples of semifinished materials.

Resources are always scarce relative to the sum total of human wants. Consider the U.S. economy. The U.S. population is about 240 million. Most U.S. citizens want more things than they now have. Can the economy increase next year's production enough to fulfill all of these wants? Obviously not. The labor force available from the present population cannot be increased substantially. Its quantity can be increased slowly over time by increasing the population, but this increases total wants, too. The stocks of buildings, machines, tools, raw and semifinished materials, and usable land are not susceptible to rapid increases either; instead they are accumulated slowly over time.

Technology refers to the known means and methods available for combining resources to produce goods and services. Given the quantities of an economy's labor and capital resources, the better its technology, the greater is the annual volume of goods and services it can turn out. Usually improvements in technology in an economic system result from increasing the scope and depth of its educational processes and from an ample supply of capital that provides a laboratory for experimentation, practice, and the generation of new ideas.

The capacity of the economy to produce

Gross national product. An economy's annual output of goods and services in final form is called its *gross national product* or GNP. For any given year, the upper limits of GNP are determined by the quantities and qualities of resources available to the economy and by the level of technology that can be utilized.

Production possibilities. Given an economy's available stocks of resources and its level of technology, there are any number of combinations of goods and services that can comprise its GNP. For simplicity, suppose that it produces only two items—bread and milk— and that all of its resources are devoted to the production of these two products. The line *AE* in Figure 1–1 represents all possible combinations of bread and milk that can be produced. It is appropriately called the economy's *production possibilities curve.* Thus, GNP may consist of 100,000 loaves of bread per year with no milk as shown by point *A,* or 100,000 quarts of milk per year with no bread as shown by point *E.* Or it may consist of any combination on the curve, such as *B,* containing 90,000 loaves of bread and 40,000 quarts of milk; or *C,* containing 50,000 loaves of bread and 80,000 quarts of milk; or some combination under the curve such as *F,* containing 50,000 loaves of bread and 40,000 quarts of milk.

If an economy's GNP is some combination of goods and services like *F,* which lies below its production possibilities curve, the economic system is not operating efficiently. Some of its resources may be unemployed, used in the wrong places, or wasted. It also may not be using the best available techniques of production.

FIGURE 1–1
Production possibilities curve for an economy

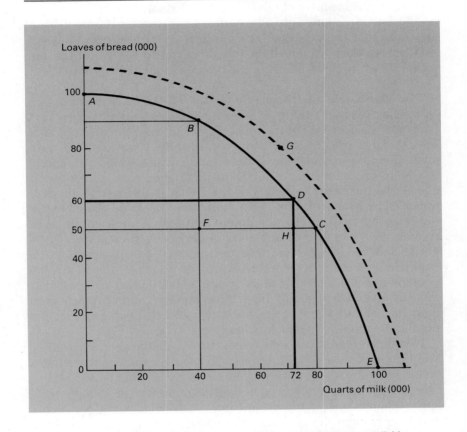

Line *AE* shows all combinations of bread and milk that the economy's available resources and techniques of production can produce annually. Combinations such as *F* imply unemployment of resources or inefficiency in production. Those such as *G* are not attainable.

If the economy were originally producing combination *D*, and then moves to combination *C*, the alternative cost of the additional *HC* of milk is the *HD* of bread that must be given up to produce it.

Combinations of goods and services, like *G*, lying above the production possibilities curve, are not currently attainable. The economy does not have sufficient quantities and qualities of resources and/or good enough techniques of production to push its GNP out to that level. Over time, perhaps, it can accumulate enough resources and/or improve its techniques and press its production possibilities curve outward to the dotted line. The combination G would become a feasible level of GNP.

The line AE represents all possible GNP combinations of bread and milk that the economy can produce when it is operating efficiently. For each combination, all of its resources would be employed, and it would be using the best technology available.

The alternative cost principle. Have you heard the expression, "There ain't no such thing as a free lunch?" Actually this is a simple way of expressing one of the most important concepts in economics, the *alternative cost*, or, as it is often called, the *opportunity cost* principle. Suppose the economy is producing combination D, containing 60,000 loaves of bread and 72,000 quarts of milk. Now let the output of milk be increased to 80,000 quarts. What is the cost of the additional 8,000 quarts of milk? The alternative cost principle embodies the often overlooked obvious point—the cost to a society of an increment in the output of any good or service is the amounts of the goods and services it must give up to obtain the increment in the one. In the present case, according to the principle, the cost of the additional 8,000 quarts of milk is the 10,000 loaves of bread that must be given up to obtain them. An economy cannot produce more than its resources and its technology will allow, so more of one product necessarily means less of others.

Note how alternative costs are measured abstractly in Figure 1–1. The increase in the output of milk and the decrease in the output of bread are represented as a movement from D to C; that is, HD of bread is given up for HC of milk. The ratio HD/HC, which is the approximate slope of the production possibilities curve between D and C, measures the (average) alternative cost per quart of milk of each of the 8,000 quarts making up the increment in the output of milk. It is 10,000 divided by 8,000, or one and a quarter loaves per quart.

Living standards

Gross national product data is reported by countries in value terms—the value of the economy's annual output—rather than in terms of so many loaves of bread and so many quarts of milk. It is necessary to multiply the number of loaves produced in a given year by the price per loaf; do the same computation for milk; and add the total values together to get the value measure of the economy's GNP. Consequently, if we look at data for a series of years and find that GNP in dollar terms is increasing, we cannot really be sure that the economy's output is increasing. The increasing numbers may be due to inflation—rising prices—rather than to rising output.

To correct for inflation, the entire series of GNP *numbers at current price levels* for each year can be converted to a base year price level. Suppose 1984 is the base year and that 1985 GNP is to be converted to the 1984 price level. Suppose also that the 1985 price level is 5 percent higher than that of 1984. This relationship can be depicted with *price index numbers*. The price index number for 1984 is 100, meaning 100 percent, while that of 1985 is 105, or 105 percent. The current year, in this case 1985, GNP is 105 percent of what it would have been had there been no change in the price level between the two years. Consequently it must be divided by 1.05 in order to convert it to 1984 price level terms. If current year price level GNPs for a series of years are all converted to a base year price level, the converted numbers are called *real* GNP numbers. They show us what is happening over time to the economy's real output—whether it is increasing, decreasing, or remaining constant.

Real gross national product data alone indicate little about how well an economy provides for its inhabitants, but if the economy's real GNP is divided by its population for any given year, the result is *per capita real* GNP. This concept is a rough measure of an economy's performance potential. For any one country, per capita real GNP for a series of years is indicative of whether or not the performance of the economy in terms of the *average well-being of its inhabitants* is improving. Among countries, the comparative per capita real GNPs are indicative of the comparative economic performances of the countries.

In Table 1–1 we track the performance of the U.S. economy for the years 1970 through 1985. Current dollar or current price level GNP is listed in column (2). The column (3) implicit price deflator or price index number uses 1982 as the base year. The real GNP data of column (4) are obtained by dividing each year's current dollar GNP by its price index number. Note that real GNP declines in 1974 and 1975, in 1980, and in 1982 even though current dollar GNP appears to indicate that the economy's output increased steadily over the years. Dividing each year's real GNP by population, we obtain per capita real GNP, our best measure of the economy's performance. This column, also, shows the declines in 1974, 1975, 1980, and 1982.

Per capita real GNP is a measure of an economy's standard of living, but it is in no sense a perfect measure. It fails to take into account such things as the distribution of the economy's output among the population. If a few people get the bulk of the output while the masses are at a subsistence level, per capita or average

TABLE 1–1
Gross national product, United States, current dollar and real, 1970–1985

(1) Year	(2) Current dollars (billions)	(3) Implicit price deflator	(4) Real or 1982 dollars (billions)	(5) Population (millions)	(6) GNP per capita 1982 dollars
1970	1,015.5	42.0	2,417.8	205.1	11,788
1971	1,102.7	44.4	2,483.6	207.7	11,958
1972	1,212.8	46.5	2,608.2	209.9	12,426
1973	1,359.3	49.5	2,746.1	211.9	12,959
1974	1,472.8	54.0	2,727.4	213.9	12,751
1975	1,598.4	59.3	2,695.4	216.0	12,479
1976	1,782.8	63.1	2,825.3	218.0	12,960
1977	1,990.5	67.3	2,957.7	220.2	13,432
1978	2,249.7	72.2	3,115.9	222.6	13,998
1979	2,508.2	78.8	3,183.0	225.1	14,140
1980	2,732.0	86.7	3,151.1	227.7	13,839
1981	3,052.6	94.0	3,247.4	229.8	14,131
1982	3,166.0	100.0	3,166.0	232.1	13,641
1983	3,405.7	103.9	3,277.9	235.5	13,919
1984	3,765.0	107.9	3,489.3	237.6	14,686
1985	3,998.1	111.5	3,585.7	238.8	15,015

Source: *Current Population Reports*, Series P-25, No. 952 (May 1984); No. 964 (February 1985); U.S. Department of Commerce, Bureau of Economic Analysis, *Business Conditions Digest*, October 1986, pp. 97–101.

figures provide a distorted picture of individual well-being. But by and large, it is the best measure currently available.

CAUSES OF POVERTY AND THE REQUISITES OF ECONOMIC GROWTH

The economic roots of world poverty become reasonably clear from an examination of the foundations of economic activity. To determine why a particular country is poor, we should look at (1) the quality of its labor force, (2) its stock of capital resources, (3) the state of its technology, and (4) the efficiency with which it employs its resources. If the economy is to provide rising living standards over time, its specific deficiencies in these areas must be determined and corrected. And in the last analysis, if living standards are to rise, the rate of growth in the economy's real GNP must exceed the rate of growth in its population.

Quality of the labor force

Almost without exception the poor countries of the world have labor forces that are not very productive compared with those of wealthy countries. Illiteracy rates are high; often 70 to 90 percent of the population will be unable to read or write. The average level of educational attainment is close to zero; expectations and aspirations of the young are low. Malnutrition and disease take their toll on the physical capacities of the unskilled labor force.

Education is the key to improvement in the quality of a country's population and its labor force. Literacy rates and average levels of education are closely correlated with living standards. To improve the health and the productivity of the labor force, it is necessary that people be able to read such signs as, "Don't urinate in the village water reservoir," and to understand the importance of sanitation for healthy productive bodies. As literacy rates increase, so do the possibilities of upgrading the skills of the labor force. A broad-based primary education system is a prerequisite for literacy, and literacy is, in turn, a basic foundation for economic growth.

Beyond the primary level, secondary and higher education is important in improving labor force quality. Both liberal arts and technical education help develop persons of higher skill levels who can think and innovate. Rather than being conflicting in purpose, they reinforce each other, contributing importantly to labor productivity. But a comprehensive educational system is hard to establish in a country whose population lives close to or at a subsistence level.

Stock of capital and capital accumulation

Small amounts of available capital resources and low capital to labor ratios in a country mean low labor productivity and poverty. The Masai family in Kenya owns little in the way of property or tools. It may own a few cattle. A farmer in India has a wooden plow and perhaps a couple of oxen to pull it. His grain will be cut and gathered by hand and threshed by the hooves of oxen driven around in a circle over a hard threshing floor instead of by mechanical harvesters. Countries without mineral deposits, tools, machines, factories, means of communications and transportation, and educational facilities usually have low per capita real GNPs.

Capital accumulation is necessary if a country is to break out of a poverty prison. Tools and machines must be accumulated and utilized. Factories and roads must be built. Telephone lines must be strung. Mineral deposits must be systematically mined. Land must be fertilized. River channels must be widened and deepened. Plant and animal life must be subjected to careful, genetically sound breeding methods.

Capital accumulation is more difficult to accomplish in a poor economy than in a wealthy one. It requires that the economy not consume its entire annual output and that some part of that output be in the form of new capital goods or resources. Of this latter part of output, some must replace capital resources used up or worn out in producing the annual output. Any extra capital resources above the amount used to keep the stock of capital intact serve to increase the total amount of capital available. It is not easy for a poor country, where many people suffer from malnutrition and starvation, to divert production effort away from food and basic consumption items toward capital accumulation.

Technology

A trip through the countryside and a visit to the industrial production sites in a poor country will reveal primitive techniques of production in use. In Egypt and India waterwheels of types used a thousand years ago are still a primary means of bringing water to the surface. Much of their cloth is produced on hand looms. Burros and ox carts are important means of transportation. Across the country, techniques in use are those requiring large inputs of human effort relative to the inputs of capital resources.

Technological development goes hand in hand with advancing educational levels and with capital accumulation. Innovative thinking and ideas germinate technological advance. And for ideas to bear fruit—or even to survive—the means of testing and proving them must be available. The capital resources of an economy provide the laboratory in which the testing and proving take place. High levels of technology are seldom developed in capital-poor countries.

It is not really essential that poor countries go it alone in improving their techniques. Usually they can borrow much from economically advanced countries. They can import complete sets of techniques as did the Japanese following World War II. And they can send students and scientists, as they do now, to be trained abroad and to bring home with them technological know-how.

Efficiency

In many poor countries, the available resources, both labor and capital, tend not to be either fully employed or most efficiently employed. Land tenure systems may hold land units to sizes too small for efficient production. Traditional ways of doing things often block the adoption of more efficient methods. Workers may be uninformed regarding opportunities for increasing their incomes. Wage systems may make it uneconomical for potential employers to hire the entire labor force, and unemployment may occur. Insufficient capital accumulation to provide new jobs needed by a growing labor force may result in unemployment. The list can be extended on and on.

Whereas improvements in labor force quality, capital accumulation, and technological development all tend to shift the production possibilities curve of Figure 1–1 outward, the achievement of higher levels of efficiency move the economy from some point below the curve toward the curve itself. If inefficiencies occur, the economy will be at a point such as *F*. Increases in efficiency will move the economy toward the curve *AE*.

Population

Are population growth and population densities serious threats to living standards? Have they kept per capita real GNP from rising, or have they been significant in holding down the rate of increase? Is there any evidence that they have caused living standards to deteriorate? Suppose we examine some GNP data to see if any answers to these questions are evident.

In Table 1–2 we classify a sample of countries as *lesser developed* or LDCs and *developed* or DCs. The classification is rough and arbitrary. We have put those with per capita GNPs of less than $1,500 per year in the LDC classification and those with per capita GNPs of $1,500 and above in the DC classification regardless of income distribution within each country.

The sample of LDCs does indeed show substantially higher rates of population growth and lower average per capita real GNP growth rates than does the sample of DCs. Most in the former sample are in the 2.0 to 3.5 percent per year population range while most of the latter are in the 1.5 percent and under range. But there are important exceptions in each classification of countries. Among the LDCs, Morocco, Nigeria, the Philippines, and Thailand all show high population growth rates *and* relatively high per capita real GNP growth rates. Among DCs, Israel, Saudi Arabia, and Venezuela show high population growth rates as well as relatively strong per capita real GNP growth rates. At the very least, we can say that relatively high rates of population growth do *not preclude* growth in per capita real GNP. It may be a factor impeding growth in some instances but is not in itself *the* problem.

Comparative population densities yield some information on the issue of whether overcrowding is a serious problem. The data of Table 1–2 may be a little surprising. Ethiopa has the lowest per capita GNP in the table along with a low growth rate in that important

TABLE 1-2 Per capita GNP and population, actual and growth rates; population density; and life expectancy for males; selected countries, 1970–1980

Country	Population estimate 1980 (millions)	Annual rate of population increase (1975–1980)	Population density per square kilometer 1980	Per capita GNP*	Percentage annual growth rate of per capita GNP (constant prices)		Life expectancy for males at age 0, latest available dates
Lesser developed							
Argentina	27.1	1.3%	10	1,388 (1977)	(1970–79)	1.1	65.2
Chile	11.1	1.7	15	421 (1978)	(1970–78)	–1.0	61.3
Colombia	27.6	2.8	24	1,237 (1980)	(1970–79)	2.9	60.0
Egypt	42.2	2.7	42	435 (1979)	(1970–79)	5.6	51.6
Ethiopia	31.1	2.5	25	91 (1978)	(1970–76)	0.3	37.5
India	663.6	2.0	202	241 (1980)	(1970–77)	1.0	46.4
Korea, Republic of	38.1	1.5	387	1,616 (1979)	(1970–79)	8.4	62.7
Mexico	71.9	3.6	36	1,749 (1979)	(1970–79)	1.6	62.8
Morocco	20.2	3.2	45	657 (1978)	(1970–77)	3.5	53.8
Nigeria	74.1	3.3	83	682 (1977)	(1970–77)	4.5	37.2
Philippines	48.4	2.7	161	457 (1978)	(1970–79)	3.6	59.1
Thailand	47.2	2.4	92	698 (1980)	(1970–79)	4.3	53.6
Average							54.3
Developed							
Canada	23.9	1.0	2	10,584 (1980)	(1970–79)	3.0	70.1
France	53.7	0.4	98	12,137 (1980)	(1970–79)	3.1	69.9
Israel	3.9	2.3	186	5,431 (1980)	(1970–77)	2.4	71.5
Italy	57.0	0.4	189	6,907 (1980)	(1970–79)	2.2	69.7
Japan	116.8	0.9	314	8,873 (1980)	(1970–79)	3.3	73.5
Saudi Arabia	9.0	4.3	4	8,845 (1980)	(1970–78)	7.2	51.5
Singapore	2.4	1.2	4,115	4,495 (1980)	(1970–79)	6.9	65.1
Sweden	8.3	0.3	18	14,881 (1980)	(1970–79)	1.6	72.5
United Kingdom	55.9	1.1	229	9,352 (1980)	(1970–79)	2.1	67.8
United States	227.6	3.0	24	11,363 (1980)	(1970–79)	2.3	69.5
Venezuela	13.9	–0.1	15	4,315 (1980)	(1970–79)	2.3	65.0
West Germany	61.6		248	13,304 (1980)	(1970–79)	2.6	69.0
Average							67.9

*At market prices (U.S. dollars) and dates in parentheses.   Sources: United Nations, *Statistical Yearbook*, 1980 and 1981, pp. 61–70, 144–55.

item. Yet its population density is a low 25 persons per square kilometer. Singapore's per capita GNP is many times that of Ethiopia, and it shows a relatively high growth rate. Its population density is 4,115 persons per square kilometer. Note that the population densities of such DCs as Japan, the United Kingdom, Singapore, and West Germany all exceed that of India, one of the major LDCs. Population densities as such, or "overcrowding," does not seem to be a major impediment to relatively high levels of per capita GNP or to economic growth.

The data of Table 1–2 are consistent with generally accepted demographic theory.[4] In premodern, poor societies, death rates were high, and for such societies to survive it was necessary that their birth rates be high too. In modern times, the lesser developed countries are succeeding—often with the help of the developed countries—in reducing their death rates. Better medical knowledge and health facilities, improvements in sanitation, and higher levels of nutrition are the responsible factors; and these are generally welcomed by the countries in question. But measures to reduce birth rates do not receive the same social approval as those that reduce death rates. Reductions in the birth rate lag behind reductions in the death rate, and it is during the lag period that so-called population explosions occur. But, as the sample of developed countries indicates, the birth rate eventually falls, and the rapid increase in population subsides. Greater affluence and higher education levels help bring the birth rates down.

The available evidence does not indicate that world poverty is *caused* by population pressure—high rates of population growth and/or population density. In some poor countries, population pressure *may be a contributing factor* to poverty, but we must look elsewhere—to the other factors cited above—for the explanation of why so much of the world's population lives in misery.

CAN GOVERNMENTS HELP?

What, if anything, can governments do to help solve world poverty problems? Over the last 55 years, populations have looked increasingly at their governments to solve their problems for them. Governments, in turn, have accepted more responsibilities for solving the economic problems of their populations. Unfortunately, people of-

---

[4]Paul Demeny, "The Populations of the Underdeveloped Countries," in *The Human Population: A Scientific American Book*, ed. *Scientific American* (San Francisco: W. H. Freeman, 1974), pp. 105–15.

ten expect more of their governments than those governments can provide. And governments promise more than they are able to deliver.

Governments of LDCs

All too often in poor countries, government is a part of the problem rather than the agency that helps to solve the problem. Without question, the greatest obstacles to economic development in LDCs are war and political instability. We need only to observe what is happening in Southeast Asia, in the Middle East, in Africa, and in Central America to see that governments of many LDCs are unstable. In their political intrigue and war activities they use up resources that could have been devoted to economic growth and elevation of living standards for their populations.

Ideally, governments of LDCs could enact measures conducive to growth and could avoid policies that impede it. Under the best of circumstances they would pursue policies that would improve the quality of the labor force, enhance capital accumulation, raise levels of technology, increase efficiency, and, perhaps, slow population growth. This is a tall order—more easily said than done.

In most countries where literacy rates are high, governments have assumed responsibilities for primary education. In many countries this responsibility has been extended to secondary and even to higher education. Insofar as it can, the government of an LDC would be well advised to emulate these countries. But universal education does not come easily or without cost. The establishment of an educational system is a slow, expensive task. Physical facilities must be built and a corps of teachers must be trained. LDCs find it very difficult to divert resources from the provision of subsistence goods to the provision of education. The immediate alternative costs of additional education are high for a hungry population.

Most government help in the capital accumulation process will be indirect rather than direct. Governments cannot create new capital resources directly, but they can establish an economic climate favorable to capital accumulation. They can pursue (monetary and fiscal) policies conducive to economic stability. They can enact tax laws that provide special incentives for capital accumulation. It is also important that those who engage in saving and investing in new capital equipment be allowed to reap the rewards for doing so. In many instances, capital accumulation is discouraged because revenue-hungry governments tax away the returns that accrue from it.

Government officials in LDCs often speak glibly about such things as raising the levels of technology and increasing the operating efficiencies of their economies. One of the most positive things they can do in this respect is to press development of *social overhead capital* to the maximum extent that their resources will allow. Transportation networks and communications networks contribute greatly to efficiency. So do energy or power systems.

Sparked by governmental activities, some positive action appears to be underway in certain parts of the world concerning population control. In India, Thailand, and the People's Republic of China, massive government educational efforts for birth control and family planning have been made. In India, voluntary sterilization of both men and women has been subsidized. In China, families are encouraged to have only one child and are heavily taxed for exceeding that number. In any case, during the late 1970s and early 1980s trends in world population growth appear to have turned downward causing population experts to become much more optimistic in their predictions of future population growth.[5]

Governments of DCs

Since World War II, the economically advanced countries of the world have provided some economic assistance to LDCs, partly for humanitarian reasons and partly in hopes of obtaining ideological allegiance from the LDCs. There has been much rivalry between communist countries and those of the Western world. Some aid to LDCs has been channeled through the World Bank. At the same time, individual countries have conducted aid programs of their own. Basically aid takes two forms: (1) loans and grants and (2) technical assistance.

Loans and grants generally are expected to help the recipient countries improve their labor forces, accumulate capital, improve their technological capabilities, and increase the efficiencies of their production processes. They are used to build educational facilities and for sanitary engineering purposes. They help construct power plants, cement plants, communications and transportation facilities, agricultural facilities, and the like. They are also used to import such things as fertilizer, raw and semifinished materials, industrial equipment, agricultural equipment, and spare parts.

Technical assistance helps in upgrading labor force skills and in advancing the technologies of the recipient countries. Much techni-

---

[5]Jan van der Tak, Carl Haub, and Elaine Murphy, "A New Look at the Population Problem," *Futurist* 14, no. 2 (April 1980), pp. 39–46.

cal assistance is turned toward increasing the productivity of agricultural resources, improving educational systems, and raising standards of public health. In addition, advisors from the DCs often assist in getting industrial projects underway.

The World Bank is an organization through which DCs can jointly assist LDCs. It provides both low-interest loans from funds supplied by the DCs and technical assistance to low income countries. Loans are made for a variety of projects, large and small, public and private. Bank officials require that the projects for which loans are made show every promise of paying off both the principal and the interest. The World Bank has been quite successful in this respect but has often been criticized as being too stingy with its loans.

SUMMARY

Abject poverty is without question the major economic problem of the world. This has always been so, but it has become the focus of great concern for nations and for large numbers of persons primarily since World War II. To understand its causes and its possible alleviation, it is necessary to understand the nature of economics and economic activity.

Economic activity is generated by the wants of human beings, which seem to be insatiable in the aggregate. The means available in any economy for satisfying the wants of its population are scarce. They consist of the economy's resources—its labor and its capital—along with its available technology. The supplies of resources, together with the level of technology available, determine the maximum GNP that the country can turn out to satisfy wants. Dividing a country's GNP by its population yields its per capita GNP, which is a rough measure of its standard of living.

The basic elements of economic activity and economic analysis provide insight into the causes of poverty. Poverty stems from low labor force qualities, little capital for labor to work with, low levels of technology, inefficiencies in the use of resources, and, in some instances, excessive rates of population growth. To break out of the poverty trap, a country must make progress in attacking some or all of the causes. But it is unlikely to make much progress unless it achieves a marked degree of political and economic stability.

Developed countries can and do assist LDCs as they strive to improve their economic lots. Aid takes two basic forms: (1) loans or grants and (2) technical assistance. Individual DCs have independent aid programs. They also engage in joint aid programs through such organizations as the World Bank.

SUPPLEMENTARY READING

Brue, Stanley L., and Donald R. Wentworth. "The Reverend Mr. Malthus and the Limits to Growth." In *Economic Scenes: Theory in Today's World*. Englewood Cliffs, N.J.: Prentice-Hall, 1980, pp. 292–304.

A novel approach to summarizing the economics of population growth, resource scarcity, and economic growth.

Ehrlich, Paul R. *The Population Bomb*. Rev. ed. New York: Ballantine Books, 1978.

A scare book written by a biologist with little understanding of economics. It is an important book, however, worthy of the attention of anyone seriously concerned with population problems.

Heilbroner, Robert L. "The Underdeveloped World." In *The Making of Economic Society*. 6th ed. Englewood Cliffs, N.J.: Prentice-Hall, 1980, chap. 12.

Discusses such diverse Third World problems as social inertia, population growth, hidden labor surpluses, lack of capital equipment, trade problems, foreign aid, social and political unrest, and ecological problems.

"Least Developed Countries." *World Health*, June 1982.

Special edition devoted to health problems of the 31 least developed countries of the world.

Mellor, J. W., and B. F. Johnston. "The World Food Equation: Interrelations among Development, Employment, and Food Consumption." *Journal of Economic Literature* 22 (June 1984), pp. 53–74.

A high-level scholarly treatment of the economic problems in developing countries, with emphasis on the question of adequacy of food supplies.

Schultz, Robert S. "Understanding Economic Growth." *Harvard Business Review*, November–December 1966, pp. 32–44, 184.

Addresses such questions as: What are the causes of economic growth? Why does one country grow more rapidly than another? Why does any particular country grow more rapidly at some times than at others?

Van der Tak, Jean; Carl Haub; and Elaine Murphy. "A New Look at the Population Problem." *Futurist* 14, no. 2 (April 1980), pp. 39–48.

An up-to-date report on one of the most critical problems of the late 20th century.

Wong, S. L. "Consequences of China's New Population Policy." *China Quarterly*, no. 98 (June 1984), pp. 220–40.

An excellent discussion of the development of China's one-child-per-couple population control program and of possible side effects of the program.

Part One

RESOURCE

ALLOCATION

GOVERNMENT CONTROL OF PRICES

Why do governments control prices?
  Price floors
  Price ceilings
Some useful economic concepts
  Market structure
  Demand
  Supply
  Competitive market price
    determination
  Price elasticity of demand
Economic analysis of price floors
  Agricultural markets
  Labor markets
Economic analysis of price ceilings
  Housing markets
  Natural gas markets
Summary and evaluation

**Checklist of
Economic Concepts**

Price floor
Minimum wages
Price ceiling
Market
Market, competitive
Market, monopolistic
Market, imperfectly competitive
Demand
Demand, changes in
Supply
Supply, changes in
Price, equilibrium
Surplus
Shortage
Elasticity of demand, price
Unemployment

2

Government Control

of Prices

A boon to the poor?

The American farmer has in many ways retained a privileged place. It's a position prompted in part by necessity; policymakers have long recognized that agriculture could not be left completely to the vicissitudes of nature and the wild price swings that could be generated by the free market. To ensure a stable, relatively inexpensive food supply for the nation's consumers and to keep farming communities intact, the government long ago stepped in, building a variety of programs designed to make sure farmers stayed in business.

Most of today's federal farm programs date from the Great Depression, when plummeting farm prices decimated much of the farming community. New Deal legislation was devised to control production and prop up prices; it also enshrined into law the concept of "parity"—the notion that the ratio of farm prices to farmers' costs should be maintained at the same robust level it reached during the prosperous farm years of 1910 to 1914. From this notion has grown a cornucopia of farm programs. The government supports prices for wheat, corn, rice, cotton, tobacco, and eight other commodities by storing farmers' produce and giving them loans so that they can wait for prices to rise. When farm prices are low, Washington also gives farmers so-called deficiency payments based on a scheme of "target" prices. The dairy industry is subsidized outright: whatever dairy farmers can't sell on the open market, the government will buy automatically, paying a fixed rate for butter, milk, or cheese regardless of how much it is forced to buy.[1]

---

[1]Susan Dentzer, John McCormick, Rich Thomas, Diane Weathers, Pamela Abramson, Daniel Shapiro, and Penelope Wang, "Bitter Harvest," *Newsweek*, February 18, 1985, pp. 55–56.

WHY DO GOVERNMENTS CONTROL PRICES?

Governments engage in fixing the prices on selected items from time to time. Sometimes they set floors under the prices of certain goods, not allowing them to be sold at lower prices. Sometimes they set ceilings on the prices of other goods, not allowing them to be sold at more than those prices. Usually, when selected price controls are set by governments, they are intended to benefit specific special interest groups in the economy.

Price floors

When price floors or minimum prices are fixed for particular items, the intent of the government usually is to increase the incomes of those who sell them. Under what circumstances are price floors likely to be set? If there are groups of sellers whose incomes are relatively low, those sellers may be able to convince legislatures or Congress that price floors are in order. Or, if there are groups of sellers that are politically strong, they may be able to get the idea across with equal effectiveness. Two classic cases come to mind.

The first case is that of agricultural price supports. From the 1920s to the present, per capita farm income has been below per capita nonfarm income. In addition, the agricultural sector of the economy has had great political clout. Consequently, from 1933 to the present, farm price supports have been a major fact of life in the operation of the U.S. economy, and farmers continue to press for still higher price guarantees.

The second case is that of minimum wage legislation. The Fair Labor Standards Act of 1938 established the first federal minimum wage for workers in designated industries. Over the years, its coverage has been extended greatly, and the minimum rates have been increased substantially. In addition, many state governments have enacted minimum wage laws of their own to cover workers not covered by federal minimums. Minimum wage laws have had wide support from the general public. They apply, of course, to workers at the lower end of the income scale. They have generally been favored by labor unions and by persons professing strong social consciences.

Price floors on certain items also may come about in ways other than through direct legislation. In the barbering trade in many states, barbers of each county or city may get together and establish minimum prices for haircuts and other services. Once determined, these joint decisions have the force of law. Labor unions, through government-approved collective bargaining procedures, may be able to establish price floors that are just as effective as legislated ones. In these and other cases, the analysis of the nature and effects of price floors is not much different from that of the two classic cases.

Price ceilings

Price ceilings or maximum prices have been put into effect from time to time in the United States for two primary purposes. They have been established across the board in attempts to hold inflation in check. They have also been used on a selective basis to keep the purchase of certain items within reach of those at the lower end of the income scale. This latter purpose may also have an anti-inflationary intent. Across-the-board ceilings in the United States have been confined largely to war-time periods except for the 90-day wage price freeze of August 1971, but selective price ceilings have been used in specific markets at other times. We shall concern ourselves in this chapter with selective price ceilings, using as illustrations rent controls and price ceilings on natural gas.

Rent controls have been used in metropolitan areas as a device to hold housing costs in check for low income groups. The outstanding example is undoubtedly that of New York City, which has had rent controls in effect since World War II. On a much smaller scale, it is common for a university to set rental rates on university apartments at relatively low levels to help alleviate problems encountered by low income students.

The control of natural gas prices at the wellhead dates from 1954 when the Supreme Court ruled in *Phillips Petroleum Co.* v. *Wisconsin* that the Federal Power Commission should regulate the price of gas that moved in interstate commerce. The FPC moved slowly and laboriously in putting controls into effect. By the early 1960s the efforts of the commission began bearing fruit. Since 1968 it has had the price of natural gas moving in interstate commerce effectively controlled. With the establishment of the Department of Energy in 1978, the Federal Power Commission became the Federal Energy Regulatory Commission (FERC), maintaining essentially the same powers and functions as before. In November of 1978 Congress passed the Natural Gas Policy Act to extend its regulatory powers to gas sold in intrastate commerce, thus giving it effective control over most natural gas prices at the wellhead until 1985. At that time, following a series of decontrol stages, FERC control over natural gas prices effectively ceased. We use natural gas price controls as an example, not because they constitute a serious current problem, but because they illustrate historically the serious disruptions that price ceilings can cause in the operation of an economy.

SOME USEFUL ECONOMIC CONCEPTS

Price floors and price ceilings have been enacted in response to specific problems of certain groups of people. Generally, they have been enacted by legislative groups in good faith and in the expectation that they would help alleviate the problems to which they were addressed. Almost invariably, the results have been unsatisfactory. The price controls have tended to generate more problems than they have solved. Why has this been so? What has gone wrong?

To analyze and assess the impact of price controls, some economic concepts beyond those developed in Chapter 1 are required. These new concepts are (1) market structure, (2) demand, (3) supply, (4) market price determination, and (5) elasticity of demand. We shall develop these in turn.

Market structure

When the buyers and sellers of a product interact with one another and engage in exchange, a *market* exists. The geographic area of any one market is simply the area within which buyers and sellers are able to transfer information and the ownership of whatever is being exchanged. Some markets are local in scope; others are national or international.

The degree of competition that exists in markets is important in economic analysis. At one end of the spectrum, markets fall into the *purely competitive* classification. At the other they are classified as *purely monopolistic*. The markets of the world range all the way from one end of the classification system to the other.

Competitive markets. For a market to be purely competitive it must exhibit three important characteristics. First, there must be enough buyers and sellers of the product so that no one of them acting alone can influence its price. To illustrate this point, consider the individual consumer buying a loaf of bread in a supermarket or an individual farmer selling wheat at a grain elevator. Second, the product price must be free to move up or down with no government or other kinds of price fixing impeding its movement. Third, buyers and sellers must be mobile. This means that any buyer is free to move among alternative sellers and can buy from whoever will sell at the lowest price. Similarly, sellers are free to move among alternative buyers and can sell to whoever will pay the highest price. Few markets are purely competitive in the sense of rigorously fulfilling all three requirements, but some may be almost so. Agriculture fulfills all but the second characteristic.

Monopolistic markets. A purely monopolistic selling market, at the other end of the spectrum, is one in which there is a single seller of a product. The seller is able to manipulate the product price to its own advantage. It is able to block potential competitors out of the market—frequently with government help. In many parts of the country, a single hospital serves an entire county. In these areas, the hospital market is a pure monopoly. While examples exist, most markets are not pure monopolies.

Imperfectly competitive markets. Most markets in the United States fall somewhere between the purely competitive and the purely monopolistic extremes. Some have predominantly competitive characteristics, but may exhibit monopolistic tendencies. Others tend toward the monopolistic pole but may show some evidences of competition. Others are a mixed bag—in some ways competitive and in other ways tending toward monopoly. Most are subject to government restrictions or rules of one kind or another. We call this broad category of markets *imperfect competition.*

Demand

The demand for a product refers to the quantities of that product that consumers or buyers will purchase. These quantities are expressed in rates per *time period,* such as 10,000 bushels of wheat per month. It makes little sense to say that demand is 10,000 bushels unless the time span for which that amount would be purchased is specified. Further, the amount purchased per month, or per year, or whatever the specified time period is, depends on the price per bushel that buyers have to pay. It also depends on (1) the *prices of substitutes* and of *complements* for the product, (2) *the purchasing power of buyers,* (3) buyers' psychological *tastes and preferences,* and (4) the *number of buyers* in the group under consideration.

Definition. Demand for a good or service is defined as the set of quantities per time period that buyers are willing to purchase at various alternative prices of the item, *other things being equal.* We can think in terms of a scientific experiment in which the "other things being equal" are the given conditions of the experiment. These are the factors (other than the price of the good) that were enumerated in the preceding paragraph. When these factors are held constant, how much will buyers purchase at each of various alternative price levels?

If we could actually consult all buyers of wheat, for example, we could devise a table something like Table 2–1, which is called a *de-*

TABLE 2–1
A demand schedule for wheat

Price (dollars)	Quantity (bushels per month)	Price (dollars)	Quantity (bushels per month)
$10	1,000	$5	6,000
9	2,000	4	7,000
8	3,000	3	8,000
7	4,000	2	9,000
6	5,000	1	10,000

mand schedule for wheat. This demand schedule is plotted as a demand curve in Figure 2–1. Both illustrate a fundamental characteristic called the *law of demand*—the lower the price of the product, the more buyers will wish to purchase; and the higher the price, the less they will wish to purchase, other things being equal.

Changes. Since demand refers to an entire demand schedule or demand curve, a *change in demand* means a shift in the position of the entire curve. The shift results from a change in one of the "other things equal" that would cause buyers to desire more or less of the product at each possible price. Suppose, for example, that an increase in buyers' purchasing power causes them to desire an additional 1,000 bushels of wheat at each possible price. In Figure 2–2, the demand curve shifts (increases) from DD to D_1D_1. An increase or decrease in the quantity buyers wish to purchase in response to changes in the price of the product, like the movement from A to B in Figure 2–2, is called a *change in quantity demanded*. It is not called a change in demand.

Supply

Definition. The *supply* of a product refers to the quantities per time period that sellers are willing to place on the market at alternative prices of the item, *other things being equal*. In the case of supply, these "other things" are (1) resource prices and (2) technology.

If the suppliers of wheat were asked how much per unit of time they would place on the market at alternative price levels, their answers would provide the information for a *supply schedule* or *supply curve* of the product, as illustrated in Table 2–2 and Figure 2–3. Ordinarily, suppliers would be expected to place more on the market at higher prices, so most supply curves slope upward to the right.

FIGURE 2–1
A demand curve for wheat

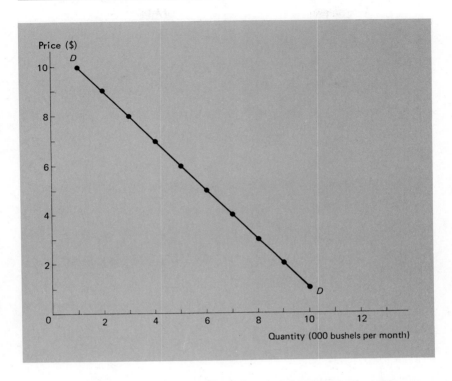

The numbers of Table 2–1 plotted graphically are points forming the demand curve
DD. The demand curve shows the quantities that all buyers will purchase at alternative
prices, other things being equal

There are two reasons for this. First, since it is more profitable to
produce at the higher prices, each individual supplier is induced to
place more on the market. Second, the greater profits earned from
higher prices induce new producers to enter the market.

Changes. The same distinction is made between a *change in supply*
and a *change in the quantity supplied* because of a price change as was
made for the corresponding demand concepts. In Figure 2–4 a shift
from SS to S_1S_1 is a change in supply, and a movement from F to G
is a change in quantity supplied. An improvement in technology
that makes it possible for each output level to be produced at a
lower cost per unit causes an increase in supply, since it also makes
it possible to produce more at each possible price level than before.

FIGURE 2–2
A change in demand

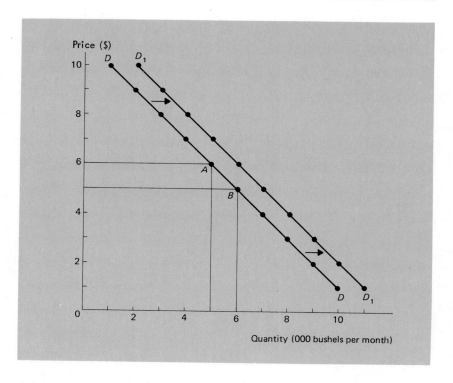

A change in demand means a shift of the entire demand curve from one position to another—say from DD to D_1D_1. A movement from A to B is not called a change in demand. Rather, it is called a change in quantity demanded because of a price change.

TABLE 2–2
A supply schedule for wheat

Price (dollars)	Quantity (bushels per month)	Price (dollars)	Quantity (bushels per month)
$1	2,000	$ 6	7,000
2	3,000	7	8,000
3	4,000	8	9,000
4	·5,000	9	10,000
5	6,000	10	11,000

FIGURE 2–3
A supply curve

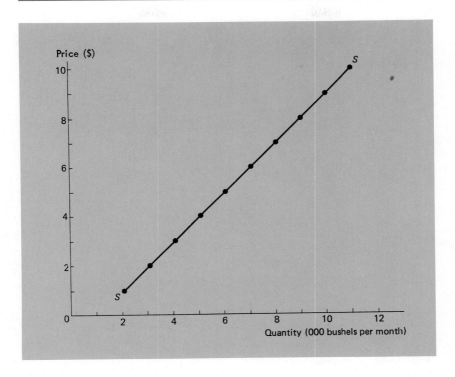

Prices and quantities from Table 2–2 are plotted as points forming the supply curve *SS*. The supply curve shows the quantities that all suppliers will place on the market at alternative prices, other things being equal.

Competitive market price determination

Equilibrium price. The price of a product in a competitive market is determined by the interaction of buyers and sellers—or, as economists like to say, by the forces of demand and supply. How this comes about is shown in Figure 2–5. The supply curve shows that at a price of $5 per bushel sellers want to sell 6,000 bushels of wheat per month. The demand curve shows that at this price, 6,000 bushels per month is what buyers want to buy. The price at which buyers want to buy the same quantity that sellers want to sell is termed the *equilibrium price*.

FIGURE 2–4
A change in supply

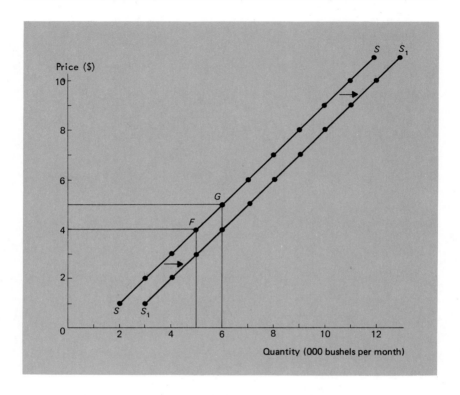

A shift in the supply curve from *SS* to S_1S_1 is called a change in supply. A movement along *SS* from *F* to *G* is called a change in quantity supplied because of a price change.

Effects of a price above equilibrium. If the price is not at the equilibrium level, market forces are set in motion that move it toward that level. Suppose, for example, that the price of wheat in Figure 2–5 were $7 per bushel. Sellers would want to place 8,000 bushels per month on the market, but buyers would be willing to buy only 4,000 bushels. Thus, there would be a *surplus* of 4,000 bushels per month. Any individual seller not able to sell all of his supplies would have an incentive to cut price a little below that at which the others sell. The price advantage would enable the seller to dispose of its surplus. As long as surpluses exist, sellers have incentives to undercut one another. When the price has been driven down to $5 per bushel, no seller is caught with a surplus, and the undercutting stops.

Effects of a price below equilibrium. On the other hand, if the price were $4 per bushel, buyers would want 7,000 bushels per month, but sellers would be willing to place only 5,000 bushels on the market. A *shortage* of wheat would exist. Individual buyers want-

FIGURE 2–5
Competitive market price determination

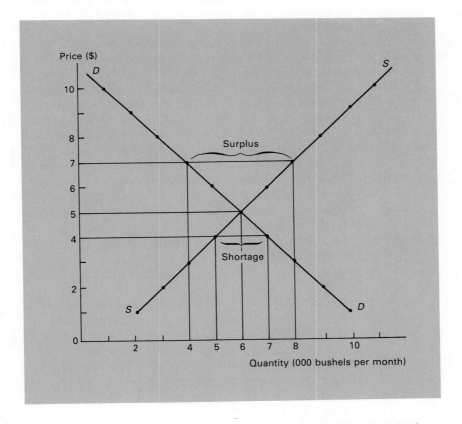

The demand curve and the supply curve together show how the equilibrium price for a product is determined in the market. If the price is above the equilibrium level, surpluses occur, and sellers undercut each other's prices until the equilibrium price is reached. If the price is below the equilibrium level, shortages occur, and buyers bidding against each other for available supplies drive the price up to the equilibrium level. At the equilibrium level there are neither surpluses nor shortages.

ing more than they can get at that price will bid up the price in an attempt to alleviate their individual shortages. An incentive exists for them to increase their offering prices as long as shortages occur. When the price reaches the $5 equilibrium level, there are no shortages, and the upward movement of the price will cease.

Price elasticity of demand

A question that comes up frequently in economic analysis is how responsive is the quantity demanded of a product to a change in its price, given the demand for the product. The measure of such responsiveness is called the *price elasticity of demand*. It is computed by dividing the percentage change in quantity demanded by the percentage change in price.

The computation of elasticity is illustrated in Figure 2–6. Let *DD* and *SS* be the original demand and supply curves. Now suppose an improvement in technology shifts the supply curve to the right, to S_1S_1. The equilibrium price was originally $5, but with the increase in supply a surplus exists at that price, causing the equilibrium price level to move downward to $4. The quantity demanded rises from 6,000 bushels to 7,000 bushels, which is a 17 percent increase. The price decrease is 20 percent. So elasticity of demand for the price change is 17/20, or 0.85, meaning that a 1 percent change in price generates an 0.85 percent change in quantity demanded.

The elasticity measurement may turn out to be greater than, less than, or equal to one, depending on the demand curve under surveillance and on the part of the demand curve for which elasticity is measured. If it is less than one, as it was in the foregoing example, demand is said to be *inelastic*. If it is greater than one, demand is said to be *elastic*. If it is equal to one, demand has *unitary elasticity*.

The magnitude of elasticity provides information on what will happen to the total receipts of sellers (or the total expenditures of buyers) if the price of a product changes. Consider the original equilibrium situation at point *A* in Figure 2–6. Total receipts of sellers, found by multiplying the quantity sold by the price, are $30,000. After the increase in supply and the decrease in price, total receipts are $28,000. This will always be the case for a price decrease when demand is inelastic—total receipts of sellers will fall because the percentage increase in quantity demanded is less than the percentage decrease in the price. Similar reasoning leads to the conclusion that a price decrease when demand is elastic will cause total receipts of sellers to rise. When demand is of unitary elasticity, a decrease in price leaves the total receipts of sellers unchanged.

FIGURE 2–6
A price change, demand elasticity, and total receipts

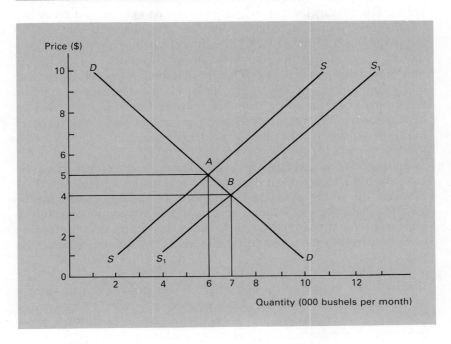

Elasticity of demand for a price change is computed by dividing the percentage change in quantity by the percentage change in price. In this example the percentage increase in quantity is outweighed by the percentage decrease in price. Demand is inelastic, and total receipts fall.

ECONOMIC ANALYSIS OF PRICE FLOORS

Agricultural markets

The relatively lower per capita incomes of farmers from 1920 to the present are rooted in the nature of the growth of the economy's GNP over that period of time. The 20th century is appropriately called the century of innovation and invention. The automobile and electricity not only have been made commercially useful, but they have provided the basis for a whole host of additional new products and services. The airplane, telephone, radio, television, and computer have served similar functions. The average level of education has been increasing. All of these factors have brought about rapid growth in GNP and rising incomes for those who provide the resources to produce it.

Demand. Demand for agricultural products tends to grow more slowly than that for industrial products and services of various kinds. The reason for the slower growth was aptly stated by Adam Smith, the father of economics, in 1776.[2] He observed that the demand for food is limited by the size of the human stomach. Demands for food and for fiber for clothing depend to a large extent on the number of people to be fed and clothed, especially after GNP has become large enough to provide a relatively nutritious diet and a reasonable degree of protection from cold and from heat. The demands for manufactured goods and for services seem, on the other hand, to expand without limits as incomes grow.

Supply. While demand for agricultural products has been increasing more slowly than demand for manufactured goods and for services, the supply of agricultural products has kept pace with the growth of supply in the other sectors of the economy. Continuous improvements in the levels of technology, invention, and innovation have occurred in the agricultural as well as the nonagricultural sectors.

Price. The impact of the relatively slower growth of demand for agricultural products on the prices of those products is represented in Figure 2–7. Suppose wheat is representative of agricultural products and automobiles are representative of manufactured products. Let $D_{w1}D_{w1}$ be the initial demand curve and $S_{w1}S_{w1}$ be the initial supply curve for wheat. The initial market price is P_{w1}. Let $D_{a1}D_{a1}$ and $S_{a1}S_{a1}$ be the initial demand and supply curve for automobiles, making the equilibrium price P_{a1}. There is no implication that the price scales of the two diagrams are identical. Let P_{w1} be $4 per bushel and let P_{a1} be $5,000 per automobile. Now, suppose that over time the demand for automobiles increases faster than the demand for wheat, while the relative supplies of the two products increase at about the same rate. The price of wheat rises to P_{w3}, or $4.50. The price of automobiles rises to P_{a3}, or $7,000.

The relatively greater demand and price increases for nonagricultural products over time makes their production more profitable than the production of agricultural products. This is reflected in the differences in incomes of those who live on the farm and those who do not. In more specific economic terms, labor and capital become worth more and are paid better prices in nonagricultural pursuits.

---

[2]Adam Smith, *The Wealth of Nations,* Cannan Edition (New York: Modern Library, 1937), p. 164.

FIGURE 2–7
Differences in the rate of growth of demand and supply for wheat
and automobiles

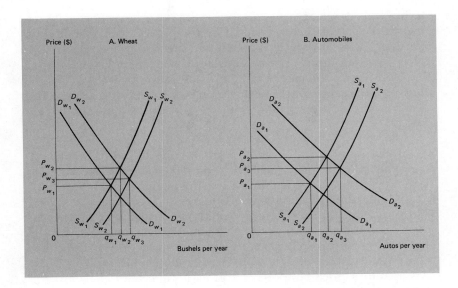

Growth in GNP and income increases demand for all normal goods and services, but
the demand for agricultural products such as wheat increases proportionally less than
the demand for nonagricultural products such as automobiles. Prices and profits
increase more in nonagricultural production, thus raising the incomes of nonagricultural
persons relative to those in agriculture and providing an incentive for resource owners
to shift some of their resources into nonagricultural production. The shift has not
occurred rapidly enough to eliminate the farm/nonfarm per capita income differential.

The differences in resource prices and in individual incomes between agricultural and nonagricultural production activities provide
incentives for resources to move out of agriculture and into manufacturing and service industries. Even though the population of the
United States has been growing rapidly during this century, the
farm population has decreased, from some 30.5 million persons in
1930 to 3.6 million in 1985.[3] Diversion of capital resources out of

---

[3] U.S. Department of Commerce, Bureau of the Census, *Statistical Abstract of the
United States*, 1986, p. 633. These numbers are not strictly comparable because the
definition of what constitutes a farm and what constitutes the farm population has
been tightened considerably over the years. They do, however, indicate a massive
movement of people out of agriculture.

agriculture has not been so dramatic. There has been a consolidation of capital into larger farms, and these enterprises can compete very effectively with nonagricultural enterprises for the use of capital.

The large, efficient farm enterprises are not where those with low per capita farm incomes reside. They represent considerably less than half of the total farm population, and they generate some 90 percent of total farm cash receipts. The rest of the farms—small, inefficient, badly managed operations—account for well over half of the farm population but generate only 10 percent of total farm cash receipts. These poverty-ridden farms constitute the serious farm problem.

The nature of price supports. The administration of Franklin D. Roosevelt inaugurated a massive program of farm price supports, beginning with the Agricultural Adjustment Act of 1933. The thinking of the administration—and Congress—seemed to be that, if prices of agricultural products could be raised relative to other prices, farmers' incomes would also increase relative to nonfarm incomes. Farm price supports were effective from 1933 to 1974; then, after a two-year lapse, they were reinstated in 1977.

Agriculture price supports are put into effect for the most part through a storage and loan program. An additional feature of the wheat support program is a so-called deficiency rate, a sum of x cents per bushel added to the loan support rate. Its primary effect is to increase wheat output as well as any surplus that may occur from the price support program. For purposes of simplicity we will confine our analysis to the basic storage and loan aspects of the program.

The government determines a support price level for a given product, such as wheat. At harvest time any farmer can place wheat in government-approved storage facilities and obtain a loan from the government equal to the support price on each bushel stored. When the loan falls due, the farmer has the option of paying it off or of letting the government have the stored wheat in repayment.

Under the program wheat farmers are given an incentive to store wheat and to borrow from the government whenever the support price exceeds the market price. When repayment is due, if the market price is still below the support price, the farmer lets the government have the wheat. If however, the market price is above the support price, the farmer pays off the loan at the support price, redeems the wheat, and sells it at the market price. In effect, the government guarantees that the farmer can receive the support level price for the wheat.

A demand and supply analysis of a storage and loan program is presented in Figure 2–8. Suppose the equilibrium price p is less than the support price level p_1 set by the government. At the support price level p_1, buyers will buy only q_1 bushels, but farmers want to place q_2 bushels on the market. But if they do so—if they sell more than q_1 bushels—the sales price will necessarily be less than p_1. Rather than sell the excess over q_1, they will store the surplus wheat—quantity q_1q_2—obtaining loans for it. Unless the market price exceeds p_1 when the loan is due, farmers will let the government have the wheat in repayment of the loans. In effect, then, when the government sets a support price above the equilibrium

FIGURE 2–8
Effects of price supports, storage and loan

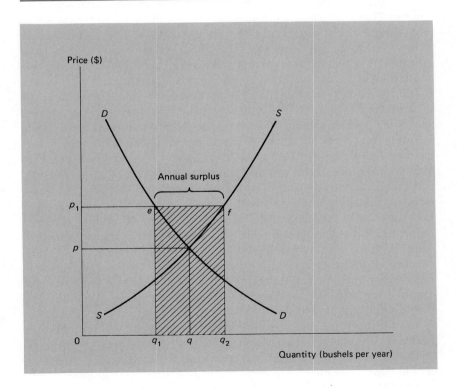

The support price p_1 is above the equilibrium price p. Buyers will purchase quantity q_1 at the support price, but farmers produce quantity q_2. The government purchases the surplus, making total payments to farmers equal to the shaded area q_1efq_2.

price level, buyers buy the quantity they want at that price, and the government buys the surplus wheat.

Economic effects of the program. A most obvious result of a storage and loan program is that if the support price for a product is effective it *must* result in the accumulation of surpluses of the product by the government. If a support price is set at or below the equilibrium price level, the equilibrium price level will prevail and the support price will not be effective. To be effective, the support price must exceed the equilibrium price; and when this is the case, the accumulation of surpluses of the product is inevitable. This is exactly what has happened, but instead of surpluses being expected by most people in the government and most of the general public, they are taken to mean that the program is in some way not being operated properly.

As the government accumulates surpluses of the product, pressure builds for the establishment of special surplus disposal programs. These take several forms. Surpluses may be sold abroad either directly or indirectly by the government at less than support prices. In 1983, for example, the U.S. government sold a large amount of wheat flour to Egypt, receiving considerably less for the flour than it had paid the farmers for the wheat from which it was made. Also, through the 1983 payment-in-kind, or PIK program, the government essentially hands farmers their payments in the form of wheat instead of making loan or deficiency rate payments in cash. Farmers can then obtain cash by selling the wheat on the private market. Surpluses are also used to provide school lunches and food stamp programs. Some are left to deteriorate in storage.

Probably the most important consequence of surplus accumulations is that they provide incentives for supply or acreage restriction programs to be established by the government. To qualify for price supports, individual farmers are required to restrict their planting in order to shift the supply curve to the left and reduce the annual surplus. But the cost of this to consumers in the economy is that some quantities of the economy's scarce resources—land, for example—are left idle, with a consequent reduction in gross national product and living standards.

In addition to the surplus disposal problem, consumers are harmed directly by a storage and loan price support program. It causes them to buy less of the price-supported product than they would otherwise choose to buy and to pay a higher price for it than would be the case under free-market conditions. In Figure 2–8, without price supports consumers get q bushels at price p per bushel. The imposition of the support price raises the price to p_1 and reduces the amount they purchase to q_1. This makes consumers worse off than they would be in the absence of the support.

Also, the direct costs of a storage and loan program must be met by taxpayers. These direct costs are of three kinds. The first is the cost of government purchase of the surplus; it amounts to the number of bushels of surplus product multiplied by the support price. In Figure 2–8 this amount is q_1q_2 multiplied by p_1, or it is the area of the shaded rectangle q_1efq_2. It represents a shift of purchasing power from taxpayers to the farmers who receive the support-price payments. The second is the costs of storage, handling, and disposal of surpluses. These costs, too, are incurred by the government and paid by taxpayers. Third, in addition to the acreage restriction required for participation in a storage and loan plan, further reductions in planting have been sought through direct payments to farmers for leaving additional land idle. Again this involves transfers of purchasing power from taxpayers to farmers.

Another important consequence of farm price supports is that they result in much larger government payments to large, wealthy farmers than to small, poor ones. The smaller the output of the farmer—the poorer the farm is—the less the amount of government payments the farmer receives. The greater the output of a farmer—the richer the farm is—the greater the payments received. These are the direct results of supporting *prices* rather than *incomes*. As a means of combatting poverty, a price support program is an upside-down welfare program providing much welfare for the rich and little for the poor!

Still a further consequence of income transfers from taxpayers to special interest groups like farmers (or airplane pilots for that matter) is that the recipients become accustomed to receiving the largess and eventually come to think that it is their right to receive it whether or not they are poor. In February 1979 a group of farmers calling themselves the American Agricultural Movement descended on Washington demanding higher price supports, greater subsidy payments, lower interest rates, and other benefits. Many were driving expensive tractors, trucks, and automobiles; some brought mobile homes; and others stayed in hotels costing some $50 a night. There was considerable doubt among those who witnessed and read of the tractorcade as to the worthiness of the farmers' cause.[4]

---

[4] Stephen Chapman, "Welfare Tractors," *New Republic*, March 3, 1979, p. 17.

Labor markets

The establishment by law of minimum hourly wage rates is looked upon favorably by a large majority of those in our society. Most of the general public see minimum wage rates as a means of helping those at the lower end of the income scale raise their wage rates and thereby raise their incomes. A widespread impression exists that low wage rates and low incomes occur because of employer exploitation of unskilled workers and that minimum wage rates will stop the exploitation. It would be wonderful if it were that simple!

Demand. The demand of employers for labor depends on what workers can contribute to the revenues of the employers. Employers will hire workers if they expect them to contribute more to their total revenues than it costs to hire them.

Suppose, for example, that in Figure 2–9 we are dealing with unskilled labor. Ignore the supply curves for the present. Each hour of labor up to 100 person-hours per week for all employers will contribute more than $3 each to employers' total revenues, but each hour can be had for a wage rate of $3. Obviously, it pays to hire 100 person-hours worth of labor. If additional hours beyond 100 per week will each add less than $3 to employers' total revenues, it is just as obvious that at a wage rate of $3 per hour it will not pay to hire them. However, if the wage rate were $2 per hour and another 200 person-hours of work will each add more than $2 to employers' total revenues, it would pay to expand employment up to the 300-hour mark. If additional hours beyond 300 would each add less than $2 but more than $1 to total revenues, they would not be hired—unless the wage rate were lowered to $1. If another 200 person-hours of work fall in this category, a wage rate of $1 per hour will induce employers to hire 500 hours but no more than that. Given the above information about how much additional person-hours will add to employers' total receipts, we have located three points—A, B, and C—on the demand curve for unskilled labor.

Ordinarily, we would expect the law of demand to apply to the demand curve for unskilled labor; that is, the higher the wage rate, the less employers would want to hire, other things being equal. In Figure 2–9, suppose that the wage rate is $1 per hour and that 500 person-hours can be hired, each of which contributes $1 or more to employers' total receipts. Suppose a minimum wage rate of $2 per hour is now imposed by law. The number of person-hours that will add $2 or more each to employers' total receipts must be less than the number that would add $1 or more. At a $2 per hour wage rate, fewer hours—300—will be employed. The number that will contrib-

FIGURE 2–9
Labor demand and supply; minimum wage rate effects

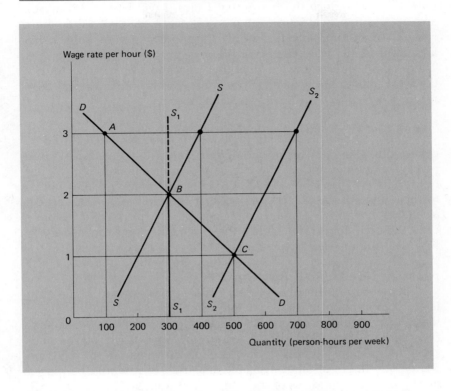

The demand curve and the supply curve for labor are DD and SS, respectively. The equilibrium price of labor is $2 per hour and the quantity employed is 300 person-hours. There is no unemployment. If a minimum wage of $3 per hour is established, unemployment of 300 person-hours will result. At that minimum wage level, unemployment would be 200 person-hours if the supply curve were S_1S_1. It would be 500 person-hours if the supply curve were S_2S_2.

ute $3 or more each to employers' total revenues must be still less. At a minimum wage rate of $3 per hour, only 100 person-hours would be hired.

Oddly enough, most people fail to remember that the law of demand applies to labor as well as to goods and services. The general public—and Congress—apparently believes that an increase in wage rates will *not* reduce employment. Yet, our analysis and a little reflection show that it will. For example, there is some wage rate low enough to induce me to hire eight hours of yard work per week on my yard; all that is necessary to bring this about is that I value the contribution to my well-being of each such hour at more than the wage rate. But an increase in the wage rate above that level will induce me to reduce the hours that I hire. I will work a bit myself and, in addition, will let the lawn and flower beds look a little more ragged. I will hire labor to do only the more important things that add more to my well-being than the cost imposed by the wage rate. There is, of course, a wage level that prices me, as a buyer, out of the market altogether. As a matter of fact, this level has already been reached, much to the regret of my neighbors.

Supply. Ordinarily, the supply curve of unskilled labor would be expected to slope upward to the right as Figure 2–9 illustrates. More person-hours of work are likely to be placed on the market at $2 per hour than at $1 per hour. At $3 per hour, still more probably will be forthcoming. The reason that more labor will tend to be forthcoming at higher than at lower rates is quite simple. People have alternative uses for their time. The higher the wage rate they can obtain by working, the more expensive it is for them to devote hours to pursuits other than work—and the less they are inclined to do so. These points are reflected in supply curve SS.

Whether or not the labor supply curve slopes upward to the right is of no great importance for our present purposes. It could be—and many people think it is—vertical, as is S_1S_1 in Figure 2–9. The supply curve will be vertical if the quantity of labor placed on the market is not responsive at all to the level of the wage rate. If there are 300 person-hours of labor available and if all of it would be placed on the market regardless of the wage level, then S_1S_1, instead of SS, would be the supply curve.

Price. If in Figure 2–9 the demand curve for unskilled labor is DD and the supply curve is SS (or S_1S_1 for that matter), the equilibrium wage rate will be $2 per hour, and 300 person-hours will be employed. Note that at the equilibrium wage rate there is no unemployment. Neither is there a shortage of labor. There is no problem of exploitation present.

Suppose that the unskilled labor supply is greater, as shown by S_2S_2. The wage rate at which the quantity of labor demanded will be the same as the quantity of labor supplied becomes $1 per hour. Note carefully that the lower wage rate is *not* the result of exploitation. It is caused by the larger supply. Wherever the supply of labor is large relative to the demand for it, wage rates will be relatively low.

The effects of a minimum wage. Suppose now that a well-meaning Congress, concerned about the low income levels of unskilled workers, enacts a minimum wage law requiring employers to pay $3 per hour for labor. If the supply curve were SS, the increase in the wage rate would coax an additional 100 person-hours into the labor market for a total of 400 person-hours seeking employment. However, employers would find it profitable to employ only 100 person-hours, so 300 person-hours would be unemployed or surplus.

Alternative positions or slopes of the labor supply curve make no difference in the analysis if the minimum wage rate is an effective one, that is, if the minimum wage rate is set above the equilibrium market level. If the supply curve were S_1S_1, the establishment of the minimum wage rate would still cause unemployment, although the amount of unemployment would be less than if the supply curve were SS. If the supply curve were S_2S_2, the effects of the minimum wage would be more problematic than in the other two cases.

Which of these outcomes is most realistic? That is, by how much does the minimum wage actually increase unemployment? While estimates of the increase in unemployment vary widely, teenagers are consistently found to be the most harmed. A general conclusion is that a 10 percent increase in the minimum wage probably increases teenage unemployment by about one-half of 1 percent. That is, if the teenage unemployment rate is initially 12 percent, a 10 percent increase in the minimum wage would increase the unemployment rate to about 12.5 percent.[5] The effect for older workers is less clear. While increased unemployment is reason enough to question the effectiveness of minimum wage legislation, perhaps the most serious criticism concerns the extent to which the legislation meets its intended goal of limiting poverty. The research in the area suggests that the minimum has very little impact on the degree of income inequality in the economy since individuals (often teenagers) who work for the minimum are equally likely to be from upper-income families as from families in poverty.[6]

These effects are not what Congress anticipates—or are they? Certainly they are not what the general public anticipates. They may very well be what labor union officials expect; such officials are often

---

[5]Charles Brown, Curtis Gilroy, and Andrew Kohen, "The Effect of the Minimum Wage on Employment and Unemployment," *Journal of Economic Literature,* June 1982, p. 487.

[6]William Johnson and Edgar Browning, "The Distributional Effects of Increasing the Minimum Wage," *American Economic Review,* March 1983, p. 204.

more knowledgeable about economic relationships than their pronouncements lead us to believe. The reasoning of Congress and the general public seems to be: If the minimum wage is put into effect, it will raise the wage rates of those receiving less than the minimum up to the level of the minimum. Therefore, their incomes will be increased. Congress and the public seem to believe that the demand curve for unskilled labor is completely inelastic—that it approaches a vertical slope. They forget the lesson that they teach themselves daily, even with respect to the cereal they eat for breakfast—the higher the price of an item, the less of it they will buy, other things being equal.

On the other hand, some people benefit from the minimum wage. First, those who remain employed are better off than they were without it. Second, those who offer skilled and semiskilled labor power for which the market wage rate is greater than the minimum wage rate gain. They gain because some of the work formerly done by those made unemployed now becomes available to them—low-wage unskilled competition is eliminated by the minimum wage rate. Many union members may fall in this category of gainers.

The economy as a whole and certain groups in the economy lose. First, because some of the labor force becomes unemployed, GNP becomes smaller, and consumers in general lose. Second, those who cannot find employment because of the minimum wage lose—they cannot find employment because they are not worth as much to employers as it would cost the employers to hire them. Especially hard hit are those groups in the economy about whom much concern is expressed—minority groups, teenage members of the labor force, and women. We are often informed by congressional personnel and by the news media that the minimum wage is designed to *help* these groups. If it is, it may miss the mark!

ECONOMIC ANALYSIS OF PRICE CEILINGS

Housing markets

Almost everyone looks with disfavor on slums. In certain areas of any city, one sees housing conditions that are distressing to say the least. Several families may be using the same bath and toilet facilities. Some families live in units that are not well-lighted or well-ventilated. Two or more families may be living in the same apartment. The buildings and apartments may be in various states of disrepair. Why do people live in them? Usually these are as much as lower income families can afford. Or, if you have tried to find an apartment in Manhattan recently, you know that they may be all that is available. Why do these problems occur? Do the rent controls that have been operative in places such as New York City serve the best interests of lower income groups? An examination of housing demand, supply, and pricing will help us evaluate the housing problems of the poor.

Demand. The demand for housing originates in households—families and unattached individuals living in the economic system. Within the confines of the incomes available to them and the prices they must pay for different goods and services, households make their choices as to what goods and services they will buy and how much of each they will purchase. Presumably, each household moves toward an allocation of its income among different goods and services that will yield it the highest level of total satisfaction. Housing is one of the large items that households purchase. For example, in 1980 for households that rent housing, almost half paid rents amounting to 25 percent of their total budgets. Almost a third of renters spent over 35 percent of their total budgets for rent.[7]

The demand for housing depends on the same set of forces that influences the demand for other goods and services. One of these is household income. Another is the psychological desires of consumers for housing. Another is the price or rental rate of housing units. Another is the prices of other goods and services that comprise households' budgets. Any given household will try to allocate its income among various goods and services in such a way that a dollar's worth of housing contributes the same to consumer well-being as a dollar's worth of anything else the household buys. If a dollar's worth of something else, say food, were more valuable to the householder than a dollar's worth of housing, the household would gain by shifting some of its expenditure away from housing toward food. On the other hand, if a dollar's worth of housing were more valuable to a household than a dollar's worth of food, the household would gain in well-being by purchasing less food and more housing with its more or less fixed income.

How does this translate into a demand curve for housing? In Figure 2–10 suppose that the rental rate is r dollars and that when households are spending their incomes so that a dollar's worth of housing makes the same contribution to household well-being as a dollar's worth of anything else, they purchase h units of housing per

---

[7] U.S. Bureau of the Census, 1980 Census of Housing, *Components of Inventory Change, United States and Regions* (Washington, D.C.: U.S. Government Printing Office, August 1983), p. 284.

FIGURE 2–10
Demand for and supply of housing

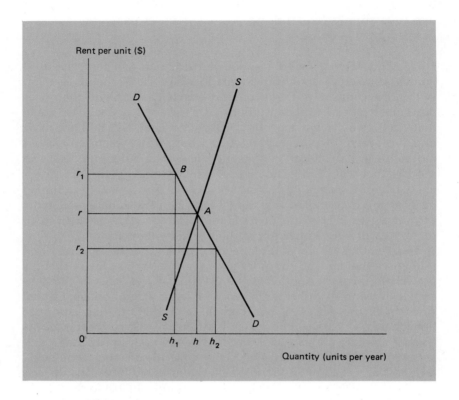

The demand curve for housing *DD* shows the value of a unit of housing to households at various alternative quantities. If the quantity available were *h* units per year, the value of a unit to households is *r* dollars per year. If the quantity available were h_1, the value of a unit to households is r_1 dollars. If h_2 units were available, the value of a unit becomes r_2.

year. What would happen to the quantity of housing if rent rises to r_1 and there are no changes in the prices of other goods, in the household's tastes and preferences, or in household's incomes? At the higher rent level, a dollar's worth of housing is a smaller quantity of housing than before; consequently, the contribution that a dollar's worth of housing makes to household well-being is smaller than it was before the rent increase. The contribution of a dollar's worth of any other item to household well-being thus is greater than that of a dollar's worth of housing. Households will shift dollars from housing to other items, reducing the amount of housing consumed to some level h_1. The entire demand curve DD is made up of such points as A and B, at which households consider that they are buying the correct amounts of housing relative to other goods and services at various different prices for housing.

One more point should be made before we leave the concept of demand for housing. The demand curve DD shows that when households take h units of housing, a unit of housing is worth r dollars to them; that is, they believe the amount a unit contributes to their total well-being is the same as the contribution of r dollars' worth of any other good or service they consume. Similarly, if only a smaller amount h_1 were available to them, they would value a unit of housing at r_1 dollars. In general terms, the less we have of any given item, the more we value a unit of it.

Supply. The supply of housing available is not very responsive to price and/or rent levels over relatively short time spans. The supply curve tends to be sharply upward sloping to the right or rather inelastic as shown by SS in Figure 2–10. The reason for this is quite evident. Most of the housing supply in any given year consists of the stock of already existing units. In the course of a year, the amount by which this stock is likely to be increased or decreased is relatively small. For example, from 1970 to 1983 the total stock of housing changed by 36.2 percent, for an average annual change of 2.8 percent.[8]

Nevertheless, some variation in the quantity supplied will occur in response to price changes. Consider, for example, the entire complex of housing units in New York City. The space they occupy is highly valuable for business purposes. A decrease in housing rental rates relative to what the space could earn if converted to business uses would cause some conversion to occur and decrease the number of housing units available. This can also work the other way around. An increase in housing rental rates relative to what the space could earn in business uses may result in conversion of some business space to housing units. It may also result in some construction of new housing units.

Price. Suppose now that in New York City the demand curve for housing is DD and the supply curve is SS as in Figure 2–11. The equilibrium rental rate is r, and the number of housing units occu-

---

[8] U.S. Department of Commerce, Bureau of the Census, *Statistical Abstract of the United States, 1986,* p. 729.

FIGURE 2–11
Effects of an increase in demand for housing

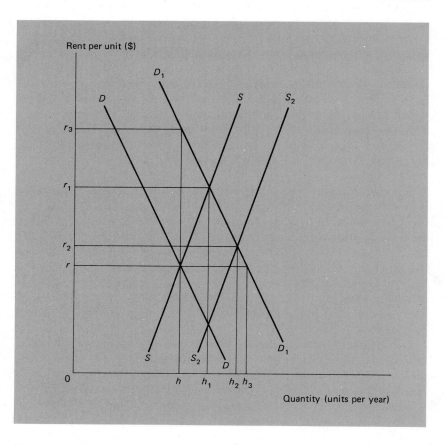

If the demand curve for housing units is *DD* and the supply curve is *SS*, the equilibrium level of rent is *r* and the equilibrium quantity occupied is *h*. An increase in demand to D_1D_1 increases the rent level to r_1 and the quantity occupied to h_1. The increased profitability of providing housing causes the supply curve to shift to S_2S_2 over time, increasing the units occupied to h_2 and lowering rents to r_2. If, however, rent controls had been enacted at level *r*, the long-run increase in housing would not take place. A shortage of hh_3 units would persist over time.

pied is *h*. Over time, economic growth and rising household incomes increase the demand for housing to D_1D_1. In the absence of rent controls, the short-run impact of the increase in demand is a rise in rental rates to r_1 and an increase in the units made available to h_1.

The rise in rental rates will make investment in housing units more profitable, and in the long run—say a period of five years or more—such additional investment will shift the supply curve for housing to the right. Rental rates will fall to some value r_2, and the number of units rented will rise to h_2. In New York City, because of space limitations and because of the alternatives of using property for business purposes, it is highly unlikely that increases in supply can keep pace with increases in demand, so the rental rate r_2 will undoubtedly exceed the original rental rate r. In other localities in which space is a much smaller problem and in which business competition for space is much less, r_2 may be very close to r.

The effects of rent controls. Following World War II, New York City elected to continue rent controls established during the war. These controlled rates were maintained in some degree, although over time they have crept gradually upward. The purpose of the controls has been to keep the price of housing within the reach of lower income groups. What are the *actual* effects of the controls?

In the first place, they generate a housing shortage. In Figure 2–11, as demand increases from DD to D_1D_1 with the supply curve at SS, if rents are not allowed to rise above r, a shortage of hh_3 units develops. Not all households looking for apartments are able to find them. Not all households desiring to add to their living space are able to do so. Much time is wasted in futile searches for apartments. Those whose employment is in New York City and who cannot find housing there are forced to outlying areas from which they must commute.

In the second place, the cost of housing is not kept down for everyone. In the normal turnover of housing units—some households vacating their apartments and others renting them—it becomes common to make undercover payments to landlords for the privilege of a new lease. For those seeking housing, the search time is extended by the shortage, and the value of the extra search time required is a cost to the searchers. Many, if not most, of those forced to commute find their costs increased in at least three ways: (1) higher rents, (2) direct costs of commuting, and (3) the value of time lost in commuting. Only those ensconced in housing before the controls were put into effect and who did not move after they became effective can be sure that the controls will not raise their housing costs.

In the third place, the long-run profit inducements that would shift the supply curve to the right to S_2S_2 are eliminated by the rent controls. The rising household incomes that serve to increase the demand for housing also increase the demand for other goods and services produced in New York City. These are not subjected to price controls. The industries producing them become relatively more profitable than the housing industry in which investors cannot capture higher returns from households. Consequently, investors in real estate are provided with profit inducements to increase the space available for business relative to the space available for housing. It is even possible that rent controls may cause the supply curve for housing to decrease in the long run, leaving even fewer housing units available than existed before rent controls were put into effect.

In the fourth place, landlords faced with rent controls tend to allow the quality of their properties to deteriorate. For any given type of good or service, lower quality sold at the same price per unit is equivalent to an increase in the price when the quality is not decreased. So quality deterioration is a disguised means of securing at least some price relief. The enactment of minimum housing standards by a municipality may block landlords from this escape route; however, omnipresent slums indicate they are not always a resounding success.

Finally, the enforcement of rent controls means that for present housing supplies the rental level of housing units is held below households valuation of those housing units. For example, in Figure 2–11, after the increase in demand to D_1D_1, the quantity of housing supplied with rent controls at r is h units. But for this quantity of housing, the value of a unit to households is r_3. The price of housing is not allowed to reflect the value that households place on a unit of it.

Natural gas markets

Natural gas is an important source of energy in the United States. The ultimate consumers of it are residential, commercial (business), and industrial users. The gas is discovered and produced by petroleum companies. Pipeline companies such as the El Paso Natural Gas Company and the Southern Natural Gas Company act as wholesalers, buying from the petroleum companies and selling to industrial users and to state and local public utility companies. These latter companies sell and distribute to residential and commercial users.

Petroleum companies engage in exploration and drilling for natural gas as well as for crude oil. Some of what they discover is "associated" gas found with, or rather in, oil pools. They also prospect for and find "nonassociated" gas in reservoirs by itself. Together, the associated and nonassociated gas discovered comprise natural gas reserves. Pipeline companies buy from these reserves.

Demand. End use energy users in the United States secure a little over one fourth of their requirements from natural gas. The major substitutes for it are coal, petroleum products, nuclear energy, and hydroelectric power. In 1984, for cooking, heating, cooling, and the like, residential and commercial users of energy obtained some 26.6 percent of their requirements directly from natural gas. Industrial users also fulfilled almost 26.5 percent of their needs directly with gas, the main substitutes being fuel oil and coal. Natural gas provided some 12.3 percent of the fuel for generating electric power, competing in this area with nuclear power, water power, coal, and fuel oil.[9]

One of the major attractions of natural gas to its users is its clean-burning, nonpolluting characteristics; however, as with any other good or service, the quantity of it demanded will vary inversely with its price. An increase in the price of natural gas relative to the prices of other energy sources will induce users to switch to those other sources. A decrease in its relative price will spur its use. We would expect long-run demand to be considerably more elastic than short-run demand because in order to switch to or from natural gas, users must convert their facilities to use the different energy sources. A representative demand curve is shown by *DD* in Figure 2–12.

The demand for natural gas has expanded rapidly over the last 25 years. Prior to the 1950s, markets were largely local, confined to the areas in which gas was discovered. The technology and plant for long-distance pipeline transmission had not yet been developed. During the 1950s and especially in the decade of the 1960s, interstate pipelines and transmission techniques were developed, opening up a national market for the product. The clean-burning nature of natural gas as compared to the polluting characteristics of coal and fuel oil made natural gas an attractive fuel. The increase in demand is shown in Figure 2–12 by the shift in the demand curve from *DD* to D_1D_1.

Supply. The key element in the supply of natural gas consists of the discovered reserves that exist. Pipeline companies enter into long-term contracts with the industrial users and the public utility gas companies that they serve. In turn, they attempt to assure that they can deliver by making long-term (5- to 20-year) contracts with the gas producers who own rights to the reserves. The time period

---

[9] U.S. Department of Commerce, Bureau of the Census, *Statistical Abstract of the United States, 1986*, p. 559.

FIGURE 2–12
Short-run versus long-run supply of natural gas

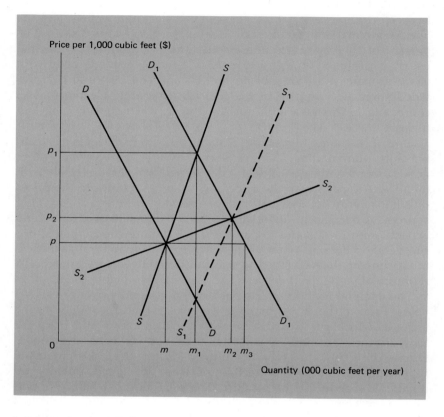

Let demand and supply for natural gas be *DD* and *SS* initially. An increase in demand to D_1D_1 increases the price from *p* to p_1 and the quantity to m_1. Higher profits induce producers to increase exploratory activity and increase supply to S_1S_1. The price falls to p_2 and the quantity sold increases to m_2. The long-run supply curve is S_2S_2. Price controls at price *p* would eliminate the inducement for the increase in exploratory activity, leaving supply at *SS* and creating a shortage of mm_3.

required for the discovery of new reserves and the tapping of those reserves for production into pipelines may be as long as five years, so pipeline companies making contracts with gas producers are careful to determine that adequate reserves exist to fulfill the contracts.

The short-run supply of natural gas thus tends to be rather inelastic since it is based on current reserves plus the current rate of discovery of new reserves. In Figure 2–12, short-run supply is illus-

trated by the curve *SS*. It is not completely inelastic since the reserves that exist—usually a 20- to 30-year supply—can serve as a
cushion between price changes and the discovery of new reserves.
If the price were to become relatively high, the annual quantity supplied can be increased to some extent by depleting reserves. If the
price were to fall relatively low, the annual quantity supplied can be
decreased, allowing reserves to build.

In the long run the supply of natural gas is thought to be rather
elastic, like S_2S_2 in Figure 2–12. At relatively higher prices, exploratory activity will be stepped up, eventually resulting in higher levels of reserves. At relatively lower prices, exploratory activity will
decline, and existing reserves will decline. It is generally thought
that the amount of potentially discoverable reserves left in the
United States is large relative to annual rates of use. Estimates vary
from 851 trillion cubic feet up to 6,600 trillion cubic feet.[10] Annual
usage has not yet exceeded 25 trillion cubic feet.

Prices. For purposes of simplicity, suppose we concentrate on
natural gas prices at the wellhead; that is, the price at which gas
producers sell the gas to pipeline companies. The demand curve for
natural gas, then, should be interpreted as the demand of pipeline
companies on the gas producers which, of course, reflects the demand of ultimate users. The supply curve shows the quantities per
year that the gas producers will produce and sell to the pipeline
companies at alternative price levels.

Natural gas prices were relatively low and more or less stable during the 1920s and the 1930s. Demand during those decades was confined primarily to the producing areas since interstate pipelines were
not yet in place. The discovery of reserves was to a large extent a
by-product of oil exploration activity. Gas was even considered a
nuisance in some areas and was burned off with flares or simply
released into the atmosphere.

Price controls at the wellhead on gas transported in interstate
commerce were inaugurated in 1954 but were not really effective
until 1960. In the meantime, following World War II, the market and
the demand for natural gas expanded rapidly because of (1) the rising affluence of the U.S. population and (2) the development of effective long-range pipeline transportation facilities. Supply did not
keep pace with the rising demand; and, as a consequence, prices

---

[10] Paul W. MacAvoy and Robert S. Pindyck, *Price Controls and the Natural Gas
Shortage* (Washington, D.C.: American Enterprise Institute for Public Policy, 1975),
p. 5.

rose rapidly. Free-market pricing on gas sold across state boundaries, or in interstate commerce, gave way to controlled pricing by
the Federal Power Commission in 1960.[11] However, gas sold within
the state where it was produced was not under the Federal Power
Commission's jurisdiction and was therefore exempt from its control.

The effects of price controls. Figure 2–12 provides us with a basis for predicting the effects of price controls. An increase in demand
from DD to D_1D_1 with no increase in supply (a situation analogous
to one in which demand is increasing more rapidly than supply) will
result in a shortage of mm_3 if the price is controlled at level p.

In the absence of price controls, there would be no shortage. The
short-run effects of the increase in demand would be a rise in price
to p_1 and an increase in quantity exchanged to m_1. The increase in
quantity would come from short-run depletion of reserves. However, the higher price would make the production and sale of natural gas more profitable. Exploratory activity would be increased, and
in the long run existing reserves and the quantity supplied would
be increased. The price would come down to p_2, and the quantity
supplied from the larger reserves would be m_2. With the existing
larger reserves, the short-run supply curve will have shifted to the
right to S_1S_1. The actual developments in the industry follow the
prediction.

The Federal Power Commission was charged with the dual responsibilities of (1) insuring adequate supplies of natural gas to consumers and (2) holding down the prices that consumers must pay
for it. Most economists thought these objectives were incompatible;
and over the last two decades adherence to the second did in fact,
prevent the first from being achieved. During the 1960s and most of
the 1970s, as the Federal Power Commission perfected, increased,
and extended its control over the wellhead price of natural gas,
shortages began to develop. In the mid-1960s, it became apparent
that the quantity of natural gas demanded at controlled prices was
exceeding the rate of discovery of new reserves. Initially, reserves
were used to cushion the shortages; but as reserves were depleted,
it became necessary for pipeline companies to curtail their deliveries
to industrial users and local gas utility companies. The gas producers found it unprofitable to provide on a continuing basis the quan-

---

[11] The preceding paragraphs are based on Robert B. Helms, *Natural Gas Regulation*
(Washington, D.C.: American Enterprise Institute for Public Policy, 1974), pp. 17–25.

tities demanded at the controlled prices. In 1973 pipeline companies were forced to decrease their supplies to customers by an amount equal to about 6 percent of total natural gas production. In 1974 the shortage was about double that, and these estimates leave out potential customers who had to be placed on waiting lists.[12] In the winter of 1976–77, natural gas shortages reached almost disastrous proportions. In November 1978 Congress passed the Natural Gas Policy Act providing for an immediate and substantial increase in the wellhead ceiling price of natural gas and for movement by stages to complete deregulation by 1985. The results speak for themselves. The shortages have disappeared; the natural gas "crisis" has evaporated.

Were consumers made better off by the price controls? The weight of evidence and logic is that they were not. It appears that consumers were made worse off. In the first place, with controlled prices the quantities of natural gas produced and consumed were less than they would have been otherwise. Those who wanted but could not get natural gas at the controlled prices were forced to turn to more costly (less efficient) substitute fuels. All this tells us that the economy's total output or GNP was held below what it would have been in the absence of controls.

In the second place, it is likely that the gas that was produced and consumed was not put to its most productive uses. The Federal Power Commission was authorized to control prices only on gas that was shipped among states; it had no control over the prices of gas sold by producers in a given state to customers in that state.[13] Thus, when shortages of gas occurred at controlled prices, where would producers be expected to sell the available supplies? Obviously, they would sell in the intrastate market where the price was not controlled. Once they had sold as much as was profitable in the intrastate market, the remainder would be sold out of state at the controlled price. Thus, the burden of shortages fell on customers and potential customers in nonproducing states. It is possible—even likely—that some of the gas sold intrastate could have been more efficiently used in interstate markets. Gas consumers in the northeast, north central, and northwest areas of the United States were especially penalized by the shortages. Their supplies were curtailed

---

[12] See Patricia E. Starratt, *The Natural Gas Shortage and the Congress* (Washington, D.C.: American Enterprise Institute of Public Policy, 1974), pp. 3–5, 21–23.

[13] Under the Natural Gas Policy Act of 1978, control of prices was extended to gas sold intrastate as well as to interstate gas. The enforcing agency, the Federal Power Commission, has been superseded by the Federal Energy Regulatory Commission.

as shortages developed and potential customers simply found natural gas impossible to obtain.

SUMMARY AND EVALUATION

Government units control the prices on selected items in the United States. This is usually done for two reasons: (1) to help the poor and (2) to help politically strong special interest groups. The objectives sought frequently are not obtained and, in addition, unanticipated side effects usually result from the price-fixing.

Demand and supply concepts are useful in analyzing the effects of price-fixing. Equilibrium prices and quantities, at which neither shortages nor surpluses occur, tend to be established in free markets. Price floors established above market equilibrium levels cause surpluses to accumulate. Price ceilings set below market equilibrium levels create shortages.

Price floors have been used extensively for agricultural products. The results have been surpluses. Resources were wasted in producing them, and problems were encountered in disposing of them. Initially intended to help a low income group—farmers—they have proven to be an upside-down kind of welfare measure, helping large, wealthy farmers much and small, poor farmers little.

Minimum wage rates set above market equilibrium levels for unskilled workers also result in surpluses—we call it unemployment. The ones that they are supposed to help—minority groups, teenagers, and women—are the ones hurt most. They must bear the brunt of the unemployment effects of the minimum rates.

Rent controls illustrate the effects of price ceilings. When these are set below market equilibrium levels, the result is housing shortages. Incentives to build new units are destroyed, and existing units are likely to be permitted by their owners to deteriorate. Rent controls do not appear to provide an avenue to improve housing for the poor.

Price ceilings on natural gas have created substantial shortages. In the process, they have inhibited the discovery of new reserves and have contributed to inefficiency in the use of existing supplies.

It would appear that government price-fixing ventures usually impose significant costs and problems on households of the economy. They may benefit some special groups, but they are unlikely to benefit all households. In determining whether or not we should have them, we must weigh the costs to the society against the benefits obtained by the special groups.

SUPPLEMENTARY READING

"As Rent Control Spreads across Country, Its Friends and Foes Watch Los Angeles." *The Wall Street Journal,* February 1, 1980, p. 34.

Describes the Los Angeles experience with rent controls, vividly depicting many of the problems described in the text.

Chapman, Stephan. "The Farmer on the Dole." *Harpers,* October 1982, pp. 18–21.

Excellent article that refutes some of the popular arguments for subsidizing farmers then goes on to explain and criticize major price support programs.

Dentzer, Susan, et al. "Bitter Harvest." *Newsweek,* February 18, 1985, pp. 542–60.

An examination of the debt crunch on the farming industry that appeared to reach crisis proportions in 1984 and 1985.

Goodman, John C., and Edwin G. Dolan. "Taking a Closer Look at the Minimum Wage." *Economics of Public Policy: The Micro View.* 2nd ed. St. Paul, Minn.: West Publishing, 1982, pp. 179–93.

Contains a brief history of minimum wage legislation and a discussion of the politics surrounding the minimum wage. In addition, a number of indirect effects of imposing a minimum wage are introduced and explained.

Leftwich, Richard H. *Elementary Analytics of a Market System.* Morristown, N.J.: General Learning Press, 1972.

A comprehensive elementary discussion of the nature of a price system and its role in guiding the operation of a private enterprise economy.

"A Perspective on the Economics of Natural Gas Decontrol." *Federal Reserve Bank of St. Louis Review* 64, no. 9 (November 1982), pp. 19–31.

A careful and thorough analysis of the effects of decontrolling the price of natural gas.

ECONOMICS OF HIGHER EDUCATION

Problems in higher education
What kinds of services?
How much service?
What institutional structure?
Who should pay?
The economic basis of the problems
The "product" of higher education
Investment in human capital
Direct consumption
Social spillovers
The incidence of the benefits
Economic concept of costs
The alternative cost principle revisited
Explicit and implicit costs
The costs of higher educational services
The explicit costs
The implicit costs
Sources of support
The incidence of the costs
Economic evaluation of the problems
What kinds of services?
How much service?
Who should pay?
An alternative institutional structure
Summary

Checklist of
Economic Concepts
Human capital
Spillover benefits, social
Spillover costs, social
Alternative costs
Production possibilities curve
Explicit costs
Implicit costs
Demand
Supply
Price, equilibrium
Surplus
Shortage
Transfer payments
Free riders

3

Economics of Higher Education

Who benefits and who pays the bills?

The atmosphere was tense in the Wilson household, but young Doug stood his ground. The problem was not new; it had been brewing all through his senior year in high school. Now that the year was almost over and decisions must be made about what college or university he would attend, the problem had come to a head.

Doug's parents wanted him to attend State University. It would be much less expensive than Private University where Doug had been accepted and where he desired to go. Tuition at S.U. for in-state students was only $1,200 per year, and at P.U. it was $4,200. With three kids to put through college, the Wilsons considered Doug's desire to go to P.U. unreasonable.

There are some intangibles, too, in the Wilson's thinking. They would be more comfortable with Doug at S.U. It offered good, solid academic work, even though it was overcrowded with students and despite the fact that the legislature never seemed to appropriate quite enough money for its operation. They would feel a little better, too, knowing that the legislature sort of kept an eye on things at S.U. so that nothing very far out—like the teaching of radical economics—was likely to occur.

Doug thought the academic challenge would be greater at P.U. It had a reputation for academic excellence and for flexibility in the programs that students could pursue. Many of its faculty had national and even international reputations in their fields. Doug had been a Merit Scholarship Finalist in high school and had done exceptionally well on his Standard Achievement Tests. He wasn't sure what major field of study to pursue—he wanted to sample several before making up his mind. At P.U. he could major in about anything he wanted to—ethnomusicology, for example. If it were not a standard major, they would help him build a nonstandard one. Doug was ready for P.U.

In addition to the appeal of P.U.'s program, Doug thought university life would be more enjoyable if he were far enough from home to be relatively independent of his family. There comes a time when one must cut the apron strings, and this seemed to Doug to be it. He believed that he was quite capable of making sound decisions on his own.

PROBLEMS IN HIGHER EDUCATION

While students like Doug wrestle with their problems of choice, colleges and universities themselves are going through troubled times. Over the last 35 years enrollments have increased greatly, placing tremendous pressure on their personnel and facilities. Enrollments peaked in 1981 and are expected to fall somewhat throughout the rest of this century. University administrators now talk of retrenchment. Though the riots, strikes, boycotts, and other disruptions of the academic processes that were so common in the 1960s have subsided, they remain as potential threats to administrators. Most institutions face serious financial problems. Some say too many degrees are being granted—there is no room for new college and university graduates to work in the fields of their choice. Others say that colleges and universities are too tradition-bound and are not responsive to the needs of society.

All of these issues (and more) call for systematic analysis of the higher education system. The economics of such an analysis center around four interrelated questions: (1) What kinds of higher educational services should be provided? (2) How much should be provided? (3) What is the appropriate institutional structure for providing them? (4) Who should pay for them?

What kinds of services?

Society expects higher educational institutions to perform multiple roles. Traditionally they have been learning centers, accumulating and transmitting knowledge of all kinds to students. University faculties are expected to engage in research and other creative activities that advance the frontiers of knowledge, and to be at the cutting edge of the intellectual, cultural, social, and technological developments of civilization.

In addition, society has come to expect colleges and universities to provide professional vocational types of training. These range from the preparation of physicians and lawyers to the training of automobile mechanics and secretaries. In many, if not most, cases, these multiple roles of colleges and universities are inextricably bound together.

How much service?

The question of how much college and university educational service the society should provide is a very live issue today. Another name for this problem is "the financial crisis" of higher education. Most administrators, faculty members, and students are convinced that a financial crisis exists, that not enough is being spent for educational services.

Over the years, legislative appropriations to public institutions have not kept pace with growing enrollments and rising costs. Tuitions have increased dramatically in both public and private schools. Many private schools have been operating with deficits, and a number face the possibility of shutting down their operations. Is all this an indication that society is unwilling to support higher education at present levels, or that it believes relatively too much is being spent for higher educational services?

What institutional structure?

The present system of higher education is a dual one made up of both private and public colleges and universities. In both components of the system, there are three types of institutions: (1) junior colleges, (2) four-year colleges, and (3) universities. The public institutions are state owned and operated, except for a growing number of community colleges and a very few municipal colleges and universities.

Is this structure conducive to providing the appropriate kinds and quantities of higher educational services relative to other goods and services desired by the society? Is it flexible? Or is it tradition-bound and susceptible to being a political football for state politicians?

Who should pay?

A related question concerns the extent to which governments (taxpayers) should pay the costs of producing the services of higher education and to what extent the costs should be paid by students and their families. If the government is to pay a substantial part of the cost, how should it go about doing so? Is the state university, with state appropriations for its capital and operating costs, the best way? Or should the state, instead of making appropriations to institutions, make funds available to students themselves, letting them and their parents choose their schools, paying tuition and fees sufficient to meet the costs of their educations? Should government payments of the costs of higher education favor poor families? These are some of the questions that bother us.

The economic basis of the problems

The basic issues outlined above are primarily economic problems. The economics of providing higher educational services was largely ignored until the 1960s because such services comprised a relatively small part of the gross national product and used small proportions of the nation's resources. In addition, it was somehow thought that education was above mundane things like analysis of economic benefits and costs.

The burgeoning enrollments since World War II changed all that. Those responsible for decision making with regard to higher education—legislators, administrators, faculties, students, and concerned citizens—can no longer ignore the economic consequences of their decisions. The provision of higher educational services requires the use of large quantities of resources, and the resources so used are not available to produce other goods and services. Higher educational services represent one of a great many competing uses for resources.

In this chapter we shall construct an economic framework of the higher education "industry" that should be useful in the decision-making processes concerning it. The present system of higher education will be evaluated within the context of that framework.

THE "PRODUCT" OF HIGHER EDUCATION

Like other producing units in the economy, institutions of higher education use resources and technology to turn out something of benefit to individuals and to society. This "something" can probably best be characterized as *educational services*. To get at what comprises educational services, we can pose the question: Why are you attending a college or university? There are at least three answers to the question. First, you expect higher education to improve your capacity to produce and to earn income, that is, to augment the quality of your labor resources. We call this *development of human capital*. Second, quite apart from improving the quality of your labor resources, you derive direct immediate satisfaction from your present participation in college or university processes and activities—it is in this respect a direct consumption service. Third, you may expect that there will be some benefits to the society as a whole in addition to the benefits that accrue to you from your obtaining higher education. We will look at these facets of educational services in turn.

Investment in human capital

A large part of educational services must consist of the development of human or labor resources. This is called *investment in human capital* because in an economic sense it is very much the same thing as investing in machines, buildings, and other material capital. We invest in additional nonhuman capital whenever we think that it will generate enough additional product output to more than repay the new investment costs. Similarly, it pays an individual to invest in human capital—additional education—if the increase in education increases the earning power of the person being educated by more than the cost of the additional education. Just as investment in nonhuman capital is expected to increase and expand the capacity of capital resources to produce, so is a large part of the investment in human capital expected to augment the capacity of labor resources to contribute to gross national product.

Investment in human capital is in no sense restricted to the provision of vocational education. Classical education—language and literature, the humanities, the fine arts, philosophy, and the like—broadens and deepens people's capacities to think, act, and enjoy, and thereby increases their productivity in an economic sense. In many cases employers of college and university graduates are just as interested in hiring students with broad liberal arts degrees as they are those trained in specific vocational majors. What they want are bright young people who know how to think and how to accept responsibility.

Direct consumption

Some part of the educational services produced by colleges and universities consists of *direct consumption benefits*. Participation in the activities of the institution and interaction with other students in university life yield direct satisfaction to many. Students who have no interest in making their education pay off through increased earning power are prime examples of direct consumers of educational services.

By way of contrast, there are students whose sole purpose in attending college is to enhance their capacities for earning income. Sometimes these are part-time students who are employed by business enterprises. Sometimes they are commuters who attend classes only and do not participate in other aspects of university life. Direct consumption benefits may be zero for them.

For most students the consumption benefits are inextricably mixed with the human investment elements of educational services. Classes, discussions, and social life combine to provide personal satisfaction as well as to increase the capacities of the human resource to produce goods and services.

Social spillovers

Sometimes the production or the consumption of a product yields benefits to people who neither produce nor consume it. Suppose my wealthy neighbor hires an orchestra to play at her garden party and I am not invited. She pays for the pleasure of her guests. But who is to stop me, a lover of beautiful music, from listening to its haunting strains from my side of the property line? The production of the music yields *social spillover benefits.*

Production or consumption of a product can yield *social spillover costs,* too. These are costs imposed on people not involved in the production or consumption of the good. If one of my neighbors opens a beauty shop at home, there will be a noticeable increase in traffic on our street. It will be necessary to supervise the kids more closely to keep them from being run over. This nuisance is a social spillover cost.

The widespread provision of educational services is generally thought to have social spillover benefits. Many believe that over and above the direct benefits to the individuals who receive them— greater productivity, earning power, and direct consumption benefits—there are additional benefits to the society as a whole. Some of the spillovers commonly cited are a better functioning democratic process stemming from greater voter literacy, more enlightened citizens who make the society a more pleasant place in which to live, better government services to the community, improved community sanitation techniques and facilities, reduced crime rates, and reduced fire hazards.

The incidence of the benefits

When individuals obtain college or university educations, to whom do the foregoing benefits accrue? Suppose we look again at the nature of the "product." The direct consumption benefits are easiest to assign. They very clearly add to the level of well-being of the individual student. There are no obvious widespread spillovers of these to others in the society as students work their way through the usual four years of undergraduate study.

The development of human capital also provides first-order benefits to individuals and their families. Individuals who develop engineering skills, medical skills, legal skills, or specialized knowledge and teaching skills increase their capacities to contribute to gross national product; however, they at the same time increase their abilities to earn income. The extra income that they can earn will be approximately equal to the value of their additional on-the-job productivity. Society as a whole benefits from this additional productivity since it makes greater supplies of certain goods and services available for consumption, or it may make some available that were previously not available, penicillin, for example. But these are not really social spillover benefits. They represent the same kind of increase in the productivity of the economy's resources that occurs when someone invests in a new, more productive machine. The resource owner is paid for the first-order increases in personal productivity. Then society receives a second-order benefit in the form of a greater gross national product.

To the extent that true social spillover benefits occur from higher education, the society, apart from individuals and their families, must receive them. It is very difficult to identify, quantify, and measure such benefits. Consequently, there is much debate and conjecture about whether they exist and the extent to which they exist for higher education.

Many people argue that the social spillover benefits associated with each additional year of education tend to decrease as an individual moves up through the educational system. They believe that the greatest spillovers come from the achievement of literacy—learning to read, write, and do arithmetic. These are associated with primary education. They expect secondary education to develop skills of interacting with others in the society and to provide some measure of sophistication in the administration of the joint affairs of those comprising the society. They do not believe that higher education provides much more in social spillovers. They believe that it benefits society mostly through the benefits it provides to those who obtain its services.

In summary, then, most of the benefits of higher educational services seem to accrue to the individuals who obtain those services. Society may receive some social spillover benefits. But the magnitude of these is debatable.

ECONOMIC CONCEPT OF COSTS

One of the most important principles of economics is summed up in the statement, "There ain't no such thing as a free lunch." We speak glibly of such things as free medical care, free housing, free food, and free education. What we mean is that those who use the "free" goods and services do not themselves have to pay money for them. All too often our chain of reasoning stops right there. But if we really think that these are free to the society as a whole, we delude ourselves. The production of the "free goods" is costly to someone—perhaps even partly to their users.

The economic costs of a product may or may not be reflected in the direct money outlays that must be made in producing it. The basic concept underlying economic costs is the *alternative cost principle*. In considering the costs of producing any given product, it is useful to classify its cost into two categories: (1) *explicit costs* and (2) *implicit costs*.

The alternative cost principle revisited

We defined and discussed the nature of the alternative cost principle in Chapter 1. The concept is particularly useful in identifying the costs of higher education.

Suppose we start with the production possibilities curve or transformation curve of Figure 3–1, which measures units of educational services along the horizontal axis and composite units of all other goods and services along the vertical axis—all of these in terms of dollar's worths. The curve TT_1 shows all alternative combinations of other goods and services and of education that the economy's given resources can produce per year. Suppose that initially combination B, made up of e_2 dollar's worth of education and g_2 dollar's worth of other goods and services, is being produced, and the economy's resources are fully employed.

What is the cost to the society of a unit of education when B represents the economy's output mix? *It is the value of the alternative goods and services that must be forgone to produce that unit.* Let the distance e_1e_2 represent one dollar's worth of education. If this unit had not been produced, the society could have had more of other goods and services, equal to the amount g_2g_1. Thus the society had to sacrifice g_2g_1 dollar's worth of other goods and services to produce the one unit of education. The sacrifice of the other goods and services releases just enough resources to produce the additional unit of education. We call the physical amounts of other goods and services sacrificed the *real cost* of producing the unit of education. The value that consumers attach to the goods and services given up is the true *economic money cost*.

Stated in a slightly different way, *the cost of producing a unit of any one good or service is the value of the resources used in producing it in their best alternative use.* A little reflection will show that this statement of

FIGURE 3–1
The costs of education

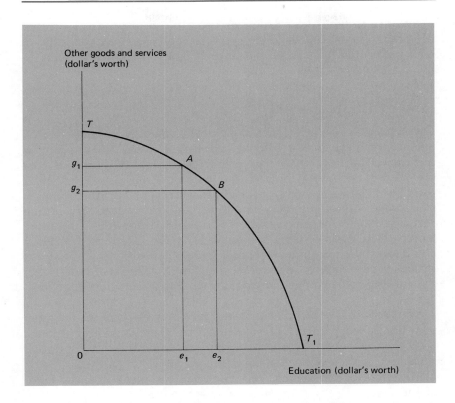

Production possibilities curve TT_1 shows all alternative combinations of other goods and services and education that the economy's resources and technology can produce per year. Two possible alternative combinations are represented by A and B. If the economy is initially producing combination B, it is obtaining g_2 units of other goods and services and e_2 units of education. If e_1e_2 represents one unit of education per year, it becomes apparent that g_2g_1 units of other goods and services must have been sacrificed to obtain it. The value of the g_2g_1 units thus measures the cost of a unit of education at the e_2 level of production.

the alternative cost principle is identical to the one developed in Chapter 1.

The alternative cost principle is capable of general application. In an economy in which resources are fully employed, an increase in the amount of medical services provided draws resources from the production of other goods and services. The value of the goods and services forgone (that is, the value of the resources that were used in their production) is the cost of the increase in medical services. The cost of a bushel of wheat is the value of the corn that must be forgone in order to produce it, if corn production is the best alternative use to which the resources used in wheat production could be put. The cost of a soldier in the society's army is the value of what one could have produced as a civilian. Thousands of such examples could be cited.

Explicit and implicit costs

The economic costs to a society of producing a good or service do not necessarily coincide with its accounting costs. As an example, consider a small family-owned grocery store for which the labor is provided by the owning family. A large part of the costs of resources used by the store to put groceries in the hands of consumers—costs of grocery stocks, utilities, and the like—are indeed accounting costs, but some resource costs may be omitted from the accounting records. The costs of labor are not likely to be listed. Amortization and depreciation costs on the land, building, furniture, and fixtures also may be omitted. The family may simply take what is left after the out-of-pocket expenses are paid, calling this remainder the "profits."

The costs of resources bought and hired for carrying on the business are called *explicit costs of production*. These are the economic costs that are most likely to be taken into account by the business, since they are usually actual cost outlays.

The costs of self-owned, self-employed resources (like the labor of the family in the example) are called *implicit costs of production*. They tend to be hidden or ignored as costs. Implicit costs of a resource can be identified by using the alternative cost principle. What the resource would be worth in its best alternative use is determined; this is its cost to the owner-user. If the family members had used their labor working for someone else, this labor would have produced other goods and services and would have earned income about equal to the value of those other goods and services. So the cost of self-employed labor is what it could have earned in its best alternative employment.

THE COSTS OF HIGHER EDUCATIONAL SERVICES

From the point of view of the society as a whole, the services of higher education are not free. Resources used in their production could have been used to produce other goods and services, and the value of those forgone goods and services is the economic cost of higher education. In this section we shall try to pin down the nature of those costs and identify who pays them.

The explicit costs

The explicit costs of the services provided by a college or university are the costs of the resources that it buys and hires to provide those services. These are the costs of capital resources and labor resources. The university uses land, buildings, equipment, and supplies. It also uses professors, maintenance personnel, administrators, secretaries, and clerks.

The institution's annual budget provides a first approximation of the annual explicit costs of its services. The budget should include amortization costs of major capital outlays, depreciation costs, small-equipment costs, maintenance costs, and the costs of hundreds of kinds of supplies. It should also include the wages and salaries of labor resources used.

The true explicit costs are the values of the resources used by the institution in their best alternative uses. This should be interpreted with some degree of caution. The economic cost of a university's buildings is not what the value of the building would be if the university were to close its doors. Rather it is the value of the goods and services that were forgone in order to build and maintain the building. Whether or not the institution's explicit economic costs are reflected accurately by its accounting records depends upon the accounting procedures it uses.

Additional explicit costs of education to students, apart from the costs of inputs used by colleges and universities in providing educational services, consist of student outlays for various items necessary or desirable in the educational process and unique to it. These include books, notebooks, calculators, pencils, pens, paper and the like. They also include clothing and entertainment costs that would not have been incurred in nonacademic life styles.

The implicit costs

The costs to a society of producing higher educational services greatly exceed the explicit costs discussed above. To obtain educational services, most students withdraw their labor wholly or partly from the labor force, thus reducing the amounts of other goods and services available to the society. In order to be students, they sacrifice some of what they could have earned as workers, and society sacrifices the value of the goods and services they would have produced had they been working. These forgone earnings, or the equivalent forgone GNP, are implicit costs to the student and to society of the educational services obtained by the student. They do not show up in the institution's budget or books of account.

Sources of support

One of the unique economic features in the production and sale of higher educational services in the United States is the diversity of the sources tapped to pay the costs. Those who have taken on the responsibility of providing higher educational services have traditionally not been willing—or able—to leave them subject to market forces. Neither public nor private universities charge their customers the full explicit costs of the educational services provided, but the extent to which they approach full costing of those services is a key difference between the two types of institutions.

Public institutions. State and community colleges and universities depend heavily on *government sources* to meet their explicit costs. For the academic year 1981–82 governments provided 75.7 percent of their current funds revenues. Almost four fifths came from state governments, almost one fifth came from the federal government, and local governments supplied the rest.[1]

Tuition and fees as a means of meeting explicit costs are relatively low at most public educational institutions. In some—those of the state of California, for example—they approach zero. Usually state colleges and universities charge higher tuition rates for out-of-state than for in-state students, indicating that state appropriations are a substitute for tuition to which they believe only the citizens of the state are entitled. About 17 percent of public institution funds came from this source in 1981–82.[2]

To a relatively small extent, public institutions depend on *private donors* to help meet their explicit costs. Funds are received from donors as endowment gifts, cash grants, scholarship gifts, and the like. The donors include foundations, corporations, philanthropists, and alumni who can be convinced that they are contributing to a worthwhile cause. To the public institution, funds from donors, rather than being a primary source of support, tend to be the frosting on

[1] U.S. Department of Health, Education, and Welfare, National Center for Educational Statistics, *Digest of Educational Statistics, 1985–86*, March 1986, p. 152. Sales and service receipts, primarily from auxiliary enterprises and athletic programs, are omitted from the calculations.
[2] Ibid.

the cake that enables it to engage in some activities that no-nonsense legislative appropriations will not permit. In 1981–82 about 4 percent of public institution funds came from private donations.[3]

Even at public colleges and universities, students and their families must pay the implicit costs of educational services. If a student does not work at all, the forgone earnings or forgone goods and services for the society as a whole are implicit costs. If the student works part time, the implicit costs are the difference between what could have been earned and what is actually earned. If the husband or wife of a student is forced to accept unemployment or less remunerative employment at the college or university site than could have been obtained elsewhere, foregone earnings will be larger than those for the student alone.

Private institutions. Private colleges and universities, since they do not receive state appropriations, must meet much of their explicit costs from the payment of *tuition* and *fees*. About 49.4 percent came from this source in 1981–82.[4] Contributions from *private donors* are also an important source of support—the more they can secure from this source, the less pressure there is to rely on tuition and the better able they are to compete with the low tuition rates of public institutions. Seeking funds from donors is always a major activity of private institutions. They obtained about 19.2 percent of their explicit costs from donors in 1981–82.[5]

Government grants to private educational institutions vary widely from school to school. Those that are research-oriented have secured sizable research grants. Many schools receive very little from government sources. For private schools in total, about 25.5 percent of their funds were obtained from government in 1981–82.[6]

The implicit costs of educational services are the same for private as for public institutions. They amount to the forgone earnings of students.

The incidence of the costs

Where do the costs of producing the services of higher education finally rest? Table 3–1 is a rough estimate of the incidence of costs

---

[3] Ibid.
[4] Ibid.
[5] Ibid.
[6] Ibid.

TABLE 3-1

Estimated per student annual cost of higher education by type of institution and source of support

	Private	Public
Explicit costs		
Tuition and fees (student and family)	$ 4,550	$ 1,500
Government appropriations, grants, and contracts (taxpayers)	2,650	7,000
Private gifts, grants, contracts, and endowment income (donors)	1,800	500
Books and miscellaneous items (student and family)	1,500	1,500
Total explicit costs	$10,500	$10,500
Implicit costs		
Foregone income (student and family)	$13,000	$13,000
Total costs	$23,500	$23,500

Note: We assume equal sizes and qualities of the public and the private institution.

for a typical good public institution and a typical good private institution. We assume that the kinds and qualities of services provided are the same for each institution and that each is equally efficient in providing them. Three features of the incidence of costs are significant.

First, implicit costs are a very large part of the total costs of the educational services provided a student. They amount to about 55 percent of the total costs. Note that they are the same whether the student attends a public or a private institution.

Second, the major source of support for the explicit costs of public institutions is government appropriations, while that for private institutions is tuition and fees. Except for scholarship holders, the burden of tuition and fees rests on students and their families. Government appropriations are made from general revenue funds in any given state and consist of money collected from taxpayers of the state; consequently, the incidence of this large part (over one half) of the explicit costs of public institutions rests on taxpayers rather than on students and their families. Public institutions, then, bring about a shift in the incidence of over one half of the explicit costs of higher educational services from students and their families to taxpayers.

Third, private institutions rely more heavily on donors as a source of support than do public institutions. To the extent that funds can be obtained from donors and substituted for tuition, the incidence of explicit costs is shifted from students and their families to donors. About 17 percent of the incidence of explicit costs of private institutions is shifted from students and their families to donors.

ECONOMIC EVALUATION OF THE PROBLEMS

While the economic framework established in the preceding sections permits the problems of higher education to be approached in a systematic and logical way, it does not always provide clear-cut, correct solutions. Economic analysis helps determine what causes what, and why. It helps determine, once goals have been set, the most efficient way of reaching those goals. However, economic analysis cannot always provide answers as to what the goals or objectives in higher education or any other activity should be. Equally intelligent people often disagree on the goals that should be sought by a particular society.

What kinds of services?

Are our expectations realistic with respect to the kinds of services higher education should produce? Of course they are! The industry can produce whatever mix of services we as a society want it to produce. The important economic problem is concerned with how well institutions respond to the society's desires or demands for those services.

Economic analysis generates questions as to how responsive the current structure of higher educational institutions permits them to be in meeting societal demands. By and large, throughout the economic system consumers register their demands for goods and services by the ways in which they dispose of or spend their purchasing power. Suppliers respond to the array of prices that results. Is this the way in which the mix of programs that are offered by colleges and universities is determined? Obviously not.

Colleges and universities make little or no use of the price system in determining what programs they will offer. Their officials usually try to offer what they think the society wants—business, engineering, computer science, and the like. Of course, the desires of students and their families must be taken into consideration; otherwise, the enrollments would not be forthcoming. In addition, in public institutions that depend heavily on legislative appropriations, the desires of the legislature are of great importance. The legislature can threaten to withhold appropriations that might be used to expand programs of which the majority of its members may disapprove. In private institutions major donors may be able to influence programs offered; however, the interests of students and their families are likely to receive prime consideration since they represent the main source of revenue to the schools.

One wonders why the price system is so completely ignored or snubbed in determining program priorities. Most colleges and universities charge the same price (tuition) to all students, regardless of the program of study pursued. College and university administrators and faculties, legislators, and students themselves seem to believe that this is the equitable way to operate the system. Yet, a little reflection will reveal its inefficiency.

Consider two possible undergraduate programs, say business administration and agriculture. Suppose that initially, student demand for agricultural programs is represented by $D_{a1}D_{a1}$ in Figure 3–2. The price per person per year is a composite of all costs except implicit costs to the student of a year of the program. The demand curve for agricultural programs would be expected to slope downward to the right as do most demand curves—the lower the price of the program, the more person-years of it students will demand. The supply curve, $S_{a1}S_{a1}$, of agricultural programs would be expected to slope upward to the right. The more money per person-year universities can obtain from sale of such programs, the more resources they can attract and use to expand them. The demand curve, $D_{b1}D_{b1}$, and the supply curve, $S_{b1}S_{b1}$, for business administration programs are conceptually the same as those for agricultural programs. Ignore $D_{b2}D_{b2}$ for the time being. Suppose that, by some great coincidence, the initial supply and demand curves for both programs are such that the person-year prices are the same for each; that is, p_{a1} equals p_{b1}. The program sizes are s_{a1} and s_{b1}, respectively.

Now, let student demand for business administration programs increase relative to that for agricultural programs. The business administration demand curve shifts to $D_{b2}D_{b2}$, and the agricultural demand curve shifts to $D_{a2}D_{a2}$. What are the effects of maintaining equal prices for the two programs as colleges and universities now tend to do? At price p_{b1}, universities cannot expand business administration programs and cover the costs of doing so. A shortage of business administration faculty and facilities will result. Classes will be larger and rooms will be more crowded. The quality of instruction will deteriorate. In agriculture programs, at price p_{a1} class sizes will decrease and facilities will be less fully utilized. There is a relative surplus of faculty and facilities. Shortages and surpluses of these types are common in colleges and universities today. They represent inefficiencies in the production of educational services.

If universities were to use a differential pricing scheme for different programs, they could increase both efficiency and responsiveness to customers. Let tuition and fees in business administration rise to p_{b2}. Additional revenue is obtained to expand to s_{b2}, taking care of the increased demand. The price increase also serves to re-

FIGURE 3-2
Effects of changes in demand for educational services

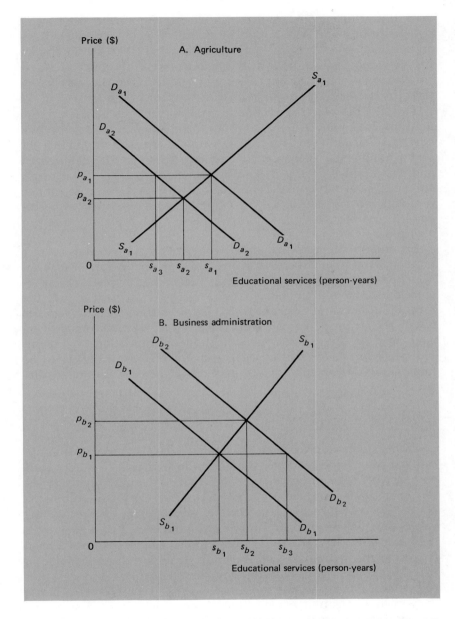

Suppose that $D_{a1}D_{a1}$ and $S_{a1}S_{a1}$ are the initial demand and supply curves for person-years of agricultural education, while in business administration they are $D_{b1}D_{b1}$ and $S_{b1}S_{b1}$. Suppose, further, they are such that the explicit costs of each kind of education are the same; that is $p_{a1} = p_{b1}$. Now, suppose that demand for business administration increases to $D_{b2}D_{b2}$ and demand for agriculture falls to $D_{a2}D_{a2}$. Maintaining explicit costs (tuition and fees) at p_{b1} results in a surplus of agricultural educational capacity and a shortage of business administration capacity. Letting the tuition and fees for business administration rise to p_{b2} and those for agriculture fall to p_{a2} will result in an increase in business administration capacity and a decrease in agricultural capacity, thereby increasing the efficiency with which both are utilized.

duce the pressure on facilities by reducing enrollment from s_{b3} to s_{b2}. Let tuition and fees in agriculture fall to p_{a2}. Universities have an incentive to cut programs back to s_{a2} at which they are once more just covering costs. Additionally, the decrease in the price of a person-year of agriculture from p_{a1} to p_{a2} will increase the enrollment after the decrease in demand has occurred from s_{a3} to s_{a2}.

To make the preceding economic analysis more general, suppose that in universities a demand arises for a program that has previously not existed—say, for ecology studies. Costs of supplying different numbers of person-years of the program can be determined and the supply curve can then be matched up with the demand curve. The resulting equilibrium price will reflect the costs of the program and the values of the program to students. It will also generate the correct program capacity reflecting neither a shortage nor a surplus.

Experience suggests that public colleges and universities will be more inclined to maintain the status quo than will private ones. Legislatures move slowly, and many functions other than education occupy their time and attention. Yet they are not inclined to give the regents, administrations, and faculties of colleges and universities under their control a free hand, since the legislatures remain "accountable" to the general public for how appropriations are spent. The programs of private colleges and universities are likely to be more flexible over time and to be more responsive to student desires.

How much service?

Economic analysis provides a conceptual answer to how much educational service the economy should produce relative to other goods and services. The resources used in producing educational services can be used to produce other goods and services, and, from the alternative cost principle, the costs of educational services are the values of those resources in their alternative uses. Consequently, if the value to society of a unit of educational services is greater than its costs—the resources used in producing it are more valuable in the production of education than in alternative ones—then the output of educational services should be expanded. On the other hand, if the value of a unit of educational services is worth less to the society than it costs to produce it, the output should be reduced.

In terms of demand-supply analysis, let DD represent the demand curve for higher educational services and SS be the supply curve for them in Figure 3–3. If the economy is presently providing a quantity of s_1 person-years, the value of a unit to demanders (stu-

FIGURE 3–3
Determination of the correct amount of educational services

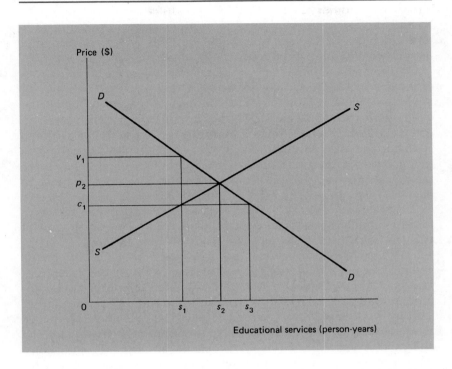

If s_1 person-years of educational services are provided in the society, the value of a person-year exceeds its cost, indicating that an expansion of services is in order. At the s_2 level of services, the value of a person-year is equal to the costs of providing it. The correct amount for the society in s_2.

dents) is v_1, but the cost of a unit to the society is c_1. The excess of the value of a year's education over its cost indicates that resources needed to produce a year of education are more valuable if they are so used than they would be in their best alternative uses. Educational services should be expanded relative to the production of other goods and services in the economy. The correct amount of educational services for the society is s_2 priced at p_2 per person-year. What can you say about quantity s_3?

The value of higher education services in relation to their costs is obscured by the way they are provided currently. Higher educational services are not priced in the marketplace in a way that will cause the quantity supplied to be adjusted to the quantity demanded. On the demand side, it is difficult, if not impossible, for students in the present system to make known how they value alternative quantities of educational services. The combination of public and private sources of support on the supply side compounds the difficulties of valuing educational services and of determining how much should be produced.

On the demand side, consider potential students who want educational services in some specific field—say medical training. In medical schools throughout the country, the annual number of openings for students is limited. At current levels of costs per student, many more want training than can be accepted; that is, there is a shortage of medical training services. This is the same thing as saying that potential medical students would be willing to pay more for the services of medical schools than they are now required to pay. However, students are not permitted to bid up the price at which these educational services are offered, and hence the price system cannot express their valuations of them. The same kind of analysis holds true for many other fields of specialization.

The supply of educational services made available by public higher education institutions is not a direct response to student demands. The amounts supplied are determined primarily by the appropriations public institutions receive from state legislatures rather than by what students are willing to pay. Colleges and universities compete with a number of other state-supported activities for the dollars that legislatures have available to appropriate; and, since state revenues are limited, they will never receive as much as educational administrators think they ought to have. At the same time, such public institutions are reluctant to supplement the funds received from the state with tuition receipts. Tuition is supposed to be kept low because of state appropriations—this is the purpose of the state-allocated funds. The higher the tuition rates set by the public institutions, the less will be their bargaining power with the legislature for state-appropriated funds.

State colleges and universities can be expected to encounter a continuous financial crisis. The services they can supply are limited by the always inadequate appropriations received from the state, while the demands for their services are augmented as they succumb to the pressure to keep their tuition rates low.

At the same time, the relatively low tuition rates of the public institutions enable them to draw students away from private institutions. The competition of public institutions limits the services that can be provided by private institutions. It also sets upper limits on the tuition rates that private institutions can charge and still remain in business. Pressure on private institutions to obtain gifts, grants, and the like is increased. Competition from public institutions makes it very difficult for private colleges and universities to stay solvent.

Who should pay?

The controversy over who should pay for higher educational services is undoubtedly the key problem faced by higher education. If this problem could be resolved, answers to "what kind" and "how much" would be much easier to determine. At one extreme of the controversy are those who maintain that educational services should be "above" market forces. Education is seen as the great equalizer, providing opportunities for self-development and self-realization. Everyone is entitled to as much education as one is able to absorb, and consequently educational services should be free. At the other extreme are those who believe that each student and family should bear the full costs of that student's education.

"Free" education. What is meant by "free" education? The economic aspects of higher education discussed in this chapter make it clear that there is no such thing from society's point of view. Neither is education free from the individual student's point of view—unless, of course, both explicit and implicit costs are covered by scholarships. Ordinarily education is said to be free if state appropriations to state colleges and universities are large enough so that no tuition is charged. This has been the case in the California system of higher education. In most states, public colleges and universities are not tuition-free; state appropriations simply permit them to charge substantially lower tuition than do private institutions.

The differences in costs between what is generally called a free education in a state college or university and what is called a full-cost education in a private college or university are nowhere near as great as tuition differentials would lead us to believe. In the example in Table 3–1, the annual costs borne by the student and family in a public institution would be about $14,700, while in the private institution they would be about $17,700.

State support of higher education. In terms of economic analysis, state support of higher education means that some part of the costs of obtaining educational services is shifted from the student who receives the services to taxpayers. State appropriations to the college or university decrease the tuition that students are required to pay.

Funds appropriated to the institution by the state are obtained from taxpayers. Thus state support constitutes a *transfer* of purchasing power from taxpayers to college and university students.

Under what circumstances do such transfers seem to be in order? It appears they are defensible: (1) to the extent that social spillover benefits are generated by higher education and (2) as a means of enabling children of the poor to develop their human resources.

When the consumption or utilization of some good or service by one or more people results in spillover benefits to others, those who receive the spillover benefits are in a good position to be *free riders*. Direct consumers of an item pay for the direct benefits they receive; otherwise, they will not be able to obtain whatever it is they want to consume. Those who receive the spillover benefits receive them whether they pay anything or not; their tendency is to be free riders and pay nothing. Direct consumers are in no position to force the free riders to pay, but what they cannot do as individual private citizens they may be able to accomplish collectively through their government. The government can levy taxes on the free riders, thus coercing them to pay for the spillover benefits they receive. The government is a unique and logical agency to accomplish this purpose.

If social spillover benefits from higher educational services exist, the use of state taxing powers and state support of higher education sufficient to pay for those benefits would seem to be reasonable. Several questions arise. The most important one is whether or not significant social spillover benefits are generated in the provision of higher educational services. If they are, they have never been unambiguously identified, much less measured in value terms. Further, if they do exist, they are generated by private colleges and universities as well as by public institutions. On these grounds, should not the higher education provided by private universities be subsidized to about the same extent as that provided by state universities?

The other major argument for state support of higher education is that it enables capable but poor students to obtain a college or university education. Education serves to increase the capacities of human resources to produce and to earn income. Since poor families do not have the means of paying for higher education for their children, and this is not the fault of the children, the state can do much to enable them to escape from poverty by providing them with the same kind of educational opportunities that are available to the children of middle and higher income families.

The case has much merit. One of the generally recognized functions of government in the modern world is that of mitigating poverty. In the United States, very substantial parts of both state and federal budgets are for this purpose. Welfare programs, along with income taxes that are intended to take larger proportions of the incomes of the rich than of the poor, provide examples. It seems reasonable that state support of higher education for the poor should be an integral and important part of any antipoverty program.

Although state support looms large in meeting the explicit costs of educational services in public institutions, the implicit costs that still must be met by the student and the student's family are a very substantial part of the total costs. The inability of a poor family to meet the implicit costs, the need for children to go to work and earn income, discourages the children of the poor from attending any college or university, public or private. For the most part, state supported colleges and universities are not devices for transferring purchasing power from taxpayers to children of the poor. Most college and university students do not come from poor families, they come from middle and upper income families. Most of the transfer, then, is from taxpayers in general to middle and upper income families.

The foregoing statement is substantiated by 1980 data on first-time college and university students in the United States as a whole. Some 14.6 percent came from families earning less than $10,000 per year. Another 26.1 percent were from families earning $10,000 to $20,000 per year. The remaining 59.3 percent came from families earning $20,000 or more per year.[7]

Student self-support. Many people believe that students and their families rather than the state should bear the costs of higher education. This does not necessarily mean abandonment of state institutions. A state-owned college or university can recover the full costs of education through tuition and fees levied on students just as a private one can. There are two main arguments why students should pay for their own education. These are that (1) those who benefit are the ones who should pay, and (2) economic resources would be used more efficiently; that is, some waste would be avoided.

The argument that those who benefit should pay is an equity argument. It asks why one group of persons—taxpayers—should be forced to pay a part of the educational costs of another group—students and their families. To be sure, there will be overlapping of the two groups; students and their families are also taxpayers. How-

---

[7] U.S. Department of Health, Education, and Welfare, National Center for Educational Statistics, *Digest of Educational Statistics, 1982*, p. 97.

ever, a much larger proportion of taxpayers are not college and university students, and neither are their children. Many of these are poor families. And, as indicated above, 59.3 percent of the freshmen entering a typical state-supported institution in 1980 came from families with incomes above $20,000 per year. Is it equitable for the state to levy taxes that rest partly on poorer nonstudent families to help pay for the education of children from middle-income and wealthy families?

The argument maintains further that investment in human capital is essentially comparable to investment in material capital. Suppose a high school graduate has a choice of investing in an education or investing in a business. One considers the payoff of each in terms of future well-being and makes the choice that one (and one's family) thinks will yield the highest return on the investment. This is the way that intelligent economic decision making should be accomplished. Ordinarily we do not expect taxpayers to bear a part of the investments of high school graduates in businesses. Why should we expect them to bear a part of such investments in higher education?

Another argument for student self-support is that people tend to waste whatever is free to them and to economize or conserve whatever they have to pay for. The greater the cost of a purchase relative to one's income, the more incentive one has to use the item carefully in order to increase the possible returns from it. This is said to be the premise underlying high charges made by psychiatrists for their services. The argument is used extensively by those who think students should pay for their own education.

If higher educational services are provided at reduced or free tuition costs to students, the incentive to economize on or make the best possible use of the resources providing those services is weakened—so the argument runs. Low tuition induces students who have no interest in learning to attend the university, whereas higher tuition charges would make them or their parents think more carefully about whether or not they should do so. Further, those who do attend would be inclined to make more of their opportunities if they cost more. There would be less inclination to waste professors' time or to destroy property.

Which way? Which of the arguments is correct? If the student and family reap the benefits of higher education—that is, if the benefits of higher education are primarily private human capital development—then a strong case can be made that the student and family should pay its full costs. If substantial social spillover benefits result from putting some part of the population through the processes of higher education, or if higher education is used effectively as a campaign against poverty, a strong case can be made for shifting a part of its costs to taxpayers.

An alternative institutional structure

When an activity such as higher education has been pursued over a long period of time, a set of institutions is developed to carry on the activity. The structure of the set that evolves becomes very difficult to change. First, people think in terms of the structure to which they have become accustomed and find it hard to think in terms of alternatives. Second, the performance of the present structure is known; the alternative might not work. Third, many people build up vested interests in the existing structure and can be expected to resist changes that would affect them.

The possibility that the institutional structure of higher education in the United States is outmoded is worth considering. Some 80 percent of college and university students in the United States are enrolled in public institutions that receive the bulk of their support from legislative appropriations. The rationale for the state-supported system is that (1) it makes higher education available to the children of poor families and (2) it increases the social spillover benefits of higher education by encouraging large enrollments. As we have argued, it does not appear to serve either of these purposes very well. The implicit costs of higher education are so great that even with the low tuition rates of public institutions, few children of the poor find it possible to attend. It seems likely that the most important effect of the low tuition rates of public institutions is to divert students from private to public institutions rather than to bring about any substantial increase in enrollment in all institutions. In addition, the present system does not enable the society to place accurate demand values on the services being provided, nor does it provide the mechanism for colleges and universities to be responsive to the demands of the society.

An alternative to the present higher education institutional structure is one that would make greater use of the price system in the production of higher educational services. A key feature of such an alternative is that students obtaining educational services would pay tuition to the colleges and universities they attend sufficient to cover the full explicit costs of the services obtained. There would be no differentiation between private and public institutions in this respect. If public institutions were to remain public, they would be required to pay their own way without obtaining direct appropriations from legislatures.

If the society desires to help the children of the poor to obtain educational services, it could do so easily and directly. Instead of allocating money to public colleges and universities, legislatures could make grants directly to the children of the poor, letting them choose for themselves the institutions they would attend. Presumably they would attend the institutions that best meet their needs. The antipoverty aspects of state support would be realized directly and efficiently. The state would not be supporting those who are not in need; with the present system, many of those it supports are not in need.

If, because of spillover benefits, the state desires to encourage larger enrollments than would occur if all students were required to pay the full costs of the services they obtain, this also can be done easily and directly. By raising the minimum income standards used to define what constitutes a poor family, the state can increase the number of students eligible for state support. Besides tuition scholarships to meet explicit costs, various devices now in use can continue to assist students from low-income families in meeting their implicit costs. These include access to loan funds, part-time employment, and the like.

Such an institutional structure should go far toward solving the problems that confront higher education. It would attack the problem of who should pay, moving toward a structure in which those who receive the benefits are the ones who pay the costs. But note that this *does not* preclude using the system of higher education as a part of an antipoverty program, nor does it preclude government (taxpayer) support of higher education. Government support would contribute more directly and more efficiently to making higher education available to the children of the poor.

Such a structure would also move toward a solution of the perpetual financial crisis of higher education. Government support of higher educational services—whatever the amount of support the society desires—would be provided to students and not to institutions. This would eliminate the primary cause of the crisis—the support of public institutions by the state, which, though usually thought to be inadequate, entails low-tuition competition and attendant financial problems for private institutions.

Further, it would tend to induce the education industry to supply the quantity of educational services the society wants relative to the quantities of other goods and services produced in the economy. Tuition would be the main source of revenue for institutions; it would cover the full explicit costs of services supplied. Colleges and universities would supply services to as many persons as are willing to pay that tuition. Persons not willing to pay the full tuition are saying in effect that alternative ways of spending that amount of money yield greater satisfaction to them.

Finally, the proposed institutional structure should be responsive to its clientele—students and their families. Institutions not responsive to the wants of students and their families would lose students to those that are. Competition among institutions for students' tuition should generate greater efficiency and a variety of innovations in programs and in the techniques of providing educational services.

SUMMARY

Colleges and universities face many problems, most of them stemming from four fundamental issues: (1) what kinds of services they should provide, (2) how much service should be provided, (3) what is the appropriate institutional structure, and (4) who should pay for it. These are issues about which economic analysis has much to say.

Institutions of higher education use resources to produce educational services. These services provide (1) investment in human capital, (2) direct consumption benefits, and (3) social spillover benefits. By far, the greatest part of educational services appears to be composed of investment in human capital. There is controversy over the extent to which social spillover benefits exist, but these are not likely to be a large part of the total. The first-order benefits of educational services accrue mainly to the student who obtains them, although society gains from secondary benefits just as it does from investment in material capital.

Higher educational services, like other goods and services, have economic costs. All economic costs are measured by the alternative cost principle. Some costs are explicit in nature, while others are implicit. The explicit costs of higher education services are the costs of the capital and labor resources used by colleges and universities. Most people view these as the total costs. However, to students and their families there are implicit costs that are greater in amount than the explicit costs. Most important of these are the forgone earnings of students and their families.

Sources of support (payment of explicit costs) for higher educational institutions in the United States are different for public than for private institutions. Structurally, the system of institutions consists of public institutions, which receive the bulk of their revenues in the form of state legislative appropriations, and private institutions, which receive the bulk of their revenues from tuition. The implicit costs to students do not enter into college and university budgets and are the same whether they attend public or private institutions. The incidence of the costs of higher educational services rests most heavily on the student and family, even in public institutions, despite their relatively low tuition levels.

An economic evaluation of the fundamental problems involved in the provision of higher educational services highlights several shortcomings of the present institutional structure of higher educational facilities. Public institutions, supported primarily by legislative appropriations, are likely to be more responsive to the demands of legislators than to the demands of students in the determination of what kinds of services should be provided. The amounts of services provided also are determined by legislative appropriations rather than by the economic factors of demand and costs. As a device for making educational opportunities available to the children of the poor, public institutions leave much to be desired.

An alternative structure for higher educational institutions that appears worthy of serious consideration is one in which the tuition rates charged are sufficient to cover all the explicit costs of providing educational services. This would tend to make institutions more responsive to the demands of students and their families. It would tend toward the production of the "correct" amounts of higher educational services, as compared with other goods and services. It would also provide a structure in which state (taxpayer) support of the educational costs of the children of the poor could be met directly and efficiently.

SUPPLEMENTARY READINGS

Bowen, Howard R. *The Costs of Higher Education: How Much Do Colleges and Universities Spend per Student and How Much Should They Spend?* San Francisco: Jossey-Bass, 1980.

> Addresses the questions raised in the title. Carefully differentiates between monetary expenditures and real costs.

Bowen, Howard R. *Investment in Learning: The Individual and Social Value of American Higher Education.* San Francisco: Jossey-Bass, 1977.

> Chapter 9, "Social Outcomes from Education," is particularly interesting. Bowen emphasizes the role of higher education in promoting social change and argues that higher education entails social spillover benefits even though there is little or no empirical evidence to that effect.

Douglass, Gordon K. "Economic Returns to Investment in Higher Education." In *Investment in Learning: the Individual and Social Value of American Higher Education,* ed. Howard R. Bowen. San Francisco: Jossey-Bass, 1977.

> Describes the decision to acquire a college education as an investment in human capital and presents estimates of the return on investment from empirical research.

Doyle, Dennis P. *The Federal Student-Aid Mess. The Wall Street Journal,* May 19, 1982, p. 30.

Reviews the Reagan Administration's position on federal aid for college students and summarizes Milton Friedman's view and recommendations on the role of government in education.

Windham, Douglas M. "The Public Responsibility for Higher Education: Policy Issues and Research Directions." In *Subsidies to Higher Education,* ed. Howard P. Tuckman and Edward Whalen. New York: Praeger Publishers, 1980.

A careful, thoughtful discussion of whether or not externalities exist in undergraduate education.

ENERGY PROBLEMS

The problems perceived by the public
The economics of energy
　Demand
　Supply
How to create energy problems
　Price controls
　Allocations of crude oil
　Conservation and other measures
Toward alleviating the problems
　The adequacy of petroleum supplies
　Alternative energy sources
　The efficiency of the price mechanism
　The role of the government
Summary

**Checklist of
Economic Concepts**

Demand
Demand, changes in
Supply
Supply, changes in
Price ceilings
Price, equilibrium
Shortage
Imports
Inflation
Rationing
Efficiency
Profits

4

Energy Problems

Must simple things be made complex?

Whenever I warn people that another energy crisis is on the way, I draw raised eyebrows and skeptical sneers.

"We thought we were through with those things," my friends hoot. "Don't we have oil and gas running out of our ears? And plenty of electricity?"

My answer is, "Yes, for the moment," but I also add this warning: energy plenty is not going to last.

I'm saying this loud and clear to anyone who will listen because I never again want to go through another day like January 23, 1974. That was when I sat embarrassed and angry in a Washington hearing room while the late Senator Henry Jackson waved a finger at me and other petroleum executives. He demanded to know whether the energy crisis that had begun the previous year was real or some kind of oil-industry concoction to raise prices.

It *was* real, but many times since, I wished I'd had the presence of mind to add: "But Senator, it need never have happened. In the three years before the 1973–74 energy crisis, we began warning of impending shortages, urging more reliance on mass transit, more domestic petroleum development and the creation of a national-energy policy. But no one wanted to hear it."

The trouble is, Congress—like all of us—tends to be complacent until crisis fires the adrenaline. Unfortunately, government's worst decisions in energy, like its ill-fated fuel-allocation program and the billions wasted on crash alternative-energy schemes, have been those responding to crisis. Sound energy decisions that avert crisis usually come in quiet times like these.

So let me say it once again, louder:

We're headed for another round of energy shortages. Certainly by the end of this century. Possibly well before that.

Planning. If a crisis even that close seems nonthreatening, remember what most people often forget: lead times in energy require very long-range planning and investment. Even when we're successful in finding a new oil or gas field, putting it into production can take five to eight years. Bringing a nuclear power plant from drawing board to start-up can often take more than a decade.

So once more, still louder:

We're seeing patterns like those that led to the 1973–74 and 1979–80 energy crises:

In 9 of the past 10 years, the United States used more natural gas than was found in this country.

After dropping for four years, U.S. crude oil and product imports rose 8 percent last year, reflecting revived domestic consumption that exceeded domestic production. Approximately one third of our oil supplies now comes from abroad, the same level as before the 1973–74 energy crisis.

U.S. energy demand is conservatively estimated to be 20 to 25 percent higher by the year 2000 than it is today. In the petroleum industry that will require finding considerably more oil and gas than we use up each year, which will be possible only with a very high level of investment.

Granted, the situation is not critical now, and there are emerging plus factors that will reduce the severity of future shortages: oil-refining capacity that's more than adequate; approximately 460 million barrels of oil in the Strategic Petroleum Reserve; increased availability of oil and gas from non-OPEC areas like Canada, Mexico, and the North Sea, and enough electricity-generating capacity in place or being built to meet immediately foreseeable needs. But that is my very point: today's relative quiet gives us a magnificent opportunity to plan energy development in a noncrisis atmosphere.

Now is the time for government, industry, and the concerned public to develop without panic those policies that will resolve future energy needs fairly and practically, responsive both to the public interest and to sound business judgment. And like the effort to revamp the tax structure, new conceptual ground may need to be broken.

How, for example, can we best halt, or at least slow, the decline in U.S. reserves of oil and natural gas—down some 20 percent in the past decade and a half?

Are there significant additional ways to conserve more fuel, or has this avenue been pretty well exhausted?

Could there be a more orderly, environmentally protected, less costly method of finding and using the oil and gas on public lands?

Might the time be ripe for a concerted government effort to restore the credibility of nuclear power plants and reduce the construction time, now that we have better inspections, improved training of operators, and other new safety measures resulting from the Three Mile Island investigation?

Taxes. Last and most important, should we not look at taxes on energy? Energy producers shouldn't be discriminated against; the arguments for tax incentives to find and produce energy are as strong as those for incentives to do research. Given the difficult times in which the oil industry currently finds itself, can we still justify taxes on so-called windfall profits that apply only to this industry? Is it fair that a special levy on crude oil should finance the clean-up of pollution created by nonoil companies? The effect of taxation on future energy security should concern us all.

With enough thoughtful attention to energy now, the crisis I'm predicting need never happen—at least not as severely as before.[1]

THE PROBLEMS PERCEIVED BY THE PUBLIC

The 1970s were difficult times in the energy industry. At the beginning of that decade, crude oil prices were somewhere around $3.50 per barrel, and most of us used oil derivatives as though they were going out of style. Then, suddenly, we were jerked up short. Spot shortages of gasoline began to appear during 1972 and became more widespread through 1973. In the winter and spring of 1973–74, Arab countries imposed an embargo on oil shipments to the United States, and shortages became acute. From late 1974 to the summer of 1979 the pressure on gasoline supplies seemed much abated. Then, in the summer of 1979 gasoline shortages severe enough to cause long lines and informal rationing once more appeared. But from the fall of 1980 until the present time petroleum supplies have seemed plentiful. These days we even hear talk of petroleum "gluts."

Even though the energy crisis is over, the average citizen still finds the energy picture confusing. Carryover from the shortages of the 1970s remains. If we can run the gamut from a plentiful supply to shortages to gluts so rapidly, isn't it reasonable to expect prob-

---

[1]Allen E. Murray, "The Impending Energy Crisis," *Newsweek*, June 10, 1985, p. 16.

lems in the future? Would it be in our best interests to be energy independent? At some time in the future are we, or our children, going to run out of energy and freeze to death in the dark?

First of all, many people worry about *shortages*. If it could happen in the 1970s, they believe it can happen again. We are highly dependent on our automobiles to get us to our jobs, to take vacations, and for many other purposes. We resent the prospects of restrictions on when we can drive, the amount of gasoline we can buy at any one time, waiting in line at the gasoline pump, and the many other frustrations that shortages imply.

Second, there is concern about heavy *dependence on foreign supplies*. The thinking is that it makes us susceptible to the inconveniences of disruptions like those from the Arab embargo in 1973–74, and the cut-off of Iranian supplies in 1979. And, of course, there are fears that it would be disastrous during wartime if a major source of supply were suddenly to become unavailable.

Third, some people still seem convinced that dwindling oil supplies in the future will force a *reduction in living standards*. They make much of our past and present energy extravagance. They note that the earth contains finite amounts of fossil fuels. When these are used up, they say, the party is over; living standards will fall.

THE ECONOMICS OF ENERGY

Basic economic analysis is useful in sorting out and evaluating the various facets of the energy situation. It indicates that the crisis of the 1970s was primarily the result of misguided policies on the part of the U.S. government—policies that ensured the development of an energy crisis. They brought about declining levels of domestic production of crude oil and natural gas, increasing levels of imports, sporadic shortages, and a sense of confusion and frustration on the part of the public.

Energy problems in the United States centered primarily on petroleum, which provided some 41.7 percent of the total energy requirements of the economy in 1985. Another 24.0 percent was filled by natural gas. Coal took care of 23.6 percent of the total requirements, and the remaining 10.5 percent came from hydro, nuclear, and other sources.[2]

---

[2]U.S. Department of Energy, Energy Information Administration, *Monthly Energy Review*, September 1986, p. 11.

Demand

Direct demand for nonhuman energy in all forms originates with *residential and commercial users, industrial users,* and *transportation users.* Some 36 percent of total demand in 1985 was by residential and commercial users. Industrial users contributed 36.5 percent of the total demand. The remaining 27.5 percent was generated by transportation users. Transportation users account for well over half the demand for petroleum energy. The rest of the demand for petroleum energy is about equally split between commercial and residential users on the one hand and industrial users on the other. Residential and commercial users account for almost half the demand for natural gas. Electric utility companies are by far the largest users of coal and the sole users of hydroelectric and nuclear sources of power. They, in turn, sell electricity to the three classes of final users, with over half their output of electricity going to residential and commercial users.[3]

In the transportation area, automobiles, trucks, buses, and airplanes are the important petroleum energy users. The number of automobiles, trucks, and buses on the road has almost tripled since World War II, and, in contrast to Europeans, our tastes have been strong for large, powerful cars that consume prodigious amounts of fuel. Our concern with environmental quality in recent years has led to mandatory antipollution devices on our motorized vehicles that have in turn reduced the miles per gallon obtained and increased total fuel consumption. In commercial aviation, piston engine airplanes have been replaced by fuel-hungry jets. Even the number of piston engine general aviation airplanes has been increasing rapidly, although quantitatively these are not yet a significant factor in the total demand for petroleum products.

Increasing residential and commercial demand for petroleum products reflects general economic expansion and rising affluence. The population is growing; greater numbers of houses are being built; and houses are larger. Central heating and air conditioning induce us to heat more rooms in our homes than we did with the space heaters and floor furnaces of years ago. Numbers of commercial establishments and the average size of the areas enclosed by them have been increasing commensurately.

Industrial demand for energy has been rising over time. The most obvious reason is the expanding industrial activity associated with

---

[3]Ibid, p. 25.

economic growth. Industrial demand for coal continues to increase, as it does for petroleum products—fuel oil.

The demand for petroleum by electricity-generating plants is shrinking. Again, economic growth and rising affluence create rising needs for electricity for lighting, heating, and cooling and for running the ever-growing number of appliances that come on the market. But, power-generating plants typically rely more heavily on coal and natural gas as fuels than on petroleum. Since 1973 their consumption of coal has increased by 68 percent; consumption of natural gas has been almost level; and consumption of fuel oil has been halved. In 1985 coal provided almost 14 times as many BTUs as did fuel oil and 4 times as many BTUs as natural gas.[4]

The pattern of energy consumption in the United States from 1973 to 1985 is shown in Table 4–1. Overall consumption peaked in 1979 and has since declined by about 6 percent. Peak petroleum consumption was reached in 1978 while that of coal was reached in 1985. Natural gas consumption has evidenced a more even pattern over time with 1973 as the highest year in the series and with 1983 as the lowest.

Supply

Energy supplies in the United States have been increasing over time but have not kept pace with the increasing demands for them. The production of bituminous coal has increased steadily over the past 10 years, but the output of the cleaner-burning Pennsylvania anthracite, a very small proportion of total coal production, has decreased. Natural gas production has been declining since 1965. Nuclear power has not yet been tapped in any sizable quantities, but its use has grown as the costs of more conventional energy supplies rise. Thus, petroleum, which accounts for almost half our energy supplies, has been the crucial element in the supply picture over the past decade and will continue to be for several years to come.

As Table 4–2 and Figure 4–1 show, the production of crude oil in the United States rose steadily until 1970. Most people believed that the annual increases in output could go on forever. However, U.S. production of crude oil peaked in 1970 and declined somewhat thereafter. Between 1974 and 1984 U.S. production remained remarkably stable. Domestic production of crude oil has dropped sig-

---

[4]Ibid, p. 33.

TABLE 4–1
Consumption of energy by type, 1973–1985 (quadrillion BTUs; percent in parentheses)

Year	Coal	Natural gas	Petroleum	Hydro electric power	Nuclear electric power	Other	Total
1973	12.978 (17.5)	22.512 (30.3)	34.840 (46.9)	3.010 (4.0)	0.910 (1.2)	0.038	74.288 (100)
1974	12.688 (17.5)	21.732 (30.0)	33.455 (46.1)	3.309 (4.6)	1.272 (1.8)	0.112	72.548 (100)
1975	12.668 (18.0)	19.948 (28.3)	32.731 (46.4)	3.219 (4.6)	1.900 (2.7)	0.086	70.551 (100)
1976	13.589 (18.3)	20.345 (27.4)	35.175 (47.3)	3.066 (4.1)	2.111 (2.8)	0.081	74.368 (100)
1977	13.925 (18.3)	19.931 (26.1)	37.122 (48.7)	2.515 (3.3)	2.702 (3.5)	0.097	76.292 (100)
1978	13.767 (17.6)	20.000 (25.6)	37.965 (48.6)	3.141 (4.0)	3.024 (3.9)	0.193	78.091 (100)
1979	15.042 (19.1)	20.666 (26.2)	37.123 (47.1)	3.141 (4.0)	2.776 (3.5)	0.152	78.900 (100)
1980	15.426 (20.3)	20.391 (26.8)	34.202 (45.0)	3.118 (4.1)	2.739 (3.6)	0.079	75.955 (100)
1981	15.908 (21.5)	19.926 (26.9)	31.931 (43.2)	3.105 (4.2)	3.008 (4.1)	0.111	73.989 (100)
1982	15.324 (21.6)	18.507 (26.1)	30.232 (42.7)	3.561 (5.0)	3.131 (4.4)	0.086	70.842 (100)
1983	15.960 (22.6)	17.352 (24.6)	30.054 (42.6)	3.871 (5.5)	3.203 (4.5)	0.117	70.497 (100)
1984	17.203 (23.3)	18.031 (24.5)	31.004 (42.1)	3.783 (5.1)	3.564 (4.8)	0.163	73.730 (100)
1985	17.482 (23.6)	17.853 (24.0)	30.922 (41.7)	3.321 (4.5)	4.160 (6.0)	0.199	73.938 (100)

Source: Department of Energy, Energy Information Administration, *Monthly Energy Review*, September 1986, p. 11.

nificantly since 1984, reaching a level in 1986 that was only slightly greater than the level of production in 1960.

Imports of crude oil complete the supply picture. Over the years crude oil imports as a percentage of total U.S. crude oil supplies (including imports) rose from 12.6 percent in 1960 to 44.5 percent in 1977. By 1985 imports had dropped to 25.9 percent of the total supply, rising to 35.6 percent in 1986. The trends are shown in Table 4–2 and Figure 4–2. Total supply trends for the same period are shown in Figure 4–3.

Where do crude oil imports come from? One frequently gets the impression that they come largely from the countries making up the

TABLE 4–2
Total supplies of crude oil in the United States, 1960, 1965–1986 (millions of barrels)

| Year | Domestic production | Imports | | Total U.S. supply |
		Total	Percent of total U.S. supply	
1960	2,575	372	12.6	2,947
1965	2,849	452	13.7	3,301
1966	3,028	447	12.9	3,475
1967	3,216	412	11.4	3,628
1968	3,329	472	12.4	3,801
1969	3,372	514	13.2	3,886
1970	3,517	483	12.1	4,001
1971	3,454	613	15.1	4,067
1972	3,455	811	19.0	4,266
1973	3,361	1,184	26.0	4,545
1974	3,203	1,269	28.8	4,472
1975	3,057	1,498	32.9	4,555
1976	2,976	1,935	39.4	4,911
1977	3,009	2,414	44.5	5,423
1978	3,178	2,320	42.2	5,498
1979	3,121	2,380	43.3	5,501
1980	3,146	1,926	38.0	5,072
1981	3,129	1,605	33.9	4,734
1982	3,157	1,263	28.7	4,230
1983	3,159	1,215	27.8	4,374
1984	3,205	1,245	28.0	4,450
1985	2,757	964	25.9	3,721
1986	2,699	1,496	35.6	4,195

Sources: U.S. Department of the Interior, Bureau of Mines, Mineral Industry Surveys, *Crude Petroleum, Petroleum Products, and Natural Gas Liquids,* 1960 and 1966–67 issues; and Department of Energy, Energy Information Administration, *Crude Petroleum, Petroleum Products, and Natural Gas Liquids,* December 1969, pp. 2, 16; *Petroleum Supply Monthly,* August 1986, pg. 24; and Department of Commerce, *Statistical Abstract, 1985,* December 1984, p. 561.

FIGURE 4–1

U.S. production of crude oil, 1965–1986

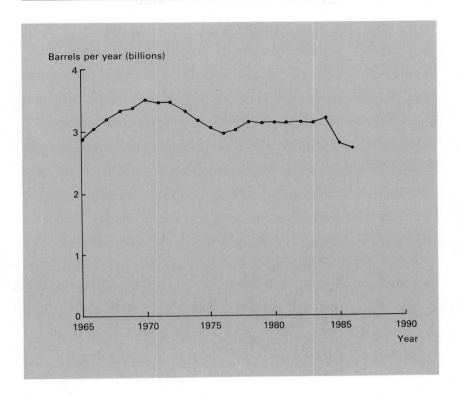

Source: Table 4–2.

Organization of Petroleum Exporting Countries (OPEC).[5] This was indeed the case until recent years. In 1979, 78.5 percent of our total crude oil imports came from OPEC countries. But as Table 4–3 shows, in 1985 only 35.8 percent of our imports came from OPEC. Arab countries accounted for 9.1 percent of total U.S. imports, with Algeria being the largest Arab supplier. Saudi Arabia the only other important Arab supplier. Non-Arab OPEC countries supplied 26.7 percent of our imports, with Venezuela, Indonesia, and Nigeria as the principal sources.

---

[5]OPEC countries are the Arab countries of Abu Dhabi, Algeria, Iraq, Kuwait, Libya, Qatar, and Saudi Arabia, and the non-Arab countries of Ecuador, Gabon, Indonesia, Iran, Nigeria, and Venezuela.

FIGURE 4–2
U.S. imports of crude oil, 1965–1986

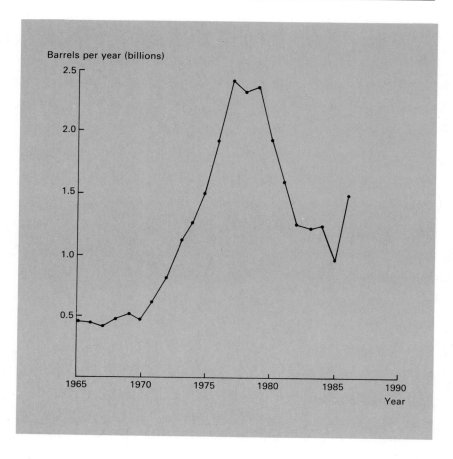

Source: Table 4–2.

The OPEC countries are much less important from the point of view of total U.S. supplies of crude oil. Our 1985 imports from them constituted 11.4 percent of total U.S. supplies. Imports from Arab OPEC countries were 2.9 percent, while those from non-Arab OPEC countries were 8.5 percent of total U.S. supplies.

Table 4–4 presents the crude oil import picture for 1985 from still a different perspective—from an individual country's point of view. The eight largest sources of crude oil imports accounted for 64.6 percent of all imports and 20.8 percent of total U.S. crude oil supplies. Mexico is the largest supplier, providing 16.1 percent of our total

FIGURE 4–3
Total supply of crude oil in the United States, 1965–1986

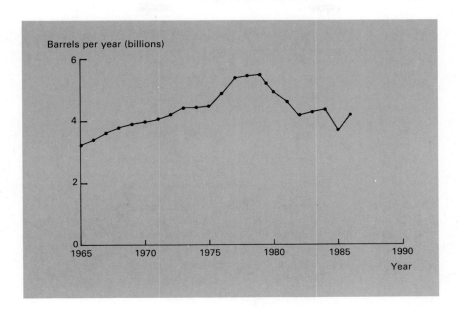

Source: Table 4–2.

TABLE 4–3
Crude oil and petroleum product imports from OPEC countries, 1985 (000s barrels per day average)

Country	Amount	Percent of U.S. imports	Percent of total U.S. supplies
Arab			
Algeria	187	3.6	1.2
Saudi Arabia	168	3.3	1.1
United Arab Emirates	45	0.8	0.2
Other	72	1.4	0.4
Total Arab	472	9.1	2.9
Non-Arab			
Indonesia	314	6.2	2.0
Iran	27	0.5	0.1
Nigeria	293	5.8	1.8
Venezuela	605	11.9	3.8
Other	119	2.3	0.8
Total non-Arab	1,358	26.7	8.5
Total OPEC	1,830	35.8	11.4

Source: Department of Energy, Energy Information Administration, *Petroleum Supply Monthly*, August 1986, pp. 2–3, 8–9.

TABLE 4–4
Crude oil and petroleum product imports from the eight largest sources of supply, 1985 (000s barrels per day average)

Country	Amount	Percent of U.S. imports	Percent of total U.S. supplies
Mexico	816	16.1	5.2
Canada	770	15.2	4.9
Venezuela	605	11.9	3.8
Indonesia	314	6.2	2.0
United Kingdom	310	6.1	1.9
Algeria	187	3.6	1.2
Saudia Arabia	168	3.3	1.1
Trinidad/Tobago	113	2.2	0.7
Total	3,283	64.6	20.8

Source: Department of Energy, Energy Information Administration, *Petroleum Supply Monthly*, August 1986, pp. 2–3, 8–9.

imports but only 5.2 percent of our total supply. Saudi Arabia was the source of only 1.1 percent of our total crude oil supplies. No country was responsible for as much as 6 percent.

HOW TO CREATE ENERGY PROBLEMS

It seems rather odd that an energy crisis arose in the 1970s when no manifestations of a serious problem had occurred previously and none seem to exist at present. We had heard, of course, from geologists, oil companies, and others concerned with energy supplies, of an inevitable day of reckoning when supplies of petroleum will fail to respond to expanding energy demands. But this warning is commonly heard from producers' special interest groups seeking government subsidization and/or protection. There were no *economic* indications prior to the 1970s that we would be unable to buy as much gasoline and fuel oil as we desired, nor are there any now. To put it in familiar economic terms, equilibrium prices prevailed in these markets until late 1971. Markets for crude oil and its products were in equilibrium, and they have been again since 1980. Using gasoline as an example, Figure 4–4 shows an equilibrium price of p_1 prevailing; buyers want quantity q_1 at that price, and suppliers are willing to place quantity q_1 on the market.

Price controls

Energy shortages—particularly petroleum shortages—began to appear following President Nixon's wage price freeze of August 17, 1971. The economic expansion of the 1960s and the inflation that

FIGURE 4–4
Equilibrium price and quantity of gasoline

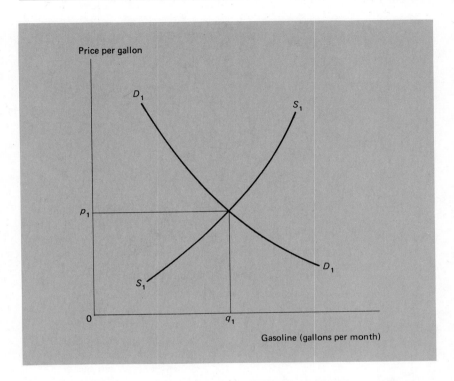

Given the demand D_1D_1 and the supply S_1S_1 of gasoline, the equilibrium price will be p_1 and the equilibrium quantity will be q_1. At the equilibrium price there is neither a surplus nor a shortage.

dates from 1967 brought rapidly increasing demand for energy—increases in demand that were not matched by greater supplies. Shortages became more acute through 1972 and 1973 as the expansion of demand continued to exceed that of supply and as price controls were continued. Then, with the Arab oil boycott beginning in October 1973, shortages suddenly began to appear catastrophic.

As we noted in Chapter 2, whenever price controls are effective in holding prices *below* their equilibrium levels, shortages occur. This is precisely what happened in the petroleum case. Petroleum product prices were held below equilibrium levels by the government, creating shortages of gasoline, jet fuel, and fuel oils. The results are illustrated for gasoline in Figure 4–5. An increase in demand from D_1D_1 to D_2D_2, which outstrips an increase in supply from S_1S_1 to S_2S_2, brings about a price increase in gasoline from p_1 to p_2. This is

FIGURE 4–5
Effects of changes in demand for and supply of gasoline with and without price controls

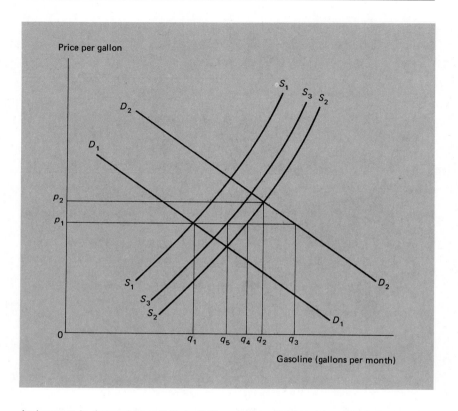

An increase in demand from D_1D_1 to D_2D_2, accompanied by an increase in supply from S_1S_1 to S_2S_2, would cause the price of gasoline to rise from p_1 to p_2, and no shortage would be created. If the price were controlled at p_1, a shortage of q_4q_3 would occur. If supply then decreased to S_3S_3 and the price were held at p_1, the shortage would increase to q_5q_3.

the nature of the inflationary process. As such, it is a part of an inflation problem, but it generates no energy crisis. When demand increases to D_2D_2 and supply increases to S_2S_2, suppose that price controls hold the price of gasoline at p_1. At that price level consumers now want q_3 gallons, but suppliers are willing to place only q_4 on the market, leaving a shortage of q_4q_3 gallons. Now, if the Arab embargo is added, the supply curve for gasoline shifts to the left, to some position such as S_3S_3. If a price ceiling of p_1 is maintained, the shortage increases to q_5q_3. Shortages would be expected to continue as long as petroleum product prices are held by the government below their equilibrium levels.

Whether or not price controls generate shortages depends upon whether or not they are effective in the marketplace. If the controlled price of a good is above its equilibrium level, the equilibrium price prevails and no shortage occurs. Price controls cause shortages only if they are in effect; that is, only if they are below the market-equilibrium level. The general wage price controls imposed in 1971 were removed in early 1974, but controls were retained on crude oil and petroleum products. From 1974 to 1979, the controlled prices of gasoline were generally *above* equilibrium levels, and the shortages of 1972–74 miraculously disappeared.

In 1979 Iranian oil supplies were cut off from the United States, shifting gasoline supply curves to the left and raising the equilibrium price level. Once again controlled prices became effective, and serious shortages appeared. In 1981 the Reagan administration decontrolled prices of crude oil and petroleum products. No shortages of crude oil, gasoline, or fuel oil have occurred since. The correlation of shortages and effective price controls between 1971 and 1981 provides a classic example of how to create problems in an important sector of the economy.

Allocations of crude oil

Controlled prices and the resultant shortages create allocation problems. Uncontrolled equilibrium prices ration available supplies of a product among buyers, and each buyer can get as much as is desired at the equilibrium price. But with effective price controls and shortages, many buyers are left out in the cold, unable to buy as much as they would like at the controlled price. Price is no longer able to perform its function of allocating as much to individual buyers as they desire.

In the crude oil case of the 1970s, the set of price controls established by the government was complex. They were established by the Emergency Petroleum Allocations Act of 1973 and the Energy Policy Conservation Act of 1975. Oil produced domestically was classified into three groups: (1) old oil, (2) new oil, and (3) oil from stripper wells. Old oil was defined as that produced by wells in existence in November 1975, up to the amounts they were producing monthly at that time. Its controlled price was about $5.25 per barrel. New oil was from wells put in production after that time, plus output from old wells that exceeded the base period output levels. The controlled price was about $11 per barrel. Oil from stripper wells was sold at free-market prices, that is, at what it cost to import crude oil from abroad. Import prices were around \$14.50 per barrel in late 1975 and early 1976 and were uncontrolled.

Obviously refiners want to purchase crude oil at the lowest possible price. Quantities of old oil supplied at controlled prices were insufficient to meet refiners' demands. At controlled prices shortages of new oil existed, too. To alleviate the shortages, refiners bought stripper oil and imported oil from abroad.

The price controls and shortages for both old oil and new oil opened up possibilities of great inequities in the cost of crude oil to different refiners. Those able to get old oil were in favored positions over those who were not. Similarly those unable to get either new or old oil and who were required to pay the import price were the most unfavorably situated.

To reduce inequities, the Federal Energy Agency established an elaborate program of entitlements and allocations among crude oil refiners. In essence each refiner was issued "entitlement" tickets, giving it the right to purchase certain amounts of domestic oil on which the price was controlled. The number of entitlement tickets that a refiner could obtain depended on the refiner's total crude oil use—both price controlled oil and that which was not price controlled. The right to purchase crude oil at the lower controlled prices was thus tied to the refiner's purchases of stripper well and imported oil at uncontrolled prices. The effective price per barrel paid by the refiner was thus an average of the controlled and uncontrolled prices.

The entitlements program in effect placed a tax on domestic production of crude oil and at the same time subsidized refinery purchases of imports of oil and stripper-well production. In Figure 4–6 suppose initially that all crude oil is produced domestically. The demand and supply curves are D_dD_d and S_dS_d, respectively. The price is p_d per barrel, and the quantity exchanged is q_4 barrels per month. Now suppose that refiners can import oil at p_f per barrel (the OPEC price). Refiners certainly would not be willing to pay domestic producers more than that price, so domestic producers would place q_3 on the market at that price, and imports will amount to q_3q_5. Note that refiners get more oil at a lower price than would be the case if they depend on domestic production only. Now consider the effect of the entitlements program. For simplicity we assume the controlled price of both old and new domestic oil is the same and is p_c. But refiners are entitled to buy it only in proportion to the quantity of oil they buy at the world price of p_f. The price of oil to refiners, p_a, is an average of the world price p_f and the domestic controlled price p_c. Refiners purchase q_6 barrels per month at the average price

FIGURE 4–6
Effects of the FEA entitlements program

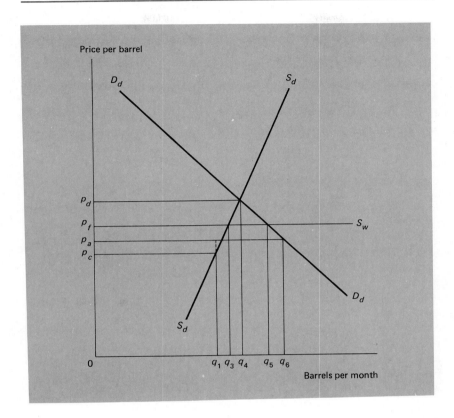

If D_dD_d and S_dS_d represent the domestic demand and supply curves for crude oil, the equilibrium price and quantity would be p_d and q_4, respectively. In the absence of price controls and a world crude oil price of p_f at which refiners can purchase as much as they want, the effective supply curve to domestic refiners becomes S_d up to quantity q_3 and S_w for larger quantities. The price of oil would be p_f and the quantity q_3q_5 would be imported. The entitlements program in effect makes imported (and stripper-well) oil available at p_a, inducing refiners to take quantity q_6. Domestic crude oil producers receive a controlled price of p_c and will place only q_1 on the market. The entitlements program increases imports to q_1q_6, whereas in the absence of entitlements imports would be q_3q_5 barrels.

p_a. Since domestic producers get only p_c per barrel, they will place only q_1 barrels on the market. The difference between the average price p_a that the refiners pay and the controlled price p_c is like a tax on domestic producers that is used to pay a subsidy of the difference between p_f and p_a to refiners for each barrel of oil that they import.

Total imports are q_1q_6 barrels per month. Refiners import more, and domestic producers produce less crude oil than would be the case if there were no price controls on domestically produced crude oil and no entitlements program.

The government's price control and allocations program had three important effects. First, it placed heavy penalties on the exploration for and production of domestic oil. Second, it subsidized and encouraged the importation of foreign oil. Third, it saddled the refining industry with a nightmarish set of bookkeeping problems as refiners attempted to keep track of the amounts they were using of foreign oil, new oil, and old oil, and to make continuous reports to the government for entitlements tickets and compliance certification.

Conservation and other measures

Price controls generate shortages and shortages lead to government allocations of short supplies among users. But government allocations do not make the shortage problem go away. It remains as long as effective price controls are maintained. The persistent energy shortages of the 1970s generated still more government action to alleviate the problems that price controls had caused.

To begin with, a bit more bureaucracy was added to the federal government. In 1978, a Department of Energy (DOE) was established by Congress to center all energy-related activities of the federal government in a cabinet-level Department of Energy instead of leaving them diffused among the Federal Energy Agency, the Energy Research and Development Agency, the Federal Power Commission, the Department of Defense, the Department of Transportation, and the Council on Price and Wage Stability.

Many utility companies were required by the government to switch from fuel oil and natural gas to coal as an energy source. These proposals met stiff opposition from environmentalists protesting the pollution that the use of coal entails. Many utility companies resisted coercion of this sort because it required them to switch from lower priced energy sources (oil and gas) to a more expensive one (coal). Interestingly enough, in 1979 the Department of Energy began encouraging, rather than discouraging, the use of natural gas. Higher wellhead natural gas prices permitted by the Natural Gas Act of 1978 largely alleviated the natural gas shortages so prevalent in the 1970s prior to 1978.

The government has enacted several measures to reduce gasoline consumption. Among these are (1) a 55-mile-per-hour speed limit, which, on rural highways, may be relaxed at the individual states' discretion, (2) mandatory improvement in gas mileage for new automobiles produced, (3) a five-cent-per-gallon increase in the federal excise tax on gasoline, and (4) substantial increases in the excise taxes on aviation fuels.

Price ceiling levels on domestic crude oil and petroleum products were raised under the Carter administration and removed entirely by the Reagan administration. But to limit the profits oil companies could make from the lifting of price ceilings, Congress passed the Crude Oil Windfall Profit Tax in March 1980. The tax is levied on the difference between the selling price of crude oil and an adjusted base price (the old controlled price); the rate varies from 30 to 70 percent. From the producer's point of view, for oil which was previously price controlled, the Windfall Profit Tax has the same economic effect as price controls but at a higher controlled price. However, stripper well oil, heavy crude, naval petroleum reserve oil, and incremental tertiary oil were not subject to price controls, and a tax on the selling price of these oils is, in effect, a reduction in the price received from the seller's point of view.[6]

In July 1980, Congress passed the Energy Development Bill authorizing $25 billion to be spent over a four-year period. The major provisions of the bill include $20 billion for the Synthetic Fuels Corporation which would administer (1) loans, (2) loan guarantees, (3) purchase agreements, (4) joint ventures with private companies and government-owned plants, (5) below-market interest rate loans and grants to help builders and home owners make buildings more energy efficient, (6) gasohol subsidies, and (7) federal loan guarantees and price supports for commercial plants that convert sewage and waste into energy.

A part of the Energy Policy and Conservation Act of 1975 established a Strategic Petroleum Reserve (SPR) to act as a cushion against shortages created by arbitrary embargos on oil sold to the United States by foreign sellers. Many problems have arisen from the SPR.

TOWARD ALLEVIATING THE PROBLEMS

Economic analysis helps us sort out the various facets of what have come to be known as energy problems. It indicates that, far from *solving* the problems, the federal government was instrumental in *causing* the problems, particularly as the problems developed in the 1970s. What light can it shed on current perceptions of and future cures of energy problems?

---

[6]Arthur Young and Company, *The Windfall Profit Tax: Summary of the Basic Provisions for Energy Producers*, March 1980.

The adequacy of petroleum supplies

Regarding the fears that future petroleum supplies will be inadequate for our energy needs, there is a great temptation—and something to be learned from it—to project future demands and future supplies forward by 5 or 50 years. But we are unlikely to come up with definitive numerical answers. Our study of economic principles tells us why this is so.

On the demand side, we can expect that in an expanding economy demand curves for petroleum (and for other energy resources) will continue shifting to the right. But we should not forget that demand curves also slope downward to the right. For any given petroleum demand curve, the higher the relative price, the smaller will be the quantity purchased. Quantities demanded in the future, then, are determined by two sets of forces: (1) the nature and the extent to which the demand curve shifts and (2) the price at which the product is sold. The greater the projected expansion of the economy, the more will be demanded at any specific price. The higher the relative price for any given state of demand, the less will be the quantity demanded.

Supply forecasts have been notoriously misleading in the past. Doomsday prophets look at U.S. proven reserves of crude oil and pronounce an early death sentence on this form of energy. But what they overlook is that proven reserves are the result of investment in exploration—they are in the nature of current inventories—and that it does not pay producers to invest in exploration and the establishment of proven resources beyond some level. We do not really know the extent of the *unproven* oil reserves of the United States— on private lands, on federal land, in Alaska, and offshore. The ultimate capability of the world to produce oil over the next 50 years is completely unknown.[7]

The era of cheap energy may indeed be over, but in the United States we are not really confronted with a problem of "running out of oil." There is nothing catastrophic in higher and relatively rising energy costs. The using up of easily available oil pools means that the supply curve is shifting to the left as in Figure 4–7 (or, what amounts to the same thing, upward). But if prices are not controlled, the price of oil will rise to equilibrium levels such as from p_1 to p_2, and there will be no shortages in evidence. Rising prices will

---

[7]See Edward J. Mitchell, *U.S. Energy Policy: A Primer* (Washington, D.C.: American Enterprise Institute for Public Policy Research, 1974), pp. 4–11.

FIGURE 4–7
The effects of declining crude oil supplies

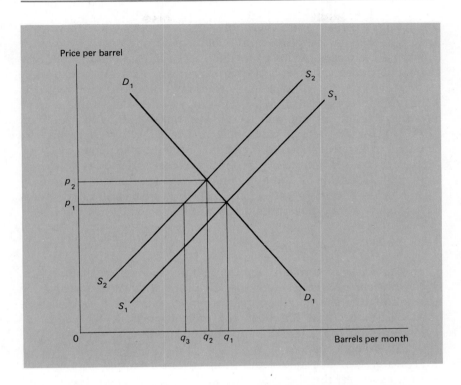

The depletion of easily available crude oil pools shifts the supply curve to the left from S_1S_1 to S_2S_2, causing the price to rise to p_2. If the price were controlled at p_1 there would be a shortage of q_3q_1 barrels. If the price is allowed to rise producers will increase output from quantity q_3 to q_2 and consumers will reduce consumption from q_1 to q_2, eliminating the shortage.

in turn generate three types of economic adjustments to the diminishing quantities of energy in the form of petroleum. First, they will induce greater recovery than would occur if the price were controlled at p_1. Such a controlled price brings forth quantity q_3, but if the price is allowed to rise to p_2, recovery from existing wells and from less accessible oil pools will increase the quantity to q_2. Second, the higher prices induce users *voluntarily* to reduce their use of oil from q_1 to q_2. As the price rises, users have an incentive to conserve, putting oil to its most valuable uses and cutting back on the amount consumed in lower value uses. Third, and most important of all, users of oil will have incentives to *voluntarily* turn to and develop alternative energy sources.

It is important to understand that in the absence of price controls, mandatory conservation measures such as controls on thermostat settings and gas-guzzling automobiles are unnecessary. If energy demand increases, or supply decreases, or both occur simultaneously, prices will rise; and each consumer, confronted with more expensive energy, will make his or her own decisions on how to cut back or conserve its use. Ms. Brown may prefer to continue using a comfortable automobile and to cool her house less in the summer. Mr. Smith may prefer a cool house and less driving. Someone else may want to use less across the board of the more expensive energy. But each does it voluntarily in the way most satisfactory to the individual. Coercion by the government cannot coincide with the diverse tastes and preferences of different individuals. It also reduces the range within which individuals are free to act as they think best.

Alternative energy sources

Petroleum is by no means the only source of energy. Natural gas, coal, nuclear processes, hydroelectric processes, wind, and the sun are among the alternative sources of power available to us. Of these sources, natural gas has been the most prominent because of its clean-burning characteristics and, more importantly, because it has been relatively cheap.

Natural gas, like petroleum, was in short supply through the 1970s; however, the shortage resulted from government pricing policies of the resource rather than from low potential reserves. After 1960 the Federal Power Commission, which became the Federal Energy Regulatory Commission with the establishment of the Department of Energy in 1978, imposed strict controls on the price of natural gas at the wellhead. The controlled price discouraged exploration and expansion of supplies while, at the same time, it encouraged expanding consumption. Like any other effective price ceiling, this one, too, resulted in shortages. But the large increases in the controlled price of natural gas sold in interstate commerce brought about by the Natural Gas Act of 1978 have virtually eliminated the shortages.

The United States has no shortage of coal. Vast reserves exist both in the older coal fields of the East and in the newer areas of Wyoming and Montana. Coal has fallen into disfavor in recent years for several reasons, the most important one being the relatively low prices of clean-burning natural gas and of fuel oil. Coal has been the target of environmentalists on two counts: (1) the relatively high sulfur content of its emissions as it burns and (2) damage to the land-scape from strip mining activities. Neither of these are insurmount-able obstacles to a significant expansion in the use of coal as an energy source. At some price, both can be successfully counteracted. In addition, a whole new technique of coal gasification is in the pro-cess of development.

Nuclear processes hold promise as an energy source, although their success to this time has been something less than spectacular. There has been considerable fear by the public that wastes from nu-clear power plants constitute a danger to the community; however, there is little hard evidence that this is so. For technological reasons relatively low-cost generating plants have not been forthcoming. In addition, the federal government has put formidable obstacles in the way of using plutonium, the most promising of nuclear fuels.

Still other potential energy sources hold promise for the future as new techniques are developed to exploit them. These include large quantities of shale oil, hydroelectric potential, the wind, and the sun. A major problem in harnessing the almost unlimited supplies of wind and solar energy is low-cost storage. But, if past experience in technological development tells us anything, we can expect that this, too, will eventually be solved.

The use of legislation and government coercion to turn energy users away from petroleum toward alternative energy sources is highly questionable from the point of view of economics. Energy users do not continue to use the petroleum source because they are addicted to it. They use it because it is still plentiful enough to be *less expensive* than equivalent energy obtained from other sources. If the price of crude oil is not controlled, diminishing supplies over time will cause the price of petroleum-based energy to rise. As it becomes more expensive relative to equivalent energy from alterna-tive sources, the shift to alternative sources will be made voluntarily and gradually. As a matter of fact, the *prospects* of relatively rising petroleum prices in the future will *induce* energy-supplying busi-nesses to engage in research and development of alternative energy sources. It makes little economic sense for the government to spend billions of dollars to develop alternative energy source industries since they will be developed anyway by the private sector of the economy when and as they can provide energy at costs comparable to the costs of petroleum energy.

The efficiency of the price mechanism

Basic economic principles—demand and supply analyses—suggest, and experience tends to bear out, that there is a rather simple solution to our energy problems. It is that the government withdraw from, rather than enter more extensively into, the markets for energy resources. When prices are permitted to rise to their equilibrium levels, shortages disappear. Government pricing, allocation, and rationing decisions become unnecessary.

The evidence with respect to gasoline and fuel oil since the Arab embargo ended in 1974 demonstrates what the market can do. Although price controls on petroleum products were retained after the wage price freeze of the Nixon administration was lifted in 1974, they were not generally effective. Market prices of gasoline and fuel oil, except for the summer of 1979, were below the controlled price levels. Since 1974 we have had no difficulty in filling our gasoline tanks or our fuel-oil tanks to whatever extent we desire. The three-level price system for crude oil created serious allocation problems among users of crude oil and inefficiencies in its use, but these disappeared when prices were decontrolled and like grades of oil and oil products were sold at equilibrium prices.

If demand for energy resources increases faster than supply, energy prices in the absence of controls will rise relative to other prices because units of energy become relatively more valuable to the economy. This will induce each of us to examine our uses of energy, to eliminate the less important uses, and to utilize available supplies for the more important uses.

Households vary a great deal in what they consider to be the most important uses for an item such as gasoline. One family likes large automobiles while another prefers compact cars. Another household places a high value on travel; some families prefer not to travel at all. Shortages, caused by government-imposed price ceilings below equilibrium levels, open the door for government officials to specify the uses to which gasoline should be put. The automobile industry can be ordered by the government to produce only compact cars—a move that will be applauded by compact car fans but not by tall people or those who like luxury cars. Travel can be curtailed. Various foolish (?) uses of gasoline can be banned. But, are government officials uniquely qualified to determine what are and what are not the most important uses for gasoline? In a shortage situation, the price system, if allowed to operate, moves the price in an upward direction; and as the price rises, each household curtails those uses of the item that are least important to it. Thus, all households together adjust to the available supply, each in the manner best suited to its own preferences.

As energy becomes relatively more scarce and as its relative price rises, there is an inducement for producers to seek out and develop additional and alternative forms of energy supplies. Removing the $5.25 price ceiling for old oil increases the rate and extent of recovery from old wells. Rising relative prices of oil encourage exploration and drilling activity for new oil. Removal of price controls on natural gas makes it economical to open up vast new reserves of this important fuel. Higher prices of petroleum energy encourage the development of shale oil recovery techniques and stimulate the development of nuclear technology. They also encourage research and development in the conversion of coal to clean-burning forms and in the development of wind and solar energy sources.

The free-market equilibrium price solution of the energy shortage problem has much to commend it. The primary argument in its favor is simply the argument for a private enterprise economic system vis-à-vis a socialistic economic system. The price system induces consumers to voluntarily limit their consumption of each good or service to the available supply. It also induces producers of each good and service to increase the quantity available, up to the point at which consumers value a unit of it at approximately what it costs to place it on the market. The price system induces buyers of goods and services and resources to put the supplies available to them to their most efficient uses. Relative prices, relative costs, and relative profits continually induce transfers of resources and goods from less valuable to more valuable uses. All of this is done automatically and impersonally. No coercion is necessary. The price system enables us to avoid putting our economic fate in the hands of government bureaucrats who may or may not be knowledgeable of the consequences of their actions, regardless of how good their intentions may be.

The role of the government

Energy problems have absorbed a tremendous amount of time for Congress and the four administrations since 1973. There is little evidence that the debate, the furor, and the consequent actions have moved toward solutions of the problems; in fact, it appears that government intervention in energy markets has tended to reduce energy supplies and efficiency in energy production rather than to increase them. Is there any positive role that the government can take in planning for the future in this area? There are several ways in which the government can contribute toward the efficient use of energy and the development of future supplies, but past experience suggests that direct intervention in the market place is not one of them.

The government can act to make energy producers more competitive. The oil industry and other energy industries can be scrutinized carefully to identify and to eliminate monopolistic practices and/or monopolistic agreements that may occur. Toward this end, the government can also put a permanent stop to its *market-demand pro-rationing activities.*[8] Prorationing has served as a government-supported monopolizing device and has been used in the states of Texas, Louisiana, New Mexico, Kansas, and Oklahoma, which collectively account for about two thirds of the crude oil production in the United States. It is accomplished by state commissions such as the Texas Railroad Commission in Texas and the Oklahoma Corporation Commission in Oklahoma for two stated purposes: (1) to conserve crude oil reserves and (2) to divide the market "equitably" among producers.

In practice, prorationing has served as a government-supported monopolizing device that enabled producers to act jointly to reduce supplies of crude oil placed on the market and to receive higher prices for their product than would be the case in competitive markets. The commission in a given state determined how much crude oil was to be produced and allocated quotas to the producers of the state. Ordinarily low-volume, high-cost wells have been permitted to produce as much as they are capable of, while production from high-volume, low-cost wells was restricted. The results were restricted production and higher costs of recovery from wells that were operating currently, as well as reduced incentives for exploration and development of new oil fields. In the interests of efficiency and of expanding domestic production of crude oil, prorationing, as well as other monopolizing or restricting devices, must be eliminated. Prorationing has not been effectively pursued in the last few years, but the machinery for its operation is still in place.

The government can also support or subsidize a small amount of research and development in the energy field. It can help finance pilot projects and experimentation with alternative energy sources. But by and large, the government's effective role in this respect is relatively small. If the expected benefits exceed the expected costs of research and development, private concerns will have incentives to accomplish it, and the government's effort will not be needed.[9]

SUMMARY

The U.S. public was confronted with an energy crisis in the winter of 1973–74 and has since been persuaded that a long-run energy

---

[8]James C. Burrows and Thomas A. Domencich, *An Analysis of the United States Oil Import Quota* (Lexington, Mass.: D. C. Health, 1970), pp. 62–68.

[9]See Murray L. Weidenbaum and Reno Harnish, *Government Credit Subsidies for Energy Development* (Washington, D.C.: American Enterprise Institute for Public Policy Research, 1976).

problem exists. The problem focuses on petroleum, which provides over 40 percent of U.S. energy supplies.

Since 1970, demand for petroleum products has been increasing faster than supply. The wage price controls of 1971–74, together with the 1973–74 Arab oil embargo and the cutoff of Iranian oil in 1979, turned these demand-supply relationships into acute shortages. The shortages, even after they ceased to exist, triggered fears of impending and future shortages as well as rising energy prices.

Although we appear to be in no immediate danger of running out of oil, its growing relative scarcity would be expected to cause the prices of petroleum products to rise over time relative to other prices in the economy. Rising petroleum prices will in turn encourage additional search and exploration for petroleum reserves. They will also encourage the development of promising alternative energy sources such as coal, synthetic fuels, nuclear power, wind, and solar power.

Direct intervention by the government has undoubtedly increased rather than decreased energy problems. General wage price controls from 1971 to 1974 brought on shortages. Price controls in gasoline were again effective in 1979 and caused shortages. The three-price system for crude oil and government allocations of domestic oil reduced efficiency in energy production and distribution and held domestic supplies below what they would otherwise have been. They also encouraged a rising volume of imports. Free-market prices for energy supplies appear to provide a better answer to the efficient use of energy and to the avoidance of shortages.

The government can play a limited positive role in the energy industry. It can act to increase and maintain competition among energy suppliers. It can help support research and development activities. However, it should probably avoid direct intervention in energy markets.

SUPPLEMENTARY READINGS

"Energy: Fuels of the Future." *Time,* June 11, 1979, pp. 72–76.

A good survey of alternative energy sources.

"Energy: How Dwindling Supplies Will Change Our Lives." *Futurist,* August 1979, pp. 258–68.

A biologist predicts that the postindustrial society will be an agricultural society. Note that his prediction is based on an incorrect assumption that technology is subject to diminishing returns.

Fowler, J. M. "Energy Policy: Toward the Year 2000." *Environment* 25 (September 1983), pp. 6–11, 35–37.

A review of the inconsistencies of United States energy policies over the last decade and a look to the future.

"Future U.S. Exploration—The Key Is Economics." *Oil and Gas Journal*, August 16, 1982, pp. 114–23.

Emphasizes the critical role of economic incentives in the development of oil and gas reserves. According to the article, the real culprit behind the 1956–71 decline in exploration and drilling was not a deterioration in the resource base but a decline in economic incentives.

LaForce, J. Claybourn. *The Energy Crisis: The Moral Equivalent of Bamboozle.* Los Angeles: International Institute for Economic Research, 1978.

Examines the role of government in creating the energy problem.

North, Douglass C., and Roger LeRoy Miller. *The Economics of Public Issues.* 6th ed. New York: Harper & Row, 1983, pp. 3–9.

Recounts the story of the first energy crisis and illustrates how market forces solved the problem of dwindling supplies of whale oil—yes, whale oil.

"Oil Prices Hit the Skids." *Business Week*, August 13, 1984, pp. 54–55.

An interesting look at how the forces of competition work in the real world.

ECONOMICS OF CRIME AND ITS PREVENTION

What is crime?
  Immorality?
  Illegality?
  Classification of criminal acts
  Causes of crime
The costs of crime
Individually and collectively consumed goods
  Individually consumed goods
  Collectively consumed goods
  Semicollectively consumed goods
  The "free rider" problem
  Government production of collectively consumed items
The economics of crime prevention activities
  The "correct" level
  Allocation of the crime prevention budget
The economics of legalizing illegal activities
Summary

Checklist of Economic Concepts

Individually consumed goods and services
Collectively consumed goods and services
Semicollectively consumed goods and services
Spillover benefits, social
Spillover costs, social
Public goods
Cost-benefit analysis
Marginal benefits
Marginal costs
Equimarginal principle
Alternative costs
"Free rider" problem

5

Economics of Crime

and Its Prevention

How much is too much?

It seemed to Linda that somehow, somewhere, things were all mixed up. The police had swarmed in on the students in her apartment last night, and three of her friends were in jail on pot possession charges. Fortunately, Linda was clean. Sure, the three who were arrested were smoking stuff, but whom were they hurting? It was a relatively quiet, peaceful gathering. They listened to a few records that may have been a little loud for the neighbors, but mostly there was just talk. A little pot never hurt anyone—why do people get all uptight about it? Everyone knows that smoking pot, if it leads to any problems at all, has much less serious consequences than the use of alcohol, and in most places it is no crime to drink.

Why don't the police go after the real criminals and leave the young people alone? Why don't they spend their time fruitfully, tracking down and apprehending murderers, rapists, muggers, thieves, and the like? Just last week two men had followed her friend, Jim, into his apartment house and pulled a gun on him, taking his watch and the little bit of money he had in his billfold. Why don't law enforcement officials do something about such serious crime problems as the Mafia and other organized crime? It seemed to Linda that the police spend their time picking on young people, while letting the real criminals get away with murder.

Criminal activities create an important set of social problems in the United States. They affect our general well-being by threatening the loss of money and property and by generating concern for one's physical safety. Yet, for most of us, crime is something we read about in the papers—something that usually affects other people, but has the potential of affecting us. We seldom look at crime from a systematic analytical point of view, but if we are to do anything about the problem, this is what we must do.

WHAT IS CRIME?

It seems almost silly to raise such a question as "What is crime?" However, if we are to look at crime analytically, we must have a solid base from which to work. The concept of what constitutes criminal activity is often not clear in the mind of any one person and may be ambiguous from one person to another. Some people think of crime in terms of that which is immoral; others think of it in terms of that which is illegal.

Immorality?

Are immoral acts criminal? It is not easy to answer this question. In the first place, many acts do not fall clearly into a moral-immoral classification. In modern societies some acts are generally considered to be immoral—murder and most kinds of theft, for example. But there are many other acts, the morality of which depends on what group in the society is evaluating them. Examples include pot smoking, drinking alcoholic beverages, betting on horse races, homosexual activities, adultery, and many more. Morality versus immorality does not provide a clear basis for defining whether or not specific acts are criminal.

Illegality?

A definition that seems to be meaningful and useful analytically is that a criminal act is one the society (or one of its subdivisions) has decided it is better off without and which it has therefore made illegal through laws, ordinances, and the like. It may or may not be immoral. For example, is it immoral to drive 30 miles an hour along a deserted street that is posted for 20 miles an hour, or to run a stop sign at an intersection where there are no other cars, or to catch a fish in a mountain stream before you have obtained a fishing license? As you quickly discover when you are caught, these acts may very well be criminal in nature. On the other hand, if gambling, drinking, and prostitution are immoral, there are many places where they are not illegal and are, therefore, not criminal.

Acts that are illegal or criminal are designated as such by legislative bodies, such as city councils, state legislatures, and Congress. There are a number of reasons for making certain acts illegal. Some acts may indeed be offensive to the moral standards of a majority of legislators and their constituents. Murder, rape, and theft are cases in point. Others may lead to consequences (in the minds of legislators, at least) of which the doer is ignorant. The consumption of alcohol, pot, cocaine, or heroin thus may be made illegal because legislators fear that those who try them may become addicted, with disastrous consequences to the users. Still other acts are designated illegal in order to prevent chaos or to promote order—violation of established traffic rules, for example. Further, some acts may carry no taint of immorality but may be made illegal because they are considered contrary to the general welfare of the society. Acts of pollution, such as burning your trash within the city limits, illustrate the point.

Classification of criminal acts

For crime rate reporting purposes, the Department of Justice classifies criminal acts as (1) violent crimes and (2) crimes against property. We can add to the classification (3) traffic in illegal goods and services and (4) other crimes. Violent crimes are crimes against persons. They include murder, rape, aggravated assault, and armed robbery. Crimes against property include such things as fraud, burglary, theft, embezzlement, forgery, arson, vandalism, and the like. Traffic in illegal goods and services is made up of dealings in such things as gambling, narcotics, loan-sharking, prostitution, and alcohol. The "other crimes" classification is, of course, a catchall for everything from nonpayment of alimony to speeding.

Crime is generally thought to be a very serious problem in the United States. In every large city, and in many small ones, people are reluctant to go out at night for fear of being robbed, raped, beaten, or even murdered. But there is some evidence of recent improvement in the situation. Table 5-1 shows over the 10-year period

TABLE 5-1
Crime rate per 100,000 inhabitants, 1975–1984

Year	Total	Violent crime	Property crime
1975	5,299	488	4,811
1976	5,287	468	4,820
1977	5,080	476	4,602
1978	5,140	498	4,643
1979	5,566	549	5,017
1980	5,950	597	5,353
1981	5,858	594	5,264
1982	5,604	571	5,033
1983	5,175	538	4,637
1984	5,031	539	4,492

Source: United States Department of Commerce, *Statistical Abstract of the United States, 1986*, p. 166.

from 1975 through 1984 a decrease in the crime rate from 1975 through 1977, an increase from 1977 through 1980 with the rate peaking in 1980, and a decrease since that time. The time patterns are slightly different for the two classifications; however, both show peaks in their respective rates in 1980 and a substantial drop since that time.

Causes of crime

Criminal activity stems from many sources. Some are economic in nature and others are not. Different kinds of crime may have their roots in different sources. The problem of the causes of crime is a hard one to attack; it is like asking what causes a society to be what it is. We can, however, identify some broad factors that tend to result in criminal activities.

Unrestrained passions or emotions are an important factor in many violent crimes. Most murders, for example, result from deep-seated, intense feelings of some sort between the murderer and the victim. The victim may be a wife, a husband, a girlfriend, or the guy who cheats in a poker game. The level of the murderer's emotion pushes aside the constraints of conscience and law that the society has established. Murders in which the victim is unknown to the murderer are the least common type.

When poverty is coupled with *high levels of economic and social aspirations*, the stage is set for criminal activities—particularly robbery and dealing in illegal goods and services. People who are thwarted in attaining desired social and economic goals legally may seek to obtain them illegally. In addition, the costs of being apprehended and convicted of a crime are less for those living in poverty than for persons from middle and upper income groups. The latter certainly have more to lose in terms of income—if not in terms of social status. Thus we find that ghettos of large cities produce a disproportionate share of criminals. The incidence of robbery and traffic in illegal goods tends to be high among members of minority groups who feel the burden of both economic and social discrimination.

The standards and social values of a society are an important determinant of criminal activities. Society's attitudes toward cheating on one's income tax, stealing from one's employer, embezzling, wiretapping, and interfering with the right to privacy help set the stage for acts that may be considered criminal. The real tragedy of Watergate was not so much what the bugging did to the Democrats, but the low level of social values shown to be held by people in positions of public trust.

THE COSTS OF CRIME

That crime has economic costs is certain. The measurement of those costs, however, is at present very inaccurate. In the first place, many criminal activities go unreported. In the second place, an accurate dollar value cannot be attached to the cost of those crimes that do occur. Nevertheless, estimates of the costs of crime are necessary if decision making regarding the level of crime prevention activities is to have any degree of economic soundness. The better the estimates, the better the decisions that can be made.

The basis for measuring the cost of crime is the alternative cost principle. The net economic cost of crime to the society is thus the difference between what gross national product would be if there were neither criminal nor crime prevention activities and what GNP currently is, given present criminal and crime prevention activities.

Current reports on crime are concerned solely with the number of crimes committed and not with dollar estimates of their costs. To estimate correctly the cost of violent crime, we would start with the loss of earnings (or value of production services rendered) of the victims and of those close to the victims. Obvious costs of crimes against property are the values of property destroyed or damaged. It is not at all clear that there is a comparable direct cost to the society of traffic in illegal goods and services—the production and the sale of these *adds to* the well-being of their consumers but may at the same time impose offsetting spillover costs on the society as a whole. Additional costs of the whole range of criminal activities consist of the costs of prevention, apprehension, and correction, since resources used for these purposes could have been used to produce alternative goods and services valuable to consumers. Many items thought to be costs are really transfers of purchasing power to the perpetrators of the crimes from their victims. In the case of theft, the thief is made better off at the same time that the person from whom the item is stolen is made worse off. Reprehensible as theft may be, it is difficult to conclude that it represents a large net economic cost to society. It may, however, represent sizable costs to the individual victims.

Criminal activities in the aggregate lower GNP below what it would be without them. *Crime prevention activities* should, if effective, raise GNP above the level that it would be in their absence. Crime prevention activities can thus be considered an economic good or service, since GNP is higher with them than it would be without them. We can think of crime prevention activities as using productive resources—labor and capital—going into the production

TABLE 5–2
Expenditures on criminal justice in the United States
by level of government, 1982

Level of government	Direct expenditure ($ millions)	Percent
Federal	$ 3,137	9
State	10,649	30.7
Local	20,922	60.3
Total	$34,708	100.0

Source: U.S. Department of Commerce, Bureau of the Census, *Statistical Abstract of the United States, 1986*, p. 175.

process. The costs of these services are measured by applying the alternative cost principle: the costs of resources used in crime prevention are equal to the value these resources would have had in their best alternative uses. From Table 5–2 we see that the expenditures of federal, state, and local governments for law enforcement and justice were an estimated $34,708 million for 1982, the latest year for which data is available.

In summary, satisfactory measures of the costs of crime, in terms of GNP lost because of it, have not yet been devised. The costs of crime prevention activities can be estimated with a fair degree of accuracy; however, these leave out a substantial part of the total costs of crime.

INDIVIDUALLY AND COLLECTIVELY CONSUMED GOODS

Would a 5 percent increase in the police force of your city be worth anything to you personally? Would an increase or a decrease in the number of patrol cars on the city's streets affect you directly? Would it benefit you if there were an increase or decrease in the number of courts and judges in the system of justice? Your answers to these questions will be "No," "I don't know," or "Possibly."

Such questions lead us logically to a useful threefold classification of the economy's goods and services. The first includes those that are *individually consumed*. The second includes those that are *collectively consumed*. The third is made up of *semicollectively consumed* goods and services.

Individually consumed goods

The concept of individually consumed goods and services is straightforward. It includes those that directly benefit the person who consumes them. Much of what we consume is of this nature—hamburgers, suntan lotion, pencils, and the like. The person doing the consuming is able to identify the benefits received. For example, eating a hamburger gives pleasure to the eater and reduces hunger pangs.

Collectively consumed goods

Collectively consumed goods and services lie at the opposite pole from those that are individually consumed; in this case, the individual is not able to isolate or identify a specific personal benefit. Consider national defense services. What part of the total defense services provided by the economy can you identify as being consumed by you, and what is your estimate of the resulting increase in your well-being? Services like this contribute to the welfare of the group to which we belong, but it is not possible to pick out the part of the benefit that accrues specifically to any one person. An additional characteristic of a collectively consumed good is that once it is provided no individual can be excluded from its benefits. Can the government exclude you from the benefits of national defense?

Many kinds of services produced and consumed by a society are collectively consumed. They include national defense, crime prevention, space exploration, some aspects of public health, and most antipollution measures.

Semicollectively consumed goods

Semicollectively consumed goods and services yield identifiable benefits to the one who consumes them, but their consumption by one person yields spillover benefits to other persons. My neighbors' consumption of the various items that lead to beautiful landscaping on their property benefits me as well as them. When other people in a democratic society consume the services of primary education—learn to read, write, and do arithmetic—they benefit directly, and I benefit, too, because a literate population improves the functioning of the democratic processes. When other people purchase sufficient medical care to avoid epidemics, I benefit from their purchases of health care.

A great many items that people consume and which yield direct benefits to them also yield benefits to others as the consumption occurs. These benefits to persons other than the direct consumers were identified in the last chapter as *social spillover benefits*. We also noted that the consumption of some semicollectively consumed goods may yield *spillover costs* to persons other than the direct consumers. Cigarette smoking in a classroom in which there are non-smokers may be a case in point. So may onion or garlic eating.

The "free rider" problem

A society may have difficulty in getting collectively consumed goods produced because of a tendency for some of the beneficiaries of the goods to be *"free riders."* The nature of the free rider problem can be illustrated by an example from the Old West. On the plains of Oklahoma, Texas, Kansas, and other frontier cattle-raising states, cattle rustling was a serious problem. In order to deal effectively with the problem in one area (say, the Dodge City environs), it was advantageous for the cattle raisers of the area to band together. They organized a vigilante group of sufficient size to make rustling in the area an exceedingly dangerous business—as a few who were caught and hanged would have testified, if they had been able. All the cattle raisers of the area contributed to the cost of organizing and maintaining the vigilante group.

As the problem was brought under control, however, it became difficult to meet the costs of holding the vigilante group together. Any one rancher was inclined to think that if the others maintained the group, they could not keep the one from benefiting from its activities. If rustlers were afraid to operate in the area, *everyone* benefited, even those who did not help pay the costs. Each rancher therefore had an incentive to withdraw support from the group and to become a "free rider," since no producer, even one who did not pay a part of the costs of protection it provided, could be excluded from its benefits.

Government production of collectively consumed items

Historically, groups of people have found that in banding together they can do things collectively that they are not able to do as individuals. One of the first things discovered was that the group provides better protection from outsiders than individuals can provide on their own. They also found that group action is well suited to protecting the members of the group from predators in their midst.

Group action on a voluntary basis is technically possible, of course. The vigilante group of the Old West provides an excellent example. But voluntary associations to provide collectively consumed goods have a tendency to fall apart because of the incentives that induce some people to become free riders and because free riders cannot be excluded from the benefits of the good. Thus the voluntary association is a tenuous mechanism for this purpose.

Supplanting the voluntary association with the coercive association that we call *government* can effectively remedy the free rider problem. A coercive government unit (and the power of coercion is an essential feature of government) simply requires that all who receive the benefits of a collectively consumed good or the service it provides should pay appropriate taxes for it. Thus, the provision of national defense, crime prevention, pollution prevention, and other collectively consumed goods and services becomes a government function. These items are often referred to as *public goods*.

Most modern governments do not confine their production of goods and services to collectively consumed goods. Name any good or service, and there will probably be a government somewhere that produces it. A major difference between a private enterprise economic system and a socialistic economic system is that the government of the latter is responsible for the production of individually consumed as well as collectively consumed and semicollectively consumed items. The government of the former leaves the bulk of individually consumed goods to private business, although it may play a relatively important role in the provision of such semicollectively consumed goods as education.

THE ECONOMICS OF CRIME PREVENTION ACTIVITIES

The "correct" level

What is the appropriate level of expenditures on crime prevention activities by any government unit? Is a $35 billion level more or less "correct" for the United States as a whole? The same question can be asked appropriately about any category of government activity and expenditure. To find the answer, *cost-benefit analysis* should be used. In this type of analysis, we must estimate the benefits of the activity, determine its costs, and look for the level at which costs of an increase in the activity begin to exceed the benefits of that increase.

The framework for such a problem is set up in Table 5–3. Suppose the annual benefits and costs of crime prevention at various levels have been investigated thoroughly and the estimates have been recorded in columns (1), (2), and (4). A "unit" of crime prevention is a nebulous concept, a composite of police personnel, patrol cars, courthouses, judges' services, prison costs, and the like. We avoid the problem of defining physical units by using arbitrary $60,000 units of crime prevention, assuming that each $60,000 chunk is spent in the best possible way.

TABLE 5–3
Estimated benefits and costs of crime prevention, typical U.S. community ($000)

(1) Units of crime prevention per year	(2) Total benefits	(3) Marginal benefits	(4) Total costs	(5) Marginal costs	(6) Total net benefits
1	$ 200	$200	$ 60	$60	$140
2	380	180	120	60	260
3	540	160	180	60	360
4	680	140	240	60	440
5	800	120	300	60	500
6	900	100	360	60	540
7	980	80	420	60	560
8	1,040	60	480	60	560
9	1,080	40	540	60	540
10	1,100	20	600	60	500

The money expense of crime prevention to the community is met by levying taxes. The *economic cost* is the value of the goods and services that resources used in crime prevention activities could have produced if they had not been drawn into crime prevention. The *benefits* of crime prevention are the community's best estimates of how much better off the suppression of crime will make them—the value of the extra days they can work as a result of *not* being raped, maimed, or murdered, plus the value of property *not* destroyed, plus the value of the greater personal security they feel, and so on. Obviously, the benefits will be much more difficult to estimate than the costs. In fact, the most difficult and vexing part of the problem is the estimation of the benefits that ensue from various kinds of crime prevention activities.

If the benefits and costs are known, and we assume in Table 5–3 that they are, determination of the correct level of crime prevention is relatively simple. Consider first whether there should be no crime prevention at all or whether one unit would be worthwhile. One unit of prevention yields benefits to the community of $200,000—keeps $200,000 worth of GNP from being destroyed by criminal activities—and it would cost them only $60,000 to obtain it. Obviously, this is better than no prevention; the net benefits (total benefits minus total costs) are $140,000.

Now consider two units of prevention versus one unit. The total benefits yielded are $380,000. But note that the increase in total benefits yielded in moving from one to two units is $180,000, somewhat less than the increase in total benefits resulting from a movement from zero to one unit. The increase in total benefits resulting from a one-unit increase in the amount of crime prevention is called the *marginal benefit* of crime prevention. As the number of units of prevention is increased, the marginal benefits would be expected to decline, because each one-unit increase would be used to suppress the most serious crimes outstanding. The more units of prevention used, the less serious the crimes to which they are applied and, therefore, the less the increase in the benefits from each one-unit increase in prevention.

It pays the community to move from the one-unit level to the two-unit level of prevention because the marginal benefits yielded by the second unit exceed the marginal costs of the increase. *Marginal costs* of crime prevention are defined in much the same way as marginal benefits—they are the increase in total costs resulting from a one-unit increase in prevention. Marginal costs of prevention are constant in the example because we are measuring units of prevention in terms of $60,000 chunks. Therefore, the total net benefits will be increased by $120,000 ($180,000 − $60,000) if the community increases the prevention level from one to two units. (Make sure you understand this before you go any further.)

Using the same kind of logic, we can determined that it is worthwhile for the community to use a third, fourth, fifth, sixth, and seventh unit of crime prevention. For each of these increases, the marginal benefits are greater than the marginal costs—that is, each adds more to total benefits than it adds to total costs. Therefore, each brings about an increase in total net benefits. Total net benefits reach a maximum of $560,000 at the seven-unit level. If the level of prevention is raised to eight units, no harm is done. Marginal benefits equal marginal costs, and there is no change in total net benefits. But if the level is raised to nine units, total net benefits will fall to $540,000.

As citizens we *must* understand the logic underlying determination of the correct amount of government activity in crime prevention—or in anything else. It is very simple, very important, and usually overlooked. If a small increase in the level of an activity yields additional benefits worth more than the additional costs of providing it, it should be expanded. On the other hand, if its marginal benefits are less than its marginal costs, it should be contracted. It follows that the correct level is that at which marginal benefits are equal to marginal costs. (Study Table 5–3 until you understand this thoroughly.)

The foregoing economic analysis suggests something about dealing with increasing crime rates. If, when crime prevention activities are stepped up, the cost of an increase in prevention is less than the benefits it realizes, we ought to engage in more crime prevention activities. We are irrational if we do not. However, if a unit of prevention is not worth to us what it costs, then it is irrational to attempt to suppress crime at present levels of crime prevention activities. Complete suppression of crime is never logical from the point of view of economics alone. There will be some level of crime prevention at which the benefits of an additional unit of prevention are simply not worth what they cost. (What about 10 units of prevention in Table 5–3?)

The *economic* analysis developed above, as important as it is, fails to touch on a very large part of the problems of crime. It does not consider, for example, such questions as: What gives rise to crime in the first place? What causes children to become delinquent and to grow up to be criminals? What causes adults to turn to criminal activities? Can criminals be rehabilitated, or should they simply be punished? These and many other questions are *psychological, social,* and even *political* in nature. Given the social milieu in which crime takes place, however, economic analysis is valuable in determining the level at which prevention activities should be pursued.

Allocation of the crime prevention budget

Economic analysis also has something to contribute in determining the efficiency of different facets of crime prevention activities. There are several facets to any well-balanced government crime prevention program. Ideally, it should deter people from engaging in criminal activities. Failing in this—as it surely will—it must first *detect and apprehend* those engaging in criminal activities. This is primarily a police function. To *determine the guilt or innocence* of those charged with criminal acts, the legal system utilizes courts, attorneys, judges, and juries. Those convicted are fined and/or put in prison to *rehabilitate and/or punish* them. Reference to the prison system as a corrections system indicates hope that those incarcerated will somehow be rehabilitated and deterred from engaging in further criminal activities. In practice, the sentences of those convicted of crimes usually take on at least some aspects of punishment.

How much of a governmental unit's crime prevention budget should be allocated to police departments? How much for courts, judges, and prosecutors? How much for corrections, rehabilitation, and punishment? Detection and apprehension of persons thought to be committing criminal acts are of little value unless there are adequate court facilities for trying them. Trying persons apprehended and sentencing those convicted presupposes an adequate system of corrections or punishment. No one facet of crime prevention can contribute efficiently unless the others are there to back it up.

The allocation of government expenditures for control and prevention of crime in 1982 is shown by function and by the level of government making the expenditure in Table 5–4. Note that local governments make the greatest total expenditures in all functions except that of corrections. In the corrections area the primary burden falls on state governments.

The most efficient mix of the different facets of crime prevention is determined logically by what economists call the *equimarginal principle*. The crime budget should be allocated among police, courts, and corrections so that the last dollar spent on any one facet yields the same addition to the benefits of crime prevention as the last dollar spent on the others. Another way of saying this is that the budget should be allocated so that the marginal benefits from a dollar's worth of police efforts will equal the marginal benefits of a dollar's worth of judicial effort and a dollar's worth of corrective effort in the overall suppression of crime.

As an example, suppose that the crime prevention system is relatively overloaded in the area of detection and apprehension. The courts cannot handle all those who are being arrested, so many of them must be set free without trial or, in the case of plea bargaining, sentenced for a lesser crime than the one committed. The mere fact of arrest will have some crime-deterring effects, but they will be much less than would be the case if there were adequate court facilities to try the persons apprehended. The contribution to crime prevention of an additional dollar's worth of police activity at this point is low. On the other hand, an expansion of court facilities would increase the likelihood of trial and conviction of those apprehended. We would expect the crime-deterring effect of a dollar's worth of such an expansion to be greater than that of a dollar spent on detection, apprehension, and subsequent freeing of those apprehended. Suppose that taking a dollar away from police work brings about enough of a crime increase to cause a 75-cent loss to the community. Now suppose that court activity was increased by one dollar's worth, and the increased activity deters criminal activity enough to make the community better off by $3. Under these circumstances, the community will experience a net gain of $2.25 by a transfer of a dollar from police activities to court activities. Such net gains are possible for any dollar transfer among police activities, court activities, and corrections activities when the marginal benefits of a dollar spent on one are less than the marginal benefits of a dollar spent on either of the others. No further gains are possible when the crime prevention budget is so allocated that the marginal benefits of a dollar spent on any one activity equal the marginal benefits of a dollar spent on any one of the other activities.

TABLE 5-4
Allocation of criminal justice expenditures by function and by level of government, 1982

	Federal		State		Local		Total	
	Amount (millions)	Percent	Amount (millions)	Percent	Amount (millions)	Percent	Amount (millions)	Percent
Police protection	$1,986	63.3%	$ 2,486	23.3%	$14,170	67.7%	$18,642	53.7%
Judicial and legal	729	23.2	2,606	24.5	3,775	18.0	7,110	20.5
Corrections	422	13.5	5,557	52.2	2,976	14.3	8,956	25.8
	$3,137	100.0	$10,649	100.0	$20,921	100.0	$34,708	100.0

Source: United States Department of Commerce, *Statistical Abstract of the United States*, 1986, p. 175.

THE ECONOMICS OF LEGALIZING ILLEGAL ACTIVITIES

Economic analysis also provides information that is useful in determining whether or not certain activities should be considered illegal. There has been much controversy historically over legalizing the purchase, sale, and consumption of alcohol. More recently, drugs have come into the picture—especially marijuana and cocaine. Abortion has also been a source of many legal questions. Although prostitution is illegal in most parts of the United States, legalizing the practice comes up for discussion periodically. Various forms of gambling also figure in arguments as to what should and should not be illegal.

The purchase and sale of abortions provide an excellent example of the contributions that economic analysis can make in a controversy over whether or not an activity should be legal. Most of the states of the United States have had laws making abortions illegal. These have been struck down effectively by Supreme Court decisions. The underlying basis of such laws is morality. Antiabortionists contend that abortion destroys a human life. Proabortionists argue that a woman should be free to make the choice of whether she wants to have a baby, and the passing of an unborn fetus is not equivalent to destroying a human life. The central disagreement is over the point at which a fertilized egg becomes a human being. It must be recognized at the outset that economics can tell us nothing about the moral issues involved. It can, however, provide important information regarding the conditions of purchase and sale when the activity is illegal, as compared with when it is legal.

In Figure 5–1, suppose that D_1D_1 and S_1S_1 represent the demand and supply curves for abortions when this type of medical service is illegal. The fact that abortions are illegal does not drive all potential customers out of the market, but it does suppress the number who would buy abortions at each possible price. Neither does it completely eliminate the supply, but it does affect the segment of the medical profession from which the supply comes. Part of it is rendered by poorly trained personnel of the midwife or unscrupulous druggist variety. Part of it comes from medical doctors who are in difficulty with their profession for one reason or another and who are more or less barred from practicing medicine legally. Almost all illegal abortions must be performed with inferior medical facilities—for example, the home "office" of the illegal practitioner—under circumstances that may be unsanitary.

Prices are likely to be very high as compared with other comparable medical services for two reasons: (1) because of the limited quantities of facilities and abortionists available, and (2) in order to

FIGURE 5–1
Economic effects of legalizing abortions

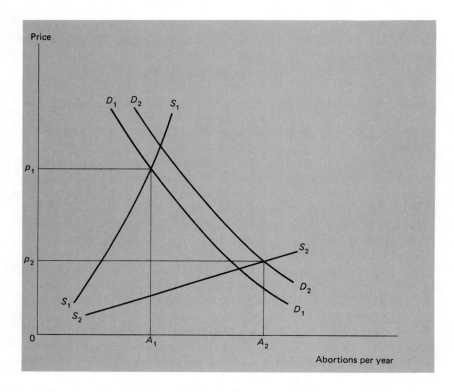

When abortions are illegal, the demand and supply curves are D_1D_1 and S_1S_1, respectively. Legalization will increase demand to some extent, shifting the demand curve to some position such as D_2D_2. Supply is likely to be greatly increased, as shown by the shift of the curve from S_1S_1 to S_2S_2. The quantity exchanged rises from A_1 to A_2 and the price falls from p_1 to p_2.

compensate the abortionist for the risk of being caught and prosecuted. An interesting side effect is that abortions will be much more readily available to the rich, for whom the high price is less important, than for the poor, who are priced out of the market. The price of an illegal abortion in Figure 5–1 is p_1, and the quantity performed is A_1.

Now suppose that abortions become legal. There will be some increase in demand, say to D_2D_2, since the taint of illegality is removed. There will, of course, still be moral constraints that prevent some women from aborting unwanted babies. The effects on supply are likely to be more dramatic. Abortions can now be performed in hospitals under controlled sanitary conditions, and in medical terms they are no big deal. They will be performed by doctors whose competency for this operation is as great as that for any other. The risk of being caught and prosecuted has been removed and no longer enters into the cost picture.

The costs of supplying abortions now are the alternative amounts that physicians could earn from operations of similar difficulty and duration. The cost spread for different quantities supplied will be very responsive to changes in the price. The price of legal abortions will be p_2, and the quantity purchased will be A_2.

To summarize the economic effects of legalizing abortions, first, the supply of the service increases. Second, there is also an increase in demand, but it is not as great as the supply increase. Third, the quantity exchanged is greater, and the price is lower. Fourth, the service becomes as accessible to the poor as any comparable operation. Fifth, there is an improvement in the quality of the service.

The economic analysis of legal versus illegal traffic in other goods and services is virtually the same as it is for abortions. When the purchase, sale, and consumption of an item—be it alcohol, prostitution, or marijuana—are made illegal, it can be expected that there will be a decrease in quantity exchanged, a rise in price, and a deterioration in the quality of the product.

SUMMARY

Criminal activities are defined as activities that are illegal. They may or may not be immoral. They are usually classified as (1) crimes against persons, (2) crimes against property, (3) traffic in illegal goods and services, and (4) other crimes.

Crime constitutes a serious problem in the United States; crime rates generally have been increasing over the years. Some of the underlying causes of crime are (1) unrestrained passions or emotions, (2) poverty coupled with high levels of economic and social aspirations, and (3) low standards of social values.

Good information on the costs of crime is not available because many criminal activities go unreported and because it is difficult to place dollar values on the results of some kinds of these activities. Some reported "costs" of crime are not really economic costs to the society as a whole but are transfers of income from the victim of the crime to its perpetrator.

In an economic analysis of crime it is useful to classify goods and services into three categories: (1) individually consumed, (2) collectively consumed, and (3) semicollectively consumed items. Governments, with their coercive powers, are in a unique position to produce such collectively consumed items as crime prevention. Consequently, collectively consumed services of this type are usually provided by governments.

Cost-benefit analysis can be used to advantage in determining the level of crime prevention activities in a society. The costs of crime prevention can be easily determined, but the benefits—many of which are intangible—are hard to estimate. Conceptually, they are the difference between what GNP would be *with* crime prevention and what it would be *without* such activities. On the basis of the best estimates that can be made, the society should seek that level of crime prevention at which the total net benefits are greatest. This will be the level at which the marginal benefits of crime prevention are equal to its marginal costs.

Once the level of the government's crime prevention budget is determined, it should be efficiently allocated among the different facets of crime prevention activities. These include detection and apprehension of violators, determination of their guilt or innocence, and corrections.

SUPPLEMENTARY READING

Federal Bureau of Investigation. *Crime in the United States.* Washington, D.C.: U.S. Government Printing Office, annual.

Sums up all reported crimes in the United States on an annual basis, providing the most complete statistical data available on types of crimes and who commits them. It also provides trend data for key types of crime statistics. There is very little analysis of the data.

Hofler, Richard A., and Ann D. White. "Benefit-Cost Analysis of the Sentencing Decision: The Case of Homicide." In *The Cost of Crime,* ed. Charles M. Gray. Beverly Hills, Cal.: Sage Publications, 1979.

A step-by-step description of applying benefit-cost analysis to a criminal justice problem. Read it for the flavor rather than the details.

McKenzie, Richard B., and Gordon Tullock. "Crime and Dishonesty." *The New World of Economics.* 3rd ed. Homewood, Ill.: Richard D. Irwin, 1981.

An analysis of the costs and benefits of crime to the criminal and of costs to the society and to the victims of crime. Traffic violations, tax evasion, lying, and cheating are also discussed.

North, Douglass C., and Roger L. Miller. *The Economics of Public Issues.* 5th ed. New York: Harper & Row, 1983.

Chapter 3 discusses the economic gains from legalizing prostitution, while chapter 28 stresses the economic nature of criminal activity. The authors argue that to reduce crime the price paid (punishment) by the criminal must be increased.

Report to the Nation on Crime and Justice. U.S. Department of Justice, Bureau of Justice Statistics, October 18, 1983.

Probably the best available survey of the many facets of crime and the criminal justice system in the United States. It reports trends over time as well as the division of labor among federal, state, and local levels of government.

POLLUTION PROBLEMS

What is pollution?
  The environment and its services
  Recycling of wastes and the concept
    of pollution
  Common forms of pollution
Economics of pollution
  Why polluters pollute
  Pollution and resource use
  The costs of controlling pollution
  The benefits of controlling pollution
  The appropriate level of pollution
    control
What can be done about pollution?
  Direct controls
  Indirect controls
  Private property rights
Summary

**Checklist of
Economic Concepts**

Collectively consumed goods
  and services
Demand
Supply
Alternative costs
Production possibilities curve
Cost-benefit analysis
Marginal costs
Marginal benefits
Spillover costs, social
Efficiency, economic

6

Pollution Problems

___

Must we foul our own nests?

The high-pitched whistle of departing jets was deafening as John Q. Smith stepped outside the terminal building and walked toward the parking lot. He located his three-year-old car, got it started, paid the parking fee, and wheeled out onto the congested freeway, adding his own small carbon monoxide and hydrocarbon contributions to the pall that hung over the city. On his left the Contaminated Steel Company was belching noxious streams of dense smoke into the heavy air, ably assisted by the nearby coal-burning power and light plant. Where the freeway joined the river's edge, a pulp and paper mill was spewing its wastes into the river. He held his breath as long as he could along the two-mile stretch of road adjoining the stockyards. Then with a sigh of relief he swerved off the freeway and turned down the country road that would take him home. Once out of sight of human habitat, he stopped the car and relieved himself at the side of the road, noting as he did so the accumulating litter of beer cans, paper, and cellophane bags on the shoulder of the road and in the ditch.

John Q.'s house was located on a lake. Since a group of industrial plants had been built along the lakeshore several miles away, it was not as pleasant to swim and water-ski in the lake as it had been previously. The fishing didn't seem to be as good either. Recently, he had been having problems with a backed-up sewer, and he wondered as he turned in the driveway if the plumber had been there to clean out the sewer line that reached from the house to the lake. John Q. had grown up in the great outdoors (this is why he had built the house on the lake), and he was much concerned about the lake's deterioration.

Most of us, like John Q. Smith, are concerned about environmental problems, but we are not quite sure what we can do about them. As individuals, we seem to believe that we can do little. In fact, we are likely to add to the problems by thinking that our own bit of pollution is just a drop in the bucket.

Public reaction to pollution varies a great deal. At one extreme are environmentalists and nature-lovers, who object to everything that decreases the purity of the air and water or that mars the natural beauty of the landscape. At the other extreme are those who seem not to value at all clean air, water, and natural beauty. Most of us are between these two extremes.

A sensible attack on pollution problems requires the use of economic analysis along with inputs from other disciplines—especially the natural sciences. In particular, economic analysis may help us (1) determine why and under what circumstances economic units pollute; (2) determine the extent to which pollution control should be exercised; and (3) evaluate alternative antipollution activities of the government.

WHAT IS POLLUTION?

We will not make much progress in an economic analysis of pollution until we are familiar with both the nature of the environment in which we live and what it is that constitutes pollution of that environment. We shall consider these two concepts in turn.

The environment and its services

The environment is easily defined. It consists of the air, water, and land around us. These provide us with a variety of important services.

First, the environment provides a *habitat* or surroundings in which both plant and animal life can survive. Temperature ranges on the planet are neither too hot nor too cold for survival. The air, the water, and the land contain the elements needed to sustain living matter as we know it.

Second, the environment contains *resources* that are usable in the production of goods and services. These include minerals such as petroleum, coal, and a wide assortment of ores that can be processed into metals and metal alloys. They also include soil properties and plant life supported by the soil. Resources include the plant and animal life yielded by water as well as the inherent properties of water used directly in production processes. They also include oxygen and nitrogen, along with other elements and properties found in the atmosphere.

Third, the environment furnishes many *amenities* that make life more enjoyable. It opens up possibilities of a walk along a river, through an alfalfa field, or in a rose garden. It provides an area in which you can fly kites or have picnics, a place to take your girlfriend or your boyfriend—or even your husband or your wife. You can sit in it and enjoy the sunset. Or, if you so desire, you can make a painting or take a photograph of it.

The services of the environment are used by production units and household units as they engage in activities of various kinds. Production units lay heavy claims on the environment's resources, but they may also make use of its habitat and amenity characteristics.

As production units engage in the process of transforming raw and semifinished materials into goods and services that will satisfy human wants, there are at least three ways in which the environment can be affected. First, some of the environment's stocks of exhaustible resources may be diminished. These include coal, petroleum, and many mineral deposits. Second, it is called upon for replaceable resources like timber, grassland, oxygen, and nitrogen. Third, it is used as a place to dispose of the wastes of the production and consumption processes—as a gigantic garbage disposal.

Recycling of wastes and the concept of pollution

The pollution problem arises primarily from the use of the environment by producers and consumers as a dumping ground for wastes. We litter the countryside with cans, paper, and the other residues of consumption and production. We dump the emissions from our automobiles and factories into the atmosphere. We empty sewage and residue from production directly and indirectly into streams, rivers, and lakes.

As wastes from production and consumption are dumped into the environment, nature sets recycling processes in motion. Animals use oxygen, giving off carbon dioxide wastes. But plants use carbon dioxide, giving off oxygen wastes. Dead plant and animal life are attacked by chemical elements that decompose them, restoring to the soil elements that the living organisms had withdrawn from it. Living organisms frequently contribute to the decomposition process. Iron and steel objects rust and disintegrate over time. So does wood and other matter. Wastes that can be decomposed in air, water, and soil are said to be *biodegradable*. But there are some wastes that are not biodegradable. Aluminum containers such as beer cans are a case in point.

Recycling—the transformation of wastes into raw materials that are again usable—requires variable lengths of time, depending on what it is that is being recycled. It takes many years for a steel pipe to rust away. Wood varies a great deal in the time it takes for its complete disintegration. But many plant and animal products require only a very short time to decompose.

Pollution consists of loading the environment with wastes that are not completely recycled, are not recycled fast enough, or are not recycled at all. It involves a diminution of the capacity of the environment to yield environmental services. Pollution occurs when recycling processes fail to prevent wastes from accumulating in the environment.

Common forms of pollution

Pollution is as old as civilization itself. Wherever people have congregated, their wastes have tended to pile up more rapidly than the forces of nature can digest them. As long as the world was sparsely populated and no permanent cities existed, no great problems were created. When the extent of pollution in one locale imposed costs on the people living there that outweighed the costs associated with moving, they simply moved away from it. Then, given time, natural recycling processes could in many cases take over and restore the excess wastes to usable form.

When towns and cities came into existence, pollution raised more serious problems. How could body wastes from humans and animals, as well as refuse from the daily round of living, be disposed of? Until fairly recent times it was not disposed of in many instances—levels of sanitation were unbelievably low, and levels of stench were unbelievably high. As the density of the world's population has increased and as it has become more difficult to move away from pollution problems, the human race has turned its attention more and more toward the development of control measures. But in order to control pollution, it must be identified as accurately as possible in its various forms.

Air pollution. In the processes of production and consumption, five major kinds of wastes are dumped into the atmosphere. Most result from combustion and have caused local problems for a long time. Since there are millions of cubic miles of atmosphere to absorb these wastes, however, air pollution has not caused great concern until the past few decades. These wastes are carbon monoxide, sulfur oxides, nitrogen oxides, hydrocarbons, and particulates.

Carbon monoxide, an odorless, colorless gas, makes the atmosphere a less hospitable habitat for animal life. In concentrated amounts, it causes dizziness, headaches, and nausea in humans. Exposure to a sufficiently high concentration—about 100 parts per 1 million parts of atmosphere—for a few hours can be fatal. In 1983,

70.6 percent of the carbon monoxide emissions into the atmosphere in the United States came from transportation sources, and another 6.8 percent came from industrial sources of one kind or another. The greatest concentrations of carbon monoxide occur in large cities. On New York City streets concentration levels as high as 13 parts per 1 million parts of atmosphere have been recorded.[1]

Sulfur oxides constitute a second major source of atmospheric pollution. Where they are heavily concentrated, they cause damage to both plant and animal life. Oxides result largely from the combustion of fuel oils and coal. Consequently, high levels of concentration are most likely to occur where these are used for the generation of electricity and for residential heating.

A third atmospheric pollutant is *nitrogen oxides*. These can cause lung damage in human beings and may also retard plant growth. The main sources of the pollutant are automobiles and stationary combustion processes such as those used in generating electric power.

Hydrocarbons constitute a fourth kind of waste emitted into the air. At their present concentration levels no direct harmful effects have been attributed to them. However, they combine with nitrogen oxides and ultraviolet rays of the sun to form petrochemical smog. The smog may produce breathing difficulties and eye irritation for human beings. In addition, it speeds up the oxidation processes to which paints and metals are subject, resulting in substantial damages to industrial plants and equipment. Almost 50 percent of hydrocarbon emissions in the United States comes from industrial sources, and another 40 percent comes from automobiles.

A fifth air pollutant consists of a heterogeneous mixture of suspended solids and liquids called *particulates*. These are largely dust and ash, along with lead from automobile exhausts. The major source of particulates, however, is fuel combustion in stationary sources and in industrial processes. Open fires used to burn trash and garbage also make their contributions. Particulates lower visibilities. Some, such as lead from automobile exhausts, may be directly harmful to human beings.

Water pollution. Water pollution is ordinarily measured in terms of the capacity of water to support aquatic life. This capacity depends on (1) the level of dissolved oxygen in the water and (2) the presence of matters or materials injurious to plant and animal life.

---

[1]U.S. Department of Commerce, Bureau of the Census, *Statistical Abstract, 1986*, p. 204.

The level of dissolved oxygen is built up through aeration of water and through the photosynthetic processes of plant life living in the water. It is destroyed in the decomposition of organic matter that originates in or is dumped into the water. The oxygen needed for decomposition purposes is referred to as *biochemical oxygen demand,* or BOD. The level of dissolved oxygen available for supporting aquatic life, then, depends on the balance between aeration and photosynthesis on the one hand and on BOD on the other.

The level of dissolved oxygen is affected by several factors. First, it tends to be higher the greater the amount of a given volume of water exposed to the atmosphere. In nature, fast-running streams, rapids, and waterfalls contribute to aeration. Artificial aeration is frequently accomplished by shooting streams of water through the air. Second, it tends to be higher the greater the amount of photosynthesis that occurs in the water. In some instances, the amount of photosynthesis that occurs in aquatic plant life may be reduced by air pollution. In this way, air pollution may be a source of water pollution. Third, it tends to be higher the lower the temperature of the water—use of the water for cooling by firms such as steel mills, oil refineries, and electricity-generating plants raises the temperature of the water and lowers its capacity to hold dissolved oxygen. Fourth, organic wastes that create BOD come from both domestic and industrial sources, so the level of dissolved oxygen varies inversely with the amounts that are dumped. The decomposition of such wastes can be greatly facilitated, and BOD can be correspondingly reduced by chemical treatment of such wastes before they are discharged into streams, rivers, lakes, or oceans.

The capacity of water to support aquatic life is reduced when various kinds of materials and matters are dumped into it. Among these are toxins which do not settle out of the water and are not easily broken down by biological means. Mercury is a toxin that has created problems of contamination in various types of fish. Phenols, herbicides, and pesticides have also contributed greatly to the water pollution problem. There have been heated discussions in recent years over the propriety of using them in large quantities. Questions have been raised also as to whether the oceans should be used for the dumping of nuclear wastes and for undersea nuclear explosions.

Land pollution. Land pollution results from the dumping of a wide variety of wastes on the terrain and from tearing up the earth's surface through such activities as strip mining. Highways are littered with refuse thrown from passing automobiles. Junkyards grow as we scrap over 7 million automobiles per year, to say nothing of the prodigious amounts of other machinery and appliances that are retired from use. Garbage dumps and landfills grow as towns and cities dispose of the solid wastes they collect and accumulate. All of these reduce the capacity of the terrain to render environmental services.

The growing emphasis on coal as an energy source creates mounting concern over the effects of mining on the landscape. Strip mining has typically left unsightly blemishes on the countryside. Can and should the mined area be restored? In pit mining areas, can and should steps be taken to make slag and rock piles more attractive aesthetically?

ECONOMICS OF POLLUTION

No one likes pollution. Almost everyone would like to see something done about it. Toward this end, we consider in this section the fundamental economics of the pollution problem. We shall examine the reasons pollution occurs, analyze the effects of pollution on resource allocation, look at the costs of pollution control, and identify its benefits. We shall attempt to establish criteria for determining the appropriate level of control.

Why polluters pollute

Why is it that pollution occurs? What is there about environmental services that causes consumers and producers to use the environment as a dumping ground? Ordinarily, pollution results from one or both of two basic factors: (1) the fact that no one has property rights or enforces them in the environment being polluted, and (2) the collectively consumed characteristics of the environment being polluted.

If no one owns a portion of the environment or if an owner cannot police it or have it policed, then it becomes possible for people to use a river, a lake, the air, or an area of land as a wastebasket without being charged for doing so. Because no one owns the air above city streets and highways, automobile owners can dump combustion gases into it without paying for the privilege of doing so. Similarly, a paper mill can dump its wastes into a river without charge because no one owns the river. But even ownership of the environment may not be enough to keep pollution from occurring. How many times have you seen litter accumulate on a vacant lot or junk dumped in a ditch in a pasture away from town because the owner was not there to prevent the dumping?

In addition, many environmental services are collectively consumed or used. It is hard to single out and determine the value of the air that one person—or an automobile—uses. Similarly, it is often difficult to attach a value to the water deterioration caused by one industrial plant when thousands dump their wastes into a river. Would any one person be willing to pay someone *not* to take an action that would destroy a beautiful view across the countryside? When values cannot be placed on the amounts of environmental services used by any one person, it is difficult to induce people not to pollute by charging them for doing so.

Pollution and resource use

In the process of polluting the environment, polluters impose spill-over costs on others. Polluters' costs are thus reduced below what they would be in the absence of pollution. Similarly, costs to others (nonpolluters) of using environmental services are greater than they would be if there were no pollution. Polluters, then, are induced to overuse environmental services at the expense of other users, and other users of the polluted environment are induced to underuse them. Thus, pollution involves inefficient use or misallocation of environmental services among those who use them.

Suppose, for example, that two industries are located along a riverbank. An industry producing paper is located upstream, using the river as a place to discharge its wastes. Downstream is a power-generating industry that requires large amounts of clean water for cooling purposes. If the paper industry were not there, the water from the river would be clean enough for the power industry to use. But since it is there—just upstream—the firm in the power industry must clean the water before using it.

Since the use of the river by one set of parties as a dumping place for wastes may reduce the value of the river's services to other users, a transfer of costs may be incurred by the dumping. If recycling of the dumped wastes occurs fast enough, or if the environment is large enough relative to the wastes dumped into it so that no one is injured by the dumping, no cost or pollution problems occur.

The use of the river for waste disposal by the paper industry decreases the value of the river's services for power production in the example, so cost transfers are involved in that dumping. In effect, the paper industry shifts some of its costs of production to the power industry. It is the power industry that must pay for cleaning the water, but it is the paper industry that makes it dirty.

Consider first the power industry situation if there were no pollution by the paper industry. In Figure 6–1, the demand curve for power is D_eD_e and the supply curve in the absence of pollution is

FIGURE 6-1
Effects of water pollution on water users

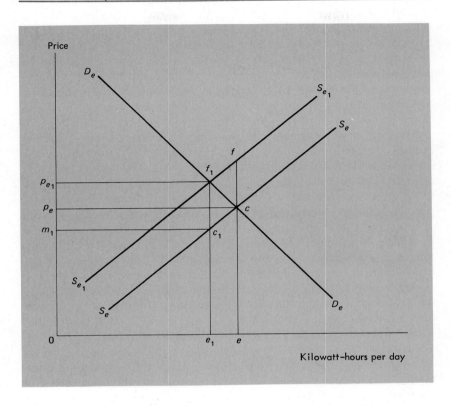

The demand curve for the output of the power industry is D_eD_e. Its supply curve, when it can obtain clean water for its use, is S_eS_e. Consequently, it will produce and sell e kilowatt-hours per day. However, if a paper industry located upstream pollutes the water, costs of cleaning the water before using it move the supply curve upward (or to the left). The power industry accordingly reduces its output to e_1 and raises its price to p_{e1}. Both the power industry and its customers pay the costs of cleaning the paper industry's wastes from the water.

S_eS_e. The equilibrium output is e and the equilibrium price is p_e per kilowatt-hour. The cost of producing a kilowatt-hour at output level e is also p_e.

Suppose, now, that the power industry must clean the water before using it. Since it must cover its costs, the price that it must receive in order to induce it to produce any specific quantity of electricity will be higher by an amount equal to the costs per kilowatt-hour of cleaning the water. The supply curve is thus shifted upward by that amount—c_1f_1 or cf—to some position such as $S_{e1}S_{e1}$. If the output of the power industry were e_1 kilowatt-hours, the price necessary to bring forth that output in the absence of pollution is e_1c_1. With pollution occurring, the necessary price is e_1f_1 or p_{e1}, with c_1f_1 being the cost per kilowatt-hour of cleaning the water. Similarly, for an output level of e, the required price in the absence of pollution is ec; with pollution it is ef; and the cost per kilowatt-hour of cleaning is cf. So the supply of electricity is decreased by the pollution of the paper industry from what it would be in the absence of pollution.

The effects of the decrease in the supply of electricity are a smaller quantity bought and sold, a higher price paid by consumers, and a lower return to producers than would be the case without the paper industry's pollution of the water. The quantity exchanged is reduced to e_1; the price paid by consumers goes up to p_{e1}; and the return to producers after paying the cleaning costs for water decreases from p_e to m_1 per kilowatt-hour. Thus, we see that the costs of pollution by the paper industry are borne by both the consumers and the producers of electricity.

In addition, the power industry is induced to underproduce. The supply curve S_eS_e shows the alternative costs per kilowatt-hour to the economy of producing various quantities of power when unpolluted water is used. For example, at output level e, it shows that ec dollars must be paid for the resources necessary to produce one kilowatt-hour. This is what those resources could earn in alternative employments; it is what they are worth in those other employments, and it represents the alternative costs to the economy of a kilowatt-hour of electricity. Similarly, at output level e_1, the *alternative cost* of producing a kilowatt-hour is e_1c_1. With the paper industry polluting the river, however, consumers pay e_1f_1 per kilowatt-hour, which is more than the costs of production. Whenever consumers are willing to pay more for an item than it costs to produce it, it is usually desirable that output be expanded. But this will not happen in the power industry because, in addition to the costs of producing electricity, it must incur an additional outlay, c_1f_1, to clean the water; that is, to undo what the paper industry has done.

The supply curve of the paper industry is increased by its access to the river for waste disposal. In Figure 6–2 let S_rS_r be the paper industry's supply curve, assuming that the river is *not* available as a "free" dumping space. The supply curve shows the alternative prices that must be received by the paper industry to induce it to produce and sell various quantities of paper. To induce it to produce and sell r reams, the price per ream must be rg. To induce it to place r_1 reams on the market, the price must be r_1g_1. Suppose now that

FIGURE 6–2
Effects of water pollution on the polluter

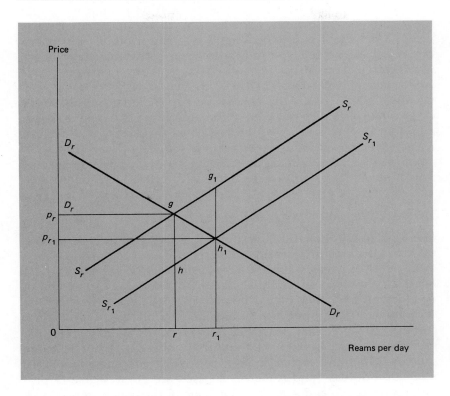

The demand curve for the output of the paper industry is D_rD_r. When it must clean its own wastes, its supply curve is S_rS_r, and its output level will be r reams of paper per day. If it can dump its wastes into the river, cleaning costs are saved, and its supply curve shifts downward (to the right). Its output will increase to r_1. It is able to shift a part of its costs to downstream users of the water.

the river is made available to the paper industry as a "free" dumping ground for wastes. The costs of producing a ream of paper are now reduced, and for an output level of r reams per day, the price need not be higher than rh—if the cost saving per ream is hg. Similarly, for r_1 reams and a cost saving of h_1g_1, the necessary price is r_1h_1. The supply curve of paper is thus shifted to the right by the accessibility of the river as a "free" place to dispose of its wastes.

The same type of reasoning that tells us the power industry underproduces because of the paper industry's pollution also tells us the paper industry overproduces. In Figure 6–2, D_rD_r is the demand curve for paper. If the paper industry were to bear the costs of its dumping of wastes by leaving clean water for the power plant, its supply curve would be S_rS_r; its price would be p_r; and its output level would be r. However, since it is able to use the river for waste disposal, its supply curve becomes $S_{r1}S_{r1}$, and it produces r_1 reams of paper per day, selling it at a price of p_{r1} per ream. The evidence of overproduction is that *alternative costs* per ream of paper exceed what consumers pay to get it. The alternative costs per ream are r_1g_1. Of this amount, r_1h_1 is the cost to the paper industry of resources other than waste disposal used in the production of a ream of paper at output level r_1, and h_1g_1 is the cost of waste disposal that is transferred to the power industry per ream of paper produced. This latter amount is not taken into account by the paper industry, so the true cost of a ream of paper exceeds what is it worth to consumers.

The costs of controlling pollution

Our reactions to pollution often motivate us to say, "Let's wipe it out." We maintain that we are entitled to clean air, clean water, and clean land. But how clean is clean? Cleanliness, like goodness, is a relative rather than an absolute quality. To determine the amount of pollution, if any, that should be allowed, the *costs* of keeping the environment clean must first be considered. Pollution control is not costless. An industrial plant that scrubs or cleans its combustion gases before discharging them into the air must use resources in the process. Labor and capital go into the making and operation of antipollution devices, and resources so used are not available to produce other goods and services. The value of the goods and services that must be given up is the cost of the plant's pollution control activities. The cost of pollution control is a straightforward application of the alternative cost principle.

The costs of pollution control to society are illustrated graphically by the production possibilities curve of Figure 6–3. Dollars' worth of all goods and services other than pollution control are measured on the vertical axis, and dollars' worth of pollution control are measured on the horizontal axis. At point A_1 the labor and capital of the economy are producing q_1 dollars' worth of goods and services and c_1 dollars' worth of antipollution activities. If still more pollution control—a cleaner environment—is desired, some value of goods and services must be sacrificed. By giving up q_2q_1 dollars' worth of goods and services, pollution control can be increased by c_1c_2 dollars' worth. Thus, q_2q_1 dollars' worth of goods and services is the economic cost of an additional c_1c_2 dollars' worth of control or of a cleaner environment.

FIGURE 6–3
The costs of pollution control

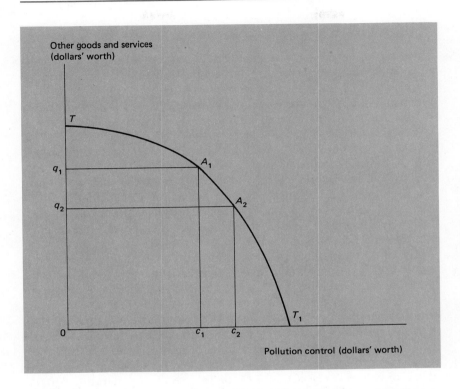

The combinations of other goods and services and pollution control that the resources of the economy can support are shown by the production possibilities curve TT_1. By giving up q_1T dollars' worth of other goods and services, the economy can have c_1 dollars' worth of pollution control, as shown at point A_1. If c_1c_2 more dollars' worth of pollution control are to be obtained, the cost will be q_2q_1 additional dollars' worth of other goods and services.

The benefits of controlling pollution

The benefits of pollution control consist of the increase in the well-being of the members of the society that results from pollution control activities. To measure the benefits of a pollution control activity, the value of the increase in well-being that it generates must be determined. Suppose, for example, that smog permeates a particular metropolitan area but that pollution control activities can reduce or perhaps even eliminate it. To determine the benefits of, say, a 50 percent reduction in smog, we can ask each individual living in the area how much such a reduction would be worth personally. By totaling all the replies we would arrive at the dollar value of the expected benefits.

The appropriate level of pollution control

Since pollution control—a cleaner environment—has costs, society must make a choice between the level of goods and services its resources will be used to produce and the degree of cleanliness of its environment. If the society experiences a level of pollution that is distasteful to it, it will be willing to sacrifice some quantities of goods and services for some level of pollution control.

The appropriate level of pollution control is determined by weighing its benefits against its costs. If the benefits of additional control—what cleaner air is worth to the citizens of the society—exceed the costs of the additional control, then pollution control should be increased. However, if the benefits of additional control are less than what it costs in terms of sacrificed goods and services, the additional control is unwarranted.

As an illustration, consider a community of 10,000 persons that is pervaded by a nauseating stench from an incinerator used to dispose of the community's garbage. Suppose that the odor can be completely eliminated by an expenditure of $100,000 per year for an alternate method of garbage disposal (carrying it away and burying it in a landfill outside the town) and that it can be partially controlled by using various combinations of burning and burying.

Suppose that the costs of different levels of partial control are those of columns (1), (2), and (3) of Table 6–1. By spending $10,000 on carrying and burying, the community can eliminate 10 percent of the stench; each additional $10,000 expenditure eliminates another 10 percent of the original total stench, until with a $100,000 expenditure the pollution is entirely eliminated.

Column (3) of Table 6–1 lists the *marginal costs* of pollution control. The concept is essentially the same as the marginal costs of crime prevention—it shows the change in total costs per unit change in the amount of pollution control. Since each increment in pollution control (an increment is defined as 10 percent of the control needed to eliminate the odor) adds $10,000 to the total cost of pollution control, the marginal cost of pollution control at each control level is $10,000.

The benefits of pollution control to the community are shown in columns (4), (5), and (6). Before any control is undertaken, each person in the community is asked for an opinion of what a 10 percent reduction in the stench is worth. Suppose each person indicates a willingness to pay $10 for it. We conclude that $100,000 measures

TABLE 6–1
Annual costs and benefits of pollution control

(1) Pollution control or eliminated stench	(2) Total cost of control ($000)	(3) Marginal cost of control ($000)	(4) Per person marginal benefits of control	(5) Community marginal benefits of control ($000)	(6) Total benefits of control ($000)	(7) Net benefits of control ($000)
1st 10%	$ 10	$10	$10.00 ea.	$100	$100	$ 90
2nd 10	20	10	8.00	80	180	160
3rd 10	30	10	6.00	60	240	210
4th 10	40	10	4.00	40	280	240
5th 10	50	10	2.00	20	300	250
6th 10	60	10	1.60	16	316	256
7th 10	70	10	1.20	12	328	258
8th 10	80	10	0.80	8	336	256
9th 10	90	10	0.40	4	340	250
10th 10	100	10	0.20	1	341	241

the total benefits yielded by the first 10 percent reduction. Since the benefits exceed the costs by $90,000, the first 10 percent reduction is clearly warranted.

The question now arises as to whether a second 10 percent reduction in the stench is worthwhile. Since the pollution is not as intense as it was with no control, a second 10 percent reduction is of less value than was the first one. Suppose each person values the move from 10 percent control to 20 percent control at $8, so that the community valuation of the extra control—or the marginal benefit of it—is $80,000. Since the marginal costs of the additional control are only $10,000, putting it into effect adds $70,000 more to the total net benefits of control and is therefore a good investment for the community.

Column (5) shows the community's *marginal benefits* at different levels of control. Marginal benefits of pollution control, like the marginal benefits of crime prevention, are defined as the *change* in total benefits per unit *change* in whatever it is that yields the benefits. Note that the *total benefits* at any given level of control are obtained by adding up the marginal benefits as the level of control is increased unit by unit up to that level.

Marginal benefits, as shown in Table 6–1, decline as the level of pollution control is increased (the level of the stench is decreased). This is what we would expect to happen in the case at hand. The greater the amount of control, or the lower the level of the stench, the less urgent additional control becomes. This will be the usual situation in controlling pollution.

The level of pollution control yielding the maximum net benefits to the people of the community is that at which the marginal benefits just cease to exceed the marginal costs. The marginal benefits of the first two 10 percent increments in the total amount of control needed to eliminate the stench exceed the marginal costs of making them. Thus, net benefits are increased by increasing control at least to the 20 percent level. The third, fourth, fifth, sixth, and seventh 10 percent increments also yield marginal benefits exceeding their marginal costs, and they increase the net benefits of control to the community. Now consider the eighth 10 percent increment. Marginal benefits are $8,000, and marginal costs are $10,000. Extending pollution control from the 70 percent level to the 80 percent level *reduces* the net benefits by $2,000. The eighth 10 percent increment is not worth to the community what it costs.

The principle is perfectly general. Net benefits will always be increased by increasing control if the marginal benefits of the increase are greater than the marginal costs of making it. Net benefits will decrease from an increase in the control level if the marginal benefits of that increase are less than its marginal costs. The appropriate level of control is the one that approaches as closely as possible the level where the marginal benefits equal the marginal costs.

WHAT CAN BE DONE ABOUT POLLUTION?

Human beings often react to problems with their emotions rather than with the capacity for logic with which they are endowed. Policies recommended to control pollution reflect this human characteristic. Typical recommendations call for direct control of pollution by the state. But this is only one of the possible avenues of reducing pollution problems. Others include indirect control by the state through a system of incentives encouraging potential polluters not to pollute or to limit their pollution, and an examination of the institutions of private property rights and markets to see if they can be modified to provide the desired limitations on polluting activities.

Direct control

An appealing simple way to control pollution is to have the government ban polluting activities or agents. If phosphates contaminate water, then ban the use of phosphates in detergents. If DDT pollutes water and land, ban the use of DDT. If the burning of fuel oil and coal increases the sulfur oxide content of the atmosphere, prohibit their use. Require industrial plants to clean the pollutants from whatever it is they discharge into the atmosphere or water. The method is straightforward and, on the face of it, seems eminently fair.

Government agencies, notably the Environmental Protection Agency (EPA) at the federal level, use direct controls to reduce many kinds of polluting activities. They set and attempt to enforce emission standards for such polluters as automobiles, power plants, and steel mills. State regulation of polluters, to the extent that it is accomplished, is in general supervised by the EPA.

The case of the city with the terrible stench shows that complete prohibition of pollutants is not likely to be worth its costs. Pollution control uses resources that could have produced goods and services, and the value of the goods and services forgone is the cost to society of controlling the pollution. If the damage done by an additional unit of pollution is less than the costs of preventing it from occurring, community welfare is greater if it is allowed to occur. Consequently, direct controls usually should aim at a less idealistic goal than a pollution-free environment. They may take the form of controlling the level of pollution by such devices as setting emissions standards or limits for industrial plants, automobiles, and other polluters.

One problem raised by the use of direct controls to limit the amount of pollution is that it presupposes the regulatory body can determine what the economically desirable levels of pollution are. This is not an insurmountable problem. Tolerance limits on the amount of pollution to be allowed can be reasonably well established. Within those limits, overall costs can be weighed continually against benefits to establish an approximation of the desirable levels of pollution.

A second problem is the difficulty facing a regulatory body in achieving an efficient allocation of the permissible pollution among different polluters. For example, it may be more costly for a steel mill to eliminate a unit of sulfur oxide from its emissions than it is for a power plant. In the interests of economic efficiency, it is best to eliminate pollution where it is least costly to do so. Thus the power plant should be required to reduce its sulfur oxide emission before the steel mill is required to do so. This is a difficult kind of decision for a regulatory body to make, since it is responsible to a political body for which economic efficiency is not a primary goal. In addition, it is unrealistic to suppose that the regulatory body has a working knowledge of the nature of costs for every polluter.

A third problem is that of enforcing the standards of emissions once it has been determined what those standards should be. Direct controls fail to provide polluters with an economic incentive not to pollute. In fact, it will pay them to seek ways and means to evade the pollution standards set for them. But we should not overstate the enforcement problem. Almost any prohibition of activities that individuals and business firms want to engage in creates enforcement problems.

Indirect controls

It is possible for the government to control many types of pollution by placing taxes on polluting activities. Where the amounts of polluting discharges can be measured for individual polluters, a tax can be placed directly on each unit of discharge. This will induce the polluter to reduce the amount of pollution that is discharged. In some cases where such measurement is not possible, polluters may be taxed indirectly—for example, automobiles not equipped with pollution control devices can be subjected to a tax on a mileage basis. This would induce their owners either to install pollution control devices or to drive less. At this time, not much use has been made of this method of control.

Figure 6–4 illustrates the use of a tax to control the amounts of pollutants discharged into the environment. Consider an industrial

FIGURE 6–4
Control of pollution by means of a tax on polluted discharges

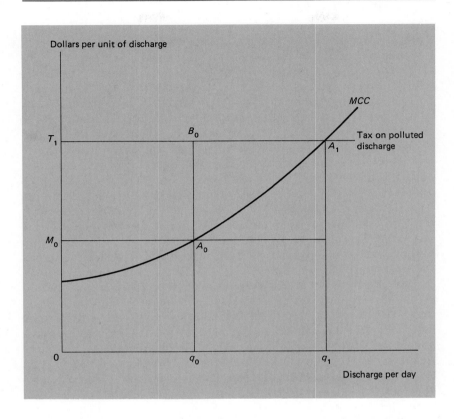

If the level of a tax on polluted discharges exceeds the marginal costs of cleaning the discharge, a firm will elect to clean the discharge. This will be the case for all discharge levels up to q_1. If the level of the tax is less than the marginal cleaning costs, the firm will elect to pay the tax rather than clean the discharge. This will occur for all discharge in excess of q_1.

concern that discharges its polluting wastes into a river. Processes for cleaning the wastes so that the pollution they cause is eliminated or diminished are available. *Marginal cleaning costs*, defined as the change in total cleaning costs per one unit change in the firm's discharge of wastes, are shown by *MCC*. For example, if the level of discharge is q_o, then q_oA_o is the *addition* to the firm's total cost of cleaning brought about when the amount of discharge is increased from one unit less than q_o to the q_o level. Similarly, the addition to total cleaning costs when the firm moves from one unit less than q_1

units to q_1 units is q_1A_1. We show the MCC curve sloping upward to the right, indicating that the larger the firm's rate of waste discharge, the greater is the cost to it of cleaning an additional unit. This may or may not be the case—we assume here for illustrative purposes that it is. The level of the tax on polluted discharge is T_1 per unit, regardless of the level of the discharge.

A tax per unit of polluted discharge will induce the firm to reduce its polluting activity if the amount of the tax exceeds the marginal costs of cleaning the discharge. If the discharge is less than q_1, say q_0 units per day, it pays the firm not to pollute. It is less costly to clean the discharge than it is to pay the tax. For the q_0 unit of discharge, q_0B_0 would be added to the firm's total costs if it elects to pay the tax and not to clean up the discharge. Only q_0A_0 would be added to its total costs if it elects to clean the discharge and pay no tax. This will be the case for any discharge level up to q_1 units per day. On the other hand, for a discharge level exceeding q_1 per day, the firm will clean q_1 units and pay the tax on the remainder of the discharge. It is cheaper to clean than to pay the tax on each unit up to that level. For units of discharge exceeding q_1, it is cheaper to pay the tax than to clean them.

The tax can be set at any desired level, depending on the amount of pollution the government decides to allow. Raising the tax will decrease the amount of pollution, and lowering the tax will increase it. Ideally, the tax should be set at a level at which the marginal benefits to society of cleaning a unit of discharge equal the marginal cleaning costs. If the level of polluted discharge permitted is such that the marginal benefits of cleaning the discharge exceed the marginal costs of cleaning it, the tax is too low and should be increased. If the level of polluted discharge permitted is such that marginal benefits of cleaning are less than the marginal costs of cleaning, the tax is too high and should be decreased.

The use of taxes to control pollution has its advantages. A major one is that it provides an incentive to the polluter to seek improved ways and means of cleaning up its discharge. Another advantage is that it prevents the polluter from shifting some of its production costs (pollution costs) to others; it reduces the incentive to over produce.

There are also disadvantages. First, it usually is difficult to determine the benefits—total and marginal—to society of cleaning the discharge. Second, enforcement of such a tax is not easy. Policing is necessary to determine that the discharge is indeed properly cleaned. Third, taxes are levied by political rather than economic bodies, and politics may well get in the way of the enactment of appropriate tax levels.

The federal government has used subsidies—the opposite of taxes—extensively as a pollution control measure. These consist primarily of grants made to state and local governments for the construction of sewage treatment facilities. For the fiscal year 1986 about 64 percent of federal outlays on pollution control and abatement were for construction of this type. This percentage is estimated to decrease somewhat during 1987–88.[2]

Private property rights

Since the absence of well-defined property rights provides an important incentive to polluters to dump their wastes in certain segments of the environment, the assignment of property rights either to firms that pollute or to those that benefit from a clean environment may provide a means of control in some cases. Consider, for example, the case described earlier about the upstream paper industry and the downstream power industry. Since neither owns the river, the paper industry is able to use it for waste disposal, and the costs of the waste disposal fall on the power industry.

Suppose that rights to the river are sold at auction by the government. These rights will be purchased by the industry to which they are most valuable. If the annual value to the paper industry of using the river for waste discharges (the costs of alternative means of disposing of the wastes) exceeds the annual cost to the power industry of cleaning the water, the paper industry will buy the rights. The river will be put to its most valuable use—that of being a sink for waste disposal. However, if the value of clean water to the power industry (the costs of cleaning it for power industry use) exceeds the value to the paper industry of using the river to discharge wastes, the power industry will purchase the rights, and the river will be put to its most productive (valuable) use—that of furnishing clean cooling water for the generation of electricity.

Regardless of which industry buys the rights, changes in the relative values of the two uses will provide incentives for the river to be put to the use in which it is most valuable. If the paper industry holds the rights to the river but the annual value of clean water to the power industry exceeds the annual value of the river as a waste disposal, the power industry will be willing to pay the paper industry enough to induce it not to pollute—to use alternative means of

---

[2]Office of Management and Budget, *Special Analysis, Budget of the United States Government, Fiscal Year 1988* (Washington, D.C.: U.S. Government Printing Office, 1987), p. A–34.

disposing of its wastes. On the other hand, if the power industry owns the rights and the annual value of the river to the paper industry as a waste disposal exceeds the annual cost to the power industry of cleaning the water, the power industry will sell the paper industry pollution privileges.

SUMMARY

The environment provides environmental services that are used by both household units and producing units of the economy. In the processes of consumption and production, wastes are generated. If the ecological system cannot recycle these wastes as fast as they are generated, wastes accumulate. This constitutes pollution.

Economic analysis of pollution provides a perspective on its causes and its effects, along with the costs and benefits of controlling it. Incentives to pollute stem from (1) an absence of property rights in the environment and (2) the collectively consumed nature of whatever is being polluted. Polluters, by polluting, transfer a part of their costs to others. Cost-benefit analysis is useful in determining how much pollution should be allowed. It indicates that it is seldom in the common interest to forbid pollution altogether.

There are three main avenues that government pollution control policies can take. First, certain polluting activities may be controlled directly through prohibitions or limitations on polluting activities. Second, they may be controlled indirectly by providing polluters with incentives not to pollute—say through taxation of polluting activities. Third, in some cases pollution can be controlled by selling or assigning individuals property rights to whatever is being polluted, then allowing them to sell pollution rights to would-be polluters.

SUPPLEMENTARY READING

Baumol, William J., and Wallace E. Oates. *Economics, Environmental Policy, and the Quality of Life.* Englewood Cliffs, N.J.: Prentice-Hall, 1979.

> An excellent and very readable exposition of the environmental dilemma. Includes topics such as the absence of property rights in causing problems, the incidence of the costs and benefits of pollution control, the appropriate level of pollution, along with the pros and cons of various environmental policies.

McKenzie, Richard B. *Economic Issues in Public Policies.* New York: McGraw-Hill, 1980, pp. 158–69.

> Describes in some detail the market answer to reducing pollution.

Millert, Robert B. "Do We Owe Anything to Future Generations?" *Futurist*, 16 (December 1982), pp. 52–59.

A philosopher looks at, among other things, conservation and environmental issues. Can you find any economic fallacies among the excellent points he makes?

North, Douglass C., and Roger LeRoy Miller. *The Economics of Public Issues.* 6th ed. New York: Harper & Row, 1983, Chapters 21, 22, 23, 24, 25, and 27.

Short chapters on several different pollution problems—air pollution, oil spills, pollution rights, and the like. Cost-benefit analysis is introduced. Considerable use is made of the concept of spillovers and the alternative cost principle.

Pasztor, Andy. "Market Booms for 'Rights' to Pollute." *The Wall Street Journal.* June 18, 1981, p. 25.

Describes ways in which many companies are beginning to acquire and trade pollution rights.

Taylor, Ronald A. "Do Environmentalists Care about Poor People?" *U.S. News and World Report*, April 2, 1984, pp. 51–52.

A set of examples in which conservation interests conflict with the use of resources to advance the interests of the poor. How active are the poor in the conservation movement?

THE ECONOMICS OF BIGNESS

The public view of big businesses
The economics of monopoly power
  What is monopoly power?
  Outputs and prices
  Entry restrictions
  Nonprice competition
Should we fear bigness?
  Bigness and monopoly power
  Outputs and prices
  Entry restrictions and resource
    allocation
  Nonprice competition
  Income distribution
Summary

**Checklist of
Economic Concepts**

Market, monopolistic
Market, imperfectly competitive
Market, competitive
Concentration ratio
Demand
Demand curve facing a firm
Marginal revenue
Marginal cost
Profit-maximizing output
Supply
Supply curve of a firm
Dead-weight welfare loss
Entry barriers
Nonprice competition

7

The Economics
of Bigness

Who does what to whom?

Taming the Giant Corporation examines the powers of giant corporations in the United States, and the ways they erode the role of law and ethical precepts. These massive institutions create serious adverse consequences for consumers, workers, shareholders, taxpayers, small businesses, and community residents; they operate without effective internal and external accountabilities to those persons so harmed. The growing damage—often latent, diffuse, or deferred—compounds the need to rethink and reshape the political economy away from these many forms of injustice.

Large corporations, commanding immense political, economic, and technological power, are different in kind and in degree from their smaller counterparts. They advance their control of political units by transcending the jurisdictions of these units, nationally and multinationally, and by financing or otherwise nourishing the political process. These corporations possess decisive market power, sometimes collusively with their giant brethren and sometimes unilaterally. Where smaller firms have to assume the bankruptcy option, these companies, controlling major resources, are considered too big to fail, despite their own mismanagement or corruption. Governments are thereby forced to socialize their losses and guarantee their tenure.

Moreover, the nonmarket impacts of giant corporations have become institutionalized. Pollution of the human environment is rationalized as an economic necessity. Subsidies have become an entrenched corporate welfare system including inefficiencies and political rewards. Such corporate excesses align big government and big business against public interests. As power begets power, large corporations are able to pursue their activities beyond the law, or against the law—a state of affairs clearly incompatible with democracy.[1]

---

[1]Ralph Nader, Mark Green, and Joel Seligman, *Taming the Giant Corporation*, New York: W. W. Norton, 1976, p. 7–8.

THE PUBLIC VIEW OF BIG BUSINESSES

The general public is highly suspicious of how big business enterprises behave. Public concern with big business goes back at least as far as the era of the "Robber Barons" in the last half of the 1800s. What are the reasons for public animosity toward big businesses? There are several possible answers—all of them related.

First, many people believe that economic activity is dominated by a few gigantic firms. They think that families and individuals have little or nothing to say about their own economic destinies or about the paths that economic events take over time. They feel impotent and frustrated, sensing that it is big business that wields the economic power.

Second, they strongly suspect that big businesses deliberately hold back output, especially whenever there are shortages. They attribute housing shortages to "holding back" by construction firms and realtors, and many believe the gasoline crunch of the summer of 1979 was contrived by the major oil companies.

Third, they commonly think that big businesses can charge whatever prices they please for their products. Steel companies, automobile companies, oil companies, and even the makers of breakfast cereals are believed to have the power to set prices in blatant disregard of consumer interests. In fact, many believe that inflation is caused by the exercise of such power.

Fourth, big businesses are thought to earn exorbitant profits— "obscene profits" is the term sometimes used in the newspapers. These profits presumably are made at the expense of (1) consumers who are charged prices that are too high and (2) employees who are paid wages **and salaries** that are too low. The relationship of presumed excessive profits to the other three beliefs about bigness is obvious.

THE ECONOMICS OF MONOPOLY POWER

In a nutshell the public is concerned about the exercise of monopoly power by big businesses. To think in a systematic way about the problem and to understand what kind of threat, if any, big businesses pose, we look first at what constitutes monopoly power. Then we analyze its impact on outputs and prices. Next, we examine the profit issue. Finally, we turn to the effects that monopoly power can have on the operation of the economy.

What is monopoly power?

As we noted in Chapter 2, *monopoly* in its strictest sense means there is a single seller of a good or service for which there are no good substitutes. Not many big businesses fit the full conditions of this definition, however. Most large enterprises operate in markets in which there are several other firms producing and selling the product. In Chapter 2 we labeled such a market structure one of *imperfect competition.* It is the monopoly power exercised by firms in imperfectly competitive as well as monopolistic markets that people worry about and to which we address ourselves in this chapter.

The monopoly power of a firm refers to the extent of its control over the supply of the product that is produced by the industry of which it is a part. The more firms there are producing and selling a given product, the less control any one of the firms can exercise over industry supply. If there are enough firms in an industry so that one firm's output and its control over industry supply are insignificant, we have a *competitive market.* On the other hand, if there is only one firm producing and selling the product, we have a market of pure monopoly. The monopoly power of a firm in an imperfectly competitive market is greater the larger the firm's output is relative to the output of the industry as a whole. It is less the smaller the firm's output is relative to the output of the entire industry.

In order to determine the degree of monopoly power in imperfectly competitive markets, we often use concentration ratios. The most common is the four-firm concentration ratio that indicates the percent of industry sales controlled by the four largest firms in an industry. Thus, an imperfectly competitive industry with four or fewer than four firms would have a concentration ratio of 100 percent and would be thought to have a very high degree of monopoly power. However, an industry with a large number of small firms might have a concentration ratio of 10 or 20 percent and would be thought to have very little monopoly power. Typically, one might suspect a significant degree of monopoly power when the concentration ratio reaches 70 or 80 percent. Table 7–1 shows four-firm concentration ratios for selected industries. As an example, consider the cereal breakfast foods industry. The concentration ratio of 90 percent indicates that 90 percent of the sales of cereal breakfast foods is controlled by the four largest firms. Consequently, this industry probably resembles the pure monopoly model more closely than the pure competition model.

The rather high degrees of concentration indicated in Table 7–1 might suggest that the economy is composed of highly monopolistic markets. However, we should be careful before drawing such a conclusion. While concentration ratios are valuable and do indicate the potential for monopoly power, they have some limitations. Consider the passenger car industry. The concentration ratio for this industry is 99 percent. In reality, however, the industry is not quite so concentrated since the ratio does not take into account the sales of im-

TABLE 7–1
Selected four-firm concentration ratios

Industry	Concentration ratio
Passenger cars	99
Cereal breakfast foods	90
Cigarettes	85
Household refrigerators	82
Primary aluminum	76
Aircraft eingines	74
Explosives	64
Synthetic rubber	60
Glass containers	54
Blast furnances and steel mills	45
Oil field machines	30
Petroleum and refining	30
Cement	25

Source: United States Department of Commerce, Bureau of the Census, *Census of Manufacturers, 1977, Concentration Ratios in Manufacturing*, MC 77–SR–9 (Washington: U.S. Government Printing Office, 1981).

ported cars. With the sales of imports included, the passenger car industry might have a four-firm concentration ratio of about 70 percent. As an example of an opposite limitation, consider the cement industry. The concentration ratio is 25 percent, indicating that 25 percent of cement sales nationally, is controlled by the four largest cement firms. The problem with this number is that, due to the product's inherent characteristics, cement producers only compete with other cement producers who are located in the same geographic area. That is, for cement, we should be interested in the percent of cement sales in one geographic area controlled by the four largest cement producers in that area. If this were done, the cement industry would appear much more concentrated than Table 7–1 suggests.

How then should the data in Table 7–1 be interpreted? Bearing in mind the limitations of concentration ratios, perhaps a reasonable conclusion might be that there is some evidence of monopoly power in the economy.

Outputs and prices

What impact does monopoly power have on the price a firm charges and on the output level it produces and sells? A useful approach to this question is to contrast the price and output of a firm that exercises monopoly power with those of a firm that does not—that is, with that of a competitive firm.

Demand. We look first at demand for the product being sold. Figure 7–1 illustrates a typical market demand curve. It can be established immediately that with any market structure—competitive, monopolized, or imperfectly competitive—sellers must take into account what buyers will do. For quantity x_1 per unit of time, buyers will pay a price not higher than p_1. If sellers try to raise the price above p_1, say to p_2, they cannot sell quantity x_1. At the higher price they can sell quantity x_2 only. Consequently, we conclude that the price that sellers are able to charge is always limited by what buyers are willing to pay. Sellers cannot escape this *law of demand*.

The more sellers there are in the market for a product, the less control any one seller has over the price that it can charge. Suppose, for example, that in Figure 7–1 four sellers of approximately equal size are selling quantity x_1. By how much can any one of the four

FIGURE 7–1
A market demand curve

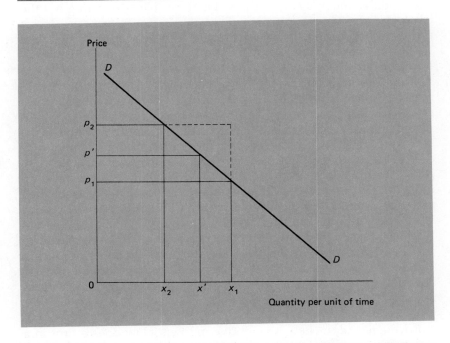

A market demand curve is downward sloping to the right like *DD*. Consumers will not pay more than p_1 per unit for an output of x_1 per unit of time. In order to sell at a price of p_2 the total sales level must be reduced to x_2 per unit of time. If four firms of equal size were producing output level x_1 one of the four could cause the product price to rise to p' only by cutting its output and sales to zero.

raise product price? If one firm reduces its output and sales to zero, the other three firms would be selling a total of approximately x' per unit of time, and the price would be p'. Price p', then, is the highest level to which any one of the four firms acting independently can force the price, and it can do this only if it ceases to produce. To stay in business it must of necessity charge less than price p'.

Using the same reasoning, if there were 100 sellers in the market, the power of one seller to raise the price would be much less. If there were 1,000 sellers, one seller would not be able to affect the market price of the product at all. If it were to drop out of the market, the total amount sold would decrease by only 1/1000 of x_1, which is not enough to cause the price to rise perceptibly. This latter case is typical of a competitive selling market.

Profit maximization. Economic entities such as consumers, resource owners, and business firms like to do the best they can with what they have. Consumers like to get as much satisfaction as possible from spending their annual incomes. As resource owners we like to get as much income as possible from selling or hiring out the labor and the capital we own. Similarly, business firms try to set prices and output levels so as to make as much profit as possible. The profit maximization principle is simply the business manifestation of a principle that affects most of us—we prefer more to less.

Profit maximization is not a goal peculiar to firms that have monopoly power. It tends to be a major objective of firms in all types of market structures. It is simply the logical conclusion that economic entities reach because they too prefer more to less and make their choices accordingly. Although profit maximization is undoubtedly a major goal of business firms, it is not necessarily the only goal. Firms may also want to build up goodwill in a community, do right by their employees, or be known for a quality product. They may also want to get rid of their rivals, collude to raise prices, or block entry into the industry.

In any case, prices and outputs tend to be set so as to maximize profits (or minimize losses) regardless of whether firms producing and selling the product are competitive or have monopoly power. But monopoly power, as we shall see, has important implications for what those prices and outputs will be.

Price and output in a competitive market. How does a firm in a competitive market determine what price to charge and what output to produce? Consider the market diagram in Figure 7–2. This is an ordinary market demand and supply diagram. The market price is p_x and the market output is X. But one individual firm selling this

FIGURE 7-2
Price and output determination in a competitive market

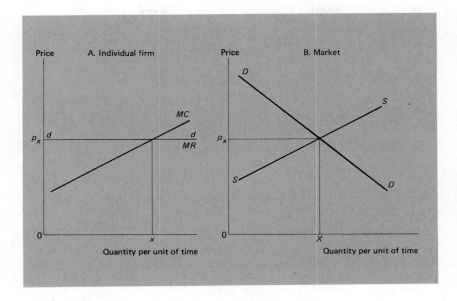

Product price p_x is determined in the market by the interaction of all buyers and all sellers. The individual firm faces the horizontal demand curve dd, which is also the firm's MR curve. The firm maximizes profits by producing output level x. Altogether the many firms in the market produce output X in the market diagram. The market quantity scale is highly compressed relative to the firm quantity scale. The price scale is the same in both diagrams.

product has *no price-setting capabilities whatsoever* since it supplies an insignificant part of the total market supply. The individual competitive firm can determine only the quantity per unit of time to sell at the market price p_x.

The competitive firm thus faces the *horizontal demand curve dd* for its possible outputs. Its level is determined by the market price of the product. Suppose the market price is $14. In Table 7-2 column (4) represents the demand schedule facing the firm, and column (5) shows the firm's total revenue *(TR)* at output levels up to 10 units per day. Although the numbers in column (6) are the same as those in column (4), the concept of marginal revenue for the firm differs from the concept of price. *Marginal revenue (MR)* is defined as the change in total revenue resulting from a one-unit change in the output level. The significance of this concept will become apparent shortly.

TABLE 7–2

Outputs, revenues, costs, and profits for a competitive firm

(1) Output (X per day)	(2) Total cost (TC)	(3) Marginal cost (MC)	(4) Price (P_x)	(5) Total revenue (TR)	(6) Marginal revenue (MR)	(7) Profits (π)
1	$ 8	$ 8	$14	$ 14	$14	$ 6
2	17	9	14	14	14	11
3	27	10	14	42	14	15
4	38	11	14	56	14	18
5	50	12	14	70	14	20
6	63	13	14	84	14	21
7	77	14	14	98	14	21
8	92	15	14	112	14	20
9	108	16	14	126	14	18
10	125	17	14	140	14	15

On the cost side, let column (2) in Table 7–2 represent the firm's total costs (TC) at different daily output levels. *Marginal cost (MC)*, a concept used in Chapter 6, is the change in the firm's total cost resulting from a one-unit change in the output level.

Determination of the output level that maximizes the firm's profits is easy once we know its TC and its TR at each possible output. *Profits* (π) are the difference between TR and TC at any given output level and are listed in column (7). Profits are maximum at either six or seven units of output per day.

An alternative means of identifying the firm's profit-maximizing output is to find the output at which MC equals MR. Consider any output below the six-unit level, say three units. A one-unit increase in output would increase TR by $14, or by the amount of MR. It would increase TC by $11, or by the amount of MC. Therefore, it would increase profits by $3, the difference between the MR and the MC of the fourth unit of output. Check the accuracy of this computation in the profit column. We have discovered an important principle: when MR is greater than MC, an increase in the output level will increase profits. Further increases in output through five and six units also increase profits since MR is greater than MC for each of the increases. An increase in output from six to seven units per day adds nothing to profits since MC = MC = $14. However, it does not cause profits to decrease. If output is increased from seven to eight or more units per day, MR is less than MC, and profits decrease—another important principle. But the most important principle of all is that profits are maximized by producing the output level at which MR equals MC. In Table 7–2 profits are maximum at an output level of seven units per day. To be sure, profits are also maximum at six units of product per day, but it will be easier to remember—and always correct—to settle on the output level at which MR equals MC.

The individual firm diagram of Figure 7–2 shows output x as the firm's profit-maximizing output. Note from Table 7–2 that if a firm's MR is plotted for each output, it will be a horizontal line coinciding with the firm's demand curve dd. The firm's MC curve can be thought of as column (3) of Table 7–2 plotted against output. The output level at which profits are maximum is the one at which MR equals MC.

The MC curve of the firm is the *firm's supply curve* for X, showing how much the firm will place on the market at alternative possible prices, other things being equal. In Figure 7–3 ignore for the present the market diagram and consider the individual firm diagram only. At a price of $14, seven units per day will be produced and sold by

FIGURE 7–3
Marginal costs and supply in a competitive industry

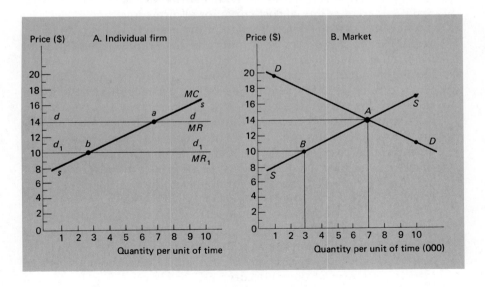

Since an individual firm produces the output at which $MC = MR = p_x$ in order to maximize profits, the firm's MC curve shows how much it will place on the market at alternative price levels like $10 and $14. The market supply curve shows the combined quantities that all firms in the market will supply at each alternative price. It is the horizontal summation of the MC curves of all the individual firms and is thus a market MC curve for the market as a whole.

the firm. What would the firm do if the price were $10 instead of $14. The firm's demand curve and MR curve become d_1d_1 and MR_1, respectively. The profit-maximizing output level falls to three units per day. Since the firm seeks to maximize its profits, whatever the market price happens to be, the firm will try to produce the output at which MC equals MR. For a competitive firm, MR and p_x are always equal, so in producing the output level at which MC equals MR, the firm is also producing the output level at which MC equals p_x. Thus, the outputs that will be produced at alternative price levels are shown by the MC curve, making it the firm's supply curve for the product.

By adding the quantities that all firms in the market will place on the market at each possible price, we get the *market supply curve*. For example, in Figure 7–3 if one of 1,000 identical firms in the market will place seven units of product per day on the market at a price of $14, all firms together will place 7,000 units per day on the market. In Figure 7–3 at the $14 price, the firm would be at point a on its supply curve. The market as a whole would be at point A. Similarly, at a $10 price level the firm would be at point b, and the market as a whole would be at point B. The market SS curve is said to be the *horizontal summation* of the individual firm MC or ss curves. It is really a market marginal cost curve for all firms together.

The simultaneous determination of the market price of a product, the individual firm level of output, and the market level of output for a competitive market now fall neatly into place. In Figure 7–3 let the market demand curve be DD and the market supply curve be SS. The price of $14 is determined by the interaction of buyers and sellers in the market as a whole. It is this price that any one firm in the market takes as given and cannot change. To maximize profits, the firm chooses the output level at which MC equals MR—seven units in this case. The market output level of 7,000 units is, of course, the sum of the output levels of all firms producing the product when they are confronted with a $14 product price.

Pricing and output in a monopolized market. To show the effects of monopoly power on the price and the quantity produced of a product, we will suppose that the purely competitive market just discussed becomes monopolized. Consider first the competitive market. The market demand curve DD of Figure 7–3 is listed as a demand schedule in columns (1) and (4) of Table 7–3. Similarly the horizontal summation of the MC curves of the 1,000 individual competitive firms, which comprises the supply curve SS in Figure 7–3, is listed in columns (1) and (3) of Table 7–3. This information is presented again as DD and SS in Figure 7–4. As we noted in the

TABLE 7–3
Outputs, revenues, costs, and profits for a monopolized firm

(1) Output (000) (X per day)	(2) Total cost ($000) (TC)	(3) Marginal cost (MC)	(4) Price (P_x)	(5) Total revenue ($000) (TR)	(6) Marginal revenue (MR)	(7) Profits ($000) ($\pi$)
1	$ 8	$ 8	$20	$ 20	$20	$12
2	17	9	19	38	18	21
3	27	10	18	54	16	27
4	38	11	17	68	14	30
5	50	12	16	80	12	30
6	63	13	15	90	10	27
7	77	14	14	98	8	21
8	92	15	13	104	6	12
9	109	16	12	108	4	10
10	125	17	11	110	2	15

preceding section, the market price of producing X is $14, and the quantity produced and sold is 7,000 units per day.

Now let the 1,000 competitive firms be merged into one gigantic monopoly. Suppose that all the production facilities of the 1,000 firms are taken over in their entireties and that they can be operated by the monopolistic firm with no loss in efficiency. What happens to the output of the industry and the price of the product?

Keep in mind the quantities the competitive firms were producing as they maximized their profits. Each firm found itself looking at a $14 product price that it could not change. Each firm saw a horizontal demand curve for its own output at the $14 level. Each firm viewed marginal revenue as constant at the $14 level—equal to the product price. Each firm produced an output level at which its MC was equal to MR *and product price*. Each firm's output level was seven units per day, and the total industry output was 7,000 units per day.

All of that is changed by monopolization of the industry. The monopolist faces the market demand curve DD, which is downward sloping to the right instead of horizontal. This fact has important implications for marginal revenue. Any firm that faces a demand curve that is sloping downward to the right will find that its *marginal revenue is less than product price* at any given output level. We demonstrate this principle in Table 7–3. If the monopolist were selling 2,000 units of product per day and were to increase sales from 2,000 to 3,000 per day, total revenue of the firm would increase from

FIGURE 7–4

Comparison of pricing and output in competitive and monopolized markets

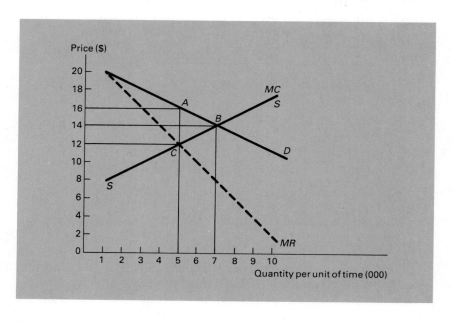

If the market is competitive, the market price will be $14 and the output will be 7,000 units. Each of the 1,000 firms in the market faces a horizontal demand curve and marginal revenue curve at the $14 level and maximizes profits by producing the output at which its *MR* equals *MC*. Monopolization of the market causes the firm to see *DD* as the demand curve it faces. Since *DD* slopes downward to the right, *MR* lies below *DD*. The profit-maximizing output for the monopolistic firm becomes 5,000 units, which will be sold at a price of $16 per unit.

$38,000 ($19 × 2,000) to $54,000 ($18 × 3,000). Since the 1,000-unit addition to output increases total receipts by $16,000, each one-unit increase in output has increased *TR* by $16. So marginal revenue for the firm in moving from the 2,000-unit to the 3,000-unit level of output is $16 and is less than the price of $18 at which each of the 3,000 units is sold. Marginal revenue in column (6) is computed in the same way for each output level listed in column (1). Compare price and marginal revenue at each level of output. Marginal revenue is plotted as the *MR* curve in Figure 7–4.

If you were the monopolist, what output would you produce and at what price would you sell if your objective were to maximize profits? You would reduce output and sales from 7,000 units per day to 5,000 units per day. You would raise the price from $14 to $16. You would do this because it would increase your profits from $21,000 per day to $30,000 per day as column (7) indicates. At the 5,000-unit output level, *MC* equals *MR* for the monopolist.

To recapitulate the analysis, in a monopolized market the price of the product tends to be higher and output tends to be less than it would be if the industry could be and were competitive. This is not because the managements of monopolized firms are inherently evil while those of competitive firms are not. The managements of firms in both types of markets seek the same general goal—profits. The monopolistic firm restricts output and charges a higher price because its managers see a different relationship between marginal revenue and price than do the managers of competitive firms.

Referring back to Figures 7–3 and 7–4, the managers of competitive firms face demand curves horizontal at the market price of the product. Consequently, they see marginal revenue curves that are also horizontal and that coincide with the demand curves. To maximize its profits, the competitive firm chooses the output level at which $MC = MR = P_x$. In the diagrams this occurs at the seven-unit output level for each firm. Since all firms in the market maximize profits in the same way, the market output is 7,000 units.

If the market is monopolized and the monopolist continues with the 7,000-unit output level, the monopolist's *MC* would be equal to the product price of $14. But *MR* for the monopolist at that output level is only $8 because the monopolist faces a downward sloping demand curve. To maximize profits the monopolist cuts the output back to 5,000 units per day and raises the product price to $16. The monopolist's $MC = MR = \$12$ at that output level.

By reducing output and increasing the product price, the monopolist imposes a significant economic cost on society in the form of reduced welfare. To see this, we must have a thorough understanding of Figure 7–4. Consider the demand curve. This curve indicates the maximum prices consumers would be willing to pay for particular quantities of the good. The fact that consumers are willing to pay a price equal to the marginal benefit they expect to receive from consuming additional units of the good indicates that the demand curve may be thought of as the marginal social benefit curve. That is, the demand curve shows the additional satisfaction, or benefit, that society expects from successive units of the good. The marginal cost curve indicates the alternative cost or opportunity cost of the resources used to produce the good. Since we are considering only one firm, a monopolist, the firm's marginal cost is also the marginal social cost of producing the good.

We now have curves in Figure 7–4 depicting the marginal social benefit and marginal social cost of producing the good. What quantity of the good should be produced? The method for answering this question was presented in the previous chapter. In that analysis, it was argued that pollution control (the good) should be produced up to the point where net benefits to society are maximized. Net benefits are increased by increasing output whenever marginal social benefits exceed marginal social cost; thus, production of a good should be carried out to the point where marginal social benefits are just equal to marginal social cost. In Figure 7–4, this logic suggests that the socially optimal level of production is 7,000 units (where marginal social benefits, DD, are just equal to marginal social cost, MC). As has been pointed out, this is the quantity that a competitive industry would produce. However, if the industry is monopolized, production is reduced to 5,000 units. In Figure 7–4, we see that when production is reduced from 7,000 to 5,000, net social benefits are reduced since, for the lost units, marginal social benefits (DD) are greater than marginal social cost (MC). Adding together the lost net benefits for each of the units between 7,000 and 5,000 yields the lost welfare for society due to the monopoly. Graphically, this is equal to the area of the triangle ABC in Figure 7–4 and is known as the dead-weight welfare loss due to monopoly.

Entry restrictions

Prices, costs, profits, and losses in a private enterprise economy provide the incentives for a continuous reallocation of resources from uses where they contribute less to uses where they contribute more to consumer satisfaction. In industries where demand is falling or costs are rising, investors will eventually receive less than average returns on their investments. Firms in these industries are said to be incurring economic *losses*. As it becomes possible for them to do so, investors and the firms producing those products will leave the industry, reducing supplies and raising prices relative to costs, until the returns to remaining investors are average for the economy as a whole.

In areas where demand is increasing or costs are falling, investors receive higher than average returns, or economic *profits*. New investment and new firms have incentives to enter the industry. If they are successful in doing so, product supplies increase, and prices fall relative to costs until the return on investment is again average. The profit and loss mechanism is thus the prime force for contracting productive capacity and output where these are not so urgently desired and for expanding them where they are more urgently desired.

Monopoly power tends to throw sand in the gears of the reallocation mechanism. Over time, firms with monopoly power in profitable industries, those that yield higher than average rates of return to investors, may be able to impede or block the entry of new investment and new firms into those industries. To the extent that they are able to do so, outputs will be lower, prices will be higher, and profits will be greater than they would be if entry were open, free, and easy. Such barriers to entry can be classified conveniently into (1) private barriers and (2) government barriers.

Private barriers. Private entry barriers arise from the nature of markets themselves or from marketplace actions of the firms that enjoy their fruits. There are many privately imposed restrictions on entry into specific industries. We shall list some of the more important ones—not necessarily in the order of their importance. First, consider a situation in which a firm or the firms already in a market own or control most of some key raw material needed for making the product. All they must do to restrict entry is deny potential entrants access to it. Second, suppose that when new firms are in the process of entering, the existing firms threaten to lower prices to the extent that the newcomers would experience substantial losses. This threat tends to discourage entry. It is also difficult on those already in the market, but they may be able to withstand temporary losses better than the potential entrants can. Third, product differentiation may be successful in retarding entry in some instances. *Product differentiation* refers to the well-known practice on the part of each firm in an industry of making its own brand of the product slightly different from that of the other firms. Then it tries to convince consumers that its brand of the product is superior to any other brand. Consumers tend to prefer the old tried and true brands and to be skeptical of purchasing the brands of new entrants. This is undoubtedly one of the many factors discouraging entry into the automobile industry. Fourth, a market may not be large enough to support more than one or a few firms of a size large enough to be efficient. Though one or a few firms may be able to make higher-than-average returns for investors, the entry of a newcomer may increase supply and reduce prices so much that none makes an average return. The list of private entry barriers could go on and on, but the ones we have included should be sufficient for illustrative purposes.

Government barriers. The firms already in specific industries have difficulty in policing and enforcing restrictions on entry. Consequently, they frequently turn to the government for help. They get city councils, state legislatures, and Congress to pass legislation restricting entry into their markets. Those government units seem not at all reluctant to take actions that confer monopoly power on certain special interest groups and help them to maintain it over time.

First, in some industries such as railroads, trucking, airlines, and communications, regulatory commissions have established entry-blocking rules that have all the force of law. Initially, regulatory commissions such as the Interstate Commerce Commission, the Civil Aeronautics Board, and the Federal Communications Commission were established to "protect" customers from certain practices of monopolistic firms. Over time, however, the range of commissions' activities has expanded to include control of entry into the industries they are regulating. In recent years one could well suspect that their primary function is to "protect" the firms from consumers.

Second, there are many occupational licensing laws on the books of individual states licensing plumbers, undertakers, physicians, barbers, and a host of other occupations. Whatever else such laws may do, one thing is certain—they restrict entry into the licensed occupations. Licensing standards and licensing examinations usually are controlled by licensed members of the occupation concerned; that is, by those who are already in it and who have a vested interest in keeping the number of new entrants relatively low.

A number of other forms of government-imposed entry barriers exist. Import duties and import restrictions limit the entry of foreign firms into many of our markets. Patent and copyright laws impede entry. Exclusive franchises to taxicab companies and casinos block the entry of new firms. Zoning ordinances and building codes are used to restrict entry into certain housing markets. Like that of private barriers, the list of government-imposed barriers to entry is a lengthy one.

Nonprice competition

In industries containing only a few firms, it is common practice for firms to compete on grounds other than price. Each such firm in a given industry can increase its profits if it can increase its monopoly power at the expense of its rivals—that is, if it can increase its own share of the total market for the product. One very obvious way for a firm to increase its market share is to reduce the price at which it sells its brand of the product relative to the prices charged by the other firms in the industry. But price-cutting presents dangers to the firm that does it. The other firms can cut their prices, too, thus preventing the first firm from accomplishing what it set out to do.

Worse yet, all firms could end up with lower prices, a larger industry output, and smaller profits. So firms in imperfectly competitive markets are reluctant to use price-cutting to increase their individual market shares. Usually they attempt to increase their degrees of monopoly power through nonprice competition.

Advertising is a major form of nonprice competition. Although it may provide consumers with important information about a firm's product, its major objective is to increase the market share or the monopoly power of the firm that does it. Unlike a price cut by the firm, a successful advertising campaign is hard for other firms to duplicate. Other firms will try to duplicate or match the advertising campaign of the first firm, but it takes time for them to do so. Meanwhile, the first firm reaps the rewards of its efforts. Eventually, if other firms succeed with effective campaigns of their own, all may end up with approximately the same market shares they had before. Much of the advertising effort will have been wasted, and since the resources used for advertising purposes are not available to produce other goods and services, consumers receive a smaller total output from the economy as a whole.

Periodic change in the design and quality of the product is another major form of nonprice competition. Annual model changes fall in this category. Model changes may incorporate new technological developments, and to the extent that they do so, they enable given quantities of resources to make greater contributions to consumer satisfaction. But they may also simply rearrange or change the chrome and the shape, making old models obsolete and new models no better. Successful design and quality innovations by one firm, like successful advertising, may be hard for other firms to imitate immediately and may increase the market share and monopoly power of the firm for a time. However, if other firms are successful over time with their own design and quality changes, all may again end up with approximately the same market shares or with some rearrangement of market shares.

SHOULD WE FEAR BIGNESS?

Does bigness of business enterprises put our economic future in jeopardy? The economic analysis that we have just completed leads to the conclusion that in industries in which monopoly power is exercised, outputs will be lower and prices will be higher than they would be if the industries were more competitive. Monopoly power also may impede the entry of additional investment and firms into industries in which profits are made. Thus, monopoly power may cause the resources or productive capabilities of the economy to be allocated poorly among alternative uses, with too little of the economy's resources allocated to the production of products made by industries in which monopoly power exists and too much allocated to products that are produced competitively. In addition, monopoly power in imperfectly competitive markets may result in some waste of resources on nonprice competition.

Bigness and monopoly power

Surprisingly enough, a business enterprise that is big in terms of the value of its assets or the value of its sales does not necessarily have a high degree of monopoly power. On the other hand, a relatively small firm may have a great deal of monopoly power. It all depends on the position of the firm in the market in which it operates. Chrysler Corporation is a very large firm in terms of its assets and annual sales volume; yet it may have very little monopoly power. If it drops out of the market, other firms will easily take up the slack. If it raises its prices relative to those of other firms in the auto industry, it will very quickly price itself out of the market. It has much actual and potential competition. Stillwater Power and Light Company in Stillwater, Oklahoma, is a small firm in terms of assets and annual volume of sales, but it comes very close to being a pure monopolist. It has no direct rivals, with the possible exception of the local gas company. We must therefore be careful not to confuse bigness with monopoly power. In assessing monopoly power of firms, we must look at specific industries and at individual firms within each industry to see whether or not they are able to affect significantly market outputs, prices, and buyers' access to the kind of product produced and sold by the industry.

Outputs and prices

When imperfectly competitive firms restrict output and increase prices, they impose an economic cost on society in the form of reduced social welfare. This reduction in welfare is the dead-weight welfare loss due to monopoly. We can better understand the issue of "fearing bigness" if we have a definitive estimate of this loss. While no definitive estimate exists, a consensus estimate places the loss at about 1 percent of gross national product per year.[2] That is, monopolistic elements within the economy serve to reduce eco-

---

[2] F. M. Scherer, *Industrial Market Structure and Economic Performance* (Chicago: Rand McNally, 1980), p. 464.

nomic welfare, as measured by GNP, by about 1 percent of GNP per year.

Is this a significant loss in welfare? This decision is for each of us to make. However, we must bear in mind two points while making the making decision. First, a basic economic truth is that while the economy's ability to produce is limited, society's desires for goods and services are unlimited. Consequently, any economic factor that tends to reduce the economy's ability to produce goods and services must be viewed as making an already difficult situation worse. Second, while 1 percent of GNP may not seem significant, 1 percent of GNP amounted to $40 billion in 1985.[3] In other words, if all vestiges of monopoly power had been eliminated prior to 1985, during that year society could have consumed $40 billion in additional goods and services. For example, if the increased production due to the elimination of monopoly were equally distributed, during 1985 each individual in the United States would have received $167 in additional goods and services.

Entry restrictions and resource allocation

Economy-wide evidences of long-run misallocation of the economy's resources because of *private* entry barriers are rather difficult to find. In recent years we have seen many evidences of easy entry. Personal computers are a case in point. Simple early models commanded relatively high prices and were produced by a very few firms. But the success of the new product and the profits that were generated soon attracted new producers into the field. Supplies increased, prices fell, and the quality and sophistication of the units increased. The same sort of thing happened with digital quartz watches. By and large, private entry barriers to markets break down rather easily.

Where entry to markets is blocked by law, it is easier to find evidences of resource misallocation. One of the more glaring instances of resources being used in quantities that are relatively too small is the medical profession. Physicians' average net incomes are at the top of the list for professions or occupations. Shortages of medical doctors have been publicly proclaimed for years and years. Yet, with their tight legal control of entry into medical training programs and into the profession itself, medical doctors continue to deter almost half of the annual qualified applicants to medical schools from en-

---

[3] U.S. Department of Commerce, Bureau of Economic Analysis, *Business Conditions Digest*, December 1986, p. 80.

tering training. In many local building markets, housing costs have soared, and profits to builders have been high because building codes have inhibited the introduction and use of new technology and prefabrication. In still another industry, try getting a taxicab in any large city during the morning and evening rush hours.

Nonprice competition

The impact of nonprice competition on the public is far from clear. The total expenditure on advertising for 1984 ran about $88 billion[4]—somewhere in the neighborhood of 2 percent of GNP. However, about a fourth of the total was for advertising in local newspapers, a type of advertising that provides information to consumers on what is available, where, and at what price. Another $15 billion was spent for television advertising and is not a total loss to consumers. It is payment—overpayment—for the "free" television programs that we see.

We also cannot be sure whether or how much the public loses from product design and quality changes. Many useful innovations are introduced in this way—the self-starter on the automobile (Yes, Virginia, they used to be cranked by hand), no-frost freezers and refrigerators, electric typewriters, and thousands of other items that make our lives more comfortable. But there are many others whose only purpose is to make the previous years' models obsolete.

Income distribution

How do bigness and monopoly power in the sale of products affect the distribution of income among economic units in the economy? It appears initially that, since entry into imperfectly competitive industries is restricted and since greater than average returns on investment may be obtained over time by firms in those industries, income is redistributed away from consumers toward those firms. Or, as it is commonly put today, those firms make monopoly profits. But on further investigation this possibility becomes shrouded in doubt. Big business firms are corporations, each having thousands of stockholders who are actually the owners of the business. The business enterprise itself provides a legal framework that enables these thousands of stockholders or investors to get together for purposes of production. Profits mean nothing to the enterprise itself.

---

[4]U.S. Department of Commerce, Bureau of the Census, *Statistical Abstract of the United States,* 1986, p. 551.

To the extent that the enterprise yields above average rates of return, those returns accrue primarily to its stockholders; they are really diffused among the thousands of households that own corporation stocks. Some of these—we do not know what proportion—are retired people, widows, old persons in rest homes, and the like; although, to be sure, the largest part of corporation returns to investors go to those in upper and middle income groups.

In addition, when a corporation yields higher than average returns on investment to its stockholders, its stock becomes attractive for people to buy. Increased demand for its stock drives stock prices up, and the rate of return consequently becomes smaller and smaller to subsequent buyers of the stock. Only those stockholders who owned the stock at the time when the higher than average returns were made stand to gain.

We cannot really be sure that bigness of business enterprises results in a distribution of income that is more unequal than would be the case if all business firms were small.

SUMMARY

Most members of the general public tend to believe that big businesses exploit them. Many people think the economy is controlled by a few business firms and that these firms restrict product outputs and charge higher prices than they should. They also think that big firms make unjustifiable monopoly profits.

To the extent that an individual firm produces a significant part of an industry's output it can exercise some degree of monopoly power. Monopoly power induces firms to produce smaller outputs and charge higher prices than would be the case if the markets in which they operate were competitive. Firms with monopoly power are frequently able to restrict entry into their industries, thus compounding the output restriction and higher price problem and inhibiting movement of resources from less valuable to more valuable uses. They also engage in nonprice competition that may result in the waste of some of the economy's scarce resources.

There is some evidence that monopolistic elements within the United States' economy have imposed, and continue to impose, an economic cost on society in terms of reduced social welfare. While this is true, it is important to realize that bigness does not necessarily imply monopoly power. To identify monopoly power requires considering the size of the firm relative to the market in which it operates. Thus, when we speak of the welfare lost due to monopoly, we should not immediately think just in terms of large firms. Much of the loss in welfare may come from rather small firms. Estimates of the dead-weight welfare loss due to monopoly place it at about 1 percent of GNP per year. In terms of 1985 GNP, this implies that monopolistic elements within the economy were responsible for a $40 billion reduction in GNP during that year. Consequently, it is important to keep a close watch on existing and potential monopoly problems. The more competition the economy can sustain, the better the price mechanism will operate in allocating the economy's scarce resources among their many uses.

SUPPLEMENTARY READING

Alpert, Geraldine. "Is Market Structure Proof of Market Power?" *Mergers and Acquisitions* 19 (Summer 1984), pp. 47–51.

An excellent discussion of the loose linkage between market structure and market power. Several case studies are cited.

Carson, Robert A. "Monopoly Power: What Should Be Our Policy toward Big Business?" In *Economic Issues Today: Alternative Approaches.* 3rd ed. New York: St. Martin's Press, 1983, chapter 4.

Presents the liberal, the conservative, and the radical answer to the question posed in the chapter title.

Friedman, Milton. "Monopoly and the Social Responsibility of Business and Labor." In *Capitalism and Freedom.* Chicago: The University of Chicago Press, 1962, p. 119–136.

A penetrating analysis of market structures with emphasis on the sources of monopoly power in the United States.

Hathaway, J. W. "Has Social Responsibility Cleaned Up the Corporate Image?" *Business and Society Review* 51 (Fall 1984), pp. 56–59.

Addresses the question of why, in the face of increasing corporate social responsibility, the public fails to get the message.

CONSUMERISM

The consumer's problem
  Shady business practices
  Why the practices occur
  Consequences of the practices
The nature of consumerism
  Description
  Private consumer advocates
  The role of the government
The economics of consumerism
  The economic benefits
  The economic costs
Evaluation
  The provision of information
  The prevention of spillover costs
  Protection from business
    manipulation
Summary

**Checklist of
Economic Concepts**

Living standards
Monopoly
Alternative costs
Consumerism
Cost-benefit analysis
Spillover costs
Profits

8

Consumerism

The regulators versus the regulatees

Fran Robinson's package was heavy, weighing almost 30 pounds. She staggered out to the car and dumped it on the right front seat. Then she slid under the wheel, buckled her seat belt, put the shift lever in the "P" position, and turned on the ignition. There was no response. What was wrong—the seat belt was buckled, wasn't it? Then she remembered that if the seatbelt is buckled when a heavy object is placed on the right front seat, it must be unbuckled and then rebuckled. With this task accomplished she tried again. No go.

Out came the *Owner's Manual* and the instructions were clear: "Turn the ignition to ON, raise the hood and turn the bypass switch on the fire wall to START." This done she closed the hood, got back in the car and buckled her seat belt. Fate was on her side, and the engine sprang to life. But then it sputtered and died. Fran turned the ignition momentarily to OFF, then tried to restart the engine. But there was only silence, broken by an occasional (deleted).

Once more the hood was raised and the bypass switch was set to START. Rather testily, Fran went through the buckle up and starting procedure and was appropriately rewarded. This time she kept the engine racing until she was moving with the traffic. But she would have given almost anything to get her hands on the diabolic maniac who dreamed up the system!

Pressure from voters has induced the government to back away from the extreme regulatory practice in which Fran found herself entangled. But the issue remains. To what extent, if any, should government shield consumers from hazards, nuisances, fraud, and the like that attend the purchase and/or consumption of thousands of products?

THE CONSUMER'S PROBLEM

Over the years some segments of the general public and some legislative groups have shown much concern for the consumer. The individual consumer is a lone voice crying in the wilderness, so the argument runs, since no single consumer is important to a giant business concern. People think that the consumer who does not like what the business firm does has no recourse. On the other hand, they think the business firm is very important to the consumer. Thus, the business firm presumably has the power to take advantage of the consumer.

Shady business practices

Consumer advocates—those who consider themselves to be speakers for consumers—usually point to four kinds of business practices that they consider adverse to the best interests of consumers. They are (1) unsafe, impure, and low-quality products, (2) deceptive advertising of goods and services, (3) techniques that obscure or hide real prices, and (4) poor or inadequate servicing of products.

Unsafe, impure, and low-quality products are nothing new to most of us. Automobiles kill hundreds of people each year. So do guns and knives. Lawn mowers slice off toes. Can openers are dangerous to fingers. Boats capsize. The use of the drug thalidomide in Europe and Great Britain several years ago resulted in the birth of a number of deformed children. Mercury found in some canned fish brought on a massive Food and Drug Administration testing and sampling program in 1971. The quality of some brands of wieners has deteriorated due to an increase in their fat content. And the list can be extended on and on.

Anyone who reads newspapers and magazines or who watches television knows that deceptive advertising occurs despite the efforts of the Federal Trade Commission to prevent it. One brand of aspirin is said to be more effective than another, although both are standard five-grain tablets. Diet supplements are advertised to ward off everything from cancer to the common cold. What do the terms *water-resistant, preshrunk, sanforized, moth-resistant,* and *shock-resistant* really mean? How can one know that the ride of one make of automobile is "smoother"? Will *XXX* dental cream really make one's teeth whiter?

Is there anyone lucky enough *not* to have been exposed to misleading or hidden pricing practices? Have you ever observed a firm that advertises a 10 percent discount from list price on its merchandise but marks the list price of the goods 10 percent higher than it would have been otherwise; or a sewing machine salesperson who sells a machine at a substantially discounted price, *provided* you purchase the five-year service policy that turns out to cost more than the machine itself? Most have seen the retailer of coffee who sells the two-pound "economy" can at more than twice the price of the one-pound can; or the firm that advertises a well-known product at a discounted price that has just sold out when you arrive, but will let you have another lesser-known brand at the same price?

Have you always been happy with the servicing of products you have purchased? Many have wondered quietly—and some not so quietly—what takes place in the auto service department while their automobiles are supposedly undergoing motor tune-ups. How long does it take to obtain the services of a repairperson from the air-conditioning shop that sold you your air-conditioning equipment? If you happen to be an airplane pilot, try finding an avionics shop that you believe does good, reliable repair work on your radios, transponder, and autopilot. Replacing the rollers on the sliding glass door that you had installed 10 years ago can be a real hassle. Are you sure that your television set really needed all those parts the repairperson put in yesterday?

Why the practices occur

Are the many consumer rip-offs that we encounter peculiar to a modern *advanced capitalistic* economic system? Not really. There were hawkers of patent medicines and hundreds of other useless things in frontier days. As far back in history as people have engaged in exchange, there have been some who try to take advantage of others, and the rip-off is not confined to capitalistic systems. But rightly or wrongly, many believe that in the modern economy the consumer's position has become more precarious than it was in the olden days. They cite several reasons why they think this is so.

In the first place, there is a much wider range of goods and services available now than there was 100 years ago, and many of these goods are more complex in design and operation. The automobile as compared with the buggy is a case in point. The mechanical features of the buggy were well understood by most people, and it was not too difficult to detect shoddy workmanship or weak points in its construction. Nevertheless, some buyers found after purchasing a buggy that the wheel spokes were tight only because they had been soaked in water before the sale. The automobile, by way of contrast, is an exceedingly complex machine. Many purchasers know nothing about ignition systems, transmissions, hydraulic systems, and the like. Some of us are inclined to wonder from time to time how much mechanics know! We don't really understand the mechanisms of our refrigerators, freezers, mixers, vacuum cleaners, and hair dryers. There are so many remedies for the common cold on the market that we have trouble choosing among them. Which make and model of single-lens reflex cameras do you think is the best buy—and why?

In the second place, large-scale factories using mass production techniques have supplanted small home and family-run production units. In the latter, craftsmanship was important. The artisans saw the whole production process through from beginning to end and were proud to attach family names to the resulting wagon, bicycle, rifle, or bathtub. In a modern factory any one worker accomplishes only one small part of the total production process and is unlikely to feel any great pride of achievement in the individual contribution made to the final product. The modern worker's contribution is impersonal and anonymous. Contact between the producer and the consumer has been lost; consequently, the producer feels little or no responsibility for the consumer.

In the third place, tremendous advances have been made in mass communications. The radio was developed, magazine and newspaper circulation has increased, and television has come on the scene. All these have increased severalfold the opportunities of sellers to advertise their wares to potential buyers. With the growth of the advertising media there has been a corresponding growth in the possibilities available to sellers for shaping consumers' desires and also for misleading consumers.

In the fourth place, many believe that growing monopoly power in the production and sale of products puts consumers in a continuously deteriorating position in the marketplace. If General Motors places an unsafe automobile on the market, the public presumably not only does not know it but would be unable to do anything about it if it did. In the 1970s supposed domestic oil monopolies were accused of making things difficult for consumers by causing gas shortages. The increasing number of industrial giants in the economy leads people to believe that they will be subjected to an ever-increasing degree of manipulation in the marketplace.

Consequences of the practices

The supposed consequences of shady or unfair business practices are, of course, losses in consumers' well-being or living standards. The primary objective of economic activity is to satisfy consumer wants as fully as the economy's resources and techniques will allow.

Shady or unfair business practices interfere with the efficiency with which this objective is carried out. These practices may occur in several ways.

Many business practices shortchange consumers on health and safety grounds. In a free market producers may take advantage of consumers by selling items that are harmful to them, that is, that will actually decrease consumer well-being. Examples include drugs and medicines that may have dangerous side effects and toys that are painted with lead paints. Occasionally producers, as well as jeopardizing health and safety by putting items on the market that should not be there, do the same thing by *not* putting some items on the market that should be there. Some believe that automobiles without seat belts and shoulder harnesses are dangerous. So are electric handsaws without blade guards and motorcycles without helmets for the rider.

A great many other products, while not actually harmful to consumers, are believed to be useless. For example, will a Geritol tablet every morning really produce the sweet, loving, understanding, sympathetic helpmate depicted on the television screen? Will STP in your gasoline really improve the engine performance of your automobile? Will aluminum siding over the present siding on your house really improve its insulating qualities? Consumers buy vast quantities of these and similar products every year.

Further, consumers may waste substantial amounts of time and effort because shady products and poor service exist. Even for products under warranty it is usually necessary to box and ship the defective item back to the manufacturer. In any case, one must make one or more trips to the retailer to return defective merchandise and to secure the appropriate adjustment for it. How often after having automobile repairs made have you discovered that they were not done properly, necessitating another trip to the repair shop and loss of the automobile's use for another day?

All the above consequences of shady business practices, to the extent that they occur, waste the resources of the economy. Double damage is done if items on balance are actually harmful to consumers. Their production and sale lower consumer well-being, and in addition, the resources utilized to produce them are not available to produce useful items. For items that are useless, but not actually harmful, the society is harmed only by losing the use of the resources needed to make them. Similarly, time and effort spent in getting faulty products repaired, replaced, or re-repaired are not available to spend in either pleasurable pursuits or in the production of useful goods and services.

THE NATURE OF CONSUMERISM

The problems of consumers vis-à-vis business firms have not gone unnoticed historically. They have given rise over time to the movement called *consumerism*. The movement is not new, going back at least to the birth of the consumer cooperative at Rochdale, England, in 1844. The movement established organizations for consumer education such as the American Home Economics Association in 1908 and the Chicago Housewives League in 1910. Consumerism was also given expression in law by the Pure Food and Drug Act of 1906 and by a number of state "truth in advertising" laws in the early 1900s. These were followed by the Federal Trade Commission Act in 1914. Two books published in the 1920s and 1930s did much to excite the public about consumer problems. These were *Your Money's Worth* by Stuart Chase and Frederick J. Schlink in 1927 and *100,000,000 Guinea Pigs* by Schlink and Arthur Kallet in 1933. Since the Great Depression of the 1930s, a flood of state and federal laws have been enacted that ostensibly protect the consumer. But the unprecedented growth of modern consumerism undoubtedly sprang from the publication of Ralph Nader's *Unsafe at Any Speed* in 1965.

Description

What is this "consumerism" that we hear so much about? The concept is somewhat nebulous with different emphasis being given to it by different people. It almost defies definition, but perhaps we can establish a working description that will suffice for our purposes.

Consumerism seems to be a movement shared by a great many people who believe that somehow the consumer is not getting a fair shake in the economic system. Several types of activities are used to "bolster" the consumer's position with respect to producers and sellers. These include consumer information and educational services performed by organizations such as Consumers' Union, the investigation of practices thought to be adverse to consumer interests and publication of reports by a number of consumer-oriented groups, lobbying by consumer advocates for legislation intended to protect consumers, and the extension of regulatory activities by government agencies for the same purpose. Consumer advocates also initiate activist programs, such as the meat boycott of early 1973. Consumerism is at least all of these—and perhaps more. It is propelled by both private consumer advocates and the government.

Private consumer advocates

There is little doubt that the best-known name among modern consumer advocates is Ralph Nader. Nader is a lawyer who was educated at Princeton and Harvard. According to reports he lives very modestly, devoting most of what he earns from his lectures and books to further investigation of practices that he believes are detrimental to consumers. He is self-employed.

Nader and a group of his followers, known collectively as "Nader's Raiders," engage in extensive and continuing investigations of business and government practices, looking for those they believe are contrary to the public interest. He buttonholes members of Congress, appears before congressional committees, writes scathing reports, confronts corporation executives, and files suits on behalf of consumers against those alleged to have harmed consumers. Businesses—particularly those in the automobile industry—take him seriously. So do senators and representatives. He is believed to be responsible for the enactment of the National Traffic and Motor Vehicle Safety Act of 1966, the Wholesome Meat Act of 1967, the Natural Gas Pipeline Safety Act of 1968, the Radiation Control for Health and Safety Act of 1968, and the Wholesome Poultry Products Act of 1968. Many other consumer advocates are active, but Nader stands head and shoulders above them all.

Much less flamboyant than "Nader's Raiders" are the private consumer information and education organizations. Three of the best known of these are Consumers' Union, Consumers' Research, and Good Housekeeping with its "Seal of Approval." These organizations engage in continual testing and evaluation of different brands of a wide range of products, publishing their results and their recommendations for their subscribers or readers.

The role of the government

Much of consumerism's power and thrust comes from the enlistment of government support to accomplish its purposes. Although private consumer advocacy can be separated conceptually from government consumer advocacy, in practice they tend to become inextricably intertwined. The primary avenue used by consumer advocates such as Nader to correct what they perceive to be wrong is the government.

The amount of legislation enacted in recent years and the number of agencies that supposedly protect consumers are rather startling. Some of the legislation attributed to Nader was listed above. In addition, agencies actively engaged in consumer affairs include the Federal Trade Commission, Food and Drug Administration, Interstate Commerce Commission, Federal Aviation Agency, Department of Agriculture Consumer and Marketing Service, Federal Energy Regulatory Commission, Consumer Product Safety Commission, National Transportation Safety Board, Federal Communications Commission, Occupational Safety and Health Administration, Federal Energy Administration, Environmental Protection Agency, Securities and Exchange Commission, and the Cost of Living Council. This list is by no means complete. Certainly one cannot say truthfully that the government ignores the consumer.

THE ECONOMICS OF CONSUMERISM

Do the activities that fall within the domain described as consumerism on balance benefit consumers? There is no unequivocal answer to this question. Some such activities will surely result in net increases in consumer well-being. Others may bring about net reductions in the level of consumer welfare. To determine which activity should be expanded and which should be curtailed, we must consider some sort of cost-benefit analysis of each of the activities making up the movement.

The economic benefits

Economic analysis indicates three possible avenues through which consumerism may lead to higher levels of consumer welfare. First, it may lead to improvements in the information made available to consumers. Second, it may cut back on the amounts of useless or even deceptive competitive advertising to which consumers are subjected. Third, it may provide increased protection to consumers as they go about their consumption activities.

More accurate and complete information. If consumers are to get the greatest possible amounts of satisfaction from the limited incomes available to them, they must be able to make intelligent choices from the vast array of goods and services available to them. Intelligent choices must be based on, but are not assured by, relatively complete and accurate information. For example, we expect by and large that weights and measures will be correctly represented by sellers, and this information is of inestimable value to us. Similarly, it is helpful to us to know the ingredients comprising a product, what the product can be used for, the way it operates, and how long we can expect it to last under average use conditions.

Information provided by independent testing agencies on comparative qualities and prices of competing product lines often prove useful to consumers. Recommended "best buys," while not infallible guides for all consumers, often provide excellent points of departure for the judicious, careful shopper. Two of the best-known sources of information of this type are *Consumers' Research* and *Consumer Reports*.

Less deceptive and useless sales promotion. Reductions in deceptive sales promotion activities in and of themselves must increase consumer welfare if we ignore the costs of bringing those reductions about. Misstatements concerning the nature of products and false claims of what those products can do obviously operate to the detriment of consumer well-being. They are the opposite of information improvement—they fog the issues and generate consumer confusion. Deceptive sales promotion activities, together with those that, while not deceptive, provide no useful information to consumers, waste resources. To the extent that they are reduced, the resources that were used to perform them can be used to produce goods and services that increase the welfare of consumers.

Although it is easy to secure agreement in principle that deceptive and useless sales promotion activities should be reduced, it is difficult to draw the line between that which is deceptive or useless and that which is not. What constitutes useless advertising? Those who want it reduced or banned have in mind activities that provide no useful information to consumers—for example, ads stating that automobile X rides smoother or dentifrice Z makes teeth whiter. However, some sales promotion activities that are useless to some consumers may not be useless to others. One person who frowns on smoking may argue that all cigarette advertising is useless. But a smoker may very well achieve higher welfare levels by discovering from advertisements or other sales promotion sources which brands contain the least amounts of tar and nicotine. Are Saturday morning television cartoons useless? It depends on the values and the tastes of the person making the judgment.

More consumer protection. The largest part of consumerism activities is directed toward protecting rather than educating consumers. They are directed toward protecting consumers from unsafe, impure, and low-quality products, and from unfair pricing practices. From the point of view of economic analysis it is useful to classify the goods that are targets of consumerism into two groups: (1) those that generate spillover costs in consumption and (2) those that do not.

Consider, first, consumerism measures intended to protect people from the spillover costs of the consumption done by others. Some obvious examples are laws that prevent smoking in public places, or that require periodic safety checks of automobiles so that drivers will not endanger the lives of others. The reduction of consuming activities that generate spillover costs for others adds to the well-being of those on whom the costs would otherwise be imposed. At the same time it places restrictions on—reducing the welfare of—those whose consuming activities are curtailed. If we believe that those who consume should pay the full costs of consumption, we will look with favor on measures that eliminate the spillover costs of consumption or that require the consumer of such goods to fully compensate or make whole those on whom the spillover costs are imposed.

Second, consider consumerism measures that curb or regulate the consumpton of goods and services where no spillover costs are generated by the act of consuming. Obvious examples include requirements that seat belts and shoulder harnesses be purchased in automobiles, that motorcycle riders wear helmets, that only Federal Aviation Agency certified parts be used to repair and maintain airplanes, that meat products sold over the counter meet certain quality standards, and that only licensed barbers be allowed to sell haircuts. The list can be extended. Most of the controversy over consumerism involves this general class of consumer goods and services.

Consumerism measures regulating the sale and consumption of individually consumed goods and services may or may not benefit consumers. Some such measures are intended to protect consumers from their own ignorance. Electrical codes for residential housing are a case in point, as is the licensing of doctors, plumbers, and barbers. Electrical codes specifying minimum wire sizes, fuses, and the like may very well benefit some consumers of residential housing. But at the same time the costs of obtaining minimum quality standards on certain goods and services may price some consumers out of markets altogether, precluding their obtaining the benefits of consuming low-cost, low-quality versions of those goods and services. Consider, for example the possible impact of requiring that all used cars sold be brought up to new car quality specifications.

Other consumerism measures are intended to protect consumers from unscrupulous sellers—sellers who presumably charge more for goods and services than they are worth to buyers. Price controls on various items fall into this category—price controls on gasoline, maximum rents on housing units, and the like. Those consumers who can get as much at the controlled price as they would purchase at an uncontrolled price clearly gain. Others who would be willing to pay more in order to obtain larger quantities than they currently can purchase lose just as clearly.

The economic costs

Consumerism activities and legislative measures are not a free service to consumers in general—not even those performed gratuitously by Ralph Nader. Two basic sets of economic costs can be readily identified. These are (1) the costs of resources used in effecting consumerism activities or measures, and (2) the costs to some consumers of providing the protection of consumerism to others.

Resource costs. The costs of resources used in effecting any given consumerism activity need not detain us long since they have been alluded to frequently throughout this chapter. The resources used by the Federal Trade Commission in monitoring advertising could have been used to produce other goods and services. The resources used by the Federal Aviation Agency in carrying out its functions of facilitating aircraft movements and enhancing aircraft safety could have been used to produce other goods and services. Among the interesting facts in this latter case is that the FAA currently employs one person for every four registered aircraft in the United States.

Costs to consumers. The direct cost to consumers of consumerism activities consists of the reductions in well-being or foregone well-being experienced by some consumers as the presumed benefits of those activities are extended to others. One of Nader's well-publicized consumerism activities illustrates costs of this type. He was able to force General Motors' Corvair automobile off the market although many purchasers had been well-satisfied with the car. The decline in value of Corvairs in existence at the time and the inability of people, who desired to do so to buy new ones after its withdrawal represent costs of a presumed increase in automobile safety. Other illustrations are easily found. The Consumer Product Safety Commission in its efforts to enhance product safety has imposed substantial costs on consumers. One case cited by Professor Murray Weidenbaum involved hearings by the commission to determine whether or not some 4 million electric frying pans were dangerous, although no injuries from the pan had ever been reported to the commission.[1] Hearings and investigations of this type use resources

---

[1] Murray L. Weidenbaum, *Government-Mandated Price Increases* (Washington, D.C.: American Enterprise Institute for Public Policy Research, 1975), p. 33.

and increase the costs of products, reducing what is available to consumers to buy. Consumerism may also prevent consumers who desire to do so from trading off some degree of product safety for lower prices—and voluntary trade-offs of this type would be expected to increase consumer well-being.

EVALUATION

On balance, what does economic analysis tell us about consumerism? Above all, the primary economic reason for consumerism is to enhance consumer welfare. Each manifestation of it should be subjected to a benefit-cost type of analysis to determine who is helped by it, what the costs of it are, and whether or not the benefits are worth the costs. Again it will be helpful to consider separately those aspects of it that are intended to (1) be informational in nature, (2) prevent the imposition of spillover costs on others, and (3) protect consumers from manipulation by business firms.

The provision of information

For any given good or service consumers generally find it useful to know the components or the ingredients that comprise it, what it can do for them, and the terms on which it is available. Against these benefits the costs of obtaining the information must be weighed. There is virtually no economic argument against consumerism measures requiring truth in advertising or a listing of ingredients on labels. The benefits are obvious, and the costs of providing accurate information are in general no greater than those of providing false or misleading information.

Consumerism activities such as testing agency activities that enhance consumer information on comparative qualities and/or durabilities of different brands of a product are also likely to enhance consumer welfare. The costs of testing must be met by consumer subscriptions to the published results. Consequently, we would expect that the benefits either exceed, or at the very least, are equal to the costs of making the information available. In addition, the extent of consumerism activities of this type will be governed by consumers themselves. They will get the approximate amount that they are willing to pay for—an amount at which the marginal benefits of additional information are approximately equal to the marginal costs of obtaining it.

The prevention of spillover costs

When the consumption of certain items would impose spillover costs on nonconsumers of those items, consumerism activities designed to prevent those spillovers from occurring seem to be on sound economic ground. If consumers of those items can pass along some of the costs to other people, they will demand—and receive—disproportionate amounts of the items. The items will tend to be overconsumed and overproduced.

Automobile transportation is a case in point. In the absence of regulation, people can drive automobiles with defective brakes, occasionally smashing into other cars, properties, and people. If drivers are allowed to impose such costs on others, driving is made less expensive to them, inducing them to indulge in more driving than they would if they were required to maintain their autos in a condition such that spillover costs would not be imposed on others. The economically correct amount of driving is that at which the marginal benefits of a mile of driving are equal to the marginal costs of doing it. This is approximately the amount that would occur if drivers are required to pay the full costs of their driving, that is, if they are not allowed to impose spillover costs on others.

There are some consumerism measures, such as banning the use of some products that are thought to generate spillover costs, where the logic is not so clear-cut. An example is provided by laws prohibiting the use of DDT and other pesticides. Prohibition of the use of DDT may preserve the purity of water and food for those farther down the watershed from the potential users of DDT. But the cost may be an outbreak of malaria or encephalitis because mosquitos are not kept under control. Weighing and balancing the costs and benefits of such prohibitions is a very imprecise and difficult business.

Protection from business manipulation

The most questionable consumerism activities are those aimed at protecting people from business manipulation—and a very large part of consumerism activities is for this express purpose. Manipulation of the individual consumer means essentially that a business firm can do with the consumer whatever it desires. It can shape the consumer's tastes and values; sell the consumer unwanted, unsafe, or low-quality products; take advantage of the consumer's ignorance; and charge exorbitant prices.

When consumer advocates succeed in obtaining legislation that requires products to meet certain quality or safety standards, the advocates—and those who pass the legislation—are supplanting consumer judgments with their own and are coercing some consumers to accept those substitute judgments. The fact that some consumers must be coerced into accepting them means that consumer well-being is decreased. Suppose that I am much less of a risk averter than is a consumer advocate and that I would rather take my chances driving an auto without seat belts and shoulder harnesses than to pay the extra costs of having them on my car. Yet the advocate is able to sway the legislature and require that all automobiles sold be equipped with these devices. I must buy them even though the benefits they yield to me are less than their costs. My welfare is decreased, and no one's welfare is increased.

Similarly, when quality standards for products are legislated, some consumers may be made worse off while no one may be made better off. Some consumers prefer a lower-quality product at a lower price than a higher-quality product at a higher price. Legislation that prevents the lower-quality product—say, hamburgers with soybean meal in them—from being sold reduces the welfare of those who would buy it. And there is no offsetting gain in the welfare of others.

What appears to be a fallacy in the reasoning of many consumer advocates is their implicit assumption that business firms profit most from manipulating consumers, that is, from taking advantage of them. To be sure there are unscrupulous and fraudulent sellers. There always have been and probably always will be. But it appears likely that the major part of the business sector of the economy will do better economically by giving the consumer a fair shake for the consumer's money. Who will take a car back a second time to a repair shop that charges for work not performed or for shoddy work? Can Detroit automakers make more money by producing styles and models that consumers do not want, attempting then to alter consumers' tastes, or by producing styles and models that meet existing tastes? Are appliance sellers with poor repair services likely to make more profit than those that excel with their repair services?

The final and important question is that of who is the best judge of consumers' interests, consumers themselves or consumer advocates? Some consumers are ignorant, and some businesses engage in shady practices. But by and large, the advocate is in the position of saying that many people ought not to want what they want—or if they do, they ought not to get it.

SUMMARY

Many people believe that consumers are at a substantial disadvantage vis-à-vis business firms in the U.S. economic system. They think that businesses take advantage of consumers by selling them unsafe, impure, and low-quality products; by engaging in deceptive advertising; by using obscure or deceptive pricing techniques; and by providing inferior servicing of products. People think these practices come about because of the wide range of products now being made available to consumers, the supplanting of small family-run production units by large mass production factories, the great advances that have been made in mass communications, and growing monopoly power. These deceptive practices are alleged to result in restrictions of consumer welfare or well-being because they do not give consumers what they want, and they utilize resources that could have been used to produce useful goods and services.

Consumerism is a movement that has developed over time to remedy the supposed inferior position of consumers. It consists of activities and efforts of private consumer advocates, consumer special interest groups, and governments.

Consumerism efforts are aimed at the provision of at least three types of benefits to consumers. These are (1) to make available more accurate and more complete information to consumers; (2) to reduce the amount of deceptive and useless sales promotion; and (3) to protect consumers from spillover costs, from their own ignorance, and from manipulation by sellers. But activities intended to provide these benefits in turn have their costs. These include the alternative costs of the resources used to provide them and the costs to consumers of not being able to obtain products or product qualities which consumerism activities have succeeded in banning from the market.

Economic analysis seems to indicate that most of the information-providing activities of the consumerism movement will on balance enhance consumer welfare, so will most activities that prevent the imposing of spillover costs by some on others. Activities intended to protect consumers from their own ignorance and/or from manipulation by business firms are of questionable value to consumers. Some such activities may result in net benefits to consumers while others will involve costs that outweigh the benefits. The primary problem in this area is that consumer advocates and those who pass legislation enforcing advocacy measures are able to substitute their values and their judgments with regard to what consumers in general want and get for the judgments of consumers themselves. This is often costly to consumers, and certainly it restricts their freedom in the marketplace.

SUPPLEMENTARY READINGS

Dreifus, Claudia. "The World According to Nader." *The Progressive* 48 (July 1984), pp. 58–61.

An interview with Ralph Nader which provides some insight into what makes him tick.

Friedman, Milton, and Rose Friedman. "Who Protects the Consumer?" In *Free to Choose*. New York: Harcourt Brace Jovanovich, 1980, chapter 7.

According to the Friedmans, the government agencies that claim to do so do not actually protect consumers. Cites examples of unintended side effects of consumer protection regulation. Recommends reliance on market forces as a preferable alternative.

McGowan, Daniel A. *Consumer Economics*. 2nd ed. Boston: Allyn & Bacon, 1984.

The first chapter provides an overview of the history of consumerism. In chapters 2 and 3 very basic macro and micro theory is developed. The rest of the book, on how to be an intelligent consumer, consists of applications to specific purchase areas.

Miller, James C. III, and Bruce Yandles, eds. *Benefit-Cost Analyses of Social Regulation*. Washington, D.C.: American Enterprise Institute for Public Policy Research, 1979.

Explains and presents results of actual benefit-cost analysis of various regulations including the labeling of donated blood, exposure of inorganic arsenic in the workplace, exposure to occupational noise, lawn mower safety, matchbook safety, crash protection for auto occupants, energy efficiency standards for household appliances, emission standards for motorcycles, and the reduction of airport noise.

North, Douglass C., and Roger L. Miller. "The Economics of Safer Products." In *The Economics of Public Issues*. 5th ed. New York: Harper & Row, 1983, pp. 22–30.

Provides a simple and clear description of the role of risk and cost in the provision of consumer protection. Also describes the built-in market forces that protect consumer interests.

Peltzman, Sam. *Regulation of Automobile Safety*. Washington, D.C.: American Enterprise Institute for Public Policy Research, 1975.

A classic study of consumer protection. The basic finding is that safety regulation has *not* reduced auto fatalities. Additional evidence suggests that such regulation has lowered the real cost of an accident and in so doing has stimulated offsetting risk-taking on the part of drivers.

Weidenbaum, Murray L. *Business, Government, and the Public*. 2nd ed. Englewood Cliffs, N.J.: Prentice-Hall, 1981.

Excellent source book by one of the leading economists working in the area of government regulation. Includes an overview of government regulation and chapters on automobile regulation, consumer product regulation, job safety regulation, and environmental regulation. Several case studies are appended.

PROTECTIONISM VERSUS FREE TRADE

The controversy over international trade
    The protectionist viewpoint
    The free trade viewpoint
The economics of international trade
    How trade takes place
    Production possibilities
    The principle of comparative
      advantage
    How international trade is financed
Analysis of the controversy
    Protection from cheap foreign
      goods
    Payments problems
    Protection of key industries
Summary

**Checklist of
Economic Concepts**

Imports
Exports
Production possibilities curve
Comparative advantage
Comparative disadvantage
Terms of trade
Demand
Supply
Exchange rates
Current account transactions
Capital account transactions
Balance of trade
   (merchandise)
Balance of payments

9

Protectionism versus

Free Trade

Can we restrict ourselves into prosperity?

More than a few theories have foundered on the rocky shoals of reality—such as one expounded by Paula Smith, assistant director of Oklahoma State University's Market Economy Education Center.

She opposes reciprocity in trade relations, saying such a suggestion has public and political appeal but could backfire if a country such as Japan retaliated instead of opening her markets to U.S. goods.

Nonsense! Japan has consistently kept her markets closed and would have nothing with which to retaliate. The vicious attempts by that country to undermine the American economy are well documented.

Tariffs are so high in Japan against American cars that they double the price paid for them in the United States. Japan now has 25 percent of the American car market. Hundreds of thousands are jobless, and the American economy limps badly precisely because good old Uncle Sam hasn't insisted on reciprocity—which Smith says would be good medicine only if it works.

Facts. The U.S. average tariff on imported autos is 2.8 percent. Australia charges a tariff of up to 57 percent on imported American cars. Austria charges 20 percent, New Zealand 55 percent, Spain 68 percent, France 10.8 percent, England 10.8 percent, Canada 14.2 percent, and Brazil up to 205 percent.

France froze the Japanese share of the French auto market at three percent and no trade war resulted. England and Germany froze the Japanese share of the market in their countries to 10.8 percent. France also charges a 33 percent value added tax and Germany and England tack on a 13 percent value added tax. Italy permits only 2,200 Japanese autos into that country per year.

Japan, until the early 1970s, prohibited all foreign cars and even today does not allow all foreign cars combined to equal more than 1 percent of sales in Japan.

It is ironic that America cracked down on Poland for mistreating the union there—invoking trade sanctions against Russia, including withholding natural gas pipeline equipment. A Japanese company immediately moved in and sold Russia the gas pipeline equipment.

Look again. Paula Smith and her free trade pals better take off the rose-colored glasses and recognize that the greatest economic threat to America today is the world markets where we're free traders and our trading partners are not.

Let her tell the unemployed auto workers that it was their outrageous salary demands that caused the collapse of the American auto market; the facts prove it is not so. It is the dirty trade tactics of alleged allies.

Would Japanese retaliation be worse than what is happening to America today?

Smith says we'd lose their cars, TVs, calculators, and the like. So what. They took over the TV market by vast dumping practices underwritten by the Japanese government (often referred to as Japan Inc.). If the price of putting America back to work is having fewer Datsuns and Sonys in America, by all means let's erect the trade barriers.

Frankly, if just once we meant what we said, we would probably get the trade barriers down without any reprisals. The reason we're in trouble is we've listened too long to the Paula Smiths and not nearly enough to common sense.[1]

THE CONTROVERSY OVER INTERNATIONAL TRADE

During the 1981–83 recession we saw a growing tide of resentment against the importation and sale of foreign goods into the United States. Actually, the resentment was nothing new; it was merely augmented, as it always is, by recession, and so far it has not been alleviated by the economic recovery of 1984–87. Historically, since the human race has organized itself into geographic groups and engaged in trade among those groups, conflict has emerged between those wanting to suppress trade relationships and those wanting to promote them. The U.S. government severely restricted product im-

---

[1]Frosty Troy, ed., *The Oklahoma Observer*, April 25, 1982, p. 9.

ports right up to the end of World War II. Since the late 1940s, import restrictions have fallen slowly and steadily but always against keen opposition. What underlies this conflict between *protectionists* and *free traders?* It is useful to consider the polar positions, recognizing that within the U.S. population one finds all shades of intermediate positions—people who are free traders in some respects and protectionists in others.

The protectionist viewpoint

For openers, protectionists want to reduce foreign competition against U.S. goods and services. They see the importation and sale of foreign goods crowding U.S. goods out of the markets in such areas as stereo and video equipment, automobiles, steel, footwear, and textiles. They note that shrinking markets for U.S. goods means less demand for U.S. labor and higher unemployment rates. Our industries cannot compete successfully, in the protectionists' view, against those in other countries that pay only a fraction of the wage rates that U.S. producers pay. The argument usually gains force during recession periods as unemployment increases.

A second argument advanced by protectionists is that import restrictions are necessary to remedy balance of trade and balance of payments problems. They point to the continuing deficits in the U.S. balance of trade, noting how much more we pay out for our imports than we receive for our exports of goods. Sometimes, as was the case in the first half of the 1970s, these deficits are viewed as driving the dollar prices of foreign currencies up, making the dollar worth less. In this case, if we were to reduce our imports, the dollar demand for foreign currencies would also be reduced, decreasing the balance of trade deficits and protecting the value of the dollar. At other times, as during the eary 1980s, the causal relationships are turned around. A strengthening dollar is seen as causing balance of trade deficits since it encourages imports and discourages exports. Protectionism is then advocated to block foreign competition from merchandise sales in the United States.

Still another protectionist argument is that there are certain key industries in the United States that are vital to our security and to our economic welfare. Among such industries we find automobiles, aerospace, steel, petroleum energy, and nuclear energy. We cannot depend on foreign suppliers during times of war. To be superior to other countries in technology of key industries, we must encourage their development and growth by restricting imports of those products from other countries.

The free trade viewpoint

Free traders generally maintain that it is in the best interests of consumers worldwide if economic units in all countries are free to engage in whatever voluntary exchanges they believe will be advantageous to them. They see trade among nations conferring the same benefits on the exchanging parties as trade among individuals in any one country. If all parties to a potential voluntary exchange fail to see gain for themselves in it, then it will never be consummated. So, why inhibit economic activity—voluntary exchange—that takes place only if every participant gains? We are all made better off, they argue, through specialization and voluntary exchange.

THE ECONOMICS OF INTERNATIONAL TRADE

What can economic theory contribute toward resolving the conflict of viewpoints? It is useful to learn and apply to the problem (1) the underlying mechanics of international trade, (2) the production possibilities of a country, without trade and with trade, (3) the principle of comparative advantage, and (4) the financing of international trade.

How trade takes place

It takes two to tango. A country cannot unilaterally import unless it also exports goods. Neither can it export unless it also imports goods.

Suppose the *only* potential international transaction that exists, now and forever, between the United States and the rest of the world is the importation by me of a West German Mercedes. This assumption is ridiculous, but it illustrates an important point. Where would I get the marks to make the purchase? The answer is obvious. There are and will be none available. Or, looking at it from the other side of the water, if I want to pay in dollars, what would the Germans do with dollars? They would have no use for dollars and, consequently, would not accept them. The transaction would never take place.

Suppose now that I want to import a Mercedes, and Cessna Aircraft wants to export a Cessna 152. If Cessna can sell the airplane for marks, then I can buy marks from Cessna for dollars, using the marks in turn to purchase the Mercedes. In order for people in one country to import, it is also necessary that they export. There is no escape from this fundamental proposition.

Production possibilities

In general why do people in different countries want to engage in exchange? The underlying reason is that it enables them to increase the levels of well-being they can get from their resources. In terms of countries as a whole, production possibilities curves can be shifted outward. Trade enables the totality of consumers in each country to achieve higher satisfaction levels with the complement of labor, capital, and technology available to them. Let's see how it works for two countries, Alpha and Omega, that can engage in trade with each other and with other countries of the world.

Without trade. Consider the production possibilities of Alpha in the absence of international trade. Given Alpha's resources and techniques, suppose its economic system can produce either 100 million loaves of bread or 200 million gallons of milk. Assuming that its resources are unspecialized to either product, the trade-off between the two products is one for two. By giving up 1 million loaves of bread, the resources released can always be used to produce an additional 2 million gallons of milk. So Alpha alone can produce any combination of bread and milk on line *AB* in Figure 9–1. Suppose its people select combination *C*, containing 50 million loaves of bread and 100 million gallons of milk.

Let Omega's resources differ somewhat from those of Alpha, but consider that they, too, are unspecialized. Suppose that Omega's economy can produce, without trade, either 100 million loaves of bread or 50 million gallons of milk. The trade-off in production between the two products is a half million gallons of milk for one million loaves of bread, or two million loaves of bread for one million gallons of milk. Thus, Omega's production possibilities curve is *MN* in Figure 9–2. Suppose its population settles on combination *P*, containing 50 million loaves of bread and 25 million gallons of milk.

With trade. What would happen if Alpha and Omega were now able to enter into international trade relationships? Under what circumstances would Alpha and Omega be willing to trade bread for milk? Or milk for bread? First we determine the limits within which the terms of trade must fall if the countries are to engage in trade. Second, we show what trade within the terms of trade limits will do for each country.

Alpha would refuse to enter into any trade relationships in which the cost of importing a gallon of milk exceeds a half loaf of bread, or in which the cost of importing a loaf of bread exceeds two gallons

FIGURE 9–1
Alpha production possibilities with and without trade

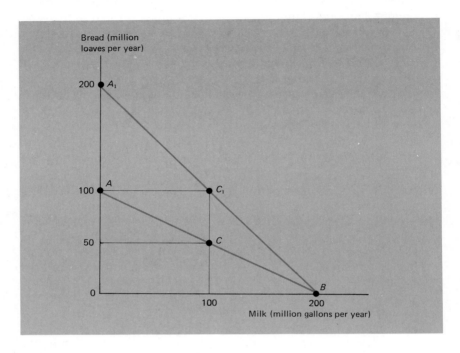

In the absence of trade, Alpha's resources will produce 100 million loaves of bread, or 200 million gallons of milk, or any combination of the two products as shown by *AB*.

If terms of trade are one for one, with trade Alpha's production possibilities curve becomes A_1B. Alpha can concentrate on milk production and can trade for bread at less than it would cost to produce it in Alpha.

of milk. A gallon of milk produced domestically costs Alpha only a half loaf of bread. Why import it if the cost per gallon of the import is greater? A loaf of bread produced domestically costs 2 gallons of milk, so Alpha would not be willing to pay more to import it. We summarize these results in Table 9–1.

Omega would not voluntarily engage in trade if the terms of trade exceed two loaves of bread for the importation of a gallon of milk or a half gallon of milk for the importation of a loaf of bread. It could do better producing both domestically. These limits are shown in Table 9–1.

Suppose now that as countries consider engaging in trade, the terms of trade between bread and milk settle at a gallon of milk for a loaf of bread. Both Alpha and Omega can gain from trade. The production possibilities curves of both countries will rotate outward.

If Alpha produces only milk and trades milk for bread, the population of the country can import one loaf of bread for each gallon of milk it is willing to export. If it were to export all its milk, it could import 200 million loaves of bread. Its production possibilities curve becomes A_1B in Figure 9–1. *Trade under these circumstances yields results identical to the discovery of a new bread-making technique that doubles the productivity of Alpha's resources in making bread.*

If Omega concentrates all of its resources on bread making and trades for milk, it can import a gallon of milk for every loaf of bread, it produces and exports. If it exports 100 million loaves of bread, it

FIGURE 9–2
Omega production possibilities with and without trade

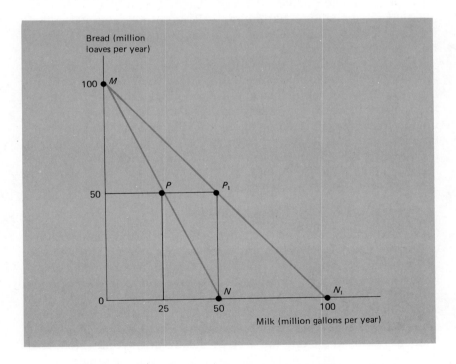

In the absence of trade, Omega's resources will produce per year 100 million loaves of bread, or 50 million gallons of milk, or any combination shown on the line *MN*.

If terms of trade are one for one, with trade Omega's production possibilities curve becomes MN_1. Omega can concentrate on bread production and trade for milk at less than it would cost to produce it in Omega.

TABLE 9–1
Limits to terms of trade between
bread and milk, Alpha and Omega

	Alpha	Omega
Bread	1	2
Milk	2	1

can import 100 million gallons of milk. Its production possibilities curve becomes MN_1 in Figure 9–2. Contrast this result with what Omega could have if it does not engage in trade.

Country Alpha will concentrate on the production of milk, and Country Omega will produce bread. Producing milk only, Alpha's people are not limited to combination C of milk and bread, which contains 50 million loaves of bread and 100 million gallons of milk. They can produce 200 million gallons of milk, trade 100 million gallons for 100 million loaves of bread, leaving themselves with combination C_1, containing 100 million gallons of milk and 100 million loaves of bread. They are 50 million loaves of bread better off than they were before trade.

Country Omega's people will be better off producing only bread and trading for milk. Before trade they chose combination P containing 50 million loaves of bread and 25 million gallons of milk. By specializing in bread they can produce 100 million loaves, trade 50 million loaves for 50 million gallons of milk, and end up with combination P_1 containing 50 million gallons of milk and 50 million loaves of bread. Trade enables them to obtain a net gain of 25 million gallons of milk.

The principle of comparative advantage

Clearly, specialization and exchange help Alpha and Omega to increase the volumes of goods and services available for their people to consume. It pays any country to specialize in producing those things in which it has a *comparative advantage* and to trade for goods in which it experiences a *comparative disadvantage*.

A country has a *comparative advantage* in the production of any good that it can produce with a smaller sacrifice of some alternative good or goods than can the rest of the trading world. Note that there is no presumption that the country can produce that good at a lower *absolute* cost than can other countries. In terms of the number of units of labor and capital necessary to produce a million gallons of milk, Alpha may use 3 times (or 10 times) more of each than other countries. Yet if Alpha must give up a half million loaves of bread for 1 million gallons of milk and can trade the million gallons of milk for *more* than a half million loaves of bread, Alpha has a comparative advantage in producing milk. Use this same reasoning to determine Omega's comparative advantage product, if any.

Symmetrically, a country has a *comparative disadvantage* in the production of any good that requires a greater sacrifice of some alternative good or goods than is required in the rest of the trading world. Country Alpha in our example has a comparative disadvantage in the production of bread. It must sacrifice 2 gallons of milk for a loaf of bread if it produces bread domestically. But it can import a loaf of bread by giving up only 1 gallon of milk to the international market. In which product does Omega have a comparative disadvantage?

Look again at the complete examples of Alpha and Omega, without and with trade. Note that if a country has a comparative advantage in the production of one good (and it most certainly will have in the real world), it must have a comparative disadvantage in the production of some other good or goods. Usually a country will have comparative advantages in the production of several goods and comparative disadvantages in the production of several others.

The reasons why every country has comparative advantages in the production of some goods and comparative disadvantages in the production of others is that countries differ in their respective resource endowments and in their states of technology. Some countries are short on certain mineral deposits such as oil, coal, copper, and the like, but they may have relatively large quantities of good capital equipment and high levels of technological know-how. Such a country, Japan for example, will likely have comparative advantages in the production and sale of goods embodying high technology and good stocks of capital with which to work. Some countries have vast quantities of good agricultural land while others do not. Some are particularly well-suited in terms of climate, terrain, and soil to grow outstanding wine grapes. Some excell in coffee production and others in growing tea. A beef industry seldom thrives in densely populated mountainous countries. Some countries have high literacy rates. In others the bulk of the population may be illiterate. All of these differences, and many more, confer on each country or region of a country certain comparative advantages and disadvantages that make specialization and exchange worthwhile.

How international trade is financed

International trade has two important characteristics that set it apart from trade within the boundaries of any given country. First, each

country has its own currency. Producers in any given country want
to be paid in that currency, and buyers want to use it to pay for
goods and services. Second, nationalism and political objectives are
invariably injected into trade relationships among nations. All sorts
of impediments to trade are enacted by governments to further political ends even though the trade, if allowed, would have been in
the best economic interests of the trading parties. Remember that
voluntary exchange will occur only if all parties to the exchange expect to gain. In this section we concentrate mostly on the problems
arising from the different currency units used by different countries.

The link between the currencies of any two trading countries is
the *exchange rate*. An *exchange rate* is the price of one country's currency in terms of the monetary units of another. It is useful for us
to think of it as the dollar price of another country's currency. We
list a recent sample of such exchange rates in Table 9–2. The dollar
exchange rate for the British pound of $1.52 is the highest one listed.
The lowest one listed is $.001 for the Mexican peso. This amounts
to one tenth of a cent.

Exchange rates, in the absence of intervention by governments,
are determined in exchange markets which arise from millions of
such transactions as the importation of a Mercedes into the United
States or the export of a Cessna 152 to West Germany. The existence
of exchange markets makes the pairing of individual import transactions with individual export transactions unnecessary. Anyone in

TABLE 9–2
Dollar exchange rates for selected foreign currencies, February
10, 1987

Country	Dollars	Foreign currency unit
Argentina	0.75	1 austral
Australia	0.69	1 dollar
Britain	1.52	1 pound
Canada	0.75	1 dollar
Denmark	0.15	1 krone
France	0.16	1 franc
Greece	0.007	1 drachma
Italy	0.008	1 lira
Japan	0.006	1 yen
Mexico	0.001	1 peso
Saudi Arabia	0.27	1 riyal
South Africa	0.48	1 rand
South Korea	0.002	1 won
Switzerland	0.65	1 franc
Taiwan	0.028	1 dollar
West Germany	0.55	1 mark

Source: *The Wall Street Journal*, Wednesday, February 11, 1987, p. 40.

the United States can buy foreign currency with dollars and can use it to import that country's goods. Similarly, anyone with excess amounts of a foreign currency on hand from selling goods abroad, or for any other reason, can sell that currency for dollars in the foreign exchange market.

In the absence of government intervention, the exchange rate of any home country currency for a foreign currency is determined, like any other price, by the forces of demand for and supply of the foreign currency. The demand curve for the foreign currency is essentially the same as the demand curve for anything else. Usually it slopes downward to the right like *DD* in Figure 9–3, indicating that the lower the price of the foreign currency the more of it the home-country people will want to buy. Similarly, the supply curve *SS* illustrated in Figure 9–3 usually slopes upward to the right since potential sellers will place more on the market at higher prices than they will at lower prices. The exchange rate r is the equilibrium price. Quantity q is the equilibrium quantity exchanged of the foreign currency.

Demand for foreign currencies within any given country is generated by any payments that those in the country want to make abroad. The summary of U.S. international transactions for 1985 in Table 9–3 illustrates the major sources of demand. The largest part of our demand for foreign currencies arose from imports of merchandise shown on line 3. This demand source is straightforward. The second largest came from increases in U.S. investments abroad on line 9. When companies like Ford or Mobil Oil invest abroad, they require foreign currencies to purchase land, build plants, and obtain equipment. The small category of line 6, entitled "Other," consists of cash gifts that persons in the United States send to relatives or friends abroad, demand for foreign services, and U.S. government nonmilitary grants. Thus, total recorded U.S. demand for foreign currencies in 1985 amounted to $383,042,000,000.

Supplies of foreign currencies, as one would expect, arise from transactions reciprocal to those generating demand. The largest supply source in 1985 was the merchandise exports of line 2. The next largest consisted of investments made by foreigners in the United States, for example, Saudi Arabia investments in hotels and land, or in financial securities in the United States. A smaller, but still a very important source of supply, was net investment income from abroad to people in the United States. Those in the United States who invest abroad expect to receive returns on that investment in the forms of interest, dividends, and capital gains. Similarly, foreigners investing in the United States expect the same kinds of returns. The net investment income of line 5 shows the excess of such income earned

FIGURE 9–3
U.S. demand, supply, and exchange rate for pounds

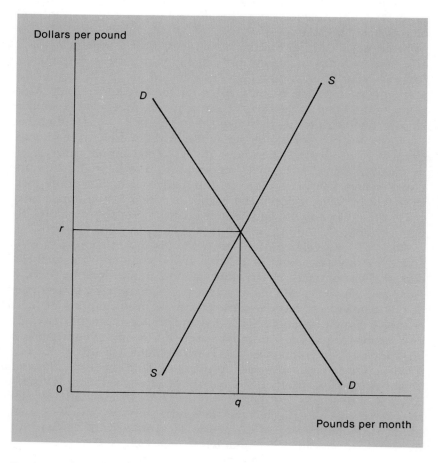

Demand for pounds is represented by *DD* and supply is *SS*. The equilibrium exchange rate is *r* dollars per pound and the equilibrium quantity of pounds is *q*.

by people in the United States over the investment income to foreign investors from their investments in the United States. Total recorded supplies of foreign exchange to the United States totaled $366,718,000,000 in 1985.

The separation of transactions in Table 9–3 into "Current account" and "Capital account" categories is simply a classification convenience. Current account items are more or less immediate and short term in character. A transaction is consummated, and that is the end of it. Others of a similar nature are occurring concurrently

TABLE 9–3
United States international transactions, summary, 1985 (millions of dollars)

Transaction type	Demand for foreign currency	Supply of foreign currency	Balance
1. Current account			
2. Merchandise exports		214,424	
3. Merchandise imports	– 338,863		
4. Merchandise trade balance			(– 124,439)
5. Investment income net		25,187	
6. Other	– 18,424		
7. Balance on current account			– 117,676
8. Capital account			
9. Change in U.S. assets abroad	– 25,755		
10. Change in foreign assets in the U.S.		127,107	
11. Other		0	
12. Balance on capital account			101,352
13. Subtotals	– 383,042	366,718	
14. Statistical discrepancy			– 16,324

Source: *Federal Reserve Bulletin,* September 1986, p. A53.

and over time. Capital account items are long-term transactions that will persist into the future and yield continuing influence on the demand for and supply of foreign exchange.

Notice the difference between the total demand for and the total supply of foreign exchanges listed in Table 9–3. It amounted to $16,324,000,000, a sizable pocketful of change. Our table shows the difference as being owed to foreigners—we used or demanded more foreign exchange than was available. Such an amount is sometimes interpreted as a balance of payments deficit. But actually it is simply a statistical discrepancy: a failure to get all international transactions on record. Suppose that for the year people in the United States end up owing some $16 billion to foreigners. If *all* transactions were recorded, those in the United States would have issued I.O.U.s of different kinds, and foreigners would have accepted them. Otherwise the extra items would not have been sold to us. Acceptance of ownership of those I.O.U.s by foreigners would increase line 10, changes in foreign assets in the United States, by $16 billion, making the demand and supply columns balance. The statistical discrepancy is not a cause for concern.

ANALYSIS OF THE CONTROVERSY

In the light of this brief survey of the economics of international trade, what light is shed on the controversy between protectionists and free traders? Should we protect ourselves from imports of Japanese and European automobiles and steel? Is it wise to limit textile imports from South Korea, Taiwan, Hong Kong, and China? Is the importation of Japanese motorcycles a threat to our prosperity? What will happen to us if we reduce the import quotas on sugar and other agricultural products? In analyzing these issues, it is important that we separate economic from political considerations. Economic analysis provides insight primarily into the former.

Protection from cheap foreign goods

The principle of comparative advantage and the economic gains ensuing from specialization and exchange make it reasonably clear that a country's population as a whole will lose from import restrictions. They will have less of all goods and services to consume. Real per capita income and living standards will be lower than they would be if all potential international voluntary exchanges are allowed to be consummated. Foreign goods cannot displace all or even a large part of the domestic production and sale of goods. A country cannot import unless, by selling domestic goods and services or other kinds of domestic assets to foreigners, it earns foreign exchange with which to buy those imports. International trade is a two-way street enabling those countries that engage in it to shift their production possibilities curves outward. It serves to *increase* the real per capita income and living standards in the trading countries

Free trade may indeed injure segments of a country's economy. It is concern for that part of the population investing in and working in the injured segments that prompts most protectionist efforts. Import quotas and/or high tariffs on steel and automobiles keep the demands for the outputs of domestic steel and automobile manufacturers higher than they would otherwise be, thus supporting profits, wages, and employment in those industries. Free trade enables foreign competitors to invade the domestic producers' markets, resulting in lower domestic profits, wages, and employment levels in those industries.

Consequently, the imposition of import restrictions leads to winners (those investing and working in the protected sector) and losers (consumers who must pay higher prices for the protected good). But do the winners "win" by more than the losers "lose"? In other words, do the benefits of the import restriction outweigh the costs? Considering the case of automobiles will help us see that in the typical case, the costs of import restrictions far outweigh the benefits. In the early 1980's, in response to poor domestic auto sales, the Reagan administration was successful in getting Japan to voluntarily limit auto exports to the United States. The major benefit of the import restriction has been the significant number of jobs saved in the auto sector (at the expense of jobs lost in the export sector.) The cost of the program has been the increased price that consumers have had to pay for autos. Which is greater? One estimate suggests that the voluntary import restriction has imposed a cost of $160,000 per job saved.[2] That is, in an effort to save a job paying $30,000 to $40,000, we spent $160,000. If the benefits of import restrictions rarely outweigh the costs, why is protectionism so popular? The gains from free trade, because they are spread over the entire consuming population, tend to be unnoticed by the average individual. The same is not true with respect to those injured by free trade. Had the import restrictions on Japanese autos not been in effect, numerous individuals would have lost their jobs. Significant personal losses of this nature are easily noticed by the entire population. Consequently, it is not strange to find that "free traders win the arguments, but protectionists win the elections," as the anonymous saying goes.

Payments problems

Protectionism for balance of trade problems appears to stem from a less than complete view of the whole set of a country's international transactions. In the United States we are reminded by the news media every month of the balance of trade deficit for that month. We are warned by many members of Congress of the dire consequences of the continuing trade balance deficits unless we curb our appetites for foreign-made goods. What seems to be overlooked is that the trade deficit doesn't really matter in the overall set of international transactions.

From current account transactions alone, the U.S. population could reasonably expect to import a greater value of goods than it exports for almost as far as one can see into the future. For a great many years we have earned much larger investment income abroad than foreigners have earned in the United States. Net investment income alone would enable us to import more than we export, even if we were to maintain a current account balance of zero. The merchandise trade balance simply doesn't tell us much.

When we take capital account transactions into consideration, the merchandise trade balance becomes even less important. Foreign investments in the United States provide us with foreign currencies to

---

[2]Robert W. Crandall, "Import Quotas and the Automobile Industry: The Costs of Protection," *Brookings Review*, Summer 1984, p. 8.

import goods if we so desire. U.S. investments abroad use supplies of foreign currencies, leaving smaller quantities available for importing merchandise. And, since much trade and investment is done by private economic units without the need of government supervision, blessing, or curse, a great many transactions never get in the official record.

Trade deficits are important only to the extent that they lead to overall balance of payments deficits. A balance of payments deficit means that a country, during a given year, is short of sufficient foreign currencies to meet its obligations. Government setting or pegging of the country's exchange rate would be necessary for such a shortage to occur.

The circumstances creating a foreign exchange shortage are illustrated in Figure 9–4. Let the equilibrium exchange rate be $1.75 for 1 pound. If the U.S. government sets an exchange rate ceiling on the pound at $1.50 each, the British will want smaller quantities of our exports (which are now more expensive to them), and we will

FIGURE 9–4
The effects of pegging an exchange rate below the equilibrium level

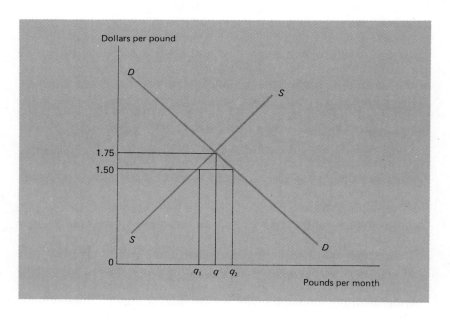

If a country pegs its exchange rate for another country's currency below the equilibrium level, the effect is the same as it is for the imposition of any effective price ceiling. There will be a shortage. If the exchange rate is fixed at $1.50 per pound, the shortage is $q_1 q_2$ pounds per month.

want to import more from them (because British goods are now cheaper for us). A shortage of q_1q_2 pounds per month occurs. Such a shortage is generally referred to as a balance of payments deficit.

The deficit can persist only if the lid is kept on the price of the pound. The $1.50 ceiling overvalues the dollar relative to the pound. If it is removed, the shortage of pounds will induce buyers of British goods to bid against each other for the available supply of pounds. The price of the pound will move toward its equilibrium level of $1.75, and the dollar will depreciate relative to the pound.

The free trade position and a free exchange rate position go hand in hand. In general, the argument runs that with free trade a freely flexible exchange market will appropriately value the currencies of different countries with respect to each other. Shortages or surpluses of foreign exchange will be short-term transitional phenomena. On the other hand, a fixed exchange rate will result in incentives to restrict trade. In Figure 9–4, for example, with the ceiling of $1.50 for the pound, the shortage of pounds provides Congress with an incentive to restrict imports. Import restriction would move the *DD* curve to the left reducing the shortage of pounds.

Protection of key industries

In an uncertain political world the protectionist viewpoint for key industries may be more frequently recommended. But the arguments are political rather than economic. It is very difficult to draw the line between what constitutes an absolutely indispensible industry for military purposes and what does not. Even in times of war, allied countries depend on one another for strategic arms and other war material.

Any one country finds it very difficult and very costly to be self-sufficient in all types of military goods. In determining where to draw the line, there should be a very careful weighing of the benefits of self-sufficiency against its costs.

SUMMARY

The recession of 1981–83 stepped up the controversy between protectionists and free traders. Protectionists argue that imports should be limited to reduce foreign competition with goods produced in the United States, to remedy balance of trade and balance of payments problems, and to encourage U.S. industries vital to national security and economic welfare. Free traders maintain that economic welfare of a country is enhanced by voluntary free exchange among countries.

A country's production possibilities are usually greater when it trades with other countries than when it does not. By concentrating on the production of goods in which it has a comparative advantage and trading for goods in which it has a comparative disadvantage, the population of the country will have a larger GNP to consume and/or invest.

International exchange markets arise from international transactions. A country's demands for foreign exchange are generated by imports of goods, investments in other countries, and any other transactions that result in payments made abroad. Supplies of foreign exchange are created by exports, foreign investments in the country, and by any other transactions that cause payments to be made to the country. Exchange rates are determined by the forces of demand for and supply of currencies used in international trade.

Economic analysis indicates that a country's population as a whole usually loses as a result of import restrictions. Gains to the protected industries come at the expense of export industries and consumers. Balance of payments problems are essentially exchange rate problems arising when countries attempt to peg exchange rates. It appears that the preferred solution to such problems is exchange rate adjustment rather than protectionism. Protection of *key* industries may have some merit—if only we could determine which industries fall in this category.

SUPPLEMENTARY READINGS

"The Consumer: A Force against Protectionism." *OECD Observer* 129 July 1984, pp. 22–25.

Explains who gains and who loses from protectionism and weighs the gains against the losses.

Heilbroner, Robert L., and Lester C. Thurow. *The Economic Problem.* 7th ed. Englewood Cliffs, N.J.: Prentice-Hall, 1984, chapters 36 and 37.

Good discussion of the protectionist as well as the free trade point of view.

Heyne, Paul. *The Economic Way of Thinking.* 3rd ed. Chicago: Science Research Associates, 1980, chapter 19.

Contains a good explanation of balance of payments accounting and exchange rates.

"The Superdollar." *Business Week,* October 8, 1984, pp. 164–76.

A series of reports on why the dollar has been gaining strength and what impact that strength has on U.S. exports, imports, investments abroad, foreign investments in the United States, and the inflation rate.

HEALTH ISSUES

Growth and nature of health services
  Health care dollars—where they
    came from and where they went
  Factors explaining the growth in
    expenditures for personal health
    services
  Special characteristics of health
    services
Health care problems
  The public view
  The economist's view
Analysis of demand for health services
  Elasticity of demand
  Factors changing the demand for
    health services
Analysis of supply of health services
  Supply characteristics: Physicians
  Supply characteristics: Hospitals
  Factors affecting the supply of
    hospital services
**Evaluation of the U.S. health care
system**
  Reducing entry barriers
  Increasing efficiency
National health insurance
  Basic issues
  Alternative proposals to national
    health insurance
A final look at rising health care costs
  Supply approach
  Demand approach
  Reform approach
Summary

**Checklist of
Economic Concepts**

Elasticity of demand
Changes in demand
Per capita income
Tastes and preferences
Relative prices
Substitution effects
Less than full-cost pricing
Elasticity of supply
Changes in supply
Principle of diminishing
  returns
Investment

10

Health Issues

Is it worth what it costs?

Even though we are a nation that places a high value on health, we have done very little to insure that quality health care is available to all of us at a price we can afford. We have allowed rural and innercity areas to be slowly abandoned by doctors. We have allowed hundreds of insurance companies to create thousands of complicated policies that trap Americans in gaps, limitations, and exclusions in coverage, and that offer disastrously low benefits which spell financial disaster for a family when serious illness or injury strikes. We have allowed doctor and hospital charges to skyrocket out of control through wasteful and inefficient practices to the point where more and more Americans are finding it difficult to pay for health care and health insurance. We have also allowed physicians and hospitals to practice with little or no review of the quality of their work, and with few requirements to keep their knowledge up to date or to limit themselves to the areas where they are qualified. In our concern not to infringe on doctors' and hospitals' rights as entrepreneurs, we have allowed them to offer care in ways, at times, in places, and at prices designed more for their convenience and profit than for the good of the American people.

When I say "we have allowed," I mean that the American people have not done anything about it through their government, that the medical societies and hospital associations have done far too little about it, and that the insurance companies have done little or nothing about it.

I believe the time has come in our nation for the people to take action to solve these problems.[1]

---

[1]Edward M. Kennedy, *In Critical Condition: The Crisis in America's Health Care* (New York: Simon & Schuster, 1972), pp. 16–17.

GROWTH AND NATURE OF HEALTH SERVICES

National health expenditures in the United States grew spectacularly in the 1950s, 60s, and 70s doubling in the 1950s, tripling in the 60s, and more than tripling in the 70s (Figure 10–1). The decade of the 1980s is expected to show a similar trend of rapid growth, although the pace is projected to slow down in the last part of the decade. The average growth rate in national health expenditures was 14 percent between 1980 and 1984, and is projected to be 10 percent between 1986 and 1990. As a percent of the GNP, health expenditures grew from 4.5 percent in 1950 to 9.4 percent in 1980 (Figure 10–2). Again, health expenditures grew faster than the economy as a whole in the first part of the current decade. They are projected to grow slightly faster than the GNP in the second part of the current decade, reaching 11.3 percent of the GNP in 1990.

FIGURE 10–1
National health expenditures in selected years, 1950–1990

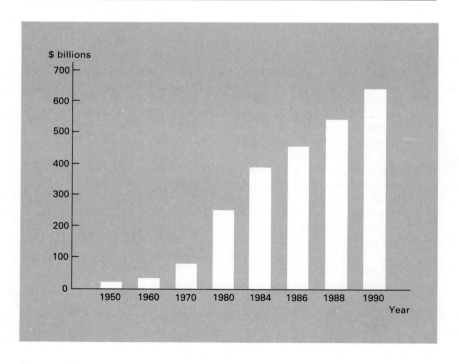

Source: U.S. Department of Health and Human Services, Health Care Financing Adminstration, *Health Care Financing Review* 7, no. 1 (Spring 1986), p. 16.

FIGURE 10–2
Health expenditures as a percent of GNP in selected years, 1950–1990

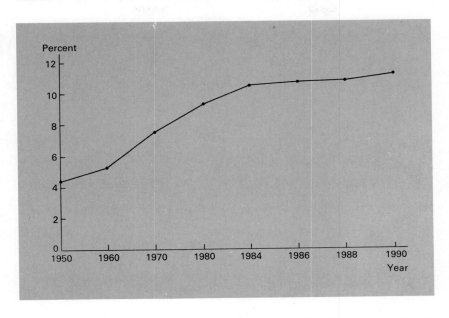

Source: U.S. Department of Health and Human Services, Health Care Financing Administration, *Health Care Financing Review* 7, no. 3 (Spring 1986), p. 6.

Health care dollars—where they came from and where they went

The $425 billion spent on health care goods and services in 1985 came from three major sources. The consumer or patient paid directly out of his or her pocket $106.2 billion, or 25 percent. Private health insurance coverage took care of $131.7 billion, or 31 percent; and government (federal, state, and local) financed the largest amount, $174.2 billion, and the largest share, 41 percent (Figure 10–3). The two largest government programs, Medicare and Medicaid, accounted for almost two thirds of government health care spending. Medicare, a federal health care program for retired people under the Social Security system, paid 17 cents of each health care dollar in 1985. Medicaid, a financially shared federal and state program for people on public assistance, paid 10 cents of each health care dollar.

National health care dollars went for hospital care, physicians' services, nursing home care, other health care goods and services (such as eyeglasses, drugs, and dental services), research, and con-

FIGURE 10–3
Health care dollars—where they came from

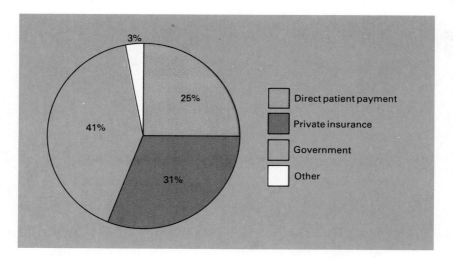

Source: Daniel R. Waldo, Katharine R. Levit, and Helen Lazenby, "National Health Expenditures in 1985," *Health Care Financing Review* 8, no. 1 (Fall 1986), p. 8.

struction. A major part of health care dollars went for hospital care—39 percent in 1985. Another large part, 20 percent, went for physicians' services. Eight percent of all health care dollars was spent for nursing home care in 1985. In the same year, 20 percent and 13 percent of health care dollars were spent for other health services, and for research administration, etc., respectively (Figure 10–4).

Factors explaining the growth in expenditures for personal health services

A number of factors explain the growth in personal health services, that is, health services for the direct benefit of the individual. In comparison to national health care goods and services discussed above, personal health services do not include outlays spent for the community, such as outlays for construction, research, and disease control. The important factors accounting for the growth in expenditures for personal services are inflation in the economy, increases in medical care prices in excess of general price inflation, increases in the intensity of health care treatment, and population growth—especially growth in the average age of the population. Table 10–1 shows the relative importance of the different factors explaining the

FIGURE 10-4
Health care dollars—where they went

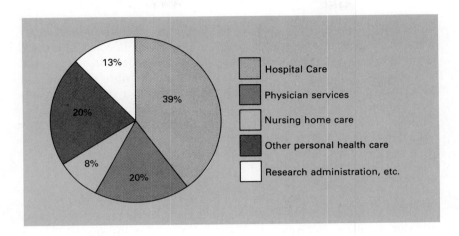

Source: Daniel R. Waldo, Katharine R. Levit, and Helen Lazenby, "National Health Expenditures in 1985," *Health Financing Review* 8, no. 1 (Fall 1986), p. 8.

rise in personal health care costs for hospital inpatient and outpatient care, and for physicians' services.

Inflation. Inflation accounts for a large part of the growth in expenditures for personal health services. For example, between 1974 and 1984, the average increase in prices accounted for 51.2 percent of the growth in expenditures for hospital inpatient care, 40.8 per-

TABLE 10-1
The relative importance of factors accounting for growth in expenditures for selected health services during the period, 1974–1984

Factors	Hospital Care		Physician's services
	Inpatient	Outpatient	
Economy-wide factors:			
General inflation	51.2%	40.8%	52.8%
Population growth	7.3	5.8	7.5
Health-specific factors:			
Growth in per capita visits	−8.5	10.9	−7.5
Growth in real services per visit or per day (intensity per visit)	33.4	29.3	27.5
Medical care price increases in excess of general price inflation	16.6	13.2	19.7
Total	100.0	100.0	100.0

Source: *Health Care Financing Review* 7, no. 3 (Spring 1986), p. 4.

cent of the growth in expenditures for hospital outpatient care, and 52.8 percent of the growth in expenditures for services provided by physicians (Table 10–1).

Medical care price increases. Medical care prices have increased faster than the general rate of inflation. So, in addition to the growth in health care costs due to inflation, health care costs have increased because of much higher charges for the same quantity of service. In the case of inpatient hospital care, 16.6 percent of the rise in costs was due to price increases in excess of the inflation rate during the 10-year period, 1974 to 1984. The fees for the services of physicians show this same pattern of growth. During the same time period, the rise in physicians' fees in excess of the rise in general inflation accounted for 19.7 percent of the growth in the cost of physicians' services (Table 10–1).

Intensity of services. Health care costs have increased because a greater quantity and quality of health care resources are used for a given treatment of illness. Intensity per hospital visit explained 33.4 percent and 29.3 percent of the growth in expenditures for inpatient and outpatient hospital care respectively between 1974 and 1984. During this same period, intensity per visit explained 27.5 percent of the rise in expenditures for physicians' services.

Use or quantity demanded. An interesting development in patient use or quantity demanded for hospital care since 1974 is the decrease in the quantity demand for inpatient care and the increase in outpatient care. The reason for this is that outpatient hospital care is a lower cost alternative to inpatient care. Between 1974 and 1984, inpatient per capita visits decreased 8.5 percent while outpatient per capita visits increased 10.9 percent (Table 10–1). During the same period, patients' visits to doctors' offices diminished 7.5 percent on a per capita basis. This may be explained by the lower out-of-pocket cost to the patient sometimes when treatment is received in the hospital than when it is received in the doctor's office.

Population growth. The final factor that explains the growth in the costs of health services is the growth in the population. The growth in the population accounted for 7.3 percent of the growth in the costs of hospital inpatient services, and approximately 7.5 percent of the growth in expenditures for physicians' services during the period (1974–84). In general, the larger the number of people, the more health care that is needed and the more resources that are channeled into health care. The current slowdown in population growth can be expected to reduce the increase in the costs of health services. However, the average age of the population will increase with a slower population growth rate; as a consequence, a larger proportion of the population may need health services.

Is there anything special about the rising costs of medical services? There is nothing special or unusual about the rising cost of medical services. Price increases, population growth, and a greater quantity and better quality of services explain the rise in costs of most, if not all, goods and services. The reason people are so nervous about the rising costs of medical services lies, in part, in the special characteristics of health services.

Special characteristics of health services

The role of the physician. A special characteristic of health services involves the role of the physician, who operates on both sides of the market. The physician is both a supplier and a demander of health services. It is the physician who provides the consumer directly with services and determines the service she or he needs from other suppliers—hospitals and suppliers of drugs and medicines. Decisions about medications, getting well at home or in the hospital, number of days spent in the hospital, and special medical services required are all made by the physician. Consumers usually do not even determine where they will receive hospital care. The selection of a hospital depends largely on where the physician happens to hold staff positions and which hospital the physician prefers.

Consumer ignorance. Consumers are probably less informed about medical services than about anything else they buy. They usually can shop around, look, try, and compare goods and services they wish to buy. *Consumer Reports* publishes the results of testing certain products and provides valuable information that can serve as a guide to rational decision making by the customers. Almost no objective information is available concerning the quality of health services, however. Physicians are reluctant to give evaluations of the work of other physicians. Hospitals' and physicians' services generally are not subject to quality controls. Human errors, mistakes, and incompetencies in the supply of medical service may go undetected until it is too late for the individual buyer.

It is not a usual practice in the health field to disclose a list of prices for units of services. In many instances, consumers do not inquire about and do not know the prices of medical services until they receive their bills—at which time their choices are narrowed down to paying the bills or going to jail. The prices, quantities, and qualities of medical services are well-kept secrets to most consumers. The suppliers of health services have done little to change this situation.

Spillover benefits. In Chapter 3, on education, it was noted that benefits that flow to the specific users of goods and services are called direct benefits. As people use the goods and services, there may be indirect or social *spillover benefits* to other individuals.

The best illustration of social spillover benefits in health services involves communicable diseases. The use of medical services to get well from a disease that may spread to others directly benefits the user of the service and indirectly benefits others. Immunization shots benefit not only the person receiving the immunity from a disease, but the benefit extends beyond the individual user to others in society.

However, benefits from many medical services flow only to the individual users of these services. A heart or kidney transplant benefits primarily the individual receiving the transplant. The increased quantity and quality of medical services from the use of new equipment and intensive-care hospital rooms increases the chances of survival to the individual buyers of these services.

A "right" to good health. Most people regard good health as a "right." They believe that a sick person should have access to medical services regardless of income. This is why people are appalled when they hear on the radio, see on television, or read in the newspaper that a person in a serious accident or with a serious illness was refused admittance to a hospital because he or she did not have either money or health insurance to pay for the services needed. The basic idea that health services are essential needs and people have a right to receive them is consistent in American thought.[2]

Unpredictability of illness. Individuals and families, through budgeting, may carefully plan what goods and services they will buy, the quantities of each, and how much they will save. Some medical and health services can be planned for in this way, and others cannot. A family may plan to fulfill medical and health needs that are predictable, such as physical examinations or immunization

---

[2] Herbert E. Klarman, "Requirements for Physicians," *American Economic Review*, May 1951, p. 633.

shots, but it is difficult to plan for illnesses or accidents. For one thing, people do not usually like to consider the prospects of illness. Second, and more critical from the viewpoint of family planning, the incidence of illness is uneven and unpredictable for a family.

Voluntary health insurance provides a way for individuals and families with the desire and ability to pay for it to plan for and cover the major risks of illness or injury. The incidence of illness is predictable, and therefore insurable, for the population or large numbers of people. Private health insurance companies cannot provide full protection against exceptional or extremely high-cost illnesses, however. The consumer remains in general unprotected against prolonged and catastrophic illnesses or injuries.

HEALTH CARE PROBLEMS

The special characteristics of health services provide a good background for an understanding of the nature of health services. They do not, however, give rise to a unique set of problems. The major economic problems in the health care industry are those of efficiency in the supply of health services and equity in their distribution.

The public view

Most people seem to view the rising costs of health care as the major health care problem. It is certainly true that the costs of treatment of a given illness, hospital room and board, routine office visits, and other health care services have risen significantly—much faster than other goods and services in general. But are rising prices and costs necessarily the major problem? Rising prices for health care services may be only the symptom of a problem and, therefore, may not be the real problem at all.

The economist's view

Economists in general do not look upon the rising costs of any good or service as necessarily a problem. Changes in prices and quantities of individual goods and services bought and sold may reflect changes in demand and supply in the market. The total amount of money spent for individual goods and services increases when the demand and supply for these goods or services rise. There is no problem here. This is what is expected in a market economy.

However, the rising costs of health care may indicate or be a symptom of factors economists are concerned about, such as the restrictions on entry into the health care industry, the response of supply to demand changes, and the impact of government subsidies on the demand for health services. A central economic problem as seen by economists involves the efficient use of scarce resources in the health care industry. The analysis of demand for and supply of health services that follows provides a framework for an evaluation of the health care industry in terms of economic efficiency.

ANALYSIS OF DEMAND FOR HEALTH SERVICES

Elasticity of Demand

Consumers of certain health services, such as hospitals' and physicians' services, are not very responsive to price changes. An increase in price will not reduce the quantity demanded very much, and a decrease in price will not increase it much. In other words, the elasticity of demand for health care services is low, or inelastic.[3] However, the elasticity of demand for specific medical services may vary from one service to another. For example, the demand for a dangerous surgery may be almost totally inelastic (if price were zero, there would be no more takers than if the price were $10,000). On the other hand, the demand for a physical examination is likely to be more elastic.

The inelastic portion of demand is illustrated in Figure 10–5. An increase in price from p_1 to p_2 decreases quantity demanded from q_1 to q_2. When demand is inelastic, the percentage decrease in quantity demanded is less than the percentage increase in price. Suppose p_1 and p_2 are $4 and $5, respectively, for a visit to a doctor's office and that q_1 and q_2 are 10 visits and 9 visits, respectively, per month. An increase in price of 25 percent [(4 − 5)/4] causes the number of visits to the doctor's office to be reduced from 10 visits to 9 visits per month—a percentage decrease in quantity demanded of 10 percent [(10 − 9)/10].[4] The elasticity coefficient is 10 percent/25 percent, or 0.40, in this illustration. The price elasticity of demand is said to be inelastic when the elasticity coefficient is less than one.

---

[3]Herbert E. Klarman, *The Economics of Health* (New York: Columbia University Press, 1965), pp. 24–25.

[4]It should be noted that elasticity more precisely refers to the response of the quantity demanded to a small change in price and that the slope of a demand curve is not a reliable indicator of the degree of responsiveness of quantity demanded to price changes.

FIGURE 10–5
An inelastic portion of demand

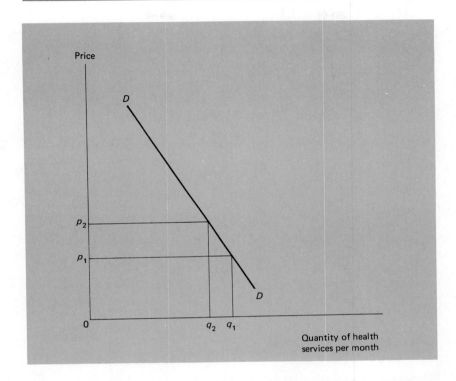

The inelastic portion of a demand curve is that over which a given percentage change in price results in a smaller percentage change in quantity demanded. For demand to be inelastic between prices p_2 and p_1, the percentage change from q_2 to q_1 must be smaller than the percentage change from p_2 to p_1.

Factors changing the demand for health services

Changes in per capita income. Rising per capita incomes in the United States have caused the demand curve for health services to shift to the right. This is illustrated in Figure 10–6. Increases in income cause the increases in demand from D to D_1 to D_2. The increases in price from p to p_1 to p_2, and the increases in quantity demanded from q to q_1 to q_2 are due to the rise in demand for health services.

Changes in tastes and preferences. Changes in consumer tastes and preferences also change demand. An increase in tastes and pref-

FIGURE 10–6
An increase in demand due to income growth

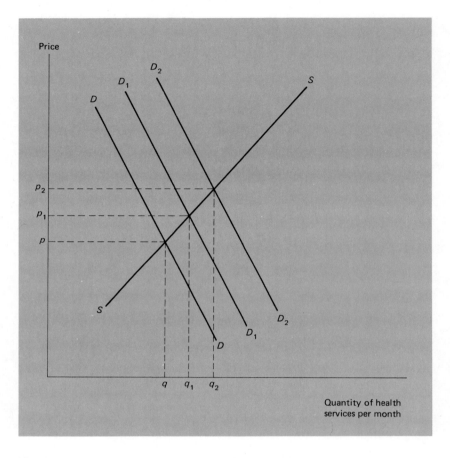

The demand curve is shifting outward because of increasing income and changing tastes and preferences. As a result, both the price and quantity demanded of health services are increasing.

erences for medical services increases demand for these services. This means that consumers are willing to buy larger quantities of medical services at every possible price. It cannot be said for certain, but an increase in tastes and preferences for medical care appears to have played at least a small part in stimulating the demand for health services.

Changes in relative price. Changes in the price of goods and services that may be substituted for medical services change the demand for medical services. For example, suppose the price of recreational services declines relative to the price of medical physical examinations. The effect of this will be to encourage consumers to substitute the less costly service for medical services, if this is feasible. The result is a decline in the demand for medical services. Since there are a limited number of substitutes for medical services, however, the demand for medical services is probably not appreciably affected by changes in relative prices.

Less than full-cost pricing. Consumers do not directly pay the full costs of health services. Direct consumer payments represent 25 cents out of each dollar spent for personal health; the remaining part of each dollar is paid by third parties—health insurance, private gifts, and government. The rise in the relative importance of third-party payments is shown in Figure 10–7. The impact of these third-party payments is to increase the demand for medical services. Consumers view medical care as a "good buy," since a dollar's worth of services may be bought for less than a dollar out of their own pockets. Of course, they have to pay the remainder of the full cost in the form of higher taxes and health insurance premium payments. A higher rate of consumption of goods and services will likely ensue when they are priced at less than full cost to the user.

Medicare and Medicaid. An important reason for the increase in demand for medical care and the rise in medical care costs has been the development since 1966 of two large government health programs—Medicare and Medicaid. The Medicare program covers the major costs of hospitals' and physicians' services provided to the aged under social security, and Medicaid pays for the costs of hospitals' and physicians' services provided to people who are poor. The combined cost of these two programs was $111 billion in 1985, paying for health care goods and services for about 50 million people, or about one fifth of the U.S. population. Medicare and Medicaid expenditures account for an important portion of the growth in medical costs in recent years. In the 15-year span from 1970 to 1985, for example, about one third of the increase in personal health costs was attributable to the rise in Medicare and Medicaid expenditures.

The growth in the cost of medical care due to Medicare and Medicaid is only one side of the coin. Health benefits are the other side. Many aged people now can receive adequate medical care because of Medicare, and many poor people can receive it under Medicaid.

FIGURE 10–7
Direct patient and third-party payments as a percent of personal health care expenditures in selected years, 1965–1985

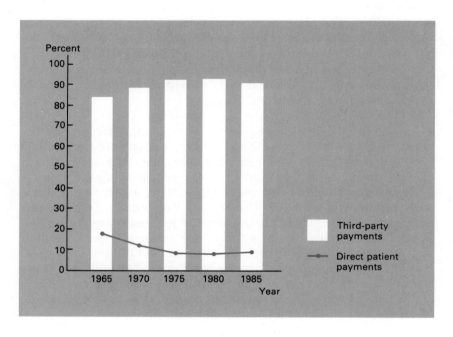

Source: Daniel R. Waldo, Katharine R. Levit, and Helen Lazenby, "National Health Expenditures, 1985," *Health Care Financing Review* 8, no. 1, (Fall 1986), p. 16.

Medicare and Medicaid are providing the means of payment for many who could not afford health care otherwise. By increasing demand, these two health programs have increased prices and the use of health services. In addition, the tradition among doctors of providing free medical care to the poor may be discouraged by the growth of government involvement in the health field. This tradition, however, perhaps was not the best way of assuring that the poor receive adequate health care.

ANALYSIS OF SUPPLY OF HEALTH SERVICES

Supply characteristics: Physicians

Source of supply. The main source of supply of physicians in the United States is American and Canadian medical schools. Among

TABLE 10–2
Number of physicians, nurses, hospital personnel, and short-term hospital beds for selected years, 1960–1983

Year	Physicians (per 100,000 population)	Nurses (per100,000 population)	Personnel (per 100 patients)	Beds (per 1,000 population)
1960	151	293	226	3.6
1965	155	321	246	3.9
1970	168	368	292	4.2
1975	187	466	339	4.4
1980	211	560	385	4.4
1983	228	600	414	4.4

Source: U.S. Department of Commerce, Bureau of the Census, *Statistical Abstract of the United States*, 1986, pp. 103 and 107.

the 20,600 newly licensed physicians in 1983, 15,800 graduated from American and Canadian medical schools, and 4,800, or 23.1 percent, graduated from foreign medical schools. The number of newly licensed physicians who received their education abroad reached a peak of 6,000 in 1975. In that year, over one third of the newly licensed physicians were trained in foreign medical schools. Since 1975, the number of physicians trained abroad has declined, falling to the 1970 level of 3,000 in 1981. However, this downward trend was reversed in 1982 and 1983 with newly licensed physicians receiving foreign medical education growing again, although remaining well below the peak level in 1975.[5]

Elasticity of supply. The supply of physicians is inelastic in the short run. Thus an increase in demand for physicians in the short run will have an impact primarily on prices. However, in the long run the supply curve of physicians is more elastic, and a rise in demand is expected to increase the number of physicians. After remaining approximately the same in the 1950s, the ratio of physicians to the population increased in the 1960s, 1970s and early 1980s.

Physician's income. The median income of physicians in unincorporated practices grew from $47,000 to $71,000 during the eight-year period between 1975 and 1983, or at an average annual growth rate of 6 percent. Physicians in incorporated practices have a substantially higher median income ($109,000 in 1983), but their median

[5]U.S. Department of Commerce, Bureau of the Census, *Statistical Abstract of the United States, 1986*, p. 109.

income grew at a slightly slower average annual pace during the same time span (5 percent). This growth in income and the relatively high income of physicians attracts foreign-trained physicians to this country to practice medicine and encourages more qualified people in this country to select medicine as a profession. Supply, then, has responded to the rising demand for physicians, but not fast enough to prevent rapidly rising prices for physicians' services. There are two reasons for this. We have mentioned one reason for the slow response of supply, namely the low elasticity of supply in the short run. The second is the restrictions on entry into the field of medicine. The first reason is a technical characteristic associated with the time it takes to train physicians. The second is a market defect attributable to the establishment of barriers to keep human resources out of the medical field.

Supply characteristics: Hospitals

The short-run supply curve of hospital services is the quantity of hospital services that will be supplied at different prices, given or holding constant the number of hospitals and hospital equipment, technology, and prices of hospital inputs. The long-run supply curve differs from the short-run curve in that hospital investment (hospital facilities and equipment) may vary in the long run. Changes in hospital investment, technology, and prices of inputs cause shifts in the short-run supply curve.

We expect the short-run supply curve of hospital services to be upward sloping, indicating that the greater quantities supplied are associated with higher prices to patients.[6] These higher quantities result in higher costs per unit because of the principle of diminishing returns. Given the fixed sizes and facilities of the hospitals, the application of more and more variable resources (nurses, medical personnel, supplies) will eventually result in smaller and smaller increases in output. These smaller increases in output associated with given increases in variable resources or inputs mean higher costs per unit. Higher costs of hospital services may eventually be encountered, also, if hospital size increases. A wider range of services and, thus, more costly services are often associated with large hospitals. In addition, there may be diseconomies connected with larger outputs, due to increasing complexities of management.[7]

---

[6]Some statistical studies indicate that the supply curve for hospital services may be perfectly elastic, indicating that additional quantities may be supplied at the same price. See Klarman, *The Economics of Health*, p. 105.

[7]Ibid., p. 107.

Factors affecting the supply of hospital services

Investment. An increase in hospital investment, that is, the construction of new hospitals, the expansion of existing hospitals, and the purchase of new equipment, increases the capacity of the hospital industry to provide hospital services. Hospital investment is a way to increase the supply of hospital services to meet the growing demand for these services.

Technology. Technological advancements increase the quantity and quality of hospital services. As a result of new technology, a greater quantity of the same services may be provided at lower prices, or new and better services may be provided at higher prices. New medical technology such as open-heart surgery, cobalt therapy, intensive care, and other new procedures and techniques usually result in both improved hospital care and higher hospital costs. Among the three specific sector factors (admissions per capita, input prices, and intensity per admission) explaining the growth in hospital costs, technological changes in the industry were a major cause for increases in these specific factors.

Wages and other costs. Hospitals are buying greater quantities of labor and medical supplies and are having to pay higher prices for these inputs. Unless higher wages and prices paid by hospitals are offset by increases in productivity, these increases represent the added cost incurred in producing the same amount of hospital services. In reference to supply, this means that the supply curve of hospital services shifts to left, indicating that the same quantities may be supplied only at higher prices.

EVALUATION OF THE U.S. HEALTH CARE SYSTEM

The U.S. health care system is under severe criticism. Herman M. Somers describes the system of health care in this country "as a technically excellent product thrown into a Rube Goldberg delivery contraption which distorts and defeats it, and makes it more expensive than it need be."[8] A committee reported to the Secretary of the Department of Health, Education, and Welfare that "the key fact about the health service as it exists today is the disorganiza-

---

[8]Herman M. Somers, "Economic Issues in Health Services," in *Contemporary Economic Issues*, rev. ed., ed. Neil W. Chamberlain (Homewood, Ill.: Richard D. Irwin, 1973), pp. 145–46.

tion . . . fragmentation and disjunction that promote extravagance and permit tragedy."[9]

The health care industry is not performing very well for two reasons: (1) entry into the industry is restricted, and (2) the industry is inefficiently organized.

Reducing entry barriers

Competition in the health care industry could possibly be restored and certainly encouraged by changing the admission practices of medical schools, by reducing the control of the American Medical Association (AMA) over the medical industry, by breaking up the influence of county medical societies, and by eliminating state licensing and examining procedures.

Admission practices of medical schools. The admission practices of medical schools check the supply of physicians and work to keep supply from catching up with the demand for physicians. Medical schools reject a high rate of *qualified* applicants. It was estimated in 1972 that half of the qualified applicants to medical schools were turned down.[10] To the extent that the high rejection rate of medical schools is due to limited capacity, a lowering of the rejection rate will require an expansion in medical school facilities.

Monopoly power of the AMA. The AMA virtually controls the supply of physicians. The source of this control is traced to the dominance of the association over medical education.[11] The AMA has controlled the number of medical schools by the use of its power to certify or fail to certify a medical school as a Class A rated school. The effects of its power to certify the quality of medical schools were never more in evidence than between 1906 and 1944, when the number of medical schools in the United States was reduced from 162 to 69. The AMA's dominance over medical education extends also to the internship and residency training programs. Its influence and power in this instance are due to the fact that it can approve or disapprove hospitals for administering internship and residency

---

[9]Ibid., p. 145.

[10]Charles T. Stewart, Jr., and Corazon M. Siddayao, *Increasing the Supply of Medical Personnel* (Washington, D.C.: American Enterprise Institute, 1973), p. 18.

[11]Reuben A. Kessel, "Price Discrimination in Medicine," in *Readings in Microeconomics*, 2nd ed., ed. William Breit and Harold M. Hochman (New York: Holt, Rinehart & Winston, 1971), p. 375.

programs. Hospitals strongly favor having interns and residency personnel because these resources are made available at prices below their productivity.[12]

Influence of county medical societies. County medical societies are private clubs which keep a close surveillance on their members. These societies have their own judicial system and may expel physicians from membership or refuse membership to physicians who do not act in the best interest of the group.[13] For example, physicians who reduce prices in order to expand business may be labeled "unethical" and expelled. Expulsion from the society may be tantamount to denying a physician access to the facilities of a hospital, for hospitals may require and usually prefer their staff to be members of the society.

State licensing systems. Physicians cannot practice in any state solely by virtue of having completed their medical education. Supported by the AMA, states require that physicians be examined and licensed before practicing medicine. Licensing and examining procedures can be an effective way of controlling the supply of physicians coming from abroad. Foreign-trained physicians and other medical personnel may be encouraged or discouraged from practicing medicine in this country by changes in the difficulty of the examinations and other costs associated with getting a license.

Summary. The supply of medical services, especially physicians' services, is kept artificially low by restrictions to entry imposed directly or indirectly by the AMA, county medical societies, and the state. Until barriers to entry are broken down, the supply of medical and health services will not be responsive to competitive market forces, and the services will not be supplied at competitive prices.

Increasing efficiency

Paramedical personnel. Paramedical personnel are medical personnel who have had less training than a doctor. The use of paramedical personnel to do some of the work that doctors usually perform can save the time of doctors, increase their productivity, reduce costs, and increase the supply of medical services.

---

[12]Ibid., p. 378.
[13]Ibid., pp. 379–80.

Although progress has been made in the use of auxiliary personnel, the idea of a lesser trained and lower paid doctor's assistant is not generally accepted.[14] Many patients prefer the expertise and the bedside manner of the licensed physician. This attitude could be changed by an education program pointing out the savings to the patient and the more efficient use of the physician's time. Health service jobs would have to be redefined so that the doctor's assistant could perform the job assigned as competently as the doctor could. One study indicates that the use of paramedical personnel could be doubled and the increase in productivity (output per physician) would be at least 20 percent.[15]

Group practice. The usual way of providing doctor's services is through a solo practice. A doctor receives an M.D. degree, obtains a license to practice medicine in a state, rents office space, buys furniture, supplies and equipment, puts up a sign, and goes to work. The chances are that business will be thriving in a short time. In some instances, a young physician may join the practice of an older one.

Solo practices are not usually efficient. Modern medical equipment may not be available and, if available, may not be fully utilized. A solo practice does not favor the maximum use of paramedical personnel and does not permit the pooling of human and capital resources. In contrast, group practices may permit better utilization of human and capital resources, as well as productivity gains from specialization and division of labor.

Group practices vary in size, type of legal organization (partnership, corporation), services provided, method of pricing, and method of financing. The one thing that is usually common to group practices is the sharing of costs and revenues.[16] A type of group practice that has attracted substantial support is a prepaid plan called a Health Maintenance Organization (HMO). Medical services are supplied for people in a certain area at fixed fees contracted for in advance. There is an incentive under the HMO for medical services to be provided at the lowest possible cost, since the net income of the organization varies inversely with the cost of providing medical services.

Hospital-based health center. An extension of the concept of a group practice is the health center. In the health-center concept pa-

---

[14]Stewart and Siddayao, *Increasing the Supply of Medical Personnel*, p. 41.
[15]Ibid., p. 43.
[16]Ibid., p. 44.

tients are tested, classified, and distributed to the area of the center that is best staffed and equipped to treat and cure them. Diagnostic tests could be handled by paramedical personnel. A computer could be used to classify patients as to the type of medical care needed and distribute them to center areas in accordance with their respective health needs.

An important role of a health center is to maintain a check on the quality of health care on its premises and throughout the community it serves.[17] Local health centers, nursing homes, first-aid stations, and clinics would be a part of the organizational structure of the health center. The center could have mobile health teams to provide advice and assistance to local health units and supply health services to areas that are without adequate health care personnel and facilities.

Health care centers can be organized and developed around the modern hospital.[18] This is logical, since the hospital is the focal point of health activities today. A hospital-based health center could mean that many hospitals in a given area would be under a single management. Each hospital could provide specialized health services. To cite a living example, in May 1975, eight hospitals in Hartford, Connecticut, joined together and formed a health consortium. Each of the eight hospitals that were highly diversified now specialized in certain services; they plan together, share facilities, and permit doctors to treat their patients in any hospital in the group. The benefits that are likely and expected from this new hospital group in the Hartford area are better hospital services and lower hospital costs.

Medical training time. It usually takes about eight years to become an M.D.—four years in college and four years in "med" school. A person who specializes, of course, receives training beyond the M.D. degree. It has been suggested that two years could be saved from the time it takes to become a doctor by admitting candidates to medical schools after three years of college and reducing the medical program to a three-year period.[19] Medical schools could thus turn out more doctors without expanding medical facilities. The supply of physicians would increase, and the price of physicians' services would thereby be reduced.

Summary. The efficiency of the present health care system could be greatly improved. This could be accomplished through the use of

---

[17]Somers, "Economic Issues," p. 149.

[18]Ibid., p. 149–50.

[19]Stewart and Siddayao, *Increasing the Supply of Medical Personnel*, p. 50.

paramedical personnel, the development of group practices and health centers, and the shortening of the period and cost of medical training. The survival of the system of health care as we know it today may depend on what improvements can be made in the supply and price of health services.

NATIONAL HEALTH INSURANCE

As a possible solution to some of the problems in the health care field, a national health insurance program has been proposed and discussed in and out of government for several decades. National health insurance, at one extreme, is regarded as a panacea; it is regarded as a bad omen at the other extreme. It is certainly no panacea. There are many issues connected with it, and many health care problems won't be completely solved by it. On the other hand, a national health insurance program doesn't necessarily mean "socialized medicine" in the pure sense as, perhaps, illustrated by programs in Sweden and England. The American version of socialized medicine could be uniquely American—a blend of private and public interest and support.

The goals envisioned by proponents of national health insurance can be summarized as follows: (1) to ensure everyone access to "adequate" health care, (2) to eliminate the financial burden connected with the acquisition of health services, and (3) to control and limit rising health care costs.[20] How to fulfill these goals is not clear. The goals may very well be in conflict. For example, it appears difficult, if not impossible, to limit the annual increases in health care costs while at the same time providing comprehensive and universal care. Several basic issues arise.

Basic issues

There are many issues involving national health insurance.[21] Among the important issues are these: *Who* will be covered? *What* will be covered? *How* will the plan be financed? *How much* will patients pay?

Who will be covered? Universal coverage means that the entire population is covered under a national health insurance program. A program that provides incomplete coverage could leave a part of the

---

[20]Karen Davis, *National Health Insurance: Benefits, Costs, and Consequences* (Washington, D.C.: Brookings Institution, 1975), pp. 2–5.

[21]Ibid., pp. 56–79.

population without access or much access to health care. A program that provides complete coverage includes both the part of the population that can afford to pay for health care and the part that cannot. The segment of the population that is of major concern is the part that cannot afford to pay for health services either because of generally low incomes or because of financial hardships associated with exorbitant medical care costs. People who can afford to pay for health care without relative financial hardship could be left with the responsibility of providing for their own health care. A difficulty with this approach is that the supply of health services to the poor is interrelated with the supply of services to the nonpoor.[22] Suppliers of health services may prefer and find it more profitable to meet the effective demand of people not covered under a national health insurance program.

A program of national insurance that provides universal coverage shifts almost the entire financial burden of health care costs to the government and redistributes income from taxpayers to the users of health services. Limiting coverage, say, to the poor, in combination with voluntary private health insurance plans for the relative nonpoor is an option to universal coverage. The benefits of this option are the reduced costs to taxpayers, and the costs are the benefits forgone that could have been associated with universal coverage.

What will be covered? There are many different kinds and a wide range of health services. *Comprehensive insurance coverage* includes almost all of them. In the determination of what will be covered under a national health insurance plan, the following priorities have been suggested: (1) medical services that have high social benefits such as immunizations and mental health care; (2) medical services that can be very expensive to the individual such as hospitalization, fees of specialists, and chronic illnesses; and (3) health services that are lower-cost substitutes for covered services, for example, services that could be rendered at the physician's office instead of in a hospital.[23]

It is difficult to draw the line as to the kinds of health services that are essential to good health and that should be covered under national health insurance. Most plans cover a wide range of services. Illustrations of health services that are usually not considered essential and are not covered are some dental services and cosmetic surgery.

---

[22]Ibid., pp. 56.
[23]Ibid., p. 58.

How will national health insurance be financed? National health insurance can be financed from premiums, payroll taxes, and general tax revenues. Unless premiums vary directly with income, premium payments are regressive; that is, they will be a smaller fraction of the income of high income patients than they will be of low income patients. Payroll taxes, as they are currently levied, would be less regressive than a fixed-premium payment, but they are also regressive on income groups above $15,000.[24] Financing an insurance scheme from state and federal general tax revenues could be made more equitable but would break the connection between individual benefits and costs that might otherwise exist. Most proposals rely on all three sources of revenue in varying degrees. Equity considerations would discourage the use of regressive methods of finance. Efficiency considerations would encourage the use of methods of finance that maintain a relationship between individual benefits and costs.

How much will patients pay? An important difference in national health insurance schemes is the extent that they vary in regard to direct payments by patients. Under health insurance schemes, direct payments by patients are generally in the form of deductibles and coinsurance provisions. A *deductible* is the amount that the patient pays of the cost up to some figure, and *coinsurance* is the fraction of the cost above the deductible that the patient pays. For example, if we assume the deductible is $100 and coinsurance is 10 percent, the total cost of a health care service of $400 would be divided between the patient and insurance as follows:

Paid by:	
Patient	$130
Deductible ($100)	
Coinsurance [30 (10% × 300)]	
Insurance	270
Total cost	$400

There are two advantages to patients paying part of the cost. The cost to the taxpayer is reduced, and the exorbitant use of health services is discouraged. The disadvantage is that deductibles and

[24]Joseph A. Pechman, *Who Paid the Taxes, 1966-85?* Brookings Institution (Washington, D.C.), 1985, p.56.

coinsurance provisions could prevent people who need it from receiving care. This disadvantage could be essentially removed by relating patients' share to the income of the patient. Also, cost ceilings could be established in regard to patients' cost. In a given year, for example, patients' cost could not exceed a given amount, say $500.

Alternative proposals to national health insurance

Congress has not found any national health insurance proposal acceptable enough to enact legislation. A more laissez-faire approach to the health-care industry is an alternative favored by the Reagan administration. There have been certain proposals, however, under the Reagan administration aimed at stemming the tide of rising health care costs. One proposal is the promotion of competition among providers and insurers through a system of financial incentives involving a *tax cap* and a *rebate*.

Under federal tax law, the cost of group health insurance plans is tax deductible to the employer and is not considered income to the employee. Thus, employers are encouraged to provide overly generous insurance plans that are highly favored by employees. The overall result is excessive insurance coverage and consumption of health care services. Under procompetition proposals as they are called, a tax cap or limit would be placed on the tax exclusion for employers. Another choice would be to establish a maximum level on the amount paid by the employer that the employee could exclude from income for tax purposes. The amount paid by the employers for health insurance above the maximum level would then be included as income by employees. This is the choice preferred by the current administration, for in the 1984 fiscal year budget a maximum level of $2,100 for family health insurance premiums was proposed.

Some procompetition proposals provide an incentive in the form of a cash rebate to employees who select a low-cost health insurance plan. Employers would contribute a given amount toward the payment of insurance premiums on various insurance plans. Employees that prefer cash, say, to higher benefit plans would choose a lower cost plan and receive a rebate equal to the employer's contribution and the low-cost plan. This rebate incentive, by encouraging the selection of health plans that would increase the price of health care services to users, would encourage consumers to be more efficient in the purchase of health care services. In addition, the rebate incentive would encourage private health insurance companies to offer consumers a wider range of health insurance plans.

Perhaps the most significant accomplishment of the Reagan administration is in regard to the implementation of proposals to stem the tide of rising costs of health services provided to the elderly and disabled under the federal Medicare program. Two actions taken in late 1982 to restrain the rise in Medicare costs were to place limits on inpatient hospital cost per admission, and to permit Medicare patients to enroll with health organizations that provide comprehensive services under a prospective payment system..[25] In 1983, the current retrospective reimbursement scheme was replaced with a prospective or prepayment system. Under the new system, hospital reimbursement payments are based on a predetermined fee schedule for diagnostic diseases. Incentives are provided to minimize costs under the new system, for losses are realized if hospital costs exceed the scheduled fees. In addition, a 15-month freeze was placed on physician fees in July 1984. These actions that have been taken thus far to reduce the growth in Medicare costs appear to have been successful, for Medicare hospital expenditures, after growing at an average annual rate of 27 percent between 1978 and 1985, grew at a rate of only 6.5 percent in 1986.

In summary, the alternative proposals to national health insurance and the implementation of some proposals may be steps in the right direction, but in general they may fall short of resolving the many issues in the health care industry.

A FINAL LOOK AT RISING HEALTH CARE COSTS

The issue of rising health care costs needs to be reexamined in light of what we have learned about the health care industry and the role of government. Rising health care costs reflect the increasing quantities and qualities of health care services supplied and demanded. Increasing prices for a unit of health care indicate that demand is rising faster than supply. The real issues are not that health care costs are rising but *why* they are rising and *what* should be done, if anything, to slow down costs.

Supply and demand analyses make it clear that there are two choices. Choice one is to increase the supply of health care services, and choice two is to reduce demand. Although these courses of action are clear, pursuing them creates issues also. We shall consider a reform approach.

---

[25]Robert M. Gibson, Katharine R. Levit, Helen Lazenby, and Daniel R. Waldo, "National Health Expenditures, 1983," *Health Care Financing Review*, Winter 1984, p. 22.

Supply approach

Suppose the health care ir ɪstry was a highly competitive industry. There would be many sellers competing with one another and all striving to combine resources so that any given output would be produced at the lowest cost. Then, each competitive seller would select an output that would maximize profits. Above-normal profits in the industry would attract more competitive sellers, thereby increasing the supply of health care services and lowering prices.

The health care industry does not fit the above description of a competitive industry. Most hospitals are not organized on a profit basis and often are controlled by another supplier, the physician. When there are several hospitals in a market—with some exceptions—they do not compete on a price basis; instead, they compete for physicians and for the latest capital equipment. In contrast to hospitals, physicians probably do behave in a profit-maximizing way. But, since the supplies of physicians and other medical personnel are controlled largely by monopolistic devices, there is little or no competition among the sellers of health care services.

Even though the health care industry is not a competitive industry, the possibility that the industry could be made more competitive should not be ruled out. First, the barriers to entry into the industry could be removed. Second, hospitals could be organized on a profit basis and/or profit-type organizations could be encouraged. Third, existing federal and state regulations that lessen competition could be eliminated. Fourth, information and advertising concerning prices, services, alternative treatments, and medications could be encouraged.

Some health economists believe that the health care industry would not perform very well even if the industry were a competitive one. There are certain problems that would not be resolved by a highly competitive health care industry, for example, the problems pertaining to externalities in the consumption of health care services, equity in the distribution of services, third-party payments, and high price inelasticity of demand and supply. Then it would seem that a realistic assessment of the industry precludes the likelihood that the issue of rising health care costs can be or will be resolved by fundamental changes in the structure of the health care industry, and, in general, precludes approaching the issue from the supply side.

Demand approach

If the real issue were rising health care costs, it would be rather easy to resolve this issue, at least in part, by reducing demand for health care services through eliminating or reducing government subsidies in-kind under the Medicare and Medicaid programs. It should be remembered, however, that these programs were developed based on the belief in equity in the distribution of health care services, and therefore, the matter of efficiency was considered to be of secondary importance. Even if these programs were cut or eliminated and the health care industry was made more competitive, there would be inefficiencies in the form of "excess" consumption of health care services because of private health insurance coverage. Both government and private health insurance lead to increased demands for health care services.

The effect of health insurance on demand. Suppose everyone in the United States has health insurance that covers one half of all health care costs. In Figure 10–8 the quantities demanded at different prices without health insurance are shown by D_o; the quantities demanded with health insurance are shown by D_1. Since it is assumed that health insurance pays one half of the price of each quantity consumed, D_1, which indicates the total price (the price paid by the consumer and the price paid by health insurance), shows a doubling of the price for each quantity over D_o. Now, at the price P_o and without health insurance, the quantities demanded and supplied would be q_o. But with health insurance the price to the consumer is reduced from P_o to P_1; hence, the quantity demanded increases from q_o to q_1. The total price, however, remains at P_o, with the consumer paying one half of P_o and the third party (health insurance) paying the remaining half. The effect of health insurance is to move consumers down their respective individual demand curves, resulting in an increase in market demand, that is, an increase in the quantity demanded at any given price. Also, it should be observed that at the quantity q_1 demanded and supplied, the consumer's marginal benefits are less than marginal costs, indicating an inefficient quantity.

Increase the price paid by the user. Based on the previous analysis of the impact of third-party payments (government and private health insurance), one way to slow down rising health care costs is to reduce quantity demanded by increasing the price that users have to pay for health care services. We know that if the consumer-user pays the full price there will be no "excess" consumption. The quantity of health care services provided under the Medicaid and Medicare programs could be regulated by changing the price paid by the users under these programs. Of course, this is tantamount to introducing the price system in part, at least, as the way to allocate resources. People in these programs who could not afford to pay the

FIGURE 10–8

The impact of health insurance on the demand for health care services

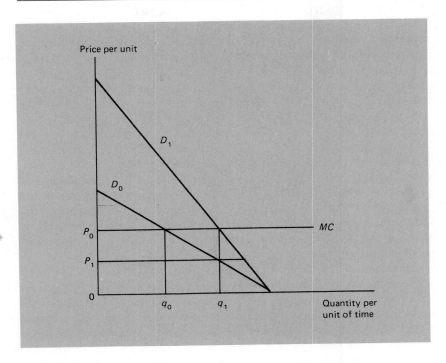

D_o shows the prices that an individual consumer will pay for different quantities of health care services. D_1 shows the combination price: the part paid by the consumer and the part paid by health insurance. At the price P_o the consumer, without insurance, will buy the quantity q_o; with insurance, the consumer will buy the greater quantity, q_1. At the quantity q_1 the consumer pays P_1 and insurance pays the difference between P_o and P_1.

price, as small as it might be, would be eliminated from the market. This would be the purpose of increasing the price to the user. To reduce the inequities that would arise, the price could be related to the income of the user.

Reform approach

It is generally agreed among health economists that little progress will be made in the improvement of the economic performance of the health care industry until the payment and delivery system is reformed. The traditional scheme is based on the fee-for-all service principle. Hospitals, physicians, and other providers are paid by users and third parties for services rendered. This scheme works well in most markets. However, this scheme is highly inefficient in a market where there are restrictions to entry, where demand is heavily subsidized, where sellers (primarily physicians) determine demand, and where users generally pay directly only a small part of the cost of services.

An alternative to the traditional system is a prepayment plan based on a negotiated schedule of fixed fees. Suppose that hospitals' and physicians' services are provided under a contract with the government, private organizations, and health insurance companies that specify the services to be provided and the cost. Under these arrangements, an incentive would be provided for services to be supplied in an efficient manner, for the net income of hospitals and physicians would depend on supplying services at a cost below the cost agreed on in the contract. Under the present system, suppliers have an incentive to provide more services, and often more services than are needed, since they are paid for the amount of services supplied whatever the amount may be.

There is a trend towards alternative payment and delivery schemes at the present time. It has been mentioned that the federal government has established a prospective payment system as the basis for reimbursement of hospitals for service provided to patients under the Medicare program. Private organizations are developing such as health maintenance organizations, primary care networks, and preferred provider organizations that are providing hospitals' and physicians' services under an alternative delivery system. Under health maintenance organizations, medical services are provided to people enrolled through a full-time group of physicians working with or working for the organization. The organization is responsible for the services provided and has an incentive to be cost conscious and to make sure that services are not provided in excessive quantities. In organizations referred to as primary care networks, participating providers typically have a fee schedule that the participating physicians are paid on a fixed per capita basis for the services provided. Sometimes the primary care physicians share the financial risk in the event that the plan exceeds the cost targets established for hospital and referral services. Preferred provider organizations are composed of a closed list of participating providers and typically have a fee schedule that the participating physicians and hospitals have agreed to accept for the services provided. A common feature of all of these organizations is a scheme that promises to represent a more efficient choice of the traditional arrangement based on the fee-for-service principle.

SUMMARY

The recent spectacular rise in the cost of medical care reflects growth in demand, slow response of supply, improvements in the quality of medical services, and the inefficient organization of the health care system. The growth in demand for health services is primarily due to the rise in per capita income in our society and the development of third-party payments. There are more people with more income who desire greater quantities of health care services and are willing to pay higher prices for them. Third-party payments, that is, payments for health care made by government and private health insurance companies on the behalf of people, have extended health care to more people and have encouraged the utilization of health services. Government payments for medical services have increased demand by providing the means of payment to people covered under Medicare and Medicaid. Prepaid voluntary health insurance reduces the out-of-pocket costs of medical care to the consumer and, consequently, increases the use of health services.

The impact of more people, higher income, and third-party payments on the prices of health services would be minimized if the supply of health services responded quickly to the rise in demand. However, supply has been slow to respond. It takes time to construct new hospitals and to train doctors, nurses, and other medical personnel. In addition, human resources cannot move freely into the health field because of restrictions on entry.

Medical services have improved in quality. New and better medical equipment has been introduced. New medical procedures and treatments are being used. A part of the rising cost of medical care, then, is due to the technically better product being supplied.

Increases in productivity can offset in part or entirely an increase in cost. Although the health care systems have had some increases in productivity, the system in general is inefficient. A great deal of progress cannot be made toward increasing the efficiency with which health services are supplied without major changes in the organization and structure of the health care system. A hospital-based health center is one type of organization within which health services may be supplied more efficiently.

It would be difficult to achieve all of the goals envisioned by the proponents of national health insurance, which are (1) to assure everyone access to adequate health care, (2) to eliminate the financial burden connected to the acquisition of health services, and (3) to control and limit the rise in health care costs. There are many national health insurance issues: Who will be covered? What will be covered? How will the plan be financed? How much will patients pay? It is doubtful that a national health insurance plan will be considered by the Reagan administration. A more laissez-faire approach to the health care industry is the alternative. Some of the procompetition proposals that have evolved under the Reagan administration could improve the economic performance of the industry such as the proposal to promote competition among providers and insurers through a system of financial incentives.

A final look at rising health care costs reveals that the most promising ways to slow down costs are to increase the price to the user and to reform the payment and delivery system. The effect of increasing the part of costs paid directly by users will be to reduce the quantities of health services demanded. A change in the payment and delivery system to the prepayment system based on fixed fees will encourage providers to be more efficient.

In conclusion, there are real problems associated with the supply and demand for health services. These problems are not going to disappear automatically. Although only symptomatic of the problems, rising health care costs will remain an important issue of the 1980s.

SUPPLEMENTARY READING

David, Daren. *National Health Insurance: Benefits, Costs, and Consequences.* Washington, D.C.: Brookings Institution, 1975.

A thorough examination of all aspects of national health insurance.

Feder, Judith; Jack Harley; and John Holahan. *Insuring the Nation's Health.* Washington, D.C.: The Urban Institute, 1981.

This monograph examines the implications of three national insurance bills before Congress in 1981—the Medical Expense Protection Plan introduced by Republican Congressman James Martin, Carter's National Health Plan, the Health Care for All Americans Plan supported by Senator Edward Kennedy and Congressman Henry Waxman.

Fuchs, Victor R. *Who Shall Live?* New York: Basic Books, 1974.

A well-written and thorough book that covers most aspects of health care.

Lindsay, Cotton M., ed. *New Directions in Public Health Care: A Prescription for the 1980s.* San Francisco: Institute for Contemporary Studies, 1980.

A collection of excellent essays concerning health care issues in the 1980s. Of special interest are essays written by Cotton M. Lindsay and Arthur Seldon on the health care systems in Britain and Canada and the essay by Congressman W. Philip Gramm and David Stockman, former Director of the Office of Management and Budget, on the Reagan administration's position concerning hospital cost containment.

Pauley, Mark V., ed. *National Health Insurance.* Washington, D.C.: American Enterprise Institute, 1980.

The major topics covered in this group of conference papers are under-insurance, overinsurance, financing national health insurance, and improving competition.

Russell, Louise B. *Technology in Hospitals: Medical Advance and Their Diffusion.* Washington, D.C.: Brookings Institution, 1979.

Examines in detail new hospital technologies. The conclusion reached is that technological changes do not explain the underlying causes of rising hospital costs.

Russell, Louise B. "Medical Care." In *Setting National Priorities: The 1984 Budget,* ed. Joseph A. Pechman. Washington, D.C.: Brookings Institution, 1983.

Chapter 5 evaluates the effects of legislative changes on medical care in the early 1980s. It also includes a discussion of the basic medicare problem and proposed solutions.

Russell, Louise B. *Is Prevention Better Than Cure?* Washington, D.C.: Brookings Institution, 1986.

Examines preventive health measures pertaining to smallpox and measles vaccination, screening and drug therapy for hypertension, and exercise. While preventive measures may improve health, they are not without cost and risks, and rarely reduce health care expenditures.

Salkever, David S., and Thomas W. Brice. *Hospital Certificate-of-Need Controls: Impact on Investment, Costs, and Use.* Washington, D.C.: American Enterprise Institute, 1979.

An empirical study of the impact of state regulations on hospital investment, use, and cost. The conclusion is that state regulations have not significantly reduced hospital investment or cost.

Part Two

DISTRIBUTION

OF

INCOME

POVERTY PROBLEMS

Poverty in terms of absolute income levels
  What is poverty?
  Who are the poor?
  The upward struggle of the poor
Poverty in terms of income distribution
  Income equality
  Income inequality
The economic causes of poverty
  Determinants of resource prices and
    employment
  Determination of individual or
    family income
  Determinants of income distribution
  Causes of differences in labor
    resource ownership
  Causes of differences in capital
    resource ownership
  Summary of the causes of poverty
Government attempts to alleviate poverty
  Government programs primarily
    for the poor
  Real growth and relative importance
    of low-income programs
  Evaluation of low-income
    programs
Negative income tax proposal
  The negative income tax
  Evaluation of the negative income tax
    scheme
Summary

Checklist of Economic Concepts

Income inequality
Demand for labor
Supply of labor
Wage rate determination
Determinants of income
  distribution
Ownership pattern of
  resources
Negative income tax

11

Poverty Problems

Is poverty necessary?

> The young today are just play-acting in courting poverty. It's all right to wear jeans and eat hamburgers. But it's entirely different from not having any hamburgers to eat and no jeans to wear. A great many of these kids—white kids—seem to have somebody in the background they can always go to. I admire their spirit, because they have a strong sense of social justice. But they themselves have not been deprived. They haven't experienced the terror. They have never seen a baby in the cradle crying of hunger . . .
>
> I think the reason for the gap between the black militants and the young white radicals is that the black kids are much more conscious of the thin edge of poverty. And how soon you can be reduced to living on relief. What you *know* and what you *feel* are very different. Terror is something you *feel.* When there is no paycheck coming in—the absolute, stark terror.[1]

"Poverty amidst plenty" is a striking feature of the American scene. Our nation is the richest in the world, yet millions of people are poor, and millions more that do not live in poverty are poor relative to others. This is not the American dream; it is the American paradox.

Poverty may be a more serious problem in our society than in societies with much less income and wealth. Poverty amidst poverty is easier to understand and even condone. But, in a land of abundance it is difficult to comprehend why some people are inade-

---

[1] Quote from Virginia in Studs Terkel, *Hard Times* (New York: Random House, 1970), p. 462.

quately fed, clothed, and sheltered. Poverty is a reality that needs to be studied, understood, appreciated, and then eradicated.

We approach our study of poverty in the United States in two ways. First, we examine poverty in reference to *absolute* income levels. This approach permits the identification of people who live below a designated poverty level of income. Second, we study it in terms of *relative* incomes, that is, the share or percent of national income that people receive.

POVERTY IN TERMS OF ABSOLUTE INCOME LEVELS

The poverty problem in the United States is essentially an income distribution problem. There is enough income to go around so that no one would have to live in poverty. But enough income does not go to everyone, and some people do live in poverty.

Figure 11–1 shows the trend in the poverty rate or the incidence of poverty between 1960 and 1985. In 1960, 22.2 percent of the population, or 39.9 million people, officially lived in poverty. The poverty rate fell steadily between 1960 and 1978, reaching a low of 11.4 percent in 1978 before turning upward again. The poverty rate increased to 14 percent in 1981, a recession year. The economic expansion that began in 1982 did not bring the incidence of poverty down; the poverty rate in 1985 was the same as it was in 1981. In 1985, 33.1 million people were classified as poor.

What is poverty?

Poverty is not easily defined. Yet, a precise definition has been implied in the statement that many Americans are poor. We shall use the definition of poverty developed by the government.

Poverty is concerned with the relationship between the minimum needs of people and their ability to satisfy those needs. The difficulty with any definition of poverty involves the meaning of "minimum needs" and the amount of money required to satisfy these needs. The approach taken by the government is essentially, first, to determine a minimum food budget and the money cost of that budget. Second, the cost of the food budget is multiplied by three because the cost of food represents about one third of consumer spending, according to studies of consumer spending patterns. For an illustration, $3,663 represents the cost of the minimum food budget for a family of four. The cost of food times three equals $10,989, the official poverty level for this size family in 1985. Poverty levels as defined for different family sizes are listed in Table 11–1.

FIGURE 11–1
Poverty rate in selected years, 1960–1985

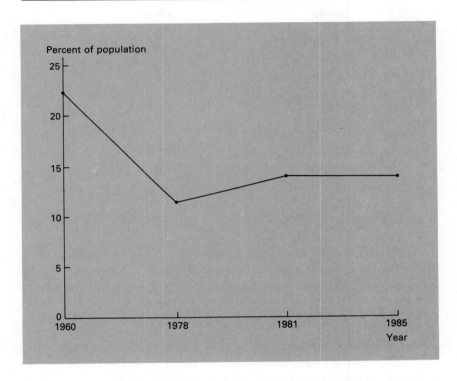

The poverty rate decreased from 22.2 percent of the population in 1960 (39.9 million people) to 11.4 percent in 1978 (24.5 million people). Then, the poverty rate increased to 14 percent in 1981—a recession year. In 1985, the poverty rate was the same as was in 1981 with 33.1 million people living in poverty.

Source: U.S. Department of Commerce, Bureau of the Census, Current Population Reports, *Consumer Income,* Series P–60, No. 124, p. 1, No. 145, p. 10, No. 149, p. 3.

Who are the poor?

In 1984, 7.3 million, or 11.6 percent of all families lived in poverty (Table 11–2). The incidence of poverty is much higher than this among certain family groupings: black families, young families, large families, and families where the head of the family is female, uneducated, unemployed, or not in the labor force. Among the 6.8 million black families in 1984, over 2 million lived in poverty. An easy way of remembering the extent of poverty among black families is to keep in mind that about one black family out of three is living below the poverty level.

TABLE 11–1
Poverty threshold levels in 1984

Family size	Poverty threshold level
1	$ 5,278
2	6,672
3	8,277
4	10,609
5	12,566
6	14,207
7	16,096
8	17,961
9 or more	21,247

Source: U.S. Department of Commerce, Bureau of the Census, Current Population Reports, *Consumer Income*, Series P–60, No. 145, p. 31.

The incidence of poverty is also extremely high for families when the age of the family head is between 15 and 24, when the size of the family is seven or more persons, when the head of the family has less than eight years of schooling, and when the family head is unemployed. In all of these cases, the poverty rate is 25.5 percent or higher.

An important aspect is the rise of high poverty rates in family groupings that are headed by women. The highest incidence of poverty is found in families headed by a black female; over half of these families live in poverty. Poverty rates are also very high in white, female-headed families (27.1 percent). The feminization of poverty is revealed further in the comparison of male and female family groupings. Over a third of the families headed by a female live in poverty, whereas only 13 percent of the families headed by a male live in similar conditions.

The upward struggle of the poor

It is often stated that a person living in poverty today will likely live in poverty in the future. The main argument is that a poor person becomes "trapped" and has little chance of breaking out of the economic conditions that put him or her there in the first place. Furthermore, some believe that a poor person does not have the motivation to advance and is even encouraged to retain a low economic status by low-income support programs of the government. There has been little research on the upward mobility of the poor. The

TABLE 11–2
Selected characteristics of families living below the poverty level in 1984

Characteristics	Total families (000)	Families below poverty	
		Number (000)	Percent
All families	62,706	7,277	11.6%
White	54,400	4,926	9.1
Black	6,778	2,094	30.9
Sex of family head:			
Male (no wife present)	2,229	292	13.1
Female (no husband present)	10,139	3,498	34.5
Male—white	1,817	189	10.4
Female—white	6,929	1,878	27.1
Male—black	344	82	23.8
Female—black	2,965	1,533	51.7
Age of family head:			
15–24	3,127	919	29.4
65 and over	9,806	713	7.3
Size of family:			
2	25,349	2,283	9.0
4	13,259	1,516	11.4
7 or more	1,229	414	33.8
Education attainment of family head:			
Less than 8 years	4,117	1,040	25.5
High school, 1 to 3 years	7,488	1,469	19.6
High school, 4 years	21,629	2,056	9.5
College, 1 year or more	22,268	1,075	4.8
Employment status of family head:			
Employed	43,921	2,853	6.5
Unemployed	2,536	879	34.7
Not in labor force	15,537	3,526	22.7

Source: U.S. Department of Commerce, Bureau of the Census, Current Population Reports, *Consumer Income*, Series P–60, No. 149.

exception to this is a 10-year longitude study of family status conducted at the Survey Research Center of the University of Michigan. The findings of this study are reported in a book entitled *Years of Poverty, Years of Plenty.*[2]

A major finding in the Michigan study is that there is an amazing amount of turnover in the low-income population. "Only a little over one half of the individuals in one year are found to be poor in the next" year.[3] In addition, only a minority of people who live in

[2]Greg J. Duncan, *Years of Poverty, Years of Plenty* (Ann Arbor, Michigan: Institute for Social Research, the University of Michigan, 1984).
[3]Ibid., p. 3.

poverty remain in poverty over a long period of time. It is concluded, also, that attitudes are not the causal explanation why some people live and remain in poverty.

The study referred to above covered a period of time (1968–79) when the poverty rate was declining. It would be expected that the upward mobility of the poor would be reduced in recent years with the increase in the number of people living in poverty. However, Greg J. Duncan, the major author of *Years of Poverty, Years of Plenty*, is confident that findings of the Michigan study will prevail in the future.[4] Assuming this is so, a high turnover among the poor does not resolve the poverty issue, although it does provide a more hopeful outlook concerning this important issue.

POVERTY IN TERMS OF INCOME DISTRIBUTION

The second approach to poverty considers the distribution of income in the United States. We have said that the poverty problem in this country is mainly one of income distribution. This means that the level of income in our country is high enough so that a more equal distribution of income should mitigate the poverty problem and reduce its significance.

Income equality

Economists usually explain income equality and income inequality by reference to a curve called a Lorenz curve, after M. O. Lorenz. Income equality among families means that any given percent of families receive an equal percent of family income: 10 percent of families receive 10 percent of income, 20 percent of families receive 20 percent of income, and 100 percent of families receive 100 percent of income. In Figure 11–2, equal percentages of families and incomes can be measured along the two axis. Income equality is shown by a 45-degree line starting at the origin. At any point on the 45-degree line, the percent of families shown receive an equal percent of total family income.

Income inequality

Income inequality can be illustrated graphically by lines that deviate from the line of income equality. A Lorenz curve derived from actual data on income distribution will usually lie to the right of the line of

---

[4]Ibid., p. 7.

FIGURE 11–2
Lorenz curve plotted with data on U.S. family income, 1984

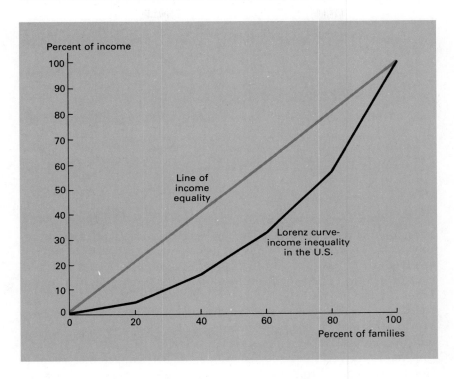

The Lorenz curve shows the degree of income inequality. The horizontal axis measures the percent of families, starting with the poorest. Thus, the 20 percent mark represents the lowest earning fifth of the population. In 1984, the lowest 20 percent earned 4.7 of the total income, and the lowest 40 percent earned 15.7 percent. This means that the second quintile (the families between the 20 percent and 40 percent marks) earned 11 percent of the total income (15.7 − 4.7). If perfect income equality existed, the Lorenz curve would be the 45-degree line.

Source: U.S. Department of Commerce, Bureau of the Census, *Statistical Abstract of the United States, 1986*, p. 452.

income equality (the 45-degree line). The further to the right of the 45-degree line it lies, the greater the inequalities in income distribution. Lorenz curves are useful in making income distribution comparisons in a given year among different countries or in the same country over time.

Table 11–3 divides U.S. families into five numerically equal groups, or quintiles, and indicates the distribution of personal income among these groups. The table also shows the income share

TABLE 11–3
Percent of income received by each fifth and the top 5 percent of families,
1960–1984

Quintile of families	1960	1965	1970	1975	1980	1984
Lowest fifth	4.8%	5.2%	5.4%	5.4%	5.0%	4.7%
Second fifth	12.2	12.2	12.2	11.8	11.3	11.0
Third fifth	17.8	17.8	17.6	17.6	17.4	17.0
Fourth fifth	24.0	23.9	23.8	24.1	24.4	24.4
Highest fifth	41.3	40.9	40.9	41.1	41.9	42.9
	100.0%	100.0%	100.0%	100.0%	100.0%	100.0%
Top 5 percent	15.9%	15.5%	15.6%	15.5%	15.4%	16.0%

Source: U.S. Department of Commerce, Bureau of the Census, *Statistical Abstract of the United States,* 1982, p. 435; U.S. Department of Commerce, Bureau of the Census, *Consumer Income, Current Population Report,* Series P–60, No. 149, p. 11.

of the top 5 percent of families. It can be observed that income is very unequally distributed. The highest 20 percent of families received 42.9 percent of income in 1984, and the lowest 20 percent received 4.7 percent. The top 5 percent of families received 16.0 percent of income. These data on income inequality are shown by the Lorenz curve in Figure 11–2.

Income inequality was reduced during the 1930s and the years of World War II. The share of income received by the top 5 percent and the highest 20 percent decreased between 1929 and 1944, while the share received by the lowest 20 percent of families increased. It is generally agreed that the two main reasons for this trend toward greater income equality were that property income fell drastically during the Great Depression of the 1930s, and the gap between low-paid and high-paid workers was reduced when full employment was reached during World War II.[5]

During the last few decades, the income shares of the low, middle, and high income groups have changed surprisingly little or not at all. The percent of income received by the lowest 20 percent of the families did increase from 4.8 percent in 1960 to 5.4 percent in 1970 but decreased to 4.7 percent in 1984. The highest 20 percent of the families in terms of income groupings lost income relative to others in the 1960s but started gaining in the 1970s, and ended up with 42.9 percent in 1984. The middle income family groupings received about the same percent of income in 1984 as they had two

---

[5]Joseph A. Pechman, "The Rich, the Poor, and the Taxes They Pay," *The Public Interest,* no. 17 (Fall 1968).

decades before. The income share of the top 5 percent of the families was 16 percent in 1984 as compared to their income share of 15.9 percent in 1960.

THE ECONOMIC CAUSES OF POVERTY

Determinants of resource prices and employment

Family incomes depend on the quantities of resources that families can place in employment and the prices received for those resources. To understand poverty, then, it is important to understand what determines the prices paid for human and capital resources and what determines the quantities that can be employed.

Wage rate determination. Under competitive market conditions, the basic principle of wage rate determination is that units (person-hours) of any kind of labor tend to be paid a price equal to any one worker's (hourly) contribution to an employer's total receipts. In other words, workers are paid about what they are worth to employers. What a worker is worth to an employer is referred to by economists as the worker's marginal revenue productivity. Suppose the marginal revenue productivity of the worker is $4 per hour; that is, an hour of labor is contributing $4 to the receipts of the employer. Then the worker is worth $4 an hour to the employer and would be paid that amount under competitive conditions. If a worker were paid less than what she or he is worth to an employer, the worker would also be paid less than she or he would be worth to *other* employers. Consequently, other employers would bid for the worker's services, driving the worker's wage rate (hourly wages) up to what she or he *is* worth. On the other hand, rather than pay $5 an hour, an employer would lay a worker off.

This principle can be seen more clearly with reference to Figure 11–3. The demand curve for labor (*DD* in the figure) shows what employers are willing to pay at different quantities of labor (worker-hours per month), or alternatively, how much a unit of labor is worth at different possible employment levels. The supply curve for labor (*SS* in the figure) shows the quantity of labor that will be placed on the market at different wage rates. Labor is paid less than it is worth at the wage rate w_o. Only q_o units of labor want to work at this wage rate. However, at this employment level, labor is worth w_2 to any employer. Thus, a shortage exists; that is, at the wage rate w_o, the quantity of labor demanded is greater than the quantity supplied, and the wage rates will be driven up to w_1. Labor is paid

FIGURE 11–3
Wage rate determination under competition

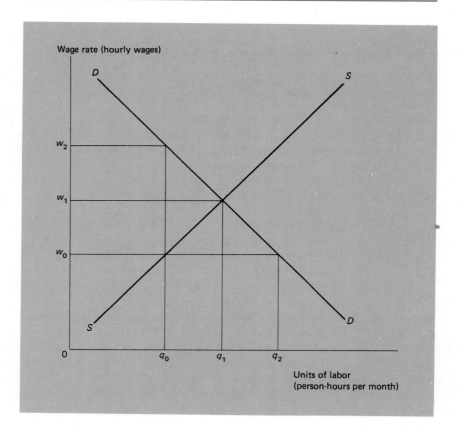

about what it is worth at w_1. At a wage rate above w_1, however, the quantity of labor supplied is not worth that wage to employers. A surplus exists; that is, the quantity of labor supplied is greater than the amount demanded. Thus the wage rate will return again to w_1.

The price of capital. In a competitive market the price of a unit of capital, say a machine, is determined in a way similar to the price of a unit of labor. The price of any kind of capital depends on the demand for and supply of units of capital, and, at market equilibrium, the price of capital equals what that capital is worth to its employer.

Determination of individual or family income

The income of a person depends on the *price* he or she receives for his or her resources, labor and capital, and the *quantities* of resources he or she can place in employment. For example, the monthly family income from labor equals the quantity of its labor employed, multiplied by the wage rate. From capital, its income equals the quantity of capital employed, multiplied by the price of each unit of capital. Total monthly family income, then, is a summation of the two monthly income flows.

Determinants of income distribution

The distribution of income among individuals and families depends on the distribution of resource ownership and the prices paid for resources of different kinds in different employments. The ownership pattern of resources is unequally distributed among individuals and families. This unequal ownership pattern of resources gives rise to an unequal distribution of income in our society. People at the bottom of the income ladder own a small share of the nation's resources on which the market places a high value.

Causes of differences in labor resource ownership

Brains and brawn. The inheritance of mental and physical talents is not equally distributed among people. Some people have greater capabilities than others. Some families' labor resources have exceptional learning abilities; others' labor resources have special talents— acting, singing, playing baseball or football. Other families are not so fortunately endowed.

Skill levels. Skill levels vary among individuals. Differences in skills among people are primarily due to differences in inherited capabilities, training opportunities, and discrimination. Some inherit specific abilities to do certain tasks better than others. Most often people with high skill levels have acquired them from their training and education. In some instances, people have low skill levels because they have been discriminated against and have not had equal opportunities for training and education. Even with the same training, certain groups, say women, may not receive the same pay as others, although they perform the same tasks. In general, those with highly developed skills are worth more and, therefore, are paid more in the market than are unskilled or semiskilled workers.

Capacity utilization rate. The capacity utilization rate is the ratio of actual earnings to earnings capacity. Utilization rates differ among people for many reasons. Among these reasons are differences among people with respect to their preferences for income and leisure, and with respect to their responsiveness to changes in their income due to, say, taxes and government transfer payments. Also, some people, such as working wives, may have low utilization rates because of certain labor supply barriers. Garfinkel and Haverman found that the major cause of income inequality is due to differences in earnings capacity among people, and that not more than 20 percent of income inequality can be explained by differences in capacity utilization rates.[6]

Causes of differences in capital resource ownership

Inheritance. Some individuals and families inherit real property and claims on real property such as stocks and bonds. These people have a head start on those who do not begin with inherited capital resources.

Luck. Luck is not evenly distributed among the population. Some families may be at or near the bottom of the income pyramid because of bad luck. A business failure caused by a depression, a prolonged illness, a fatal accident, or a natural disaster may leave persons and families without income or the ability to earn an adequate income.

Propensities to accumulate. People vary as to their propensities or tendencies to save and accumulate capital resources. Those who are strongly motivated are willing to forego consumption today in order to enjoy greater income in the future. Others are more concerned about their current consumption standards. They do not save and do not accumulate capital resources.

Summary of the causes of poverty

Several things are clear about the poor and about low-income families. They have small quantities and low qualities of resources. The market places a low value on the services they provide in the mar-

---

[6]Irwin Garfinkel and Robert H. Haverman, *Earnings Capacity, Poverty, and Inequality* (New York: Academic Press, 1977), p. 39.

ket. The low productivity and, therefore, the low pay of the poor are due to low levels of training and education, misfortune, relatively small inheritances, and discrimination. The poor are in a vicious circle that is difficult to escape. What they need in order to move out of poverty they do not have and cannot afford to acquire. So they remain poor.

GOVERNMENT ATTEMPTS TO ALLEVIATE POVERTY

Two approaches to poverty are suggested by the foregoing analysis. First, the productivity of the employable poor can be increased. This can be accomplished through subsidized education of the children of the poor, adult training and education programs, counseling and guidance, job placement programs, and the elimination of discrimination. Second, a minimum annual income can be guaranteed. This is essential if no one is to live in poverty. Some people, such as the very young, the very old, the disabled, and the ill, are poor because they cannot produce at all, and others are poor because they cannot produce enough. Income-support programs are required to aid those who are unproductive and those who have low productivity.

Government programs primarily for the poor

Federal government programs that seem to have the most to do with attempting to alleviate poverty in a major way are enumerated in Table 11–4. These programs were selected essentially on the basis that more than half of the outlays benefit people in low-income groups, and in some instances 80 percent or more of the outlays will be for the purpose of easing the pain of poverty. Outlays that are not included in the total may benefit low-income groups, such as some federal aid to college students and some veterans' benefits. However, since some of the outlays on the programs selected may not go to those living in poverty, the estimate of federal spending on programs for the poor may be overestimated if anything.

Training and employment. The federal training and employment program is in the form of grants to states for the purpose of assisting people, such as displaced persons, who have the greatest difficulties in the job market. The program includes subsidized jobs for youth in the summer and the operation of the Employment Service. Under the Job Training Partnership Act (JTPA), states have the major responsibility for the program; however, JTPA requires that a major portion of the block grant be used for training the economi-

TABLE 11–4
Federal government programs primarily for low–income groups in selected
fiscal years, 1980–1988 (in billions)

Program	1980 (actual)	1986 (actual)	1987 (estimate)	1988 (estimate)
Training and employment	$10.3	$5.3	$5.0	$ 5.2
Social services	6.1	7.2	7.5	7.9
Health care services (primarily Medicaid)	18.0	28.8	32.0	31.5
Housing assistance	5.6	12.4	12.9	13.4
Food and nutrition assistance (primarily food stamps)	14.0	18.6	19.4	18.6
Other income security (primarily aid to the blind, aged, disabled and to families with dependent children)	17.2	24.4	25.5	26.8
Total outlays	$71.2	$96.7	$102.3	$103.8

Source: Office of Management and Budget, *Budget of the United States Government,* fiscal year
1988, pp. 5–22, 5–24.

cally disadvantaged and that welfare recipients be treated fairly. The
federal training and employment program was cut from $10.3 billion
in 1980 to $5.3 in 1986 and is estimated to remain at this lower level
in 1987 and 1988.

Social services. The Federal program of social services is a program of grants to states and local and private institutions. The poor,
elderly, disabled, children, youth, and Native Americans are the
beneficiaries of a variety of social services that include day care,
child welfare, foster care, and child abuse intervention. The program
of social services increased about $1 billion between 1980 and 1986,
reaching $7.2 billion in 1986. The projection is for the cost of this
program to reach $7.9 billion in 1988.

Health care services. The major program under the heading of
health care services is the Medicaid program. Medicaid accounts for
about 85 percent of the federal outlays for health care services. Medicaid pays for a major part of the cost of hospital care, physician
care, and other health care services for people living in poverty. In
1987, 23.6 million poor Americans received health care under the
jointly financed federal and state Medicaid program with the federal
government paying $25.9 billion and states paying $21.3 billion. The
cost of all federal health care services more than doubled between
1980 and 1986, soaring to $28.8 billion in 1986. These services are
estimated to top $30 billion in 1987 and 1988. New government pol-
icy proposals have been made to slow down the cost of health care

services especially in regard to Medicaid. Under the proposals, states would be encouraged through fiscal incentives to initiate an optional capitation program that would place Medicaid beneficiaries into Health Maintenance Organizations. Additionally, it has been proposed that a limit be placed on the growth of federal Medicaid payments.

Housing assistance. Federal housing assistance takes two forms. Historically, federal housing assistance to low-income families has been in the form of construction subsidies, that is, subsidies to finance housing units for low or near low-income families in urban and rural areas. More recently, under the Reagan Administration, more emphasis has been placed on housing assistance in the form of housing vouchers. The major problem faced by most low-income households is not a lack of housing units but a lack of income to afford decent housing. Housing assistance in the form of vouchers addresses this problem directly, and provides low-income families with the opportunity to choose among public and private-owned rental units. Federal outlays on housing assistance jumped from $5.6 billion in 1980 to $ 12.4 billion in 1986, and is estimated to reach $13.4 billion in 1988 (Table 11-4). Over 6 million households or about 18 million people received housing assistance in 1986.

Food and nutrition assistance. Approximately 70 percent of the federal outlays on food and nutrition assistance is in support of the federal food stamp program. An estimated 19.5 million people will receive food stamps each month in 1987 at a cost of about $12 billion. Food stamps enable low-income households to purchase food and maintain a nutritious diet. In addition to the food stamp program, meals are subsidized for children in schools, child care facilities, and other institutional settings under the child nutrition program. This program will cost about $5.8 billion in 1987 and benefit 12.7 million young Americans. The total outlays for the programs mentioned above and for other food and nutrition assistance increased from $14 billion in 1980 to $18.6 billion in 1986. It is estimated that these outlays will be in the range of $18.6 to $19.4 billion in 1987 and 1988.

Other income security. Other income security includes federal programs traditionally known as public assistance: namely, aid to the blind, disabled, and aged who are poor, and aid to poor families with dependent children (AFDC). The official name for aid to the blind, aged, and disabled is supplemental security income (SSI). The aid for both SSI and AFDC is in the form of cash payments. These payments are intended to help the eligible poor maintain a subsistence living standard. However, to be eligible, a person has to be not only poor but has to be also either blind, old, disabled or be a member of a family headed by a female with children. When someone says that a person or family is on welfare, he usually has reference to SSI or AFDC. It is estimated that in 1987 there will be 4 million needy blind, aged, and disabled persons. The cash payments to these people are expected to be $10.5 billion in 1987. In the same year, about 3.7 million are estimated to receive AFDC benefits, with the cost of these benefits and the benefits from child support enforcement estimated at $8.9 billion. Other income security programs include the earned income tax credit program and the low-income energy assistance program. With the earned income tax credit, wage earners (with children) that earn less than $11,000 may receive tax credits. A cash payment is made to these wage earners when earned tax credits exceed tax liabilities. Total federal outlays on all programs listed under the heading of other income security increased from $17.2 billion in 1980 to $24.4 billion in 1986, an average annual growth rate of 7 percent. In 1987 and 1988, total outlays are estimated to grow slightly over $1 billion in each of these two years.

Real growth and relative importance of low-income programs

Federal outlays on low-income programs examined above totaled $71.2 billion in 1980. Between 1980 and 1986, federal outlays for these programs grew $25.5 billion or 36 percent. It is estimated that federal outlays primarily for poor people will exceed the $100 billion mark in 1987. These data may suggest to some that a poor person is better off today than in the past. However, this is not necessarily the case. Two adjustments to these data should be made. The first one is to adjust for the rate of inflation, and the second one is to adjust for the growth in the number of poor people. Also, it is interesting to discover the changes that may have incurred in the relative importance of low-income programs. This can be done by expressing outlays on low-income programs as a percent of total federal outlays over time.

Real growth in low-income programs. The rate of inflation between 1980 and 1986 was 30.2 percent. Thus, almost all of the growth in federal spending on programs for the poor was due to inflation. In constant prices or in real terms, the growth in spending was $2.1 billion, an increase of only 2.9 percent over the six-year period. However, there were about 4 million more poor people in 1986 than in 1980. The average dollar amount given to a poor person in 1980 was $2,430; whereas, the dollar payment per poor person in constant 1980 prices was $2,215 in 1986.

FIGURE 11-4

Federal outlays on poverty programs as a percent of total federal outlays in
selected fiscal years, 1980–1988

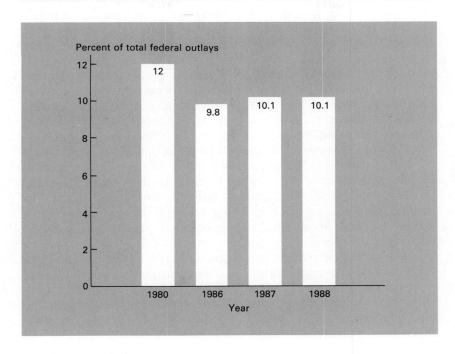

Source: Office of Management and Budget, *Budget of the United States Government*, fiscal year
1988, pp. 5–22, 5–24.

Relative importance of low-income programs. Figure 11-4
shows federal outlays on low-income programs as a percent of total
federal budget outlays in selected years. The relative importance of
these programs fell between 1980 and 1986 and are slated to stay
about the same in relative importance in 1987 and 1988. In 1980,
spending on these programs accounted for 12 percent of the total
federal budget as compared to 9.8 percent in 1986. The estimated
spending share on low-income programs is set at 10.1 percent in
1987 and 1988.

Evaluation of low-income programs

Federal programs designed for low-income groups should have two
major goals. The first goal is to provide a minimum living standard
for people who otherwise would live below the minimum. The sec-

ond goal is to provide the opportunity for those currently living in poverty to move out of poverty, and, at the same time, provide the opportunity for people currently not living in poverty to remain living above the poverty level. Most of the programs examined seem to be directed towards trying to accomplish the first goal. Federal health care services, housing assistance, food and nutrition assistance, and other income security are programs that account for over four fifths of the outlays on low-income programs. They are intended primarily to provide income support either in-kind or in cash to the poor or near-poor people. If 80 percent of the low-income federal budget were allocated equally among persons estimated to live in poverty in 1987, each would receive financial support of about $2,400. A family of four would be able to have a living standard equal to the money cost of $9,600, which would be reasonably close to the official threshold poverty level. Thus, it appears that the first objective of low income programs is close to being reached. However, the same cannot be said about the second objective which is equally as important.

The second goal may be more difficult to reach than the first goal. It seems that it is more difficult to design programs that will enable poor people to move out of poverty than it is to mitigate the hardships of poverty through in-kind and cash payments. About the only way to increase upward mobility of the poor and prevent downward mobility is through training and education. Training and educational programs may not appeal to everyone living in poverty. Some poor individuals may not be able to take advantage of them, and some may not desire to take advantage of them. Federal spending on training and employment programs were cut in half between 1980 and 1986, reflecting failures and disappointments in these programs.

In conclusion, government programs for the poor should be constantly evaluated in order to find out how they may be improved. Reforms and alternative proposals should be considered. An efficient reform does not mean that a program will be necessarily eliminated or outlays on it reduced. Instead, it means that the program will be changed so that the benefits per dollar spent are higher.

NEGATIVE INCOME TAX PROPOSALS

In this final section, we examine the negative income tax proposal. First, we present the essential features of this reform proposal, followed by an evaluation of the negative income tax proposal.

The negative income tax

There are three variables common to every negative income tax scheme. These variables are the guaranteed level of income, the tax rate on earned income, and the break-even level of income. In the example in Table 11–5, the guaranteed level of income is $6,000, and the tax rate on earned income is 50 percent. The break-even level of income, that is, the level of earned income at which the negative tax payment or cash payment is zero, is $12,000.

The relationship among these variables may be seen from the formulas $Y = rB$, $r = Y/B$, or $B = Y/r$, where

Y = Guaranteed annual income
r = Tax rate on earned income
B = Break-even level of income

It may be observed in the table that the negative tax payment varies inversely with earned income. A family with earned income of $3,000 receives a cash payment from the government of $4,500, a family with earned income of $6,000 receives a cash payment of $3,000, and so on. The cash payment or negative tax payment is equal to the guaranteed income ($6,000) minus the tax on earned income (0.5 × earned income). The total income of the family is the earned income of the family plus the cash payment from the government. Thus, the family with earned income of $3,000 has total in-

TABLE 11–5
Negative income tax plan for a family of four

Guaranteed income	Earned income	Negative tax*	Total income†
$6,000	$ 0	$6,000	$ 6,000
6,000	1,000	5,500	6,500
6,000	2,000	5,000	7,000
6,000	3,000	4,500	7,500
6,000	4,000	4,000	8,000
6,000	5,000	3,500	8,500
6,000	6,000	3,000	9,000
6,000	7,000	2,500	9,500
6,000	8,000	2,000	10,000
6,000	9,000	1,500	10,500
6,000	10,000	1,000	11,000
6,000	11,000	500	11,500
6,000	12,000	0	12,000

*The negative tax is the cash subsidy payment and is equal to $6,000 minus 50 percent of earned income.
†Total income is equal to earned income plus the negative tax payment.

come of $7,500 ($3,000 plus $4,500), and the family with earned income of $6,000 has total income of $9,000 ($6,000 plus $3,000).

Evaluation of the negative income tax scheme

The negative income tax scheme has some attractive features. It is based on the idea that when a household has income above the poverty threshold, the household pays positive taxes; and when a household has income below the poverty level, the government pays the household (negative taxes). The scheme is designed for individuals and families that have one and only one characteristic—they live in poverty. It is not necessary to be old and poor or blind and poor. To be eligible, you need only be poor. A negative income tax program is more simple and probably easier to administer than most of the current programs for the poor since the only consideration is money income. Under this reform proposal, people are always better off if they earn income than they are if they do not earn it; and the more they earn, the better off they will be.

The cost of a negative income tax plan will depend upon the number of eligible households, the earned income of each eligible household, the minimum annual income level guaranteed, and the negative tax rate. Given the first two variables, the cost of the plan will vary directly with the guaranteed level of income and inversely with the negative income tax rate. In the illustration presented in Table 11–5, the minimum guaranteed income is $6,000 for a household of four, and the tax rate on earned income is 50 percent. A negative tax payment or cash payment would be made to these households until their earned income reached $12,000. Assuming an average household of four, the number of poverty households in 1987 would be about 8 million. If these households earned on the average $3,000, the cost of the negative income tax plan would equal $36 billion in 1987 (the negative tax payment of $4,500 times 8 million households). Adding an estimated cost of Medicaid of $30 billion and a cost of a training and education program of $25 billion to the cost of the negative income tax plan gives a total cost of $91 billion. This is significantly below the scheduled outlays of $100 + billion in 1987 for the current programs for the poor with five times more available to increase the upward mobility of the poor.

SUMMARY

The number of people living in poverty in the United States was significantly reduced from 39.9 million to 24.5 million between 1960 and 1978. This downward trend in poverty was reversed between

1978 and 1981 with the poverty rate increasing from 11.4 percent in 1978 to 14 percent in 1981. Although the ratio of poor persons to the total population remained the same between 1981 and 1985, there were 1 million more people living in poverty in 1985 than in 1981. A slowdown in the real growth in the economy and, eventually, a recession caused the increase in the incidence of poverty between 1978 and 1981. A decrease in the poverty rate, instead of a constant rate, would have been expected with the economy expanding during the 1981–85 period. However, the unemployment rate remained relatively high during the period, and the real absolute and relative reductions in some federal programs for the poor may explain why the incidence of poverty did not decline during this expansionary period.

About one out of every nine families lived in poverty in 1985. Perhaps, more difficult to imagine than this is the fact that families with certain social characteristics have an incidence of poverty generally more than double that of all families. Families with much higher than average incidence rates of poverty are black families (30.9 percent), families headed by a female (34.5 percent), young families (29.4 percent), very large families (33.8 percent), families with the family head having less than eight years of education (25.5 percent), and families with the family head not in the labor force (22.7 percent). To deal with problems of poverty and low income, programs should be designed to (1) increase the upward mobility of the poor and near poor and (2) guarantee a minimum annual income to families and individuals who cannot work and those that cannot earn the minimum when they do work.

Changes and improvements are needed in current federal programs for the poor. Many current programs have developed in a piecemeal fashion, and many were not designed strictly for the poor. A guaranteed annual income plan in the form of negative income tax scheme would appear to be more efficient than the current in-kind and cash payment programs.

SUPPLEMENTARY READING

Brown, Peter S.; Conrad Johnson; and Paul Vernier. *Income Support*. New Jersey: Rowmand and Littlefield, 1981.

> This collection of readings includes excellent passages on the proper goals of government with regard to assistance to low-income groups, on the objectives of income-support policies and welfare rights, and on the current policy debate.

Cowell, F. A. *Measuring Inequality*. New York: Holsted Press, 1977.

> A good coverage of the meaning and measurement of inequality.

Duncan, Greg J. *Years of Poverty, Years of Plenty.* Ann Arbor, Michigan: Institute for Social Research, the University of Michigan, 1984.

Reports on the findings of a longitude study of family status conducted by the Survey Research Center of the University of Michigan. The introduction and chapters 1 and 2 are recommended. The major finding is that there is upward mobility among the poor.

Garfinkel, Irwin, and Robert H. Haverman. *Earnings Capacity, Poverty, and Inequality.* New York: Academic Press, 1977.

The concept of earnings capacity is developed and used as a measure of poverty to explore many important poverty issues.

MacDonald, Maurice. *Food Stamps and Income Maintenance.* New York: Academic Press, 1977.

This monograph covers all aspects of the food stamp program. The history and how the program operates are covered in chapters 1 and 2, respectively.

Robbins, Philip K.; Robert G. Spiegelman; and Samuel Weiner, eds. *A Guaranteed Annual Income: Evidence from a Social Experiment.* New York: Academic Press, 1980.

The focus of this selection of essays is on the issues of welfare reform and the effects of welfare reform alternatives based on experiments, especially experiments with negative income tax plans.

Rodgers, Jr., Harrell R. *Poor Women, Poor Families.* New York: M. E. Sharpe Inc., 1985.

This is a good account of the economic plight of families headed by a female.

Thurow, Lester C. *Poverty and Discrimination.* Washington, D.C.: Brookings Institution, 1969.

Extent of poverty is covered in chapter 2, and the income distribution patterns for whites and blacks are examined. Chapter 3 is good on the causes of poverty.

DISCRIMINATION

What is discrimination?
  The public view
  A working definition
Economic analysis of discrimination
  Sources of market discrimination
  Kinds of market discrimination
  Economic costs of discrimination
Nonmarket discrimination
  Social discrimination
  Educational discrimination
What can be done about discrimination?
  Reduce tastes for discrimination
  Reduce market imperfections
  Reduce discrimination in
    development of human
    capital
  Reduce occupational segregation
The comparable worth controversy
  Proponents
  Opponents
  Comparable worth: a definitive
    conclusion?
Summary

**Checklist of
Economic Concepts**

Market discrimination
Wage discrimination
Employment discrimination
Occupational discrimination
Price discrimination
Nonmarket discrimination
Monopoly power
Exploitation
Comparable worth

12

Discrimination

The high cost of prejudice

> The real reason back of the refusal of some of you to mingle with Negroes at the canteen isn't nearly so romantic and dramatic as you think it is. The real reason has nothing to do with rape, seduction, or risings in the night. The real reason can be summed up in two extremely unromantic little words: cheap labor. As long as you treat Negroes as subhumans, you don't have to pay them much. When you refuse to dance with Negro servicemen at the canteen, you are neither protecting your honor nor making sure that white Southerners won't have their homes burned down around their ears. All you are doing is making it possible for employers all over the country to get Negros to work for them for less money than those employers would have to pay you.[1]

Discrimination shows its ugly face through varied expressions. At its worst, discrimination takes away freedom and rights, robs people of human dignity and, in the end, enslaves them. In its milder form, discrimination is an unintentional by-product of decision making. For example, a famous restaurant in the French Quarter in New Orleans will not take a reservation unless there are at least four people in the party. Parties of three or less are denied access to a service because of the decision of the restaurant to exclude or discriminate. However, the decision of the restaurant to restrict reservations to parties based on size was undoubtedly motivated not by the desire to discriminate but by the desire to use its facilities efficiently. Also, this form of discrimination leaves open access to the restaurant to everyone in a party of four or more.

---

[1]Margaret Halsey, *Color Blind* (New York: Simon & Schuster, 1946), pp. 56–57.

WHAT IS DISCRIMINATION?

The public view

Most people relate discrimination to what they consider to be unfair treatment of some sort. Discrimination is viewed as the opposite of social justice. A person who is discriminated against is one who is treated unjustly.

There is nothing wrong in relating discrimination to unfair treatment. The shortcoming of this view is that it does not go far enough. It leaves unanswered the vital question: What is unfair treatment?

A working definition

Discrimination as we use it means that equals are treated unequally or that unequals are treated equally. More specifically, discrimination exists in a labor market when people with equal productivity are paid different wages or people with differences in productivity are paid equal wages. Discrimination exists in the product market when consumers pay different prices for the same product.

Market discrimination exists, then, when the terms on which market transactions are based are not the same for all. A seller who charges different prices to different consumers for essentially the same product or service is practicing price discrimination. A buyer who pays different wages for identical units of labor provides another illustration. Sellers who cannot sell in a certain market and buyers who cannot buy in a certain market for reasons other than price provide examples of complete market discrimination.

ECONOMIC ANALYSIS OF DISCRIMINATION

Sources of market discrimination

Market discrimination may be traced to two primary sources. These are the power to discriminate in the market and the desire to discriminate.

Monopoly power. Monopoly power may exist on the selling and buying sides of markets. In Chapter 2 we defined a monopolistic market as one in which the seller is able to manipulate the product price to his or her own advantage and can keep potential competitors out of the market. A monopsonistic market is a market in which the buyer is able to control resource prices. This *monopoly* control over price and impediments to entry in markets that are not competitive makes it possible for consumers and workers to be *exploited*. Consumers are exploited when the price of a product is above the cost per unit of producing it, and workers are exploited when the wage rates paid are below their marginal productivity—below their contributions to the receipts of their employer.

Exploitation may exist without discrimination. For example, both blacks and whites with the same productivity may be paid equal wages that are below their productivity. However, monopoly power is a source of discrimination. In the exercise of monopoly power, a seller may segregate the market and charge consumers different prices for the same product. A monopsonistic buyer may segregate the job market and practice discrimination by paying workers on bases other than merit or productivity.

Desire to discriminate. Some people have a taste for discrimination and strive to satisfy this taste or desire. An employer who desires to discriminate acts as if nonmonetary costs were connected with hiring women, blacks, Chicanos, Indians, Puerto Ricans and other minorities.[2] The result is that resources are allocated on bases other than productivity, and the incomes of minority groups are reduced.

Kinds of market discrimination

There are different kinds of market discrimination. The major ones are wage, employment, occupation, and price discrimination.

Wage discrimination. Full-time working women earn, on average, about 60 percent of what full-time working men earn. The situation is only slightly better for blacks, with the typical full-time black worker earning about 70 percent of the earnings of full-time white workers. These statistics do not, however, suggest that there is a 40 percent discrimination gap in earnings by gender or a 30 percent discrimination gap by race. To determine the importance of discrimination in earnings, we need a better understanding of what constitutes wage discrimination.

The meaning of wage discrimination can be elucidated by the slogan "equal pay for equal work." Suppose a man and woman complete their Ph.D. degrees at the same time and place, have identical

---

[2]Douglass C. North and Roger Leroy Miller, *The Economics of Public Issues* (New York: Harper & Row, 1971), p. 136.

records and recommendations, are hired by the same university to teach speech, and differ in only one respect—the man is paid $20,000 a year and the woman is paid $18,000 a year to teach. This is a case of discrimination. Two workers have the same productivity but are paid unequal wages.

It is often difficult to be sure that wage discrimination exists because the person who discriminates may deny it, and the relative productivities of labor may be difficult to measure. A discriminator may say that qualified blacks cannot be found or that females are paid less than males because their productivity is less. In some instances, discriminators may be right; in others, they may only be trying to hide discriminatory behavior.

The meaning of wage discrimination is clear enough—unequal pay for equal contributions. But the proving of discrimination depends on being able to distinguish among individuals on the basis of individual efforts and productivity. Generally speaking, human resources, like any other resources, are paid approximately what they are worth in a competitive economy. Thus, wage differences where competition exists reflect differences in labor productivity. Wage discrimination that does exist in the economy means that the market is not working perfectly in allocating resources among alternative uses.

What can we conclude with regard to the importance of discrimination in earnings gaps according to race and gender? Some part of these gaps is no doubt due to "legitimate" factors such as differences in productivity and occupations. If we were able to determine the part of the earnings gaps that is due to these factors, the part of the gap that remained would serve as a rough estimate of the degree of discrimination in earnings. Researchers have spent much time doing just this. A general conclusion of this research is that legitimate factors explain only about half of the earnings gaps.[3] In other words, if women were comparable to men with regard to productivity, occupation, and other legitimate factors, they would still earn only about 80 percent of what men earn, while blacks, under the same conditions, would earn about 85 percent of what whites earn.

Employment discrimination. Employment discrimination means that some people are not hired because of noneconomic characteristics such as race or sex. Two individuals with the same training,

---

[3]Mary Corcoran and Greg Duncan, "Work History, Labor Force Attachment, and Earnings Differences between the Races and Sexes," *Journal of Human Resources*, Winter 1979, p. 3.

education, and experience apply for a job. One is black and one is white. If both do not have the same chance of getting the job, discrimination has entered into the decision-making process.

Employment discrimination, like wage discrimination, is difficult to identify positively. Differences in unemployment rates among whites and minority groups and between males and females may suggest discrimination but do not prove that it exists. However, when you consider all low-productivity families and discover that unemployment rates are much higher among blacks than whites, or when you look at families with identical education levels and find unemployment rates higher among black families than white families, the evidence of employment discrimination becomes more conclusive.

Occupational discrimination. There is a growing belief that discriminatory differences in pay, especially sex differences in pay, occur largely because of occupational segregation. In general, men work in occupations that employ very few women, and women work in occupations that employ very few men. Barbara Bergman points out that the economic results of occupational segregation for women are low wages.[4] She observes that women are relegated to occupations where productivity and experience have little to do with their status as they advance in age.[5] Another study confirms the concentration of women in low-paying occupations and points out further that women are found in occupations where opportunities for overtime and premium pay are limited.[6]

Why do women fail to enter the high-paid occupations? Male prejudice has been an important factor, but in some cases women imposed discrimination upon themselves along occupational lines. Many women were taught early in life that their economic role would be unimportant. "They are socialized to expect that they will spend their lives as housewives and mothers—for toys they are given the tools of their trade: dolls, tea sets, frilly dresses, and so on."[7] Now that women are beginning to think in terms of careers,

---

[4]Barbara R. Bergman, "The Economics of Women's Liberation," *Challenge*, May–June 1973, p. 12.

[5]Ibid.

[6]Mary Hamblin and Michael Prell, "The Incomes of Men and Women: Why Do They Differ?" *Monthly Review*, Federal Reserve Bank of Kansas City, April 1973, p. 10.

[7]Marilyn Power Goldberg, "The Exploitation of Women," in *Economics: Mainstream Readings and Radical Critiques*, 2nd ed., David Mermelstein, ed. (New York: Random House, 1973), p. 52.

prepare themselves for them, and break away from self-imposed economic exile, the male-female pay gap should narrow in time.

There is some evidence that women are beginning to move into traditional male occupations at a faster rate. Analyzing data through 1981, Andrea Beller concludes that the pace at which the degree of occupational segregation is declining accelerated significantly during the 1970s.[8] Although progress is being made, a large degree of occupational segregation still exists.

Price discrimination. A shopping study in New York City revealed that an Admiral 19-inch screen, portable television set varied in price from $179 to $200 on the lower east side and that an identical set was sold in a downtown discount house for $139. Three different prices were quoted for a set by one lower east side store— $125 for a white law student, $139 to a Puerto Rican housewife, and $200 for a black housewife.[9] Is this evidence that the lower east side consumers are discriminated against?

The price differential for the identical TV set between the lower east side store and the downtown discount store does not by itself indicate price discrimination. The price difference between the lower east side store and downtown discount store may reflect cost differences. The former may have higher costs in the form of higher insurance rates, higher bad-debt rates, and/or higher theft rates. It may be an inefficient supplier of TV sets.

There is evidence of price discrimination on the part of the lower east side store because different prices were quoted to different customers for the same set. Even here more information is needed about the payment record of each customer. We have defined price discrimination as charging different prices to different consumers for the same product or service. We need to qualify this definition of price discrimination. We must add the assumption that costs in the form of risks of nonpayment are constant or do not account for the differences in price.

Price discrimination may take the form of preventing a person, because of race, from having access to a given market. The housing market is a market where some sellers may not sell at any price to certain buyers. Another illustration is the refusal to allow blacks equal access to the capital or credit markets. The purchase of real

---

[8]Andrea H. Beller, "Changes in the Sex Composition of U.S. Occupations, 1960–1981," *Journal of Human Resources*, Spring 1985, p. 235.

[9]Warren G. Magnuson and Jean Carper, *The Dark Side of the Market Place* (Englewood Cliffs, N.J.: Prentice-Hall, 1972), p. 37.

capital—equipment, machinery, buildings—is usually financed from borrowed money. The complete or partial barring of blacks from the credit market may result in low ratios of capital to labor for blacks and, consequently, low productivity. Their production efforts are thus limited to products and services where high ratios of labor to capital are required.

Economic costs of discrimination

The economic costs of discrimination are both individual and social in nature. The individual costs of discrimination are those imposed on individuals or groups who lose one way or another because of discrimination. The social cost of discrimination is in the form of a reduction in total output in the economy due to discrimination.

Individual losses and gains. Individual losses and gains flow from discrimination. Individuals discriminated against, or the discriminatees, suffer losses in the form of reduced living standards. They tend to be paid less for what they sell, to pay higher prices for what they buy, to have fewer employment opportunities, and to be segregated in low-paying occupations. Individuals who discriminate, the discriminators, may gain and may lose. An employer-discriminator may gain if a female worker can be hired at a lower wage than a male worker, assuming both are equally productive. The wages of whites may be kept artificially above blacks if blacks are shut off from jobs and occupations because of race. Discriminators, however, may lose by having to forfeit income in order to satisfy their taste for discrimination. For example, an individual who refuses to sell a house to a black may end up selling the house at a lower price to a white. Or, an individual who refuses to hire a woman may end up paying a higher price for a man with the same productivity.

Output reduction. We have said that the cost to society of discrimination is the reduction in the nation's output of goods and services (GNP) resulting from discrimination. In this way, discrimination causes a dead-weight welfare loss much like that attributed to monopoly in Chapter 7. We concluded that monopolistic elements within the economy reduced GNP by about 1 percent per year. A fairly recent study estimates that the loss in GNP due to racial discrimination is about 4 percent per year![10] That is, race discrimination

---

[10]Joint Economic Committee, *The Cost of Racial Discrimination* (Washington, D.C.: U.S. Government Printing Office, 1980), p. 2.

FIGURE 12–1
Production possibilities with and without discrimination

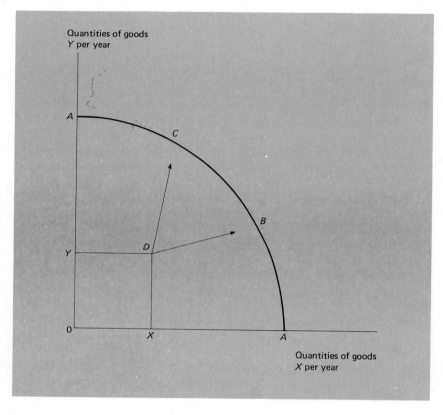

Point *D* = combination of *X* and *Y* with discrimination.
Points *B* and *C* = combination of *X* and *Y* without discrimination.
Line *AA* = production possibilities curve.

reduced the nation's output of goods and services by about $160 billion in 1985. Add to this discrimination against women, Chicanos, Puerto Ricans, and Indians, and you have an annual loss of goods and services to the American society that could easily exceed one quarter of a trillion dollars per year.

Discrimination causes losses of goods and services to society because it results in unnecessarily low levels of economic efficiency. Without discrimination, resources would tend to be allocated on the basis of their productivities. Units of any given resource would tend to be used where their productivity is the greatest.

The production possibilities curve shown in Figure 12–1 illustrates the impact of discrimination on the production of goods and services in the economy. Point D represents the combination of goods X and Y produced in the economy when discrimination exists, with its resultant inefficiency. Without discrimination, the quantities of goods X and Y may be expanded to such points as B and C.

Discrimination prevents the efficient use of resources, causing the combination of goods and services that is produced to lie below the production possibilities curve. The elimination of discrimination makes possible the production of those combinations of goods and services that lie on the curve. The social cost of discrimination is equal to the difference between the gross national product represented at point D and that represented by points on the production possibilities curve, such as points B and C.

NONMARKET DISCRIMINATION

Social discrimination

Social tastes and attitudes, customs, and laws are the bases for social discrimination. Social discrimination may take the extreme form of preventing certain individuals or groups from engaging in social interaction. A Little League rule that prohibits girls from playing baseball in Little League games provides an illustration. Fraternities and sororities that have rules limiting membership to certain races provide another. Segregated schools are examples of discrimination based on customs and laws. Societies such as South Africa are structured along lines of social discrimination. Under these arrangements, discrimination by race is a way of life, sanctioned by custom and frequently enforceable by law. Deviations from the legal segregated manner of behavior are crimes, and severe punishment may be handed out to offenders.

Social discrimination is difficult to root out, since it is based on deep-seated beliefs and customs often supported by law. In contrast to market discrimination, it is difficult to associate monetary costs with social discrimination. Members who may with joy vote to keep certain people from joining their country club often with the same joy sell products to them in the market. Although the source of much market discrimination is social discrimination, the self-interest motive in the market tends to overcome and reduce the effectiveness of discrimination in the marketplace.

Educational discrimination

It is generally believed that if everyone had equal access and opportunity to training and education, many of the major issues in our society, such as poverty and extreme income inequality, would be significantly alleviated, perhaps even eliminated. Unfortunately, however, inequality and discrimination exist even in our public school system.[11]

A great deal of the inequality in public education is due to the way it is financed. The public school system is a highly decentralized system composed of thousands of school districts charged with the responsibilities of providing education. School districts pay for education with revenues from the local property tax and grants-in-aid, primarily from the state. Variations in the market value of property give rise to variations in per pupil expenditures on education within a given state and among states. A poor district (one with low property values) within a poor state will have low per pupil expenditures and may have high property tax rates. This regional and state inequality in the allocation of resources for the purpose of public education has led to court decisions opposing the way public education is financed. In the meantime, however, resources are unequally distributed, and the rich receive a better financed education than the poor.

Discrimination in the public school system is indicated by the allocation of experienced and highly paid teachers.[12] The worst teachers, the least experienced, and the lowest paid, are concentrated in the ghettos. Also, there is a regional bias to discrimination. Effective discrimination in public schools is more evident in the South; in some cases it reaches complete segregation, "with all black students taught by black teachers and all white students taught by white teachers."[13]

WHAT CAN BE DONE ABOUT DISCRIMINATION?

Markets and humans are not perfect. Perfection may be beyond reach. However, movements in the direction of perfection are pos-

---

[11]John D. Owen, "Inequality and Discrimination in the Public School System," in *Economics: Mainstream Readings and Radical Critiques,* ed. David Mermelstein and Robert Lekachman (New York: Random House, 1970), pp. 137–44.

[12]*Ibid.,* p. 141.

[13]*Ibid.,* p. 144.

sible. What courses of action can be taken to move in the right direction? What policy implications can be drawn from our analysis?

Reduce tastes for discrimination

If tastes for discrimination are to be reduced, people must be persuaded that they should alter their views and behavior. These tastes may be reduced by education, by legislation, and by the use of government subsidies to discourage discrimination.

Education. A task of education is to teach people to understand one another so they will not be prejudiced. Unfortunately, this task of education is hampered by discrimination in education itself, especially in regard to the allocation of resources for primary and secondary education. Although not a panacea, a more equal distribution of resources for public education would reduce inequality in per pupil educational services, and it could contribute toward reducing tastes for discrimination.

Legislation. It is difficult to change the tastes of people by coercion, that is by passing laws. Laws are usually only effective when they are supported by or coincide with people's beliefs. However, the framework for reducing tastes for discrimination can be established by laws. The Equal Pay Act of 1963 was the first major federal attempt to control discrimination. The act makes it illegal for employers to pay different wage rates for "equal work." Since the Equal Pay Act only applies to wage discrimination, it is quite limited. To broaden the impact on discrimination, the Civil Rights Acts of 1964 and 1965 were enacted. These laws require not only equal treatment in wages but also equal treatment in hiring, promotion, and ultimately firing. These laws may reduce discrimination by imposing greater risks and higher costs on discriminators. For example, a person who satisfies a taste for discrimination by refusing to sell a house to a black breaks the law and risks prosecution.

Government subsidies. If the sole goal is to eliminate discrimination, government subsidy payments may be used to encourage employers not to discriminate. Subsidy payments would be made to employers who do not practice discrimination in hiring, wages, and promotions. Employers who discriminate would be sacrificing subsidy payments. Thus, an incentive is provided not to discriminate. The alternative cost of discrimination is equal to the subsidy payment. Government subsidy payments will reduce discrimination if the subsidy payments are equal to or greater than the nonmonetary gain the discriminator receives from discrimination.

Reduce market imperfections

Market defects such as scarce labor market information, imperfect competition, and immobility of labor constitute a major source of market discrimination. Some people receive low wages, that is, wages below what they could earn in alternative employments, because they are unaware of other job openings. Better access to job information would make it less likely for a person to receive income below what he or she would be paid on a similar job.

The market for goods and the market for resources may not work well at all if there is little competition in these markets. In imperfect markets, discrimination may be prevalent. A seller or a buyer has control over the price of what he or she sells or buys in highly monopolized markets. Other potential sellers or buyers are shut out of the market. Price, wage, employment, and occupational discrimination may remain unchallenged in the absence of competitive forces and in the presence of monopolistic controls. Antitrust action to strengthen competition and reduce barriers to entry into markets would be an important way to eliminate or at least lessen discriminatory market behavior.

The government has an important role to play in the elimination of discrimination when it is due to the use of monopoly power. First, it is the responsibility of the government to reduce monopoly power and restore competition in markets where competition is lacking through the vigorous use of antimonopoly laws. Second, a great deal of monopoly power is derived from and granted by government. Thurow noted that "The institutions of government are an important link in implementing discrimination. Either directly through legal restrictions or indirectly through harassment and expenditure decisions, the coercive power of the white community flows through local, state, and federal government institutions."[14]

Reduce discrimination in development of human capital

Investment in human capital, that is, spending on education, training, and health, provides a high rate of return in the form of increased productivity and income. Blacks and other minority groups

---

[14]Lester C. Thurow, *Poverty and Discrimination* (Washington, D.C.: Brookings Institution, 1969), p. 158.

generally do not and cannot invest enough in human capital, and public investment in human capital is unequally distributed. The elimination of human capital discrimination would tend to make most forms of market discrimination, such as wage and employment discrimination, less effective. The reason is that it is difficult to treat human resources unequally if they are productive and have access to other jobs. Thurow, who believes human capital investment holds the key to nondiscrimination, states, "Attacking human capital discrimination will not raise Negro incomes by itself, since wage, employment, and occupational discrimination would also have to be eliminated, but eliminating human capital discrimination would make the enforcement of these other types difficult in the absence of government discrimination."[15]

Reduce occupational segregation

Women, blacks, and other minority groups have been pushed into low-wage occupations. The effect of segregation by occupations is twofold. First, the supply of labor is increased in those occupations restricted to minority groups, depressing wages in those occupations. Second, the supply of labor is decreased in those occupations closed off to minority groups, thus increasing wages in those occupations. The result of these effects is to create a wider gap between low and high wage occupations.[16]

In addition, if a member of the minority group crosses over into segregated occupations usually closed to members of the group, he or she has typically not received equal pay for equal work. For example, a black male with a Ph.D. in chemistry who works as a research chemist for an oil company may be discriminated against in wages and opportunities for advancement because he has a position typically reserved for whites. In recent years this situation has been reversed in many cases by the Equal Opportunities Act. Employers are virtually required to bid for minority group personnel. The small supplies available of these workers who are qualified assure they will receive salaries *above* those of white employees.

However, segregation by occupations would be difficult to maintain if minority groups were relatively well educated and well trained. Education and training open up job opportunities. Those who have job opportunities cannot easily be forced into designated

---

[15]*Ibid.,* p. 138.
[16]Daniel R. Fusfeld, *The Basic Economics of the Urban Racial Crisis* (New York: Holt, Rinehart & Winston, 1973), p. 64–68.

occupations; they are mobile and can cut across occupations. Providing improved job opportunities for minority groups is one way to break up segregation by occupations.

THE COMPARABLE WORTH CONTROVERSY

Frustration over the slow progress toward equality that women have experienced has lead to a call by some for more aggressive approaches to reducing discrimination. One such proposal is to replace market determination of wages with comparable worth pay systems. The essence of comparable worth pay systems is a realization that women and men do not do the same work. As mentioned earlier in this chapter, women are concentrated into a very few low paying jobs while men are disproportionately represented in the higher paying occupations. Given this, laws such as the Equal Pay Act can do little to improve the economic position of women since they only require "equal pay for equal work." The comparable worth doctrine would extend the "equal pay for equal work" principle to require "equal pay for similar or comparable work." Would such an approach be desirable? Strong arguments are made on each side of the debate.

Proponents

Comparable worth advocates argue that the occupations dominated by women (nursing, elementary and secondary school teaching, clerical, etc.) are low paying not due to "market forces" but purely because they are jobs held by women. That is, in a male-dominated society, the work done by women is of necessity valued less than comparable work done by men. A logical extension of this argument suggests that if a job currently dominated by females (such as nursing) switches and becomes primarily male, the average pay of nurses would increase substantially. Consistent with this view, comparable worth advocates often cite Margaret Mead who once wrote, "There are villages in which men fish and women weave and in which women fish and men weave, but in either type of village the work done by men is valued higher than the work done by women."[17]

The remedy proposed is to require employers not only to pay equal wages for equal work but also to require equal wages for jobs of comparable worth, where the comparability of jobs is determined

---

[17]June O'Neill, "Issues Surrounding Comparable Worth: Introduction," *Contemporary Policy Issues*, April 1986, p. 1.

by factors such as the skill, effort, and responsibility requirements of the jobs. For example, suppose that it is determined that secretaries (primarily female) and truck drivers (primarily male) do jobs which are comparable in terms of skill, effort, and responsibility. The comparable worth doctrine would require that employers pay secretaries and truck drivers the same salaries. While comparable worth pay systems have not made significant inroads in the private sector, a number of state and local governments have started the process of evaluating jobs, determining their "intrinsic value," and paying workers accordingly.

Opponents

While the arguments of the comparable worth adherents are logical and to some extent consistent with evidence concerning occupational segregation and the pay of women, comparable worth may not be the panacea its advocates hope for. A number of fundamental policy questions have been raised in regard to comparable worth. Overlooking the difficulties involved with determining the "intrinsic value" of a job, opponents suggest three shortcomings of comparable worth. First, the essence of comparable worth is to increase the pay of women relative to men. To the extent that the program is successful, the outcome must be to reduce the employment of women. This argument is directly parallel to the argument raised with reference to the minimum wage in the second chapter of this book. While some women will gain (those who remain employed), a significant number of women may lose. Second, opponents suggest that what is truly needed is for women to move into the higher paying male occupations and that comparable worth, by making the female occupations more attractive, will do just the opposite. Thus, the policy would serve to reinforce occupational segregation rather than reduce it. Finally, opponents argue that comparable worth treats a symptom of a disease rather than the disease itself. Specifically, opponents argue that women are low paid because they work in low-paying jobs, and to the extent that this occupational segregation is due to discriminatory hiring and promotion factors, the appropriate remedy is more strict enforcement of existing law rather than comparable worth legislation.

Comparable worth: A definitive conclusion?

While no definitive conclusion may be reached with regard to the comparable worth controversy, the debate points out several things of importance with regard to discrimination and attemps to deal with it. First, even when problems of discrimination are perceived, the development of remedial actions which generate widespread support is very difficult. Second, before policy actions are undertaken, careful consideration must be made of all of the possible effects of the policy. In many cases, those we wish to help most, may end up being harmed. Beyond this, we can be sure that the comparable worth controversy will continue and may intensify.

SUMMARY

Market discrimination means that people with the same economic characteristics are not treated equally. For example, workers who have the same productivity receive different wages, and consumers are charged different prices for the same product.

Discrimination comes from two sources—market and human imperfections. Market imperfections are due to imperfect knowledge, immobility of resources, and imperfect competition. Human imperfections are revealed in the tastes and preferences that some people have for discrimination. Market discrimination exists in the form of wage, employment, occupational, and price discrimination.

Discrimination is costly both to individuals and to society. There are individual welfare gains and losses from discrimination. It is difficult to say who gains and who loses. Sometimes the discriminator can lose. It is certain that there is a loss to society from discrimination, in the form of a reduction in output.

The economic analysis of market determination stresses two related points: (1) the observed differences in wages and prices may reflect differences in productivity, and (2) market discrimination exists only to the extent that wage and price differences cannot be explained on the basis of productivity. Competitive markets tend to minimize the extent and degree of discrimination. Occupational segregation explains to a large extent differences in wages and income, and social discrimination, especially in the field of public education, is the source of much inequality.

Several policy conclusions may be drawn from our analysis. One, tastes for discrimination have to be reduced. This can be done by changing the tastes of people concerning discrimination through education, preventing by law the fulfillment of tastes for discrimination, and encouraging people not to discriminate by the payment of subsidies to employers who refrain from discrimination. Two, the source of exploitation and much discrimination—the exercise of monopoly power—has to be reduced. The way to reduce the use of monopoly power is to reduce that power itself through vigorous enforcement of antimonopoly laws. A great deal of market discrimination is primarily due to human capital discrimination. If there were no discrimination in regard to investment in human capital (education, training, and health), segregation by occupations would be dealt a serious blow. It is difficult to discriminate in the market against people who are productive and have job choices.

SUPPLEMENTARY READINGS

Alvarez, Rodolfo, and Kenneth G. Lutterman. *Discrimination in Organizations*. San Francisco: Jossey-Bass, 1979.

Examines opportunity and power in organizations and discusses sex segregation of jobs and male-female income differentials.

Arvey, Richard D. *Fairness in Selecting Employees*. Reading, Mass.: Addison-Wesley Publishing, 1979.

Evaluates the employee selection process and examines discrimination in employment.

Chafetz, Janet S. *Sex and Advantage*. Totowa, New Jersey: Rowman and Allandheld, 1984.

A thorough analysis of the variables that determine sex stratifications.

Hartman, Heidi I., and Donald J. Treiman. *Women, Work and Wages: Equal Pay for Jobs of Equal Value*. Washington, D.C.: National Academy Press, 1981.

Provides evidence regarding wage differentials and introduces wage-adjustment approaches to overcome discrimination.

Jain, Harish C., and Peter J. Sloane. *Equal Employment Issues: Race and Sex Discrimination in the United States, Canada, and Britain*. New York: Praeger Publishers, 1981.

Examines the complex human resources problems faced by policymakers regarding minority employment. Uses economic analysis to point out where we might expect discrimination to be more extensive.

Mermelstein, David, ed. *Economics: Mainstream Readings and Radical Critiques*. 2nd ed. New York: Random House, 1973.

Includes several good essays on discrimination, particularly "The Structure of Racial Discrimination," by Raymond Franklin and Solomon Resnick, and "The Economic Exploitation of Women," by Marilyn Power Goldberg.

Thurow, Lester C. *Poverty and Discrimination*. Washington, D.C.: Brookings Institution, 1969.

Covers the economic theories of discrimination. In chapter 7, various kinds of market discrimination are presented and analyzed.

Vanderwaerdt, Lois. *Affirmative Action in Higher Education*. New York: Garland Publishing, 1982.

Demonstrates how affirmative action has changed employment practices regarding faculty and staff on college and university campuses.

Part Three

STABILIZATION

UNEMPLOYMENT ISSUES

Some effects of unemployment
  Effects on GNP
  Effects on social relations
What is unemployment?
  General definition
  Involuntary unemployment
Analysis of the unemployment problem
  Types of employment
  Further dimensions of the
    unemployment problem
What causes people to lose their jobs?
  Circular flow of economic activity
  Aggregate demand
  Aggregate supply
  Aggregate demand and supply
  Reasons for deficient aggregate
    demand
  Reasons for weak aggregate supply
Combating unemployment
  Aggregate demand policies
  Aggregate supply policies
    and the economy in the 1980s
Summary

**Checklist of
Economic Concepts**

Potential GNP
GNP GAP
Involuntary unemployment
Frictional unemployment
Structural unemployment
Cyclical unemployment
Circular flow of production and
  income
Leakages
Injections
Aggregate demand
Aggregate supply
Aggregate demand policies
Aggregate supply policies

13

Unemployment Issues

Why do we waste our labor resources?

I'd get up at five in the morning and head for the waterfront. Outside the Spreckles Sugar Refinery, outside the gates, there would be a thousand men. You know dang well there's only three or four jobs. The guy would come out with two little Pinkerton cops: "I need two guys for the bull gang. Two guys to go into the hole." A thousand men would fight like a pack of Alaskan dogs to get through there. Only four of us would get through. I was too young a punk.

So you'd drift up to Skid Row. There'd be thousands of men there. Guys on baskets, making weird speeches, phony theories on economics. About 11:30, the real leaders would take over. They'd say: OK, we're going to City Hall. The mayor was Angelo Rossi, a dapper little guy. He wore expensive boots and a tight vest. We'd shout around the steps. Finally, he'd come out and tell us nothing.

I remember the demands: We demand work, we demand shelter for our families, we demand groceries, this kind of thing. . . .

I remember as a kid how courageous this seemed to me, the demands, because you knew that society wasn't going to give it to you. They'd demand that they open up unrented houses and give decent shelters for their families. But you just knew society wasn't yielding. There was nothing coming.[1]

SOME EFFECTS OF UNEMPLOYMENT

Both economic and social effects are associated with unemployment. The economic effects are related to the impact of unemployment on

---

[1]Studs Terkel, *Hard Times* (New York: Random House, Pantheon Books, 1970), p. 30.

the nation's production of goods and services, that is, the GNP. The social effects of unemployment are more difficult to pin down and measure, but they are just as real as the economic effects.

Effects on GNP

Idle human resources represent a waste, a loss of goods and services, and, therefore, a loss of real income. Unemployed resources could have contributed to society's well-being; the economic value of this lost contribution of goods and services is the economic cost of unemployment. The difference, then, between what may be produced at full employment and what is produced at less than full employment measures the total cost of unemployment. In 1986, the estimated gap between actual and potential GNP was about $30 billion.

Unemployment may affect not only current production of goods and services but also future production. During periods of unemployment, machines as well as workers are idle. Capital goods, plant and equipment, become obsolete and are not replaced. The productivity of labor and the overall ability of the economy to produce in the future are reduced during periods of unemployment.

Effects on social relations

Unemployment threatens the stability of the family as an economic and social unit. Without income or with a loss of income, the head of the family cannot play the role in which he or she was cast. Family wants and needs are not fulfilled, and family relationships suffer as a consequence. Economic and social dependency and important family ties may be in jeopardy and may eventually be severed by prolonged unemployment.

Human relationships outside the family are also seriously affected by unemployment. An unemployed person loses self-respect and influence among the employed, may be rejected by working companions, and loses pride and confidence. In the end, the unemployed may become spiritually disabled.

Although there may be a few families that are economically and socially prepared for unemployment, it tends to strike families least capable of withstanding either its economic or its social effects. Also, the incidence of unemployment, like family instability and crime, is high among low-income groups.

The social and economic effects of unemployment extend beyond the period in which it occurs. During a period of high unemployment, consumption and savings are reduced, debt is incurred, and, for many unemployed people, home and auto loans may be defaulted. Afterwards, when work is available and income is earned, debts must be paid and savings replenished. It may take a long time before the living standards that prevailed prior to the unemployed period can be retained and even longer before self-esteem is restored.

WHAT IS UNEMPLOYMENT?

It would seem that unemployment could be easily defined. However, there are many complexities and ramifications concerning its meaning. The first thought about unemployment may be that the unemployed are people without jobs. This may be true, but many people without jobs are not considered unemployed. What about a person who prefers leisure to work? Are persons over 65 to be considered unemployed? Is a college student included in the unemployment count?

Our approach to unemployment in this section is, first, to give a general definition of unemployment, and, second, to elucidate the meaning of *involuntary* unemployment—the unemployment that is of major economic concern. The subsequent section probes deeper into the meaning of unemployment.

General definition

In general, unemployment may be defined as a situation in which people who are qualified for a job, willing to work, and willing to accept the going wage rate cannot find jobs without considerable delay. There are three important aspects to this definition.

First, a person has to be qualified for a job. A person is not involuntarily unemployed if one seeks jobs which one is precluded from obtaining because of a lack of training, experience, and education. For example, one cannot be considered an unemployed truck driver if one is unable to drive a truck.

Second, a person is not considered unemployed if he or she is not seeking a job and willing to work at the market wage rate. Some may decide to withdraw their labor services because they prefer leisure to work at the market rate. These people represent a type of unemployment, but not the kind that usually presents a problem.

Third, it may take time to find a job that a person is qualified for and is willing to accept at the going wage rate. However, the delay in finding a job should be of a short duration. The time delay should probably not extend beyond a 30- or 60-day period for most occupations. Some may believe that this time period is too long for people to be without jobs.

Involuntary unemployment

The economic aspect of unemployment originates from a situation in which the quantity of labor demanded is less than the quantity supplied at the market wage rate. This results in involuntary unemployment. Involuntary unemployment occurs when wage rates are too high, that is, above competitive levels. The solution to involuntary unemployment is to expand demand or, if competitive forces are operating, to rely on automatic market forces to drive wage rates down to the level at which the amount of labor demanded equals the amount supplied.

Figure 13–1 is shown to clarify the meaning of involuntary unemployment in a competitive economy. DD and SS are the demand and supply curves for labor. The wage rate is w_1. The amount of labor demanded at this wage rate is e_0, and the amount supplied is e_1. This difference between e_0 and e_1 is the involuntary unemployment at the wage rate of w_1. In a purely competitive situation, wage rates would be forced down to w, and involuntary unemployment would disappear.

ANALYSIS OF THE UNEMPLOYMENT PROBLEM

Types of unemployment

The meaning of unemployment may be elucidated further by distinguishing between different types of unemployment. Three major types are frictional, structural, and cyclical unemployment.

Frictional unemployment. Frictional unemployment is transitional or short run in nature. It usually originates on the labor supply side; that is, labor services are voluntarily not employed. A good illustration is the unemployment that occurs when people are changing jobs or searching for new jobs. The matching of job openings and job seekers does not always take place smoothly in the economy, and, as a consequence, people are without work.

The important thing about frictional unemployment is that it does not last. Frictional unemployment may exist at all times in the economy, but for any one person or family it is transitional. Therefore, frictional unemployment is not considered a significant economic

FIGURE 13–1
Involuntary unemployment in a competitive market

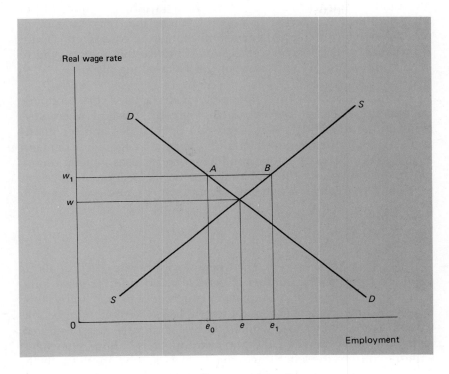

DD	= Demand curve for labor.
SS	= Supply curve for labor.
e_0	= Amount of labor demanded at w_1.
e_1	= Amount of labor supplied at w_1.
$e_1 - e_0$	= Involuntary unemployment.

problem, it can be reduced by improvements in the flow of information concerning job openings.

Structural unemployment. Structural unemployment is usually long run in nature and usually originates on the demand side of labor. Structural unemployment results from economic changes that cause the demand for specific kinds of labor to be low relative to the supply in particular markets and regions of the economy.

A relatively low demand for labor in a given market may be due to several factors. Technological change, although expected to reduce costs and expand the productive capacity of the overall economy, may have devastating effects in a particular market. Changes in consumer preferences for products expand production and employment in some areas but reduce them in others. Immobility of labor prolongs the period of unemployment that may have originated due to technological change and changes in consumers' tastes. A reduction in job opportunities should induce the unemployed to move, but immobility may prevent this from taking place.

Cyclical unemployment. Unemployment caused by economic fluctuations is called cyclical unemployment. Cyclical unemployment is due to reductions in aggregate or total demand for goods and services in the overall economy. A decline in aggregate demand in the economy reduces total production and causes general unemployment throughout the economic system. Cyclical unemployment is usually the culprit when the unemployment rate goes above 6 percent.

Further dimensions of the unemployment problem

The unemployment rate. The unemployment rate (UR) equals U/L, where U equals the number of people included in the labor force who are unemployed and L equals the number of people in the labor force. The unemployment rate underestimates the number of people without work. Only those who are in the labor force are considered to be unemployed when they are without jobs. Those who have withdrawn from the labor force, that is, people who are not actively seeking employment, are not included in the labor force.

Full employment is often defined for policy purposes in terms of a minimum unemployment rate such as a rate of 4, 5, or 6 percent unemployment. The economy is considered to be operating at less than full employment at unemployment rates above the minimum rate. The unemployment below the full employment rate is supposed to measure frictional and structural unemployment. The unemployment above the full employment rate is supposed to measure cyclical unemployment, the unemployment that fiscal policy is directed toward reducing or eliminating. In the 1950s and 1960s, full employment was defined in reference to a 4 percent unemployment rate. In the 1970s, the rate was increased to 5 percent, and in the early 1980s it was increased to a range of from 6 to 6.5 percent. The basic reason for defining full employment in reference to higher unemployment rates is to account for structural changes in the labor force such as the increasing number of women in the labor force.

FIGURE 13–2

Unemployment rates: all workers, 16- to 19-year-old workers, male and female workers, and workers with different ethnic backgrounds in selected years, 1960–1986

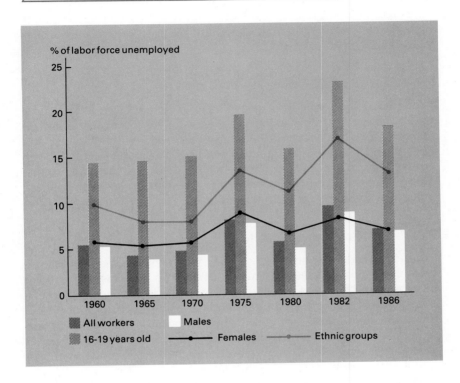

Source: *Economic Report of the President*, January 1987, p. 285.

Who are the unemployed? Unemployment rates vary by age, sex, and ethnic groups. Young people between the ages of 16 and 19 have the highest unemployment rate (Figure 13–2). The unemployment rate is usually about two and a half times higher for these young workers than for all workers. For example, the unemployment rate was 18.3 percent among 16- to 19-year-old workers as compared to 7 percent among all workers in 1986. The next highest unemployment rate is among ethnic groups; 13 percent were without jobs in 1986. The unemployment rate is higher usually among female workers than among male workers; however, in 1986 the female and male unemployment rates were approximately the same as the unemployment rate of all workers. The highest unemployment rate in all categories in recent times took place in 1982. In the recession year of 1982, 1 out of every 10 workers was without a job. The economic expansion in the economy reduced the jobless rate to 6.7 percent in early 1987. However, this unemployment rate was still high by historical standards, especially for an economy in the fifth year of economic expansion.

WHAT CAUSES PEOPLE TO LOSE THEIR JOBS?

People lose their jobs in a recession when production in the economy is falling. But what causes the recession? What causes a decline in production? Economists have searched for a single answer and have found many—not enough spending, too much saving, or relatively high wages. Thus, the answer is neither simple nor single. There are many contributory causes; we shall try to explain those that seem to be the most important.

Circular flow of economic activity

To understand why people lose their jobs it is necessary to understand how jobs are created. This is not difficult in terms of the forces of supply and demand pertaining to products in individual markets. We have established an understanding of equilibrium prices and quantities demanded for individual commodities such as wheat, automobiles, dresses, televisions, ice cream, necklaces, and all other commodities produced in our economy. We now move from demand and supply curves for individual products to a demand and supply curve representing all commodities. Thus, we present an overview of the operation of the economy, which economists call the *circular flow of economic activity.*

The circular flow is illustrated in Figure 13–3. The relationships it shows are important in understanding the operation of the economy. (Study this figure carefully.)

Income and jobs are created in a society when goods and services are produced. Owners of resources—labor, capital, and natural resources—sell their productive services to producers who, in turn, pay them money in the form of wages, interest, rent, and profits. The flow of productive services to producers represents the supply of resources, and the flow of money payments from producers represents the demand for resources. Producers transform productive services or resources into goods and services through the production process and sell the goods and services to households. They receive a flow of money payments from households in exchange. The flow

FIGURE 13–3
Flow of production and income in a stationary economy

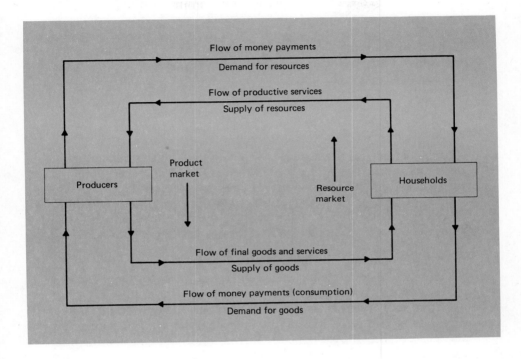

from producers to households represents the aggregate supply of goods and services, and the flow of money payments from households to producers represents the aggregate demand for them.

There are several points to remember about the circular flow. First, there are two markets—a resource market and a product market. The prices of resources and employment are determined in the resource market, and the prices of goods and production are determined in the product market. Second, the resource and product markets are interrelated. The demand for goods creates a demand for the resources that are used to produce goods. The costs of producing goods depend on the prices paid and the quantities of resources used in production. Third, there are two circular flows involved in the economy—a real flow of productive services (labor, capital, and natural resources) and products (autos, dresses, medical services), and a flow of money payments to owners of resources for productive services and to producers for goods and services. Fourth, real income is determined by the physical goods and services produced, and money income is the money value of the physical goods and services produced.

The circular flow of economic activity shows in a simple way how the overall economy operates. It emphasizes the interdependency of economic variables—the dependency of income on production, production on spending, spending on income, demand for resources on the demand for products, and so on. Now we shall turn to the product market in order to find possible reasons why people lose their jobs.

Aggregate demand

Aggregate demand is a schedule showing total output demanded in the economy at different prices. Since we are concerned with the prices of all goods and services, we must view prices as an average, or as a price level. Since we are also concerned with the quantities of all goods and services, we must view the quantities demanded as composite units of goods and services—each unit composed of shirts, tables, food, fuel, and other items that comprise the real output of the economy.

Aggregate demand is illustrated in Figure 13–4. At the price level p_1, 200 units of goods and services are demanded; at the price level p, output demanded is 400 units, and so on. The output demanded of goods at any price level is the sum of the output of goods and services purchased by *consumers*, such as shoes and steaks; the output purchased by *investors*, such as new plant and equipment; and the output purchased by *government*, such as highways and recreational services. A change in the output demanded at a given price level by these groups—consumers, investors, and government—will change aggregate demand. For example, if consumers begin to buy greater quantities of consumer goods at all prices than they did previously, aggregate demand will increase—shift to the right, indicating that greater output is demanded at all prices.

It is important at this time to mention some of the important determinants of aggregate demand. Consumer spending depends upon prices, the real income and wealth of consumers, the rate of interest, and other objective and subjective factors that influence decisions of consumers to spend and save. Output demanded by consumers at a given price level would be expected to vary directly with real income and wealth, and inversely with the rate of interest—that is, the higher the rate of interest the lower the output demanded. Investment spending depends upon the rate of interest and the expected profit rate on new investment. Investment spending will be higher the lower the interest rate and the higher the profit rate. The

FIGURE 13–4
Aggregate demand

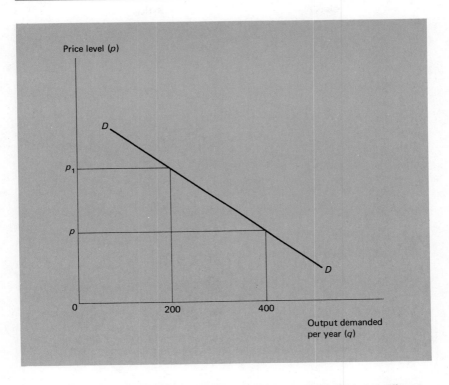

DD is an aggregate-demand schedule which shows the output demanded at different price levels. For example, at price level p_1, 200 units of goods and services are demanded.

final part of aggregate demand, government purchases of final goods and services, depends primarily on social priorities and government policies.

Aggregate supply

Aggregate supply is a schedule showing the output supplied at different price levels. It is generally shown as an upward sloping curve, reflecting increasing marginal costs of producing higher levels of national output. It is profitable to produce higher levels of national output only at higher price levels when higher marginal costs are associated with higher levels of national output.

FIGURE 13–5
Aggregate supply

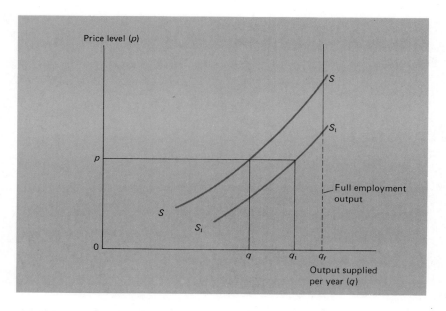

Aggregate supply shows the output supplied at different price levels. At the price level *OP*, output supplied is *Oq* given aggregate supply, *SS*, and is *Oq*₁ given aggregate *S₁S₁*. Aggregate supply, *S₁S₁*, represents a greater aggregate supply.

The determinants of aggregate supply are the same as the determinants of individual supply curves, namely, resource prices and techniques of production. Aggregate supply varies inversely with resource prices; that is, higher resource prices decrease aggregate supply, and lower resource prices increase aggregate supply. Improvements in production techniques that increase the productivity of resources increase aggregate supply.

Two aggregate supply curves, SS and S_1S_1 are shown in Figure 13–5. Both of these supply curves indicate the positive relationship between output supplied and the price level. At the price level, op, output supplied is oq, given SS, and oq_1, given S_1S_1. In reference to aggregate supply SS, aggregate supply, S_1S_1, indicates an increase in aggregate supply. The output supplied at oq_f is full employment.

Aggregate demand and supply

Employment and job opportunities depend on both aggregate demand and supply. Figure 13–6 shows three aggregate demand curves and two aggregate supply curves. Beginning with aggregate demand *DD* and aggregate supply *SS*, the equilibrium price level is *op*, and output demanded and supplied is *oq*. The economy is experiencing unemployment at this equilibrium level of national output as indicated by the difference between *oq* and oq_f, the full employment level of output. Given aggregate supply *SS*, the economy could reach full employment output only with a greater aggregate demand as represented by D_2D_2. At this level of aggregate demand, the equilibrium price level is op_2—much higher than it was at the lower level of aggregate demand. However, given the higher level of aggregate supply, S_1S_1, and the higher level of aggregate demand, D_1D_1, full employment could be reached at the price level *op*.

It can be said that at price level *op*, and at the output level *oq*, both aggregate demand and aggregate supply are deficient; for, the

FIGURE 13–6
Aggregate demand and supply

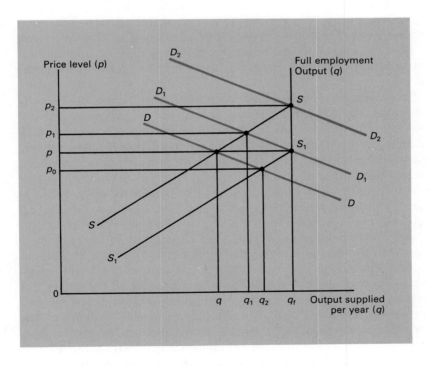

Starting with *DD* and *SS*, the equilibrium price level is *Op* and the national output is *Oq*. Full employment output, oq_f, can be reached by an increase in aggregate demand to D_2D_2. Full employment output can be reached at a lower demand D_1D_1, if aggregate supply can be increased to S_1S_1.

economy is not operating at full employment when *DD* and *SS* represent the strength of aggregate demand and supply. What are some of the reasons for a relatively weak aggregate demand and supply?

Reasons for deficient aggregate demand

Aggregate demand may not be high enough to provide for a full employment economy for many reasons. A deficient aggregate demand may be due to an inadequate level of output demanded by consumers. Consumers may reduce their rate of spending because of high prices, reductions in their real income and wealth, and high interest rates. The weakness in aggregate demand may be traced to the level of investment spending that falls short of the investment spending that would be required for a full employment economy. Finally, the deficiency in aggregate demand may be related to reductions in government purchases or increases in taxes that discourage private spending.

In order to understand more thoroughly why the economy may not operate at full employment, let's return to the circular flow of economic activity. The circular flow of economic activity shows that income is created in the process of production, and income created in production may return to producers in the form of spending for the products produced. However, there may be breaks in the circular flow.

These breaks are called *leakages* and *injections*. Figure 13–7 shows the leakages and injections in the circular flow of economic activity. Leakages, or withdrawals from the flow of economic activity, may be offset by injections to the flow of economic activity. An example of a leakage is *saving*, and an example of an injection is *investment*. Saving means that people are not spending part of the income created in production on the purchase of consumer goods such as radios, apples, cigarettes, ties, or refrigerators. This may turn out all right. Saving is required for the economy to invest in new plant and equipment and to grow. If the rate of saving at full employment returns to the circular flow of economic activity through investment (that is, the purchase of investment goods such as plant and equipment), aggregate demand will be sufficient to buy all the goods and services produced. If full-employment saving is greater than full-employment investment, then aggregate demand will be deficient unless other injections into the circular flow happen to be greater than other leakages by the amount of difference between saving and investment. When aggregate demand is deficient, part of the income created by production does not return to producers in the form of spending. This results in surpluses at current market prices and em-

FIGURE 13–7
Breaks in the circular flow of economic activity: Leakages and injections

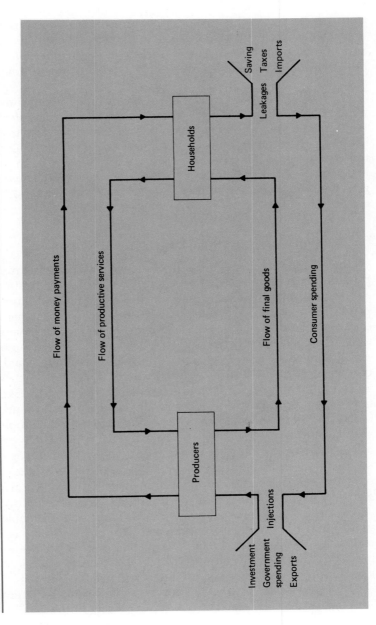
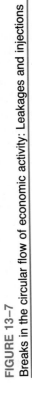

ployment levels. Producers respond to a surplus market situation by reducing production (and, therefore, income) causing people to lose their jobs.

Another example of a leakage is government *taxes*, and the corresponding example of an injection is *government purchases*. Taxes are similar to saving in the sense that they represent a withdrawal from the circular flow of economic activity. Taxes reduce private spending and, therefore, reduce aggregate demand. Aggregate demand may be deficient because taxes are too high in relation to government purchases.

Do you know why we have been so concerned about the *deficit* in the U.S. international balance of payments? A deficit in international trade means we are buying more products and services from other countries than they are buying from us. An *import* is a leakage from the circular flow of economic activity, and an *export* is an injection. A deficit, an excess of imports over exports, tends to decrease aggregate demand and contributes to the difficulty of reaching the level of aggregate demand required for full employment.

Reasons for weak aggregate supply

We have said that aggregate supply depends essentially on resource prices and techniques of production. The weakness or strength of aggregate supply depends, then, on these two factors. Suppose the price of a resource such as labor increases and is not offset by productivity increases. Under these circumstances, as we have said before, aggregate supply would decrease and cause unemployment. As we have also said previously, the weakness in aggregate supply may be attributable to the low productivity of labor.

The motivating force behind aggregate supply in a market economy is the profit motive. Producers are not going to expand output if it is not profitable to do so. The relationship between employment and wages and productivity may be extended further. It is profitable to expand employment out to the point where the real wage equals the marginal productivity of labor. In Figure 13–8 with the demand or the marginal product of labor shown by DD and the real wage equal to $0w$, the equilibrium or profitable level of employment is equal to $0n$. There are two ways that it would be profitable to expand output and increase employment to $0n_1$. One way is for the real wage to decrease to $0w_1$. The second way is for the marginal product of labor to increase to D_1D_1. Again, the weakness of aggregate supply is closely linked to wages and productivity.

The weakness of aggregate supply can be related to incentives to save and work. The stock of real capital assets in the economy cannot increase unless there is an adequate flow of savings to finance

FIGURE 13–8
Real wages, marginal product of labor, and employment

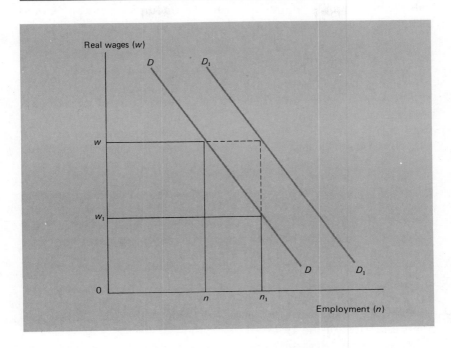

Given the demand or marginal product of labor, *DD*, and the real wage, *0w*, the level of employment is *0n*. There are two ways to increase employment to *0n₁*. One way is to reduce the real wage to *0w₁*. The second way is to increase the marginal product of labor to *D₁D₁*.

real investment. It is the stock of real capital assets that determines the general productivity of the economy. If incentives to save are seriously reduced by taxes, say, saving could be inadequate to provide for the replacement, modernization, and additions to the economy's capital stock. Certain taxes and certain government expenditure programs may reduce incentives to work by lowering the relative price of leisure. As a consequence, people may work less and take more leisure, resulting in a decrease in the supply of labor and a weaker aggregate supply.

COMBATING UNEMPLOYMENT

Unemployment has to be approached from both sides of the market since it may arise from the demand side or the supply side of the market. In the 1950s, 60s, and 70s, an aggregate demand approach was taken to cope with unemployment. More attention has been given to the supply approach in recent years because of some aggregate demand policy failures and because unemployment appears to stem more from the side of supply than in the past.

Aggregate demand policies

Aggregate demand policies are based on aggregate demand theory. This theory develops and explains the determinants of private consumer and investment spending. Two policy views have emerged from this theory. The first view is to stabilize aggregate demand over the business cycle. This means that government spending would be increased and/or taxes cut when private spending is contracting, and government spending would be decreased and/or taxes increased when private spending is expanding. The effect of these changes in government spending and taxes would be to smooth out economic fluctuations in the economy by stabilizing aggregate demand over time. The second policy view is to stabilize aggregate demand at a high level of employment and production, say, at the full employment level. This would mean that government spending would be increased and/or taxes decreased anytime the economy was not operating at the full employment production level. This latter view seems to have dominated the policy thinking during the 1960s and most of the 1970s.

The aggregate demand approach to unemployment is to increase aggregate demand directly by increasing government purchases and to increase aggregate demand indirectly by reducing taxes. Policies based on this approach have not been an unqualified success. The economy experienced a long period of growth and low unemployment rates in the 1960s under aggregate demand policies. However, the inflation rate increased in the late 1960s and very little was done about it, and what was done was done too late. After the 1973–75 recession, the economy expanded but encountered strong inflationary pressures that erupted into an inflation rate above 10 percent in 1979 and 1980.

Aggregate supply policies and the economy in the 1980s

Aggregate supply policies are based on aggregate supply theory. This theory provides the framework for analyzing the determinants of aggregate supply. The implication of the theory is that an alternative approach to unemployment is to pursue policies that would increase aggregate supply. The drawback in the supply-side approach is not in the theory but in being able to design a policy that will increase aggregate supply. What sort of economic policy will reduce resource prices and increase productivity in the economy?

The Reagan administration did set into action, beginning in 1981, policies that were at least inspired by supply-side thinking, even though the policies had an impact on aggregate demand as well as aggregate supply. The most significant policy from a supply-side viewpoint was the reduction in federal tax rates, especially the reduction in the marginal income tax rate from 70 percent to 50 percent, and more recently (1986) to 28 percent. The stated purpose of these marginal tax rate reductions was to increase aggregate supply by increasing incentives to save, work, and produce. In addition, incentives to invest were provided through an accelerated cost recovery system that allowed a much faster write-off of investment assets. An increase in investment will surely increase aggregate demand since it is an important component of demand, and it may indirectly increase aggregate supply by increasing the productivity of labor.

The economy responded to the above policy incentives (and to other underlying forces in the market) and started to expand in 1983. The real growth rate in the gross national product (GNP) was 3.6 percent and 6.4 percent in 1983 and 1984, respectively. The expansion continued in 1985 and in 1986 but at a slower growth rate, approximately 2.5 percent. This slow growth rate is predicted to continue in 1987. Figure 13–9 shows the role that the different component parts of the GNP have played in the expansion.

Consumer spending played an important role in bringing the economy out of the 1982 recession and in sustaining the expansion into 1987. Consumption was maintained, even during the recession, and increased steadily from 1982 to 1987. Investment, as usual, was more volatile in nature, decreasing and contributing to the recessionary forces in 1982, but increasing and contributing to the rapid real growth in the economy in 1983 and 1984. Since 1984, investment has remained at about the same rate. Government purchases of goods and services (federal, state, and local) were a stimulating force throughout the period from 1980 to 1986 while net exports (exports −imports) were a contractionary force. In 1983, 1984, 1985, and 1986, net exports were negative, indicating an export deficit; and the export deficit increased from $19.9 billion in 1983 to $149.7 billion in 1986. Unless the trade deficit had been offset by increases in the other components of the GNP, the economy expansion would have come to an end.

What role did federal economic policy play in the economic expansion that began in 1983? The cut in income tax rates, the tax incentives given to investment, and the increase in federal pur-

FIGURE 13–9
GNP, consumption, investment, government purchases, and net exports in constant 1982 dollars, 1980–1986

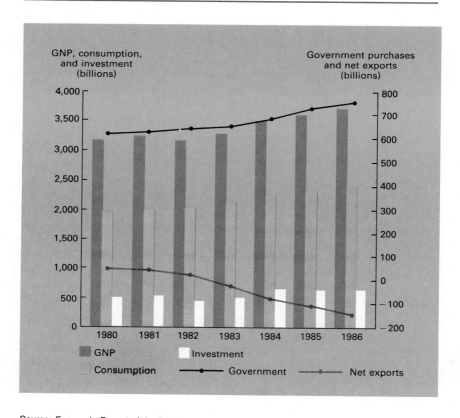

Source: *Economic Report of the President,* January 1987, pp. 246–47.

chases of goods and services together had stimulating effects on both aggregate demand and supply. However, the private sector not only had to respond to these policies and other market forces, such as the decline in oil prices, it also had to introduce new products and services and efficiently supply them in order for the economic expansion to have been as long-lasting.

SUMMARY

There are economic and social effects of unemployment. The economic effect involves the waste and loss of goods and services when resources are unemployed. The social effect involves the breaking up of human relationships within the family and outside it.

There are three types of unemployment—frictional, structural, and cyclical. Frictional unemployment is transitional in nature and is not a major economic issue. Structural and cyclical unemployment are major economic issues. Structural unemployment results from fundamental changes in demand and supply for products in specific sectors of the economy. Cyclical unemployment is associated with the ups and downs in the overall economy.

Aggregate demand and supply theory are developed to explain why people lose their jobs. Aggregate demand is composed of the output demanded by consumers, investors, and government. The determinants of consumer spending are prices, income, wealth, and rate of interest. At a given price level, the output demanded by consumers will vary directly with income and wealth, and inversely with the rate of interest. The determinants of investment spending are the expected profit rate and the rate of interest, with investment spending related directly to the expected profit rate and inversely with the interest rate. Government purchases, the final part of aggregate demand, depend on social priorities and policies.

A deficient aggregate demand or a weak aggregate supply may explain why the economy may operate at less than full employment. An aggregate demand approach to unemployment would be to pursue fiscal policies that would increase aggregate demand, namely increase government expenditures related to taxes. An aggregate supply approach would be to pursue policies that would increase aggregate supply, namely policies that would increase the productivity of resources and decrease the price of resources. The best possible approach is to pursue consistent aggregate demand and supply policies since unemployment may be caused from both a deficient aggregate demand and weak aggregate supply.

SUPPLEMENTARY READINGS

McConnell, Campbell R. *Economics.* 8th ed. New York: McGraw-Hill, 1981.

Chapters 10, 11, and 12 are suggested for students that desire to probe further into employment theory.

Miller, Roger LeRoy. *Economics Today.* 4th ed. New York: Harper & Row, 1982.

The circular flow of income is presented in chapter 9, and issues related to consumption, saving, and investment are presented in chapter 11. These two chapters and chapter 12 would add to the student's background in regard to what causes unemployment.

Schiller, Bradley R. *The Macro Economy Today*. New York: Random House, 1983.

Supply-side policies are examined in chapter 13. This chapter and chapter 15, "Reagan Economics," are recommended.

Swartz, Thomas R.; Frank J. Bonello; and Andrew F. Kozak. *The Supply Side*. Guilford, Conn.: Dushkin Publishing Group, 1983.

This paperback book provides numerous essays on supply-side economics and on the philosophical thinking behind the supply-side approach.

INFLATION

Meaning and measurement of inflation
  Inflation defined
  Further aspects of inflation
  Measurement of inflation
  Rate of inflation
Economic effects of inflation
  Equity effects
  Efficiency effects
  Output effects
What is money?
  Functions of money
  The basic money supply (M1)
  Other money measures
The process of creating money
  Commercial banks
  Other depository institutions
  Balance sheet of a bank
  The fractional reserve banking
    system
  Demand deposit creation
The issue of control
  The Federal Reserve System
  Federal Reserve controls
  Federal Reserve targets
Inflationary causes and cures
  Quantity theory of money
  Demand-pull inflation
  Cures for demand-pull inflation
  Cost-push inflation
  Demand-pull and then cost-push
    inflation
  Is there a cure for cost-push
    inflation?
Summary

**Checklist of
Economic Concepts**

Inflation
Price index numbers
Equity
Efficiency
Money supply
Creating money
Money multiplier
Legal reserve ratio
Discount rate
Open-market operation
Equation of exchange
Quantity theory of money
Demand-pull inflation
Cost-push inflation
Incomes policy

14

Inflation

How to gain and lose at the same time

We had sold out almost our entire inventory and, to our
amazement, had nothing to show for it except a worthless bank
account and a few suitcases full of currency not even good
enough to paper our walls with. We tried at first to sell and then
buy again as quickly as possible—but the inflation easily
overtook us. The lag before we got paid was too long; while we
waited, the value of money fell so fast that even our most
profitable sale turned into a loss. Only after we began to pay with
promissory notes could we maintain our position. Even so, we
are making no real profit now, but at least we can live. Since
every enterprise in Germany is financed in this fashion, the
Reischsbank naturally has to keep on printing unsecured
currency and so the mark falls faster and faster. The government
apparently doesn't care; all it loses in this way is the national
debt. Those who are ruined are the people who cannot pay with
notes, the people who have property they are forced to sell,
small shopkeepers, day laborers, people with small incomes who
see their private savings and their bank accounts melting away,
and government officials and employees who have to survive on
salaries that no longer allow them to buy so much as a new pair
of shoes. The ones who profit are the exchange kings, the
profiteers, the foreigners who buy what they like with a few
dollars, kronen, or zlotys, and the big entrepreneurs, the
manufacturers, and the speculators on the exchange whose
property and stocks increase without limit. For them practically
everything is free. It is the great sellout of thrift, honest effort,
and respectability. The vultures flock from all sides, and the only
ones who come out on top are those who accumulate debts. The
debts disappear of themselves.[1]

---

[1]Erich Maria Remarque, *The Black Obelisk* (New York: Harcourt Brace Jovanovich,
1957), pp. 54–55.

Inflation is considered by most people as equal to or second only to unemployment among the nation's major aggregate economic problems. In almost every presidential campaign, candidates call inflation a bad thing and vow to control it once elected. The rising cost of groceries, auto repairs, medical services, clothes, travel, and everything else is a main topic of conversation among consumers. Business firms realize that higher prices for materials, labor, equipment, and other things they buy will reduce business profits unless they are successful in passing these higher costs on to the consumer in the form of higher consumer prices. Inflation is a prime bargaining consideration in labor union negotiations. A stated national goal of government economic policy is to stabilize the price level. All groups comprising the population— consumers, unions, business firms, and government—are concerned about inflation.

MEANING AND MEASUREMENT OF INFLATION

Most people have a good idea of what is meant by inflation. They know that it causes a sack full of groceries to cost more money. They know that buying Christmas presents costs more. They know that it is more expensive to eat out, to go to a movie, to take a vacation, or to buy a car. They know they will be generally worse off in the future unless their pay can keep up with inflation.

Inflation defined

Inflation means that the general level of prices is rising. That is, enough commodity prices are rising so that, on the average, prices in general are rising. During inflation some commodities may be falling in price and some may be rising, but the commodities rising in price are dominant, and they exert an upward force on the general price level.

Further aspects of inflation

Dynamic aspects. Inflation has dynamic and self-sustaining properties. Increases in the price level induce economic groups to react to rising prices, causing further increases in prices. For example, consumers expecting increases in prices may increase current consumer spending, causing current market prices to rise. During periods of rising prices, producers are not inclined to resist increases in wages and other costs, since higher production costs may be shifted forward to consumers in the form of higher prices. These increases in prices, however, become the basis for further increases in production costs and still higher prices.

Inflation without rising prices. Inflation is not always observable in the form of rising prices. It may be suppressed; market prices may not always reflect the inflationary forces operating in the economy. *Suppressed inflation* is usually associated with an attempt on the part of government to control prices. During the control period, market prices remain the same. Inflationary forces, however, continue to exist because the government is not doing anything to alter the underlying inflationary forces in the market. Under these circumstances, it is difficult to keep prices under control, and prices in general will rise rapidly when price controls are lifted.

Measurement of inflation

Inflation is measured by price index numbers. Price index numbers indicate the general level of prices in reference to a base year. For example, the consumer price index in 1986 was 328.4, using 1967 as the base year. This means that consumer prices on the average were 228.4 percent above the level in 1967 (1967 = 100). The consumer price index was 322.2 in 1985. What was the rate of inflation between 1985 and 1986? The answer is 1.9 percent. This was derived as follows:

$$\text{Rate of inflation} = (328.4 - 322.2)/322.2$$

Price indexes. The consumer price index, sometimes referred to as the cost-of-living index, includes commodities that city wage earners and clerical workers buy, such as food, housing, utilities, transportation, clothing, health services, and recreation. The wholesale price index includes hundreds of commodities such as farm products and processed foods, as well as industrial commodities such as textiles, fuel, chemicals, rubber, lumber, paper, metals, machinery, furniture, nonmetallic minerals, and transportation equipment. Another price index that is used often by economists is the implicit price deflator. The implicit price deflator includes the components of the gross national product—consumer services, durable and nondurable goods, residential and nonresidential fixed investment, exports and imports, and goods and services purchased by governments.

Construction of a price index. Since inflation is measured by price index numbers, it is important to understand how price index numbers are derived. A simple illustration can point out the essential principles underlying the construction of the consumer price index. Suppose a family spends $20,000, $21,000, and $22,000 in 1985, 1986, and 1987, respectively, for identical baskets of goods. If 1985 is used as the base year, the index number for the goods for that year is 100. It is 105 for 1986, calculated by dividing the cost of the basket in the base year ($20,000) into the cost in 1986 ($21,000) and multiplying by 100 in order to remove the decimal. Using the same procedure, the index number in 1987 is 110, or

$$\frac{\text{Cost of market basket (1987)}}{\text{Cost of market basket (1985)}} \times 100 = \frac{\$22,000}{\$20,000} \times 100 = 110$$

The basket of goods used to compute price index numbers is a representative sample of the quantities of each good in the basket— the number of dresses, shirts, loaves of bread, gallons of gasoline, movie tickets, television sets, autos, and so forth—bought during the year specified. The sum of the price times the quantity of each good in the basket gives the value of the basket. After the value of the basket is calculated, the final step in the construction of a price index is to select the base year and compute the index numbers as illustrated.

A set of price index numbers is not a perfect measure of inflation. Only a sample of commodities is included in the index. What constitutes a representative sample is difficult to determine, and it changes over time in response to changes in tastes and preferences of people. It is also difficult to account for changes in the quality of goods that occur over time; for some goods and services, higher index numbers reflect higher costs for a better commodity rather than higher costs for the same commodity. Despite these imperfections, price index numbers are still useful indicators of trends in the level of prices.

Rate of inflation

Figure 14–1 shows the rate of growth in consumer prices since 1960. Prices were generally stable during the first part of the decade of the 1960s. However, inflationary forces began to grow in 1966 and continued to grow throughout the rest of the decade. The inflation in the 60s was mild overall, averaging 2.3 percent on a yearly basis. However, the inflation rate did reach 5.4 percent in 1969, and the underlying forces causing this higher rate continued into the early 1970s.

The decade of the 1970s not only inherited inflationary forces from the late 60s but added inflationary forces of its own. Wage and

FIGURE 14–1
Inflation rate (consumer prices) in selected years, 1960–1986

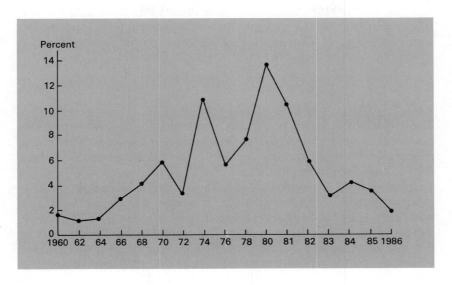

Source: *Economic Report of the President,* January, 1987, p. 311.

price controls were enacted to cope with the inflationary problem in the early 1970s. The year that controls were removed, 1974, the rate of inflation was 11 percent. The inflation rate was 5.8 percent or higher during the last half of the decade with a two-digit rate of inflation occurring again in 1979 (11.4 percent). The average annual inflation rate for the entire period between 1970 and 1980 was 7.1 percent—over three times the average annual rate of the previous decade.

The economy was in the worst possible state at the beginning of the 1980s. The inflation rate hit a high mark of 13.5 percent, and production in the economy was stagnated in 1980. A recession came next in 1981 and 1982. Inflation was brought under control by 1983; the inflation rate was 3.2 percent in that year. The rate of inflation remained in the 3 to 4.5 percent range in 1984 and 1985. However, the inflation rate fell to the lowest rate since the early 60s in 1986— 1.9 percent. It is predicted that the inflation rate will return to the 3 to 4 percent range in 1987. For the period between 1980 and 1986, the average annual rate of inflation was 6.1 percent.

ECONOMIC EFFECTS OF INFLATION

Inflation affects the distribution of income, the allocation of resources, and the national output. The effects of inflation on the distribution of income are referred to as the *equity* effects, and the effects on resource allocation and national output are called the *efficiency* and *output* effects of inflation, respectively.

Equity effects

The impact of inflation is uneven. Some people benefit from inflation, and some are made worse off. Because inflation alters the distribution of income, a major concern is the degree of equity or fairness in the distribution of income.

Anyone who is on a fixed income is hurt by inflation, since it reduces real income. For example, a person who earns $10,000 a year during an inflationary period in which there is a 25 percent increase in the price level suffers a cut in real income equivalent to the rate of inflation—$2,500 in this illustration. Examples of those whose incomes often do not rise as fast as the price level are retired people on pensions, white-collar workers, civil servants, people on public assistance, and workers in declining industries.

People who hold assets in the form of money and who have fixed claims on money may be worse off by inflation. Suppose a person deposits $1,000 in a savings account and receives a 5 percent interest rate, or $50 during the year. If the rate of inflation is in excess of 5 percent, the real value of the original savings of $1,000 plus the $50 earned on the savings for a year is reduced to less than the original $1,000. Creditors and owners of mortgages and life insurance policies are hurt by inflation, since the real value of their fixed money claims is reduced. People who bought government savings bonds for $18.75 and were paid $25.00 at maturity 10 years later have sometimes discovered that the $25.00 would not buy the same quantity of goods and services as the $18.75 would have bought 10 years earlier.

Inflation benefits people who have incomes that rise faster than prices and those who hold assets whose values rise faster than the price level. Wages and salaries of workers in rapidly growing industries are likely to rise faster than the price level. Strong unions are sometimes successful in bargaining for wage increases that are greater than the increases in the price level. People who depend on income in the form of profits—owners of stocks and business enterprises—may have increases in real income, depending upon the rate of increase in profits in comparison to prices. The value of land

and improvements on land may rise during inflation; if they rise in value faster than the rate of inflation, owners of property will benefit.

In summary, inflation alters the distribution of income and wealth.[2] Inflation is like a tax to some people and like a subsidy to others. People whose real incomes are reduced by inflation are those who have fixed incomes and hold assets in the form of money. People whose real incomes are increased by inflation are those who have money income that increases faster than prices and hold real assets that appreciate in value faster than inflation. The arbitrary manner in which inflation may change the pattern of income distribution gives support to the claim that inflation is inequitable.

Efficiency effects

Inflation tends to change the pattern of resource allocation. In a competitive market the prices of different goods and services reflect differences in consumer valuations of the quantities made available. Inflation causes demands for different goods and services to increase, but demands for some increase more rapidly than those for others. Increases in demands evoke supply responses, the extent of which varies from product to product. Thus, inflation changes relative demands, relative supplies, and relative prices of different goods and services. The pattern of resource allocation, then, is not the same pattern that would exist in the absence of inflation. It is not certain that the pattern of resource allocation with inflation is less efficient (that is, results in lower economic welfare) than the pattern without inflation.[3] However, many economists argue that inflation distorts the pattern of resource allocation, implying a less efficient allocation of resources.

Inflation encourages economic groups to spend time and resources in an attempt to adjust to inflation. Since inflation reduces the purchasing power of money, it encourages everyone to economize or minimize their money balances, that is, assets held in the form of money. The time spent and the resources used in adjusting to inflation could have been used to produce goods and services. Inflation, by encouraging everyone to make adjustments and divert time and resources away from production, reduces economic efficiency.

---

[2]It is assumed that inflation is unanticipated. A fully anticipated inflation may not alter the distribution of income and wealth.

[3]Frank G. Steindl, "Money Illusion, Price Determinancy and Price Stability," *Nebraska Journal of Economics and Business*, no. 10 (Winter 1971), pp. 26–27.

Output effects

The preceding discussion of the equity and efficiency effects of inflation assumes that the levels of real output and production lie on the economy's production possibilities curve. This assumption is made in order to focus attention on how inflation may alter the distribution of real income among people (equity effects) and the allocation of resources (efficiency effects). Simply stated, a certain size pie is assumed in the previous discussion, and the concern is how inflation alters the slices of pie and affects the use of resources in making the pie. Now we consider the effects of inflation on the size of the pie. What are the effects of inflation on the level of output of goods and services?

Inflation may have a stimulating effect on production and employment in the economy. The argument in support of this proposition can be presented as follows. During inflation money wages lag behind price increases. Real profit income is increased. Under the stimulus of higher profits, producers expand production and employ more people.

The argument that inflation may stimulate production and employment should be qualified. Runaway or hyperinflation may depreciate the value of money so drastically that it loses its acceptability as a medium of exchange. Under these circumstances a barter economy develops, accompanied by lower production levels and higher unemployment. If the economy is operating at full capacity and full employment, then, of course, inflation cannot stimulate them further. Inflation at full employment is referred to usually as *pure* inflation.

The impact of inflation differs depending upon whether or not inflation is associated with increases in production and employment. As long as production is rising, there is a check on inflation since, although lagging behind demand, supply is increasing and inflationary forces are mitigated. The equity effects of inflation are also minimized if production and employment are rising. However, as the economy approaches full employment, the seriousness of inflation increases. The possibility of an accelerated rate of inflation is nearer, and the possible beneficial effects of inflation on production and employment are remote.

WHAT IS MONEY?

It is sometimes stated that inflation is a situation in which "too much" money is chasing "too few" goods. As a first step to understanding inflation, we need to be able to answer the question, what is money?

Money is anything that is generally accepted as a means of payment for goods, services, and debt. Many things have been used for money such as sea shells, bullets, and metals. Money is much more than just cash. There are several measures of money, and what is included in the money supply and the functions of money are the points of interest in this section.

Functions of money

Money serves three basic functions: a medium of exchange, a measure of value, and a store of value. Goods and services are paid for in money, and debts are incurred and paid off in money. Without money, economic transactions would have to take place on a barter basis, that is, one good traded for another good. Thus, the use of money as the *medium of exchange* simplifies and facilitates the exchange process. Second, the values of economic goods and services are measured in money. Money as a *measure of value* makes possible value comparisons of goods and services and the summation of quantities of goods and services on a value basis. It is not possible to add apples and oranges, but *it is possible* to add the *values* of apples and oranges. Third, wealth and assets may be held in the form of money. Money serves as a *store of value.*

The basic money supply (M1)

The basic money supply, called M1 for short, includes currency and coins in circulation, traveler's checks, demand deposits at commercial banks, and other transaction accounts or checkable deposits, such as NOW accounts, ATS accounts, credit-union share drafts, and demand deposits at mutual savings banks. NOW accounts are negotiable orders of withdrawal, and ATS accounts are automatic withdrawal of savings accounts. NOW and ATS accounts are similar to a regular checking account in the sense that goods and services can be paid for by writing checks on these accounts. ATS accounts can be both checking and savings accounts; however, the bank will automatically transfer balances from savings to checking accounts when necessary to cover checks that have been written. The effect is the same as if all balances were held in a regular checking account. Credit-union share drafts and demand deposits at mutual savings banks are also the same as regular checking accounts at commercial banks.

Figure 14–2 shows the growth in M1 in selected years since 1960. The first observation that can be made about the money supply growth rate is that it is erratic. The average annual growth rate in the money supply was 3.5 percent during the decade of the 1960s.

FIGURE 14–2
Money supply (M1) growth rate in selected years, 1960–1986

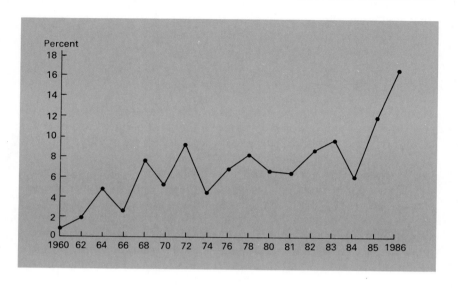

Source: *Economic Report of the President,* January, 1987, p. 319.

However, the growth rate of the money supply fluctuated from a low of less than 1 percent in 1960 to a high of about 8 percent in 1968. The ups and downs in the growth in the money supply were repeated in the 70s and in the 80s. In the 1970s, the average annual money supply growth rate was 6.6 percent, and the low rate and high rate ranged from 4.4 percent in 1974 to 9.2 percent in 1972. The swings in the growth in M1 have been even more extreme in the current decade. In 1981 and 1982, the money supply growth rate was slightly above 6 percent. Then, the growth rate in M1 acceler-ated to 9 and 10 percent in 1982 and 1983, respectively. After declin-ing to 6 percent in 1984, it jumped to 12.2 percent in 1985 and 16.6 percent in 1986.

The second observation that may be made concerning the growth in the money supply is that the long-run trend in the average annual growth rate is significantly upward. The average annual growth rate in M1 increased from 3.9 percent in the 60s to 6.6 percent in the 70s, and to 9.5 percent from 1980 to 1986. Most economists would prob-ably like to see the annual growth rate in M1 stabilized at about 6 percent. The reason for this is that excessive growth in the money supply leads to serious inflation, and erratic growth in the money supply may contribute to economic instability.

Other money measures

The basic money supply, M1, is composed of assets that are easily accessible and completely liquid. There are other assets possessing almost these same features. Two examples are time or savings deposits and money-market mutual funds. A phone call or a trip to a bank is often the only difference between a demand and time deposit. Some savings accounts may have more stringent conditions placed on them such as the loss of interest if they are withdrawn early, but, in general, savings accounts are like money. Many people find it convenient and can earn more interest by buying shares of money-market mutual funds. These funds are invested in an almost riskless, interest-yielding asset, namely, U.S. Treasury bills. Money-market mutual funds are easily accessible and, under certain conditions, checks can be written against these funds. A broader definition of money, called M2, includes M1 plus savings accounts, small denomination time deposits, money-market mutual funds, and overnight Eurodollars.

There are still broader definitions of money referred to as M3 and L. Time deposits of over $100,000 are included in the definition of M3, and L includes other liquid assets such as Treasury bills, U.S. savings bonds, and commercial paper. The purpose of these broader measures of money is to have a measure of near-money and a measure of the overall liquidity in the economy. However, the basic money supply, M1, is what is generally meant by the money supply, and this is the definition of money that we use throughout the text.

THE PROCESS OF CREATING MONEY

The major part of the money supply is in the form of demand and other checkable deposits. Checking deposits are held in commercial banks and other depository institutions, namely, savings and loan associations, mutual savings banks, and credit unions. In this section, the focus is on the way these deposits are created and destroyed.

Commercial banks

There are about 15,000 commercial banks. Banks are private firms that are in business to make a profit by providing a full range of banking services, including checking accounts, savings accounts, loans, automatic transfers from savings to checking accounts, and electronic banking services. Commercial banks are either state banks or national banks. State banks receive their charters to engage in the banking business from the state; whereas, national banks receive their charter from the federal government.

Goldsmiths, the original bankers, provided the important service of a safe and convenient place to keep money or gold deposits, generally storing them in a vault. Depositors received a receipt for the gold deposited and used the receipt to buy goods and services. These receipts were the early form of paper money. Goldsmiths discovered early that it was not necessary to have a dollar in gold for each dollar issued in the form of receipts since only a *fraction* of the gold deposited was required to meet gold withdrawals. This discovery led to two more important services. Loans were made to individuals and businesses, and paper money was created in the form of the issue of goldsmiths' receipts. The three main functions of banks today as then are (1) to provide a safe place for depositors to keep money and other assets, (2) to make loans, and (3) to create money as a group.

Other depository institutions

The traditional distinctions between commercial banks and other depository institutions or banks are disappearing. The Monetary Control Act of 1980 allows more flexibility in providing a full range of banking services. Prior to this act, savings and loan associations and mutual savings banks were restricted to offering savings accounts. These institutions now offer checking account services and are expanding other banking services. Historically, savings deposits of savings and loan associations were used primarily to finance the purchase of homes. Now with checking deposits, savings and loan associations will probably make other types of loans as well. Mutual savings banks are very much like savings and loan associations; however, they were originally intended to serve small savers and used their funds for different purposes, such as investment in stocks and bonds.

Another depository institution is the credit union. A credit union is a cooperative banking venture where the members or owners have a common employer or union. Credit unions have savings and checking accounts and use their funds primarily for small consumer loans. The services of credit unions can be expected to expand in the future.

Balance sheet of a bank

A balance sheet of a bank shows the relationship among the bank's assets, liabilities, and net worth. The important feature of a balance sheet is:

$$\text{Assets} = \text{Liabilities} + \text{Net worth}$$

When there is a change on one side of the equation, there is an offsetting change either on the same side of the equation or on the other side of the equation. For example, if there is an increase in a liability of $10,000, there is a decrease of $10,000 in another liability or net worth or an increase in an asset of $10,000.

The major assets of a bank are cash reserves, loans and investments, and fixed investments, such as a building and equipment. The major liabilities of banks are demand or checking deposits and time or savings deposits. The net worth of a bank is the owner's equity or the capital stock of the bank.

The balance sheet of a bank appears as follows:

Assets	Liabilities and net worth
Reserves:	Liabilities:
Legal reserves	Demand deposits
Excess reserves	Time deposits
Loans and investments	Net worth
Fixed investments	

In order to focus on the way money is created, we are concerned only with reserves and loans of banks on the asset side and demand or checking deposits on the liability side.

The fractional reserve banking system

Banks are required by law to keep only a part of their deposits in reserves. These reserves are held primarily in the form of deposits at Federal Reserve Banks but also include the cash that banks have on hand, sometimes referred to as vault-cash. The legal reserve requirement is expressed in percentage terms and is called the *reserve ratio* since it is the ratio of required reserves to bank deposits. For example, if the reserve ratio for a particular bank with demand deposits of $40 million is 10 percent, this bank must have in legal reserves 10 percent of $40 million or $4 million. Banks are classified by size into two classes. As of January 1985, reserve ratios are 3 percent and 12 percent for the two classes. Today, most banks are large enough to be subject to the 12 percent reserve ratio.

Banks may have *excess reserves*, that is, reserves above what is required to meet the legal reserve requirement. Banks must have excess reserves to make new loans. When banks, as a group, expand loans, they create demand deposits; and when banks, as a group, contract loans, they destroy demand deposits. Now, let's turn more specifically to the process of creating and destroying demand deposits or money.

Demand deposit creation

Suppose there is a new demand deposit of $10,000, and the reserve ratio is 10 percent. The demand deposits of the bank increase $10,000, and reserves increase $10,000. If the new deposit was made from withdrawing currency in circulation, there is no change in the money supply since the money supply is composed of currency in circulation and demand deposits. Given a 10 percent reserve ratio, the bank has to keep $1,000 in legal reserves and has $9,000 in excess reserves.

Now, let's say you go in the bank and borrow $9,000 in order to buy a car. You sign a piece of paper called a promissory note agreeing to pay back the loan plus interest over a period of time in monthly installments. The new auto is used as collateral for the loan. After you sign the promissory note, the bank increases your checking account by the amount of the loan or $9,000. You write a check for $9,000 to pay for the new auto. Your balance at the bank remains unchanged. Demand deposits at another bank increase $9,000 when the auto dealer deposits your check. A loan of $9,000 to pay for a new auto has created new demand deposits of $9,000 in the banking system.

The process of demand deposit creation does not have to end after your loan of $9,000 creates new demand deposits of $9,000. The increase in demand deposits of $9,000 generates bank reserves of this same amount. With the assumed legal reserve ratio of 10 percent, $900 ($9,000 × .10) is required to meet the legal reserve requirement. Thus, excess reserves of $8,100 ($9,000 − $8,100) remain in the system. By the same process as your loan, a new loan of $8,100 may be made that creates a new deposit of $8,100. This process may be repeated over and over again until excess reserves become zero.

The multiple expansion of demand deposits from a $10,000 deposit withdrawn from currency in circulation assuming a reserve ratio of 10 percent is shown through four stages in Table 14–1. Could you continue the stages through five, six, seven, and so on? In the final stage, observe demand deposits are $100,000, but the maxi-

TABLE 14–1
A $10,000 new deposit is made from currency in circulation
(legal reserve ratio = 10%)

Stage 1: Bank 1

Assets	Liabilities
Reserves:	
Legal + $1,000	Demand Deposits + $10,00
Excess + $9,000	

A $9,000 loan is made
Stage 2: Bank 2

Assets	Liabilities
Reserves:	
Legal + $900	Demand Deposits + $9,000
Excess + $8,100	

An $8,100 loan is made
Stage 3: Bank 3

Assets	Liabilities
Reserves:	
Legal + $810	Demand Deposits + $8,100
Excess + $7,290	

A $7,290 loan is made
Stage 4: Bank 4

Assets	Liabilities
Reserves:	
Legal + $729	Demand Deposits + $7,290
Excess + $6,561	

At the end of Stage 4: Sum Total of Loans + $24,390

Assets	Liabilities
Reserves:	
Legal + $3,439	Demand deposits + $34,390
Excess + $6,561	

Final Stage: Sum Total of All Stages
Sum Total of Loans + $90,000

Assets	Liabilities
Reserves:	
Legal + $10,000	Demand Deposits + $100,000
Excess $0	

mum demand deposit *increase* or money supply increase is $90,000 since $10,000 is currency withdrawn from circulation. In a symmetrical way, there may be a multiple contraction in demand deposits and the money supply when demand deposits are reduced in the banking system by a new currency withdrawal of $10,000.

The maximum demand deposit creation possible from a given new demand deposit can be calculated based on the following equation:

$$D = E(1/r)$$

where D = maximum deposit creation; E = excess legal reserves; and r = reserve ratio.

In our illustration, the $10,000 new demand deposit increases legal reserves $1,000 and excess reserves $9,000. The increase in excess reserves times the reciprocal of the reserve ratio or the *money multiplier* equals the maximum deposit creation possible ($9,000 × 10 = $90,000).

THE ISSUE OF CONTROL

It is apparent that with a fractional reserve banking system the money supply can expand and contract rapidly. The system works well when money growth is controlled. The Federal Reserve Act of 1913 established the Federal Reserve System. The main purpose of the Fed is to control the money supply.

The Federal Reserve System

There are 12 Federal Reserve banks located in various regions of the country. Each Federal Reserve bank acts as a central bank for private banks in the region. A central bank is a bank for private banks. Just as a private bank provides you with a full range of banking services, the Fed provides private banks with many services. Among these services are the clearing of checks, the holding of bank reserves or deposits, the providing of currency, and the making of loans to private banks.

The Board of Governors manages the Federal Reserve System. The board consists of seven members appointed by the president and confirmed by Congress. The appointments are for 14 years, and reappointments are prohibited after serving a full term. The president selects the chairman of the board, who is the chief spokesperson and architect of Fed policy. The chairman of the board, Alan Greenspan, was appointed by President Reagan in 1987. Greenspan replaced Paul Volcker, who had been chairman since 1979.

An influential policy committee is the Federal Reserve Open Market Committee (FOMC). This committee is composed of all seven members of the Board of Governors plus five regional Reserve bank presidents. The FOMC meets about once a month in Washington, D.C., to discuss and determine open-market operations. Open-market operations are the buying and selling of government securities in order to influence the level of bank reserves.

The Monetary Control Act of 1980 brought all banks and depository institutions under the regulations of the Fed. Prior to this act, state-chartered banks could choose whether they wanted to be "members" of the Fed. This distinction between member and nonmember banks no longer has economic significance. All banks are subject to the Federal Reserve legal reserve requirements, and all banks are provided with Fed services.

Federal Reserve controls

The Federal Reserve has three major policy instruments. They are the legal reserve requirement, the discount rate, and open-market operations. Each of these controls influences excess reserves and the lending ability of banks. The discount rate is not generally a powerful control but is important because it may indicate the direction of the Federal Reserve policy with respect to interest rates. The legal reserve ratio is a powerful weapon, but changes in the legal reserve ratio are not made frequently. Open-market operations have a direct impact on excess reserves and are the most important way that the Fed controls the money supply.

Legal reserve ratio. The legal reserve ratio is the ratio of reserves that banks are required to maintain to demand deposits. An increase in this ratio reduces excess reserves and the lending potential of banks. Banks that are fully loaned out, that is, banks with zero excess reserves, are required to reduce loans and borrow from the Fed or from other banks with excess reserves in order to meet a higher reserve requirement. A decrease in the legal reserve ratio increases excess reserves and the lending potential of banks. Thus, a contractionary Federal Reserve monetary policy could be in the form of increasing the legal reserve ratio, and an expansionary policy could be in the form of reducing the ratio.

Discount rate. The discount rate is the rate of interest that Federal Reserve banks charge when banks borrow from the Fed. An increase in the discount rate tends to discourage bank borrowing from the Fed and to increase interest rates on bank loans generally. The Fed increases the discount rate when it desires to tighten credit and slow down growth in the money supply. In contrast, the Fed decreases the discount rate when it desires to ease money and credit. Sometimes changes in the discount rate are viewed as signals indicating whether the Federal Reserve is pursuing or planning to pursue a policy of monetary ease or monetary tightness. A change in the discount rate not supported by appropriate changes in other monetary weapons may not have much impact on the economy.

Open-market operations. The Federal Reserve Open Market Committee (FOMC) buys and sells federal securities in order to influence bank reserves, loans, and demand deposits. An open-market purchase means that the Fed is buying federal securities from banks or from the nonbank public. In either case, banks' excess reserves are increased. The primary impact of the purchase of federal securities from banks is to increase excess reserves and decrease federal securities held by banks. The primary impact of an open-market purchase from nonbanks is to increase demand deposits and excess reserves of banks. The FOMC makes the decision to buy federal securities when it desires to expand the money supply. An open-market sale has the opposite effects. Excess reserves and the lending ability of banks are reduced by open-market sales. Thus, the FOMC makes the decision to sell federal securities when it desires to contract growth in the money supply.

Federal Reserve targets

The two most often discussed monetary policy targets are the interest rate target and the money growth rate target. Federal Reserve policy has often focused on interest rates. When interest rates were believed to be "too high," the Fed pursued a policy of monetary ease; and when interest rates were believed to be "too low," the Fed pursued a policy of monetary tightness. These policy actions are sometimes referred to as a policy of "fine tuning," that is, pursuing a policy that in effect changes the growth rate in the money supply in order to maintain interest rates at a level that will promote economic stability and growth. This focus on interest rates as the prime basis of Fed policy has at times led to serious inflationary problems. During periods of economic expansion, interest rates generally rise because of the increase in the demand for money and credit. To prevent interest rates from rising in these circumstances, the Fed may pursue a policy that increases the money growth rate. Also, political pressures on the Fed to keep interest rates low or to prevent interest rates from rising tend to increase inflationary expectations and eventually lead to a higher money growth rate and inflation. The major criticism of using interest rates as the main policy target is that the Fed would be relinquishing control over the growth in the money supply.

Primarily in response to the high rate of inflation in the late 1970s, the Federal Reserve began in October 1979 to focus on money growth as the prime policy target. Money growth rates were established for the various measures of money. For example, the growth rate for M1 in 1986 was set within a range of 3 to 8 percent. The money growth rate of M1 was not kept close to this range in 1986.

A growing number of economists support the money growth rate target. They make two major points. First, they argue that it is the growth in the money supply that ultimately determines the inflation rate. Second, they argue that erratic movements in the money growth rate are primarily responsible for the economic instability in the economy. For these reasons, a Fed policy that concentrates on a stable money growth rate is favored by these economists.

The experiences with Fed policy based on money growth targets raise certain policy questions. The money growth targets set by the Fed in 1981 and 1982 resulted in a monetary policy that was, perhaps, too restricted. Some economists argued that the restricted Fed policy contributed to the severity and duration of the 1981–82 recession. On the other side and in support of Fed policy, the restricted policy was successful in significantly slowing the inflation rate. More recently, in 1985 and 1986, the M1 money growth target was greatly exceeded. The argument used by the Fed in defense of its policy was that it is not as important to keep M1 within its target range as it is to keep the broader monetary aggregates, M2 and M3, within their growth target ranges. Although an accelerated rate of inflation did not occur in 1985 and 1986, as would have been expected from rapid growth in M1, some feared that a higher inflation rate would take place in 1987 and in future years. Then, even if it is accepted that the money growth rate is the best alternative policy target, the problems of selecting the correct monetary aggregates and the correct money growth target for these aggregates, and staying within the targets, are policy problems yet to be resolved.

Another policy issue related to the money growth target is the ability or inability of the Fed to pursue a *stable* money growth rate policy. In some periods, money growth rates vary widely on a monthly basis from the established targets. Critics of Fed policy believed that the Fed was not focusing on controlling the money supply and was basing policy on other considerations. It may be that this criticism was in part justified. It may also be that money growth rates cannot be precisely controlled in the very short run.

In summary, the issue of the appropriate monetary policy target is not resolved among policymakers. Among economists, there is somewhat more agreement that monetary stability can be best accomplished by a Federal Reserve policy that strives to maintain a stable and reasonable money growth rate.

INFLATIONARY CAUSES AND CURES

Two approaches will be taken to explain the causes of inflation and to present possible methods of stopping it. The quantity theory of money is the first approach. This theory stresses the importance of money in the inflationary process. Aggregate demand and supply analysis provides a framework for approaching the causes of inflation.

Quantity theory of money

The starting point for the quantity theory of money is the *equation of exchange:*

$$MV = PQ$$

where M = the money supply; V = the income velocity of money or the number of times, on an average, a dollar is used to buy final goods and services in a year; P = the price level or the average price of final goods and services; and Q = the quantity of final goods and services produced during the year.

The left-hand side of the equation, the money supply (M) times the velocity or turnover of money (V), measures total money spending in the economy. The right-hand side of the equation, the price level (P) times the national output (Q) equals the money value of the national output or nominal income. The two sides of the equation are equal since the total spending for goods and services is the same as the total sales value of goods and services.

The quantity theory of money states that increases and decreases in M cause increases and decreases in P and Q, respectively. The assumption of this theory is that V is constant. If it is further assumed that the nation's output is fixed, it follows that the price level will rise or fall at the same rate that M rises or falls. More relevant than this extreme assumption concerning output is that, given a constant or relatively constant V, the inflation rate is closely connected with the growth rate in the money supply as the economy expands and nears full employment.

An increase in the money supply will certainly increase prices unless either velocity of money decreases and/or output increases. In the event of no changes in V and Q, the price level is the equilibrium variable that moves the economy toward a new equilibrium where the increase in M is offset by an increase in P. That is to say, when there is "excess money" created by an increase in M, the excess money, assuming a constant V, flows into the final goods market resulting in inflation. A decrease in V or an increase in Q could partially or wholly eliminate the excess money, and therefore, could partially or wholly offset the inflationary pressure. The quantity theory of money teaches, however, that growth in the money supply is the basic cause of inflation, and the cure for inflation is to control the growth in the money supply. The control can be achieved, of course, through the appropriate use of Federal Reserve controls over the money supply.

Demand-pull inflation

An alternative approach to the quantity theory of money is the aggregate demand approach. In this approach, the stress is on excess demand as the major cause of inflation. The two approaches are similar in most important respects, but there are some differences in points of emphasis and in policy recommendations. The aggregate demand approach places more emphasis on total consumer, investment, and government spending in the economy (MV) and less emphasis on growth in the money supply. The money supply is viewed primarily as an *accommodating* variable instead of an *initiating* variable. According to aggregate demand analysis, demand-pull inflation is initiated by an increase in aggregate demand and is self-enforcing by further increases in aggregate demand. A demand-pull inflation is associated with increases in production and employment until the economy reaches full employment. Once full employment is reached, further increases in demand increases prices only.

Figure 14–3 depicts demand-pull inflation. Beginning at the price level p and production q, an increase in aggregate demand to D_1 means that all of demand cannot be satisfied at p. Thus, the price level rises to p_1, and production rises to q_f. An increase in demand to D_2 causes the price level to rise further to p_2. This inflationary process continues as long as aggregate demand increases, since all of demand can be satisfied only at higher prices. Pure inflation, an increase in the price level without an increase in output, is shown when aggregate demand increases to D_2.

Cures for demand-pull inflation

Demand-pull inflation can be stopped by the appropriate use of Federal Reserve monetary policy and federal fiscal policy. We know now that demand-pull inflations are caused by "excess money" leading to excess spending or that they are caused by "excess demand" accommodated by expansions in the money supply. In either case, this type of inflation can be slowed down or stopped completely by Federal Reserve policy that slows down the growth in the money supply: namely, a policy employing a combination of Fed controls that reduce excess reserves in the banking system and the ability of banks to expand loans and create money.

The appropriate federal fiscal policy in periods of demand-pull inflations is some combination of government expenditure cuts and tax increases; that is, federal budget deficits should be reduced. A decrease in government purchases directly reduces total spending in the economy. A decrease in government transfer payments or an increase in taxes indirectly reduces aggregate demand by decreasing

FIGURE 14–3
Demand-pull inflation

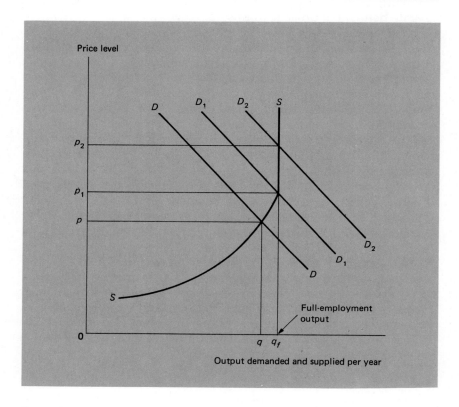

Demand-pull inflation is due to increases in aggregate demand from DD to D_1D_1 to D_2D_2.

private spending. In addition, increases in the federal debt brought about by budget deficits should be financed in a way that does not create money.

Demand-pull inflations are difficult to stop without causing unemployment. The same economic forces causing inflation also increase production and employment. The secret to controlling demand-pull inflation is not to let it develop in the first place. Once inflation develops and is out of control as in the late 1960s and 70s, it seems almost inevitable that the opportunity cost to stop inflation is rising unemployment.

Cost-push inflation

It is difficult to explain some of the inflationary periods in the 1960s and 70s only on the basis of demand-pull inflation. The economy has experienced both inflation and recession together at certain times. How can this be? Demand-pull inflation is characterized by rising prices and rising production until full employment is reached. Inflation and recession at the same time mean rising prices and falling production.

The only way the economy can experience simultaneous inflation and recession is for inflation to be initiated by a decrease in aggregate supply. This type of inflation is called cost-push inflation. Increases in costs cause aggregate supply to decrease, reducing the quantity of goods produced and increasing prices.

Figure 14–4 illustrates cost-push inflation. Beginning at price level p and production q_f, aggregate supply decreases to S_1. Now all of demand cannot be satisfied at p; that is, aggregate output demanded is greater than aggregate output supplied. As a consequence, the price level rises to p_1. Aggregate supply decreases further to S_2. Again, all of demand cannot be satisfied, and price rises to p_2. This inflationary process continues until there are no further decreases in aggregate supply. In Figure 14–4, cost-push inflation is characterized by rising prices and falling production.

Cost-push inflation occurs because of decreases in aggregate supply. But what causes aggregate supply to decrease? The answer is an increase in resource prices not offset by productivity increases. If a resource, such as energy, increases in price, it is not profitable to produce the same levels of output at the same price levels unless the higher energy costs are offset. For another illustration, an increase in the price of labor increases labor unit costs and, therefore, decreases output supplied at every price level. Sometimes the blame for cost-push inflation is placed on monopoly power—the power of unions to negotiate successfully for wage gains in excess of productivity gains and the market power of monopoly firms to restrict output and increase prices. In the absence of inflationary demand pressures, the monopoly powers of unions and producers to bring about cost-push inflations are exaggerated. The major point to remember about cost-push inflations is that they are caused by resource price increases or productivity decreases regardless of the reason or reasons why these things may occur.

Demand-pull and then cost-push inflation

It may be misleading to look upon demand-pull and cost-push as two separate inflationary processes. In fact, a single inflationary pe-

FIGURE 14–4
Cost-push inflation

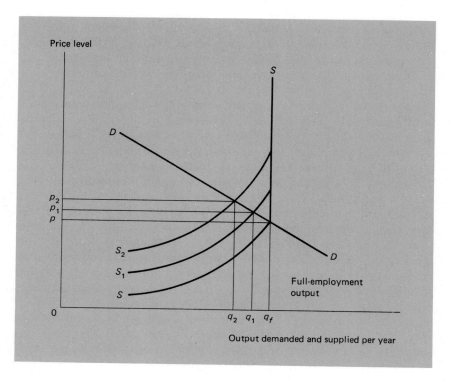

Cost-push inflation is due to a decrease in aggregate supply from SS to SS_1, and SS_2.

riod may result from both demand-pull and cost-push pressures. Increases in aggregate demand start the inflationary process. Prices, production, and employment rise in response to the pull of demand. Money wages rise, but with a lag behind prices. Unions realize eventually that wages have lagged behind prices and begin to try to catch up by demanding wage increases in excess of productivity increases. Once this happens, cost-push pressures begin to reinforce demand pressures.

The end of an inflationary process may not coincide with the moment that demand-pull pressures no longer exist. Prices may continue to rise for a period because of cost-push pressures. These pressures operating alone sustain the inflation temporarily, even though production and employment are falling. However, without demand-pull pressures, inflation eventually stops.

Is there a cure for cost-push inflation?

Monetary and fiscal policies can deal, theoretically anyway, with demand type problems. They are more designed for these purposes. However, they cannot cope effectively with cost-push inflationary pressures. Certain other policies have been advocated by some economists to deal with cost-push inflationary pressures that stem from wage and price increases connected with monopoly power of unions and business firms. These policies are often referred to as *incomes policies.*

An incomes policy may range from the president of the United States inviting labor and business leaders to the White House in order to persuade them to use wage and price restraint to wage and price controls. President John F. Kennedy adopted a policy of wage and price guidelines in the early 1960s. President Johnson abandoned guidelines for jawboning when inflationary pressures mounted in the late 1960s. President Nixon resorted to wage and price controls between 1971 and 1974. President Carter announced voluntary wage-price standards in 1978. President Reagan did not have to deal with cost-push inflationary pressures during his first several years in office. Cost-push inflationary pressures do not exist or are weak when the economy is declining or when the economy is in a weak recovery as it was in early 1983.

Incomes policies have been far from successful thus far. The main criticism of almost any incomes policy is that it does not eliminate the cause of the inflation. Assuming the monopoly power of unions and business firms is the major cause of cost-push inflationary pressures, these pressures do not disappear unless this cause is eliminated. Also, the monopoly power of unions and business firms cannot be effectively used anyway unless there are inflationary pressures caused by expansionary monetary and fiscal policies.

An incomes policy that has not been tried but has support among some economists is called a tax-based incomes policy or TIP.[4] The general economic thinking behind a tax-based incomes policy is that prices are determined by an average markup of prices over labor unit costs. When labor unit costs rise, say, because of wage increases in excess of productivity increases, prices rise generally in the economy. In the TIP proposal, incentives are provided to discourage "excess wage" increases.

---

[4]Sidney Weintraub, *Capitalism's Inflation and Unemployment Crisis* (Reading, Mass.: Addison-Wesley Publishing, 1978), pp. 121–44.

The TIP proposal would work simply as follows. A wage increase guideline would be established, say, 5 percent at the beginning of the year. At the same time, the government would announce a TIP tax schedule. Suppose the tax schedule is that for each percentage point a corporate firm grants over the wage guideline, 4 percentage points is added to the corporate income tax rate. A firm giving a 6 percent increase in wages, then, would be subject to a 4 percent added tax to its income tax rate.

There are variants to the TIP proposal. One variant is to reward firms that give wage increases less than the wage guideline. Another alternative is to apply the reward and penalty system to prices or to both wages and prices. The innovating feature of the TIP proposal and its variants is the use of an incentive system that would tend to foster noninflationary wage and price behavior. However, it remains uncertain as to how effective a tax-based incomes policy would be if implemented sometime in the future.

SUMMARY

Inflation means that the general level of prices is rising. It means that it takes more money to buy the same quantity of goods and services. Inflation may be suppressed. This occurs when output demanded is greater than output supplied at the current price level, but the price level does not rise because of government price controls.

The three effects of inflation are the equity, efficiency, and output effects. The equity effects are the results of inflation on income distribution. The people who lose during inflation are those who receive fixed incomes and have fixed money claims. The people who gain during inflation are those whose money incomes rise faster than prices and who hold assets that rise in value more than the increase in prices of goods and services.

The efficiency effects of inflation are the results of inflation on the allocation of resources. Inflation changes the allocation of resources, since inflation alters relative commodity prices. It is not certain that this change in resource allocation is a less efficient allocation. However, some economists argue that the allocation of resources is distorted by inflation and results in a less efficient allocation.

The impact of inflation on the national production of goods and services may be to encourage production. Before the economy reaches full employment, rising prices tend to go hand in hand with rising production. The same forces that cause prices to rise cause production to rise. However, the continuation of inflationary forces at full employment leads to pure inflation—that is, rising prices not associated with rising production.

Money plays an essential role in the economy. Money is anything that is generally accepted as a means of payment for goods, services, and debt. Money serves three functions. First, money serves as a medium of exchange; second, the value of goods and services are measured in money; and third, money serves as a store of value. The supply of money in the economy includes currency and coins in circulation, traveler's checks, demand deposits at banks, and other checkable deposits. There are broader measures of the money supply that include other near-money assets.

The money supply expands when banks, as a group, expand loans, and contracts when banks, as a group, contract loans. The Federal Reserve System, which has the responsibility of controlling the money supply, attempts to fulfill this responsibility through the use of policy controls over excess cash reserves of banks. The three policy controls are the legal reserve ratio, the discount rate, and open-market operations. When the Federal Reserve thinks it is desirable to slow down growth in the money supply, the Fed can increase the legal reserve ratio, increase the discount rate, and increase open-market sales of government securities. These policy actions decrease excess cash reserves and reduce the lending ability of banks. The opposite policy actions can be taken if it is desirable to increase the growth in the money supply—namely decrease the legal reserve rate, decrease the discount rate, and decrease open-market purchases of government securities. These actions increase excess cash reserves and increase the lending ability of banks.

Two approaches are taken to explain the causes of inflation and the cures to inflation. The first approach is the quantity theory of money. This theory stresses the importance of money in the inflationary process. The second approach is an aggregate demand and supply approach. The central message of the quantity theory of money is that behind every inflation there is a rapid growth in the money supply, and the way to stop inflation is to control the growth in the money supply. In a demand-pull inflation, it is excess aggregate demand that initiates and causes inflation. In a cost-push inflation, aggregate supply decreases resulting in upward pressures on prices. The cure for demand-pull inflation is the appropriate use of monetary and fiscal policies. There is no certain solution to cost-push inflationary pressures other than restoring competitive markets and making sure that inflationary pressures do not exist because of an excessive growth in the money supply. An incomes policy that provides incentives to foster competitive wage and price behavior has been recommended as a possible solution to cost-push inflation but has not yet been implemented.

SUPPLEMENTARY READINGS

Anderson, W. H. Locke; Ann Putallaz; and William G. Shepherd. *Economics.* Englewood Cliffs, N.J.: Prentice-Hall, 1983.

Chapter 26 is recommended for a good coverage of cost-push and demand-pull inflations.

Schiller, Bradley R. *The Macro Economy Today.* New York: Random House, 1983.

Chapter 6 has a thorough discussion of the different types of inflation, and chapters 13 and 15 have an extensive coverage of supply-side policies and the policies of the Reagan administration, respectively.

Weintraub, Sidney. *Capitalism's Inflation and Unemployment Crisis.* Reading, Mass.: Addison-Wesley Publishing, 1978.

Sidney Weintraub is one of the pioneers of the tax-based incomes policy. Chapter 3 presents the underlying theory behind the TIP proposal; chapter 6 discusses the proposal.

Part Four

THE

PUBLIC

SECTOR

GOVERNMENT EXPENDITURE AND TAX ISSUES

What are people afraid of?
  Size of government
  Tax inequities
The problem of size
  Government expenditures
  Government receipts
Economic analysis of the problem of size
  An efficient level of government
    expenditures
  Collective goods and services
  External benefits and costs
  Income distribution
  Summary
Tax principles and analysis
  Tax equity
  Tax efficiency
  Principles of shifting and incidence
Who really pays taxes?
  Federal, state, and local tax
    distribution in 1980
  Federal tax incidence versus state
    and local tax incidence
  Tax rates by type of tax
Policy reforms
  The problem of size
  Income tax reform: a dream
    come true
Summary

**Checklist of
Economic Concepts**

Government purchases
Government transfer
  payments
Collective goods
External benefits and
  costs
Progressive tax rates
Proportional tax rates
Equal tax treatment
  doctrine
Relative tax treatment
  doctrine
Horizontal equity
Vertical equity
Ability-to-pay principle
  of taxation
Benefits-received
  principle of taxation
Tax efficiency
Tax incidence
Forward and backward
  tax shifting

15

Government Expenditure
and Tax Issues

Who wins and who loses?

I am reminded of the mythical Midwestern farmer retired Senator Stephen M. Young (D-Ohio) used to tell about.

He rode free to public schools on free buses, studied agriculture under the GI bill, bought his home with a VA loan, got his power through Rural Electrification Administration lines and sent his kids to government-subsidized colleges on government loans.

He eventually made it big in the farming business, joined the John Birch Society and finally, disgusted with his high taxes, wrote to his senator, one Stephen Young:

"I believe in rugged individualism. People should stand on their own two feet, not expect government aid. I stand on my own two feet. I oppose all those socialistic trends you have been voting for and demand return to the free enterprise system of our forefathers."[1]

WHAT ARE PEOPLE AFRAID OF?

A great concern of people seems to be related to the involvement of government in their daily lives in the forms of questionable government services, regulations and controls, and the payment of taxes. As is apparent from the introductory quote, many people do not object when they receive government services free or below the market price, but they do object when others are on the receiving line and when they have to pay taxes to support government. On a broader, more philosophical plane, people fear that the increasing

---

[1] William Raspberry, " 'American Way' OK, for the Other Guy," *Tulsa World*, Section A–13, February 16, 1979.

scope of government narrows their individual choices and reduces their individual rights.

Most fears of people are related to the *size of government* and to the *distribution of taxes*. Issues connected to government size and tax distributions, then, are the focal points of this chapter.

Size of government

There appears to be a growing feeling among people that government is too big. If this is so, it could certainly be argued that government services and taxes should be cut. Is there a basis for this feeling?

Some of the fears of people concerning government size are well-founded. Government activities have extended into areas of society not deemed necessary many decades ago. Taxes have risen to pay for these activities until today almost all families have to part with a significant amount of their income in order to pay taxes. The worry that people have about government waste and the abuse that is connected with government expenditures is not imaginary. People have found out about these things through the various means of communication. A day, a month, and certainly a year rarely passes without a report on unnecessary government expenditures or on abuse of some sort in the operation of one or more government expenditure programs.

Some fears of people concerning government size are not well-founded. Although the history of many government expenditure programs is a story of growth, waste, and some abuse, there is also the other side that shows at least in part the success of many government expenditure programs, including the provision of benefits to many people and the fulfillment of the needs of people living in a changing society. For example, since the beginning of the social security program in 1936, social security taxes have grown rapidly and have become a heavy tax burden to many taxpayers. At the same time, however, this program has been enlarged in scope and coverage and now includes not only retirement income and unemployment benefits to those covered but also health care benefits. Still, people may be correct in their fears that government is doing too much in regard to the social security program or any other government expenditure program. More public debate and scrutiny of government activities are needed, not less, if unneeded programs are to be eliminated and needed programs are to be improved.

The source of some fears is not specific and concrete but more general and philosophical. Fear of too much government is an important aspect of the American heritage. The idea that "the least government is the best government" encourages individual choice making and problem solving in the marketplace. In a market-oriented economy, the supposition is that the market will solve problems impersonally and efficiently. It is this belief that underlies the concerns of people when the government interferes in the market.

Tax inequities

A major concern of people involves the question of tax equity, that is, tax justice. Tax equity refers to the way taxes are distributed among people. Even if tax collections were exactly the right amount to pay for government goods and services demanded by people, there could be concern that tax distributions were not fair. Some taxpayers may be paying more than what they believe is a fair amount, and some may be paying less than what others believe is a fair amount. So, in addition to the fear that government is too big and taxes too high generally, there is the fear that taxes are "too low" for certain taxpayers and "too high" for certain others.

There is ample evidence that there are tax inequities in the tax system at all levels of government. The concept of equity will be developed, and illustrations of tax inequities are presented later in the chapter. It may suffice here to point out that the fears that people have concerning the fairness of tax distributions are in part justifiable.

THE PROBLEM OF SIZE

Our approach to the problem of size is, first, to provide background information concerning this problem and, second, to analyze the problem of size in reference to the economic criteria of efficiency and equity.

Government expenditures

The concern that people have over the size of government becomes evident when certain indicators of the size of government (federal, state, and local) are examined. One way to indicate the size of government is to look at the expenditures of government and to compare these expenditures to the nation's income or the GNP. Figure 15–1 shows the hugeness of government in 1986 and the absolute and relative growth of government since 1960. An examination of this figure reveals that government is rapidly increasing in size and, more importantly, that government is growing faster than the rest of the economy. To substantiate this latter point, government expen-

FIGURE 15-1

Total, federal, state and local government expenditures in billions of dollars, and total and federal government expenditures as a percent of the GNP in selected years, 1960–1986

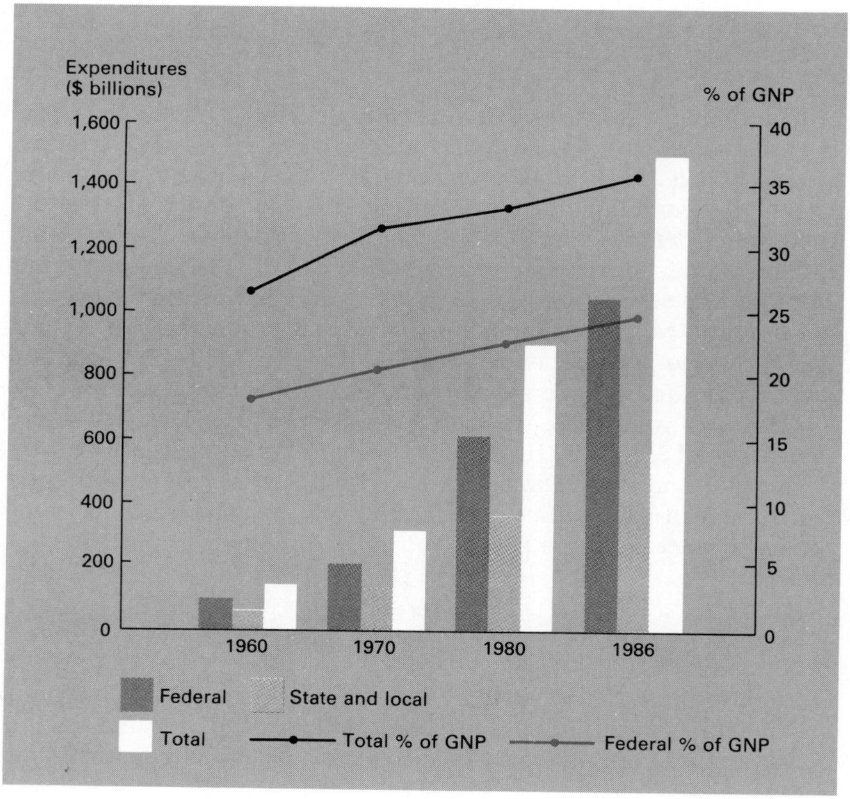

Source: *Economic Report of the President,* January 1987, p. 335.

diture was 27 percent of the GNP in 1960 as compared to 35 percent in 1986. Government, then, is big and getting bigger as measured by the expenditures of federal, state, and local governments.

It seemed that the relative size of government had reached a plateau in 1960 with government expenditures nearing but staying less than 30 percent of the nation's income. However, Figure 15–1 shows that the 30 percent plateau was broken in the 1960s. Why?

Part of the answer to the question can be found by dividing government expenditures into what are called *transfer payments* and government *purchases of goods and services*. Transfer payments are payments to people who have not made a contribution to current production of goods and services, while government purchases are expenditures for currently produced goods and services. Figure 15–2 shows this breakdown between transfer payments and government purchases. In the 1960s, both government purchases and transfer payments grew relative to the GNP; however, transfer payments increased much faster than the GNP, increasing from 5.7 percent of the GNP in 1960 to 8.3 percent in 1970. In this era, Medicare and Medicaid were introduced and many social domestic programs expanded rapidly. During the decade of the 1970s, government purchases declined as a percent of the GNP from 21.5 percent in 1970 to 19.4 percent in 1980 while transfer payments continued to grow faster than the GNP, reaching 11.7 percent in 1980. These trends

FIGURE 15–2

Total government purchases (G) and transfer payments (Tr) in billions of dollars and as a percent of the GNP in selected years, 1960–1986

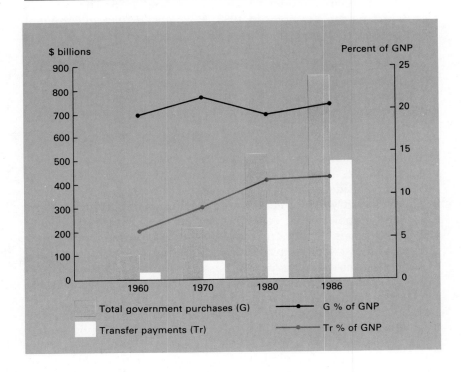

Source: *Economic Report of the President*, January 1987, p. 336.

have been reversed so far in the 1980s with transfer payments staying about the same percentage and government purchases increasing as a percentage of GNP (Figure 15–2). These trends reflect the change in priorities from transfer spending programs to the national defense program.

Government receipts

The other side of the government expenditure-revenue system, receipts, shows a somewhat different growth pattern with respect to GNP than government expenditures. Government receipts grew faster than the nation's income between 1960 and 1970 but stayed about the same percentage of GNP since 1970. In 1970, total government receipts represented 30.2 percent of the GNP, and in 1986 they were 31.9 percent (Figure 15–3). This slight increase in total government receipts was due to the growth of state and local government receipts; federal government receipts as a percent of the GNP fell from 20.3 percent in 1980 to 19.6 percent in 1986.

As a percent of GNP, the gap between total government expenditures and receipts widened between 1980 and 1986. The gap was less than 1 percentage point in 1980. However, in 1986 government expenditures as a percent of GNP were over 3 percentage points above government receipts as a percent of GNP. Thus, the government budget deficit, primarily the federal deficit, has not only grown in absolute terms but has grown faster than GNP thus far in the 1980s.

ECONOMIC ANALYSIS OF THE PROBLEM OF SIZE

Economic efficiency and equity are two concepts that have been used to analyze many issues previously discussed. Efficiency was the major consideration in dealing with government price controls in Chapter 2. It was the basis for evaluation in the examination of the energy problem, the economics of crime, pollution problems, and health issues. Equity came directly into play in the treatment of poverty and discrimination. Efficiency in the use of scarce resources of society causes society to produce as many goods and services and satisfy as many human wants as possible. Equity is concerned with the distribution of goods and services among people. Both equity and efficiency considerations are involved in an analysis of the size of government, for the size of government is determined by expenditure programs aimed at redressing the unequal distribution of income and at providing goods and services that would not be pro-

FIGURE 15–3
Total, federal, and state and local government receipts, and total and federal government receipts as a percent of the GNP in selected years, 1960–1986

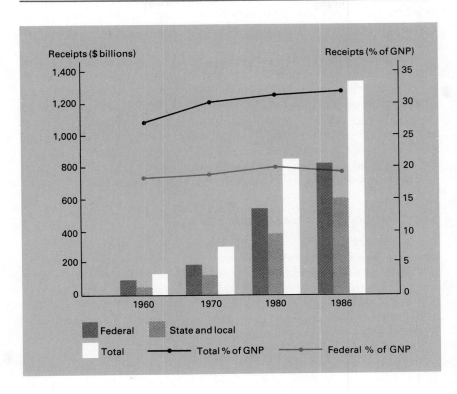

Source: *Economic Report of the President*, January 1987, p. 335.

vided at all, or at least would not be provided in efficient quantities, in the marketplace.

An efficient level of government expenditures

An efficient level of government expenditures is that level at which the *net* benefits to society are maximized, that is, the level at which benefits and costs are equal at the margin. The maximization of net benefits and the equation of marginal benefits and costs were illustrated in Chapter 5 in analyzing the correct (efficient) level of crime prevention activities. To move to an efficient level, government expenditures would be increased (decreased) when the marginal benefits per dollar spent in the public sector of the economy is greater (less) than the marginal benefits per dollar spent in the private sector. Finally, the efficient level of government expenditures would be reached when the marginal benefit per dollar spent in the public sector is equal to the marginal benefit per dollar spent in the private sector.

Although cost-benefit analysis has practical application in many instances and is the guide to an efficient allocation of resources, it must be acknowledged that benefits and costs of government expenditures can seldom be precisely quantified, and often government programs are developed without any attempt to estimate benefits and costs. Thus, there is no way of knowing for certain whether the present size of government is too big or too small. Further insight can be gained, however, into the question of efficiency and the size of government by discussing the proper scope of government.

Collective goods and services

It was said in Chapter 5 that collective goods and services lie at the opposite pole from private goods and services since an individual is not able to isolate or identify a specific personal benefit. Let's take the meaning of collective goods and services a step further in the context of this chapter.

Collective goods and services, such as defense and crime prevention services, have two identifying characteristics: (1) demand for collective goods and services is not generally divisible on the basis of individual quantity demanded, and (2) supply of collective goods and services is not generally divisible into small units. These characteristics make it difficult, if not impossible, for these goods and services to be supplied and demanded in the marketplace. Thus, it is widely accepted that collective goods and services fall under the domain of government to provide.

The main issue, then, in the supply of collective goods and services is for the government to provide these goods and services efficiently. For economic efficiency to be obtained, government has to provide collective goods and services at the lowest possible cost, and the output supplied has to equal output demanded. Even assuming collective goods and services are provided at the lowest possible costs, inefficiencies may arise if the output demanded is less than or greater than the output supplied. The only way people can reveal their preferences for collective goods and services is through the ballot box, which may not be a perfect indicator of the true preferences that people have for collective goods and services. However, assuming true preferences are revealed, the efficient amount of collective goods and services is the amount corresponding to the point when collective demand intersects the cost (marginal) of supplying collective goods and services.

External benefits and costs

The line of demarcation between what government should provide and what private producers should provide would be clear if all goods and services were either collective or private goods and services. But, you have already learned that in the production of certain goods there can be social spillover costs, and in the consumption of certain goods and services there can be social spillover benefits. The existence of *externalities*, that is, social spillovers in production and consumption, broadens the scope of government beyond collective goods and services.

Market demand indicates marginal private benefits *(MPB)*, and market supply indicates marginal private costs *(MPC)*. Assuming no externalities, marginal private benefits and costs equal marginal social benefits and costs. However, if either external benefits or costs are present, a divergence will exist between private and social benefits or between private and social costs. This divergence means that government action is required for resources to be used efficiently.

Figure 15–4 shows private demand and supply of good A. Assuming no external benefits and costs exist, the efficient quantity would be Q, and the price would be P. Suppose, now, that in the consumption of good A, there are external benefits. In Figure 15–4 the demand curve D_T shows both marginal private and external benefits *(MPB + MEB)*; that is, D_T shows the total marginal social benefits. The demand curve that indicates all benefits is the relevant one. Thus, the efficient quantity in Figure 15–4 is Q_E, not Q. What can government do to guarantee that the efficient quantity is provided?

The government could consider two choices. One choice would be for the government to produce good A and attempt to produce the efficient quantity. This type of action presumes that government will be an efficient supplier and can accurately estimate marginal social benefits. The second choice of action does not depend on government being an efficient supplier but still depends on precise estimates of benefits. Government action could be in the form of subsidies to consumers of good A so that they would be willing to purchase the efficient quantity. In Figure 15–4, consumers would buy the correct amount at P_o. The total subsidy payment would be equal

FIGURE 15-4
The efficient quantity assuming external benefits in consumption

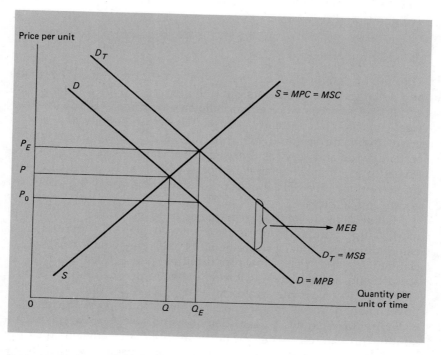

D represents marginal private benefits *(MPB)*, and D_r represents *MPB* and marginal external benefits *(MEB)*. Given the supply curve, *S*, the optimum or efficient quantity is at Q_E where *MSB* equals *MSC*. The government could ensure that the efficient quantity would be demanded by giving a subsidy payment to consumers equal to $[(P_E - P_o) \times Q_E]$.

to $[(P_E - P_o) \times Q_E]$. A subsidy payment greater than this would result in too much production of good A, and a subsidy payment smaller would mean that less than the efficient quantity is produced.

The case of external costs in production was examined in Chapter 6 and illustrated in the case of water pollution in the production of paper. In this instance, the market price was too low and the production of paper was too high since external cost in the form of water pollution was not taken into account in the supply of paper. To correct this situation, the government could levy a tax on each unit of paper supplied. The effect of the tax would be to increase the marginal cost of supplying paper and, therefore, decrease supply. Assuming the tax equals marginal external costs, an efficient but lower quantity of paper will be supplied at a higher price. The price elasticity of demand for paper will determine how much the price of paper will rise as a result of the tax.

Income distribution

Government actions thus far have been rationalized on economic efficiency grounds. The scope of government has been greatly extended and defended based on the belief that income inequality needs to be reduced. The distribution of income, and therefore consumption, would be largely based on the productivity of people in a highly competitive economy. A social problem arises because some people have no or low productivity. What should be done to alter the distribution of income so as to help people who cannot work and those who can work little?

Shifting income from those who are relatively productive to those who are relatively unproductive, say through taxes and subsidies, must be based on the values of people as to what constitutes a "fair" distribution. It is not surprising that government programs aimed directly or indirectly at altering the distribution of income are under constant attack. Evidently there is general support for programs aimed directly at helping low-income people, such as public assistance and the food stamp programs, and for programs that only indirectly help certain low-income groups, such as the social security program, for these programs have expanded relative to other government programs. Paralleling this growth has been the increased controversy concerning income transfer programs. Although the debate is not likely to end, the responsibility of government in the area of income redistribution is seemingly established. No private institutions could thoroughly cope with the problem.

Summary

The major ideas that have evolved from our discussion thus far are these: (1) collective goods and services must be supplied by government; (2) government actions are needed to improve the efficiency of the market system, especially where there are externalities; and (3) government may alter the distribution of income in order to move in the direction of an equitable distribution as determined by the beliefs of people in our society.

TAX PRINCIPLES AND ANALYSIS

The first part of this section develops a theoretical framework based on the criteria of equity and efficiency. The second part examines tax principles pertaining to the shifting and incidence of taxes.

Tax equity

Everyone agrees that taxes should be "just." The problem that arises, however, is over the exact meaning of justice or fairness in taxation. An idea that runs strongly through western thought is that tax justice means that taxpayers in equal economic circumstances should be treated equally. This is called the *equal tax treatment doctrine* and pertains to *horizontal* equity; that is, people in identical economic positions should pay equal taxes.

In the application of the equal tax treatment doctrine, the best indicator or measure of economic circumstances has to be determined. Generally, economists interpret economic circumstances to mean a person's real income, namely, consumption plus changes in net wealth. Assuming real income is the best measure of economic circumstances, then horizontal equity is achieved when all taxpayers with the same income pay exactly the same amount in taxes.

What about taxpayers in different economic circumstances? How should they be treated? These questions are related to the idea of *vertical* equity, that is, the tax treatment of taxpayers in different economic circumstances. The *relative tax treatment doctrine* now emerges. Taxpayers in different economic circumstances should be treated differently. But how differently? Two principles of taxation have been developed to shed light on this question—the *ability-to-pay principle* and the *benefits-received principle*.

Ability-to-pay principle. The ability-to-pay principle of taxation suggests that taxpayers with more ability to pay taxes should pay more taxes. Again, using income as the measure of ability to pay, this means that taxpayers with more income should pay more taxes. But how much more? Progressive and proportional income tax rates are always consistent with the ability-to-pay principle because if the rate of taxation (the percent of income paid in taxes) is rising as income rises (progressive rates) or constant as income rises (proportional rates), the amount paid in taxes will always be higher as income is higher. On the other hand, regressive tax rates can violate the ability-to-pay principle since the percent of income paid in taxes decreases as income rises.

Benefits-received principle. Do you recall the way the market distributes the costs of producing private goods and services? The market distributes costs based on marginal private benefits. The benefits-received principle of taxation is an attempt to apply the rule of market and is thus a guide to an efficient allocation of taxes rather than to an equitable allocation. However, efficient and equitable tax distributions are not always in conflict, and when equity in the distribution of income is not a concern, the benefits-received principle of taxation is an important tax standard. This principle is more limited than the ability-to-pay principle because private benefits received from government goods and services are usually more difficult to measure than the ability to pay. Illustrations of taxes that are defended on the benefits-received principle are the gasoline tax and local street assessments. The gasoline tax is used primarily to pay for highways. Thus, the demander of highway services, the automobile user, pays for the benefits received from highway services through a tax levied on gallons of gasoline consumed. It is argued that well-maintained local streets benefit property owners by enhancing the value of property. Thus, it is reasoned that property owners should pay in the form of property taxes for the benefits they receive from streets.

Tax efficiency

There are two aspects to tax efficiency. First, tax efficiency is concerned with the *administration* and *compliance* cost of taxes. Taxes should be economical to collect and to enforce. They should also be convenient and certain to the taxpayer.

The second and more important aspect of tax efficiency involves minimizing what economists call the *excess burden* from taxes. The idea of an excess burden from taxes can be grasped easily with an illustration. Suppose the government transfers $10 billion worth of resources from the private sector to the public sector via taxes and provides marginal benefits equal to $10 billion. Further, suppose that in the levy of taxes, tax rates are used that discourage incentives to work so that private production is less than what it would have been by $1 billion. It becomes clear in this example that there is a net loss of $1 billion even though the government is using the resources transferred as efficiently as they would be used in the private sector. This net loss in production resulting from the disincentive effects of taxes is the excess burden that has arisen because of the imposition of taxes.

If there is no excess burden or if the excess burden is small, then it can be said that taxes have *neutral* effects or near neutral effects on the operation of private economy. Unfortunately, taxes seldom have completely neutral effects. However, certain taxes adhere to the idea of neutrality better than others, and these are the taxes that we are searching for to put into an ideal tax scheme. Taxes that directly alter relative commodity prices or that do so indirectly through altering consumption and income patterns are taxes that have strong nonneutral effects and do not adhere to the concept of tax efficiency. For example, a tax levied on a specific commodity will increase the price of that commodity and result in a shift of spending away from the taxed commodity to nontaxed commodities. Progressive and regressive income tax rates change the pattern of income distribution as well as alter the price of work relative to the price of leisure.

Principles of shifting and incidence

Taxes may be levied on one taxpayer and shifted to another taxpayer. A tax that is shifted *forward* is a tax that falls on the consumer in the form of higher prices; a tax that is shifted *backward* falls on the owners of resources in the form of lower resource prices. The *incidence* or burden of a tax that is not shifted, then, remains on the original taxpayer.

Two kinds of taxes are to be considered in the following analysis. The first is an output tax, and the second is a tax levied independent of output.

An output tax. An output tax is a tax that is levied on each unit of output produced, such as a tax on each pack of cigarettes or on each gallon of gasoline. An output tax increases the cost of producing each unit and, therefore, decreases supply. Given the demand for the taxed commodity, a decrease in supply will increase the price of the commodity. How much of the tax will be shifted forward?

The extent of the forward shifting of an output tax depends essentially on the price elasticity of demand. If demand is *perfectly* inelastic (Figure 15–5), the entire tax is shifted forward. The incidence of the tax, under these circumstances, is *completely* on the consumer in the form of higher prices. If demand is *perfectly* elastic (Figure 15–6), none of the tax is shifted forward; or, in other words, all of the tax is shifted backward to resources in the form of lower prices (lower wages, etc.). The elasticity of demand for most products will not be either of these two extremes. We can generalize, then, by saying that an output tax will normally be shifted forward and back-

FIGURE 15–5
Demand perfectly inelastic—complete forward shifting of an output tax

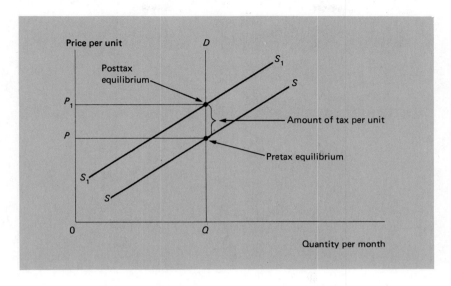

The pretax equilibrium is at a price of P and at a quantity of Q where supply, S, intersects demand, D. An output tax on each unit produced is levied with the amount of the tax shown above. The effect is to decrease supply to S_1. Thus, price rises to P_1 where S_1 intersects D. The full amount of the tax is shifted forward since the rise in price from P to P_1 equals the amount of the tax.

ward, with more forward shifting when demand is more inelastic and more backward shifting when demand is more elastic.

Independent of output tax. A tax levied on income, say the net income or profits of a business, is a good illustration of the tax we are to consider. Suppose a business has selected the best output, that is, the output where profits are maximized before a 25 percent profits tax is imposed. Now, after the tax, is there a better output? The answer is no. If the best output is selected before the tax, it remains the best output after the tax. There is no short-run shifting of a tax levied independently of output. The incidence of such a tax is on the owners of the business in the form of a reduction in profits. The difference between an output tax and a tax independent of output is that the former increases costs and decreases supply, whereas the latter does not. For taxes to be shifted, a change in supply has to occur.

FIGURE 15-6
Demand perfectly elastic—complete backward shifting of an output tax

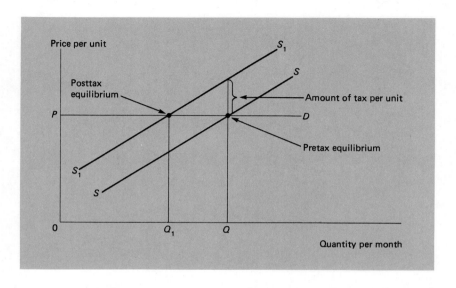

The pretax equilibrium is at a price of P and a quantity of Q where supply S, intersects demand, D. An output tax decreases supply to S_1. The posttax equilibrium is at a price of P and a quantity of Q_1 where supply, S_1, intersects demand, D. There is no forward shifting of the tax since price does not change. Thus, the entire tax is shifting backward to owners of resources.

WHO REALLY PAYS TAXES?

The question above is an empirical question. Thus, we rely on an empirical study by Joseph A. Pechman to answer the question.[2] We first examine the findings in regard to the distribution of total federal, state, and local taxes. Then we look into the tax incidence of federal and state and local taxes separately. Finally, we present the tax burden of specific taxes.

Federal, state, and local tax distribution in 1980

The American tax system can be best described as proportional or mildly progressive; that is, the tax rate or the ratio of taxes to income by income class is the same or rises only slightly as you move from

[2]Joseph A. Pechman, *Who Paid the Taxes, 1966–85?* (Washington, D.C.: Brookings Institution, 1985).

low-income classes to high-income classes. Under the most progressive set of incidence assumptions, it was found that the tax rate increased from only 20 percent in the lowest income group to 27 percent in the highest income group.[3] Most taxpayers pay a tax rate between 20 and 25 percent.

A tax system that is proportional will not alter the distribution of income. Under such a tax system, taxpayers in each income group will have proportionately less income after taxes than before taxes, but they will be in the same relative income position. The U.S. tax system, then, has only a small impact on reducing income inequality since it is only moderately progressive at best. The statement sometimes made that taxes significantly redistribute income away from the rich to the poor is not verified by the data.

Federal tax incidence versus state and local tax incidence

It is often stated that the incidence of federal taxes is highly progressive, and that the incidence of state and local taxes is highly regressive. It is true that the federal tax system is more progressive since it relies more heavily on income taxes; but with the relative growth in payroll taxes, the relative decline in corporate income taxes, and recent changes in the federal tax code, the federal tax structure is much less progressive than generally believed. Also, state and local tax structures are much less regressive than generally believed because of the relative growth in state income taxes and because of the assumption that the incidence of the state corporate income tax and the local property tax fall primarily on capital instead of consumption.

Table 15–1 shows the effective tax rate of federal taxes and state and local taxes by family income class. Federal tax rates are between 12 and 14 percent in the lower income classes and then rise to 21 percent in the highest income class. The rate of state and local taxes is the highest (18 percent) at the lowest end of the income scale. However, between this lowest income class and the highest income class, state and local tax rates are largely proportional, varying only between about 7 and 10 percent.

Tax rates by type of tax

Individual income taxes, corporate income taxes, and property taxes are the most progressive tax sources. Individual income taxes are the

---

[3]Ibid., p. 4.

TABLE 15-1
Federal and state and local tax distributions by famiy income class, 1980

Income class ($ 000)	Federal tax	State and local taxes	Total taxes
0–5	14.2%	18.3%	29.8%
5–10	12.2	8.1	20.3
10–15	13.3	7.2	20.5
15–20	14.5	7.0	21.5
20–25	15.7	6.9	22.7
25–30	16.2	7.0	23.2
30–50	17.4	7.2	24.5
50–100	19.1	7.4	26.5
100–500	19.2	8.1	27.3
500–1,000	18.2	8.9	27.1
1,000 and over	21.4	9.7	31.0
All classes	17.3	7.5	25.3

Source: Joseph A. Pechman, *Who Paid the Taxes, 1966–1985?* (Washington, D.C.: Brookings Institution, 1985), p. 60. Reproduced with permission. Data shown are based on the most progressive set of incidence assumptions.

most progressive of all taxes but are not nearly as progressive as the statutory rates indicate. Corporate income taxes and property taxes are mildly progressive under the assumption that these taxes are paid by the owners of capital. Sales and excise taxes and payroll taxes are regressive taxes under any set of incidence assumptions.

Individual income tax rates are about 3 percent on the two lowest family income groups, steadily rising to about 14 percent on family income between $100,000 and $500,000. Then the effective rate falls to approximately 11 percent in the two highest income groups (Table 15–2). Corporate income tax rates are much lower than individual income tax rates at each income class, with the exceptions of the two highest income groups, and are less progressive than individual income taxes. The effective tax rates of corporate income taxes start at less than 1 percent in the lower income groups but eventually reach 13 percent in the highest income group.

Property taxes at best are only slightly progressive with the effective tax rate about 1 percent at the low end of the income scale, rising to about 6 percent at the top end (Table 15–2). Property taxes, at worst, are regressive at the low end of the income ladder and largely proportional over other income groups. This last statement is made based on the assumption that property taxes are shifted in part to consumers.

The effective tax rates of sales and excise taxes and payroll taxes decrease as you move from the low- to the high-income families. Sales and excise taxes are very burdensome on the very lowest in-

TABLE 15–2
Effective tax rates of federal, state, and local taxes by type of tax, 1980

Income class ($ 000)	Individual income tax	Corporate income tax	Property tax	Sales and excises	Payroll taxes
0–5	3.2%	0.8%	1.0%	17.9%	9.4%
5–10	2.7	0.5	0.6	7.7	8.7
10–15	4.9	0.7	0.9	6.2	7.7
15–20	6.5	0.8	0.9	5.6	7.6
20–25	7.8	0.8	1.0	5.2	7.6
25–30	8.6	0.9	1.2	4.9	7.3
30–50	10.5	1.2	1.4	4.5	6.7
50–100	13.1	2.3	2.2	3.3	5.4
100–500	13.9	5.7	3.9	1.6	2.1
500–1,000	10.8	9.7	5.2	0.7	0.5
1,000 and over	11.3	13.1	5.8	0.6	0.2
All classes	10.8	2.5	2.0	4.0	5.8

Source: Joseph A. Pechman, *Who Paid the Taxes, 1966–1985* (Washington, D.C.: Brookings Institution, 1985), p. 56. Reproduced with permission. Data shown are based on the most progressive set of tax incidence assumptions.

come families, representing a tax rate of approximately 18 percent (Table 15–2). In comparison, the tax rate of these taxes varies from only 3 to 6 percent over most income classes. In the two highest income groups, the tax rate of sales and excise taxes is less than 1 percent. Payroll taxes, also, fall heavily on low-income families. The tax rate of payroll taxes begins at about 9 percent and declines steadily to less than 1 percent on very-high-income families.

POLICY REFORMS

The concluding section of this chapter examines two sets of policy reforms. The first set is in the proposal stage and pertains to limiting the size of government. The second set is the 1986 Income Tax Reform Act. We attempt to discuss these reforms based on previous economic analysis.

The problem of size

Concern over the bigness of government has prompted certain groups to advocate limits on the level of government expenditures and on the rate of taxation. Two proposals are to be considered— the balanced budget proposal and the proposal to limit the relative size of federal expenditures.

The balanced budget proposal. Traditionally, a balanced budget has been viewed as a guide to an efficient allocation of resources from the private sector of the economy to the government sector. Early economists, called the classical economists, believed that unbalanced budgets in the form of budget deficits invited unnecessary government expenditures. Thus, they advocated the rule of a balanced budget. Some economists today favor a balanced budget because they fear that many government expenditures are wasteful and inefficient. Some states have passed balanced budget laws. These state laws can be easily circumvented because they pertain to only certain kinds of state debt. There has been much debate in Congress concerning the issue of a balanced budget. This debate has intensified in recent years because of huge federal budget deficits of about $200 billion. Although a balanced budget law was not passed, Congress did pass the Gramm-Rudman-Hollings deficit reduction plan. This plan sets a deficit reduction target for each fiscal year from 1986 to 1991. In addition to a timetable, procedures for meeting the targets are incorporated in the plan. It will be interesting to see if the timetable is kept and the procedures are followed, especially in the event of a recession. President Reagan has endorsed in words a balanced budget amendment to the Constitution. His budget policy actions, however, suggest thus far that his support is limited to words. Nevertheless, chances are good that with the support of the president Congress will pass a balanced budget amendment sometime in the near future. The odds are even better that when the amendment becomes law there will be ways of getting around it, say, in times of war and recession.

Balanced budget laws do not seem to be the solution to the problem of the size of government for several reasons. One, a balanced budget does not necessarily limit the size of government because budgets can be balanced at any level of government expenditures and taxes. Two, a balanced budget would tend to cause economic instability under certain circumstances; for example, if the economy were in an economic decline, tax rates would have to be increased or government expenditures cut in order to balance the budget. This would have the effect of encouraging further declines in economic activity. Three, it is rational for government not to balance the budget and to incur debt to finance viable capital projects. Four, it is a responsibility of the federal government to pursue a fiscal program that promotes economic stability. This means that an unbalanced budget is required when the economy is confronted with either a serious inflationary problem or a serious unemployment problem.

Limiting the relative size of government. There have been discussions and considerations to limit the size of government by limiting increases in government expenditures to some maximum or by fixing a maximum legal rate of taxation. The latter approach was taken in California. In that state people voted in favor of limiting the property tax rate to 1 percent of the market value of property. There has been some movement of a similar nature in other states, but it is too early to assess these movements. At the federal level, there is some support to tie increases in federal expenditures to the GNP. The way this could work is that federal expenditures by law could not exceed a given percentage of the GNP, say, 20 percent. Thus, each year growth in federal expenditures would be limited by the growth in the GNP so that the ratio of federal expenditures to the GNP would remain constant. There may be some merit to this proposal. However, many problems would certainly arise. In the first place, the correct ratio of federal expenditures to the GNP would have to be determined. It is hoped that the ratio selected would be the efficient one, that is, the ratio corresponding to the point where benefits and costs of federal expenditure programs are equal at the margin. But, if this is done, there is no need to have the ratio since the size of government would be the efficient size anyway. Second, legal rules such as the rule to limit the size of government to a constant percent of the GNP will probably not be flexible enough to meet the changing economic and social problems of society. If there are inefficient federal expenditure programs, it would seem more realistic to eliminate them directly rather than to use an indirect rule to prevent them.

Income tax reform: A dream come true

Many believe that a major income tax reform is an impossible dream. The reasons given are that people in general and their representatives do not understand what is meant by an equitable and efficient income tax and that even if they did they would not support such a tax. Perhaps the difficulty in implementing tax reform in regard to the federal income tax is best expressed in the following quotation reportedly delivered by Senator Russell Long: "Don't tax you. Don't tax me. Tax that fellow behind the tree."

Congress made a dream come true by passing a major income tax reform program in 1986. There may have been several reasons for the passage of the 1986 Income Tax Reform Act. (1) Special tax treatment to certain groups of taxpayers had been well publicized and had made the income tax system unfair. (2) A carefully prepared income tax reform based on tax equity and efficiency, called Treasury 1, was presented to the public by the Secretary of the Treasury in early 1985, giving vested interest groups and the public ample time to react to the tax reform proposal. (3) A modified version of Treasury 1, called Reagan 1, was presented to the public by the president of the United States, and strongly supported by him. Finally, income tax reform was generally endorsed by both political parties.

Historical background leading to income tax reform. The federal income tax has been viewed historically by most people as the most equitable federal tax source. However, in more recent times, the income tax has lost much of its support as a fair tax. In 1954, the federal income tax was levied on a rather broad income tax base. This means that taxpayers with equal incomes were generally treated equally; that is, they paid the same taxes. Taxpayers with unequal incomes were treated unequally; that is, they paid unequal taxes depending on their income differences. In addition, a comprehensive income tax base usually means that the income tax will be relatively more neutral with respect to investment decisions. As a consequence, the income tax was considered by most taxpayers to be both equitable and efficient. However, there was a major flaw in the federal income tax in 1954. This flaw was the extremely high marginal tax rates that could have adverse effects on incentives to save and work. But Congress did not approach this weakness directly by reducing marginal tax rates. Instead, since 1954, it essentially reduced the effective marginal tax rates by granting a growing number of tax breaks every year, thus eroding the tax base. These tax breaks or subsidies were rationalized sometimes on economic grounds and even benefited the economy sometimes, but the result was an income tax system that was unfair and an income tax system that was replacing the market as the major determinant of investment. A change in the income tax system had to be made.

Income tax rates under tax reform. Individual income tax rates are drastically cut under the new tax reform act. When fully phased in (1988), there will be only 2 rates, 15 and 28 percent, instead of the 15 rates ranging from 11 to 50 percent under the previous law. Corporate income tax rates are reduced also. The top corporate income tax rate is reduced from 46 percent to 34 percent. With a more comprehensive tax base, these lower rates are estimated to bring in about the same tax revenues. The main benefit from lower marginal tax rates is the movement of the income tax system toward a more neutral and efficient system. The result should be an increase in incentives to work, save, and invest.

The income tax base under tax reform. The 1986 reform act broadens the income tax base. The investment tax credit is eliminated. The long-term capital gain income tax exclusion is repealed. The accelerated depreciation of capital assets is reduced. Losses from tax-sheltered investment cannot be deducted from other income. State and local government sales taxes cannot be deducted. Interest on consumer loans are phased out as a tax deduction. Mortgage interest is deductible only for the principal and second residence. Investment interest is deductible only against investment income. The dividend tax exclusion, the two-earner couple deduction, and income averaging are disallowed. Many people will lose their $2,000 deduction from contributing to an individual retirement account (IRA). Even people who receive prizes and awards for their achievements will no longer be permitted to exclude these monetary gifts as income for tax purposes. Charitable contributions are to be scrutinized and limited to taxpayers who itemize their deductions. The list of tax deductions, income exclusions, and credits repealed under the new reform law does not end here, but most of the controversial ones are included in this list. The ones on the list that are the most controversial among economists are the ones that may have an adverse effect on investment, such as, the repeal of the investment credit. When the economy is not doing well and the investment rate is low, the investment tax credit may stimulate investment and therefore improve economic conditions in the economy. However, if a comprehensive income tax base is the surest way to reach both an equitable and efficient income tax system, then the temporary benefit that may flow from the investment credit may have to give way to a more long-run benefit that will flow from a more neutral income tax system.

All income groups gain under tax reform. Figure 15–7 shows the projected reduction in federal income tax liabilities in 1988 by income classes when reforms are fully phased in under the 1986 tax reform act. Every income class gains under tax reform. There will be a 6.6 percent decrease in taxes for all income classes. The lowest income groups will have the greatest percentage reductions in their taxes. In the $0 to $10,000 and the $10,000 to $15,000 income classes, tax liabilities will be reduced 56.2 and 27.8 percent, respectively. The reason for these large percentage reductions in the lowest income groups is that personal exemptions will be increased from $1,080 in 1986 to $2,000 in 1988. The almost doubling of the personal exemption for the taxpayer and dependents, plus the increase in the earned income credit for low-income families, will take many low-income and near-low-income households off the tax rolls. Income

FIGURE 15–7

Percent reduction in income tax liabilities under tax reform by income class

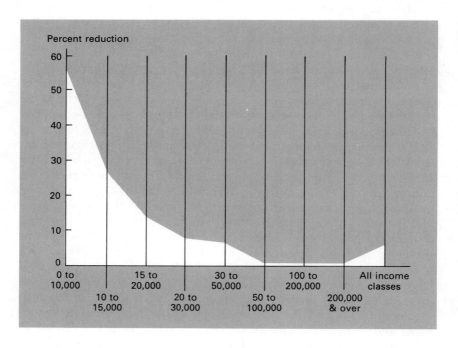

Source: *Economic Report of the President*, January 1987, p. 85.

classes from $30,000 to $50,000 will have reductions greater than the average for all classes. Figure 15–8 shows the average income tax rates by income classes before and after income tax reform. Again, average income tax rates will be lower in all income groups when tax reform is fully implemented in 1988, although the average tax rate will be about the same in the upper-income groups. These data clearly indicate the positive impact of a more comprehensive tax base on the distribution of income taxes among income groups and the resulting improvement in tax equity.

Conclusion. The income tax reform that was passed by Congress in 1986 represents a landmark in the history of tax legislation. Even now it is difficult to believe that tax reform is a reality. However, many believe that Congress will revert in the future to the traditional practice of eroding the tax base by granting tax subsidies to certain groups. Although the reforms reflect some compromises and

FIGURE 15–8
Average income tax rates before and after tax reform by income class

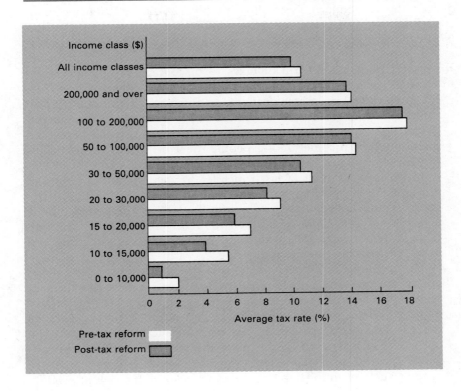

Source: *Economic Report of the President*, January 1987, p. 85.

deviate from an ideal income tax system, in general the reforms are in the right direction and will move the federal income tax system toward an equitable and efficient tax system.

SUMMARY

Many fears of people are related to the size of government and to inequities in the distribution of taxes. Thus, this chapter focuses on the problems of government size and of tax distributions. After discussing the fears of people and concluding that some worries are well founded and some are not, both the problem of government size and the problem of tax distributions were approached in the same manner. First, relevant facts were presented; second, an economic framework was developed based essentially on the concepts of efficiency and equity; and finally, policy proposals were discussed to deal with these problems.

In the economic analysis of the problem of size, efficiency considerations justify government expenditures in the form of provisions of collective goods and services, in the form of subsidies to encourage more consumption when external benefits in consumption are present, and in the form of taxes to discourage production when external costs in production are present. Equity considerations justify government programs designed to enhance the economic opportunities of people who do not earn adequate income in the marketplace. The "adequacy" of income as well as the socially accepted distribution of income among people must be based on the beliefs of people.

In the development of tax principles, it was pointed out than an efficient tax is one that has neutral effects on the allocation of resources, and an equitable tax is one that can be defended on the ability-to-pay principle or the benefits-received principle. An equitable system would adhere to the equal tax treatment doctrine and to the relative tax treatment doctrine.

The incidence or burden of a tax is the final resting place of the tax. A tax may be shifted forward to consumers in the form of higher prices or backward to the owners of resources in the form of lower resource prices. The shifting of an output-type tax, such as the gasoline tax, depends on the price elasticity of demand. The more inelastic demand is, the more the tax will be shifted to consumers in the form of higher prices. A tax that is independent of output, such as an income tax, does not increase the cost of producing goods and services; therefore, this type of tax is not shifted, at least, in the short run. For a tax to be shifted, supply has to decrease.

An empirical study of tax incidence was examined in order to answer the question: "Who really pays taxes?" It was discovered in this study that the effective tax rate of combined federal, state, and local taxes is proportional or mildly progressive. In addition, it was found that the tax rates of individual income taxes, corporate income taxes, and property taxes tend to be progressive, whereas the tax rate of sales and excise taxes and payroll taxes are regressive.

Policy reforms were examined with respect to the size of government and the Tax Reform Act of 1986. The two reforms presented and evaluated concerning the size of government were the proposal that would require the federal government to balance the budget every year and the proposal that would restrict the growth in federal spending to the growth in GNP. Special attention was given to income tax reform. When the Tax Reform Act of 1986 is fully phased in, the major features of the income tax system will be much lower tax rates, 15 and 28 percent, and a much broader tax base. As a consequence, the income tax system will be more equitable and efficient.

SUPPLEMENTARY READINGS

Aaron, Henry J.; Michael J. Boskin, eds. *The Economics of Taxation.* Washington, D.C.: Brookings Institution, 1980.

A collection of essays on the economics, politics, and legal problems of taxation.

Aaron, Henry J.; Joseph A. Pechman, eds. *How Taxes Affect Economic Behavior.* Washington, D.C.: Brookings Institution, 1981.

The view of various authors are presented in order to determine the possible effectiveness of tax policy to stimulate economic growth.

Dworak, Robert J. *Taxpayers, Taxes, and Government Spending: Perspectives on the Taxpayer Revolt.* New York: Praeger Publishers, 1980.

Examines the results of the taxpayer revolt of 1978 and offers alternatives to higher taxes for all levels of government.

Pechman, Joseph A. *Federal Tax Reform.* 4th ed. Washington, D.C.: Brookings Institution, 1983.

This reference covers the major deficiences in the federal tax system and discusses various tax reform measures.

Pechman, Joseph A. *Who Paid the Taxes, 1966–85?* Washington, D.C.: Brookings Institution, 1985.

The distribution of taxes by income groups under various shifting and incidence assumptions is shown. This is the best tax incidence study to date.

Sharp, Ansel M.; Kent W. Olson. *Public Finance.* St. Paul, Minn.: West Publishing, 1978.

Chapters 7 and 8 provide a more thorough examination of the principles of taxation and shifting and incidence of taxes.

THE BIG NATIONAL DEBT

The course of the national debt
The relative growth in the national debt
  Gross federal debt as a percent of GNP
  Federal debt held by the public as a percent of total credit market debt
What is the national debt?
  Types of federal securities
  Who owns the national debt?
Problems with a large national debt
  The views of the public
  The concern of economists
  Summary in regard to national debt problems
Economic analysis of national debt financing
  Methods of finance
  Economic effects of government debt financing
  Differing effects of tax and debt financing
Managing a large national debt
  Debt management policy
  Debt management principles
When should the government borrow?
  Public investments
  Economic instability
  Is government debt accumulation necessary during wartime?
  A budget proposal
Summary

Checklist of Economic Concepts

Gross federal debt
Federal debt held by the public
Credit market debt
Primary burden
Secondary repercussions
Balanced budget
Budget deficit
Budget surplus
Monetizing the debt
Debt management policy
Near money
Public investments
Recurrent expenditures
Fiscal rules
The current account
The investment account
The stabilization account

16

The Big National Debt

Is it bad?

> Mythology distracts us everywhere—in government as in business, in politics, in economics, in foreign affairs as in domestic affairs. . . .
>
> The myth persists that Federal deficits create inflation, and budget surpluses prevent it. . . .
>
> Obviously, deficits are sometimes dangerous—and so are surpluses. But honest assessment plainly requires a more sophisticated view than the old and automatic cliché that deficits automatically bring inflation. . . .
>
> There are myths also about our public debt. It is widely supposed that this debt is growing at a dangerously rapid rate. In fact, both the debt per person and the debt as a proportion of our gross national product have declined sharply.
>
> Moreover, debts public and private are neither good nor bad in and of themselves. Borrowing can lead to overextension and collapse—but it can also lead to expansion and strength. There is no single slogan in this field that we can trust.[1]

The national debt, the debt of the federal government, is big. For every woman, man, and child, the national debt was $6,652 in 1984. It will be much higher in years to come if history repeats itself.

THE COURSE OF THE NATIONAL DEBT

People probably became very concerned when the national debt topped $1 billion for the first time. It did this about 120 years ago

---

[1]Office of the Federal Register, National Archives and Records Service, General Service Administration, *Public Papers of the Presidents, John F. Kennedy, 1962* (Washington, D.C.: U.S. Government Printing Office, 1963), pp. 471–73.

when we were fighting each other over the question of slavery. Can you guess when the Civil War national debt high of $2.75 billion was exceeded? It occurred during the first World War. The debt of the U.S. government reached $27 billion in August 1919. During the decade of the 1920s, the national debt was reduced, distinguishing this period for decades to come as the decade to reduce the national debt. The national debt shot upward again during the decade of the 1930s. The cause was another war, but a different kind of war. The war was a fight against a domestic enemy— unemployment. To wage this fight, the government tried spending what seemed at that time to be a lot. The part of the spending not paid for by taxes was paid for by government borrowing. This is the way the national debt was increased then and the way it is increased now.

The $32 billion increase in the national debt between December 31, 1930, and June 30, 1940, was small in comparison to the increase in the debt of over $200 billion during World War II. The highest World War II debt was $280 billion reached on February 28, 1946. After reductions in the debt for several years after the war, the debt started climbing again during the 1950s. This story was repeated in the 1960s and has continued to the present. The national debt reached $2.133 trillion in fiscal year 1986, and is estimated to be $2.4 trillion in fiscal year 1987.

A major point surfaces in this scenario of the history of the national debt: namely, the growth in the debt is generally associated with wars and economic slumps. The most recent upsurge in the national debt is due to recessionary-induced budget deficits and to structural budget deficits. Structural budget deficits are deficits that occur at high employment levels because of tax cuts and expenditure increases.

THE RELATIVE GROWTH IN THE NATIONAL DEBT

In order to place the historical rise in the national debt in perspective, this section relates the growth in the debt of the U.S. government to the growth in the nation's income, to the growth in private debt, and to the growth in state and local debt.

Gross federal debt as a percent of GNP

The national debt as a percent of the nation's income, the GNP, declined steadily between 1945 and 1974. Near the end of World War II, in 1945, the national debt soared to over 100 percent of the GNP. After this war and during the 1950s, the 60s, and the first part of the 70s, the nation's income grew faster than the national debt,

FIGURE 16–1
Gross federal debt as a percent of GNP in selected fiscal years, 1945–1987

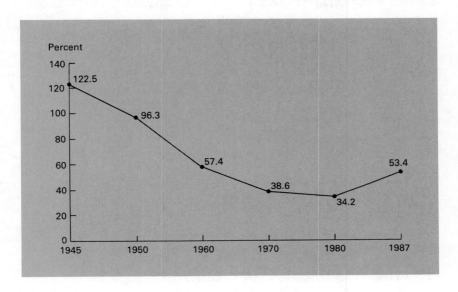

Source: *Economic Report of the President*, January 1987, p. 331.

with the national debt declining to 35 percent of the GNP in fiscal year 1974 (Figure 16–1). The national debt–GNP ratio increased slightly in 1975 and 1976, reflecting primarily the impact of the 1973–75 recession on the national debt and on the GNP. The downward trend in the ratio of the national debt to the GNP continued again in 1977 until the 1981–82 recession. This recession, coupled with major tax cuts and the growth in federal outlays, caused huge federal budget deficits that resulted in, of course, large increases in the national debt. The national debt as a percent of the GNP is estimated to be approximately 53.4 percent in fiscal year 1987.

Federal debt held by the public as a percent of total credit market debt

Another way to understand the relative importance of the federal debt is to compare the growth in the federal debt held by the public to the growth in total credit market debt. The federal debt held by the public is the federal debt held by Federal Reserve Banks and private investors such as individuals, businesses, banks, and state

FIGURE 16–2
Federal debt held by the public as a percent of total credit market debt in selected fiscal years, 1929–1986

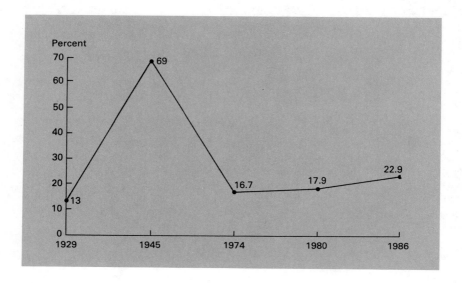

Source: Office of Management and Budget, *Special Analysis*, Budget of the United States government, Fiscal Year, 1988, pp. E 10–11.

and local government. Total credit market debt is composed of federal, state, and local government debt and private debt—namely, mortgage debt, consumer credit, and business borrowing. Figure 16–2 shows the publicly held federal debt as a proportion of total credit market debt in selected years since 1929.

The federal debt held by the public grew much more rapidly than credit market debt between 1929 and 1945, increasing from 13 percent in 1929 to 69 percent in 1945. The reasons for the faster growth in the federal debt were the depression in the early 1930s and World War II. During depressions, private debt is restricted by bad economic conditions; and during wars, especially a major war, private credit is scarce because of the huge demand for credit by government. During the period from 1945 to 1974, the average annual growth rate in federal debt was only 1.1 percent, while state and local government and private debt grew 10 percent and 9.7 percent, respectively. As a result, the federal debt held by the public decreased to 16.7 percent of the credit market debt in 1974. The impact of the federal debt on the credit market was much smaller in 1974 than it had been in the period following World War II.

A new federal debt growth trend emerged in 1975. The federal debt held by the public started to grow faster than the growth in state and local government debt and in private debt. The new trend in the federal debt started in 1975 because of the increases in federal deficits associated in part with the 1973–75 recession. Federal budget deficits continued to be incurred in the last part of the 1970s. The publicly held federal debt reached 17.9 percent of the credit market debt in 1980. Federal deficits accelerated in the 1980s. During the six years between 1980 and 1986, cumulative federal deficits were $1.1 trillion, and, as a consequence, the federal debt held by the public soared from $715 billion in 1980 to $1,746 billion in 1986. Even though the economy and private debt expanded rapidly after 1982, the federal debt held by the public as a proportion of total market debt increased to 22.9 percent in 1986.

What are the major causes of this new federal debt trend? Wars and recessions are usually the causes for the federal debt to rise as a share of total market debt. There has been no recession since 1982, and there has been no official war declared. But, there have been war-like increases in defense spending, continued increases in domestic spending programs, and major cuts in income tax rates.

WHAT IS THE NATIONAL DEBT?

The data on the national debt already referred to are in reference to the gross federal debt. It includes all securities issued by the federal government—interest-bearing and noninterest-bearing securities, securities held by citizens of this country, securities held by citizens of other countries, securities held by government agencies and trust funds, those held privately (individuals, businesses, insurance companies, etc.), securities held by the Federal Reserve, and those held by commercial banks. A federal security is a promissory note stating that the federal government will pay the holder or the owner of the note the principal, the amount of money borrowed, plus interest over a specified period of time. It is an obligation of the federal government to pay the holder so much money plus interest for the money borrowed. The government is the debtor or the borrower, and the owner of the federal security is the creditor or lender.

Types of federal securities

There are two major types of federal securities. They are marketable securities and nonmarketable securities. Marketable federal securities are bought and sold in the market by investors. The price of these securities is determined by market forces similar to those determining commodity prices, such as wheat, in competitive markets. Nonmarketable federal securities are nonnegotiable debt instruments and cannot be bought and sold in the market. However, they may be redeemed in cash or converted to another security.

Marketable securities. In 1986, marketable securities represented 73.7 percent of the interest-bearing debt. Examples of marketable securities are Treasury bills, notes, and bonds. The basic distinction among these securities is the difference in the period of time in which they come due or mature. Bills are usually of short maturity, less than one year, while notes range from one to five years, and bonds mature over longer periods of time. The shorter the maturity of the security, the more liquidity it provides the owner and the more frequent is the need for the federal government to refinance it. Most of the marketable debt is concentrated in bills and notes; bonds represented only 15.4 percent of the marketable debt in 1986.

Nonmarketable federal securities. Nonmarketable securities include convertible bonds, state and local government series, foreign issues, savings bonds, and the government account series. The most important nonmarketable securities are savings bonds and the government account series, which is held almost entirely by government agencies and trust funds. Together, these issues represented 80.9 percent of the nonmarketable debt in 1986. Savings bonds and notes are generally issued to attract the savings of the public and are redeemable in cash after specified periods of time. An example of nonmarketable securities in the government account series is the securities held by the social security trust fund. When a tax surplus occurs in the social security trust fund, the surplus is transferred to the U.S. Treasury in exchange for special issues in the form of nonmarketable securities.

Who owns the national debt?

Federal securities are held by U.S. government agencies and trust funds, Federal Reserve Banks, and private investors. Private investors include commercial banks, mutual savings banks, insurance companies, other corporations, state and local governments, and individuals. Private investors hold U.S. government securities because they represent a relatively safe income-yielding asset.

A significant change has taken place in the composition of holders of federal securities. The adage "we owe it to ourselves," meaning that the federal debt is held by U.S. citizens and institutions, is no longer generally true. Foreign holders of federal securities are now the single largest group of U.S. creditors. Private investors held $1,553.3 billion of federal securities in June 1986, and foreign holders accounted for $256.3 billion, or 16.5 percent of this total. Between June 1976 and 1984 alone, foreign holdings of the debt rose $170 billion. This spectacular growth in foreign-held federal securities in recent years reflects the relative growth in U.S. imports, especially the growth in oil imports. Most of these debt securities are short-term securities and are held by central banks. In recent years, a great deal of the acquisition of federal securities by central banks in other countries has been a part of their general operations to stabilize the dollar exchange rate. However, since most of these federal issues mature in less than one year and could be liquidated, strong pressures could be exerted on the dollar in years ahead.

PROBLEMS WITH A LARGE NATIONAL DEBT

Now that we know what is meant by the national debt and who owns it, we are perhaps in a better position to identify problems associated with it. Two views will be presented—the views of the general public and the views of economists.

The views of the public

Why is the public aroused and alarmed about a large national debt? The public fears that a huge national debt will bankrupt the economy and future generations will have to bear the burden of the federal debt. Are these fears justified?

The bankruptcy argument. The argument that a large national debt will lead to bankruptcy is primarily based on an analogy. An individual or a business that has a large debt may go bankrupt. It happens all the time. It is reasoned, then, that like an individual or business, the federal government may become bankrupt.

Unlike individuals and businesses, the federal government cannot go bankrupt in a legal sense. The federal government can always meet its debt obligations. It has the power to tax and the legal right to print money. Individuals and businesses do not have these sources of revenue and therefore are not like the federal government.

Shifting the debt burden. Many people are concerned about the national debt because they are worried about its burden on future generations. They would argue that, when the debt is incurred, the current generation is postponing paying for government goods and services and shifting the cost or burden to the future. This is not entirely untrue as far as it goes. The difference between tax financing and debt financing is that in the former case individual taxpayers pay money today for government goods and services today, while in the latter case taxpayers pay money in the future for government goods and services today. However, is debt financing, which shifts money costs to the future, necessarily a bad deal for future taxpayers? Suppose the government develops an irrigation project for $1 billion and finances it from selling securities. In the future, the government will have to service the debt by raising taxes to pay $1 billion plus interest. But what about the flow of benefits or income in the future? There is no *net* burden shifted to the future if income from the irrigation project is in excess of the costs of servicing the debt. As a matter of fact, there is a net gain to future taxpayers in this event.

The concern of economists

Economists, like the public, are concerned about a large national debt. Economists don't think much of the argument that a large national debt will bankrupt the government and the economy; however, they have had a great deal to say about the primary burden of the national debt. Unlike the public, economists are generally more concerned about the secondary repercussions of a large national debt, that is, the economic impact of the debt on prices, output, and distribution of output.

The primary burden of an internally held national debt. Two time periods should be distinguished in trying to locate the primary burden of the national debt—the *present*, when the debt is incurred, and the *future*, when the debt is serviced. Most economists agree that the primary burden of an internally held federal debt is in the present in the form of a sacrifice in private production. Assuming full employment, federal debt or tax-financed expenditures withdraw resources from private production. The value of goods and services that could have been produced is the primary burden or real cost. Since these goods are foregone in the present, the burden or real cost is in the present. What about the future when the national debt is serviced, that is, when interest charges have to be paid? Economists have reasoned that there is no primary burden in the future since the reduced incomes of taxpayers having to pay higher taxes are offset by the increased incomes of bondholders who received the interest payments. There is no decrease in private income. Economists realize, of course, that paying interest charges on the national debt may redistribute income. However, the income redistribution effects of servicing the national debt are considered a secondary effect, not a primary effect.

The primary burden of an externally held national debt. Economists do agree that the primary burden of an externally held national debt is shifted to the future. The essential difference is that the sacrifice in private real income and production does not take place until the future in the case of an externally held national debt. For example, suppose the government buys goods and services produced in another country and pays by selling government securities. This is no sacrifice in domestic private real income when the debt is incurred. However, in the future, when the national debt is serviced, a part of domestic private income is reduced since taxes are increased to service the external debt. It is not possible to offset the reduced income of taxpayers with the increased incomes of bondholders as in the case of an internally held national debt, for government securities are held in this case by people outside the country.

Income redistribution effects. The secondary effects of the national debt are the *income redistribution effects*, the *output effects*, and the *inflationary effects*. Servicing a national debt redistributes income and, therefore, alters the distribution of the nation's output among people. The income redistribution impact of servicing the national debt depends on the distribution of taxes among people and the ownership pattern of the federal debt. Suppose the federal tax system is less progressive than the ownership pattern of federal securities; or, stated more extremely, suppose only poor people pay taxes and only rich people own federal securities. What happens to the distribution of income if the government pays $10 billion in interest by increasing taxes by $10 billion? The answer is obvious; the distribution of income is shifted away from the poor to the rich. It is generally believed that a shifting in income from lower to upper income groups occurs because of the national debt, although the actual degree of redistribution could be determined only after a thorough examination of the relevant data.

Output effects. Our large national debt may reduce productivity and output. Taxes have to be increased in order to meet interest costs on the national debt. In this instance, the economy would be less efficient. It will not produce as much as it would if the national debt did not exist. These disincentive effects of taxes and other distortion effects that taxes may have are a worry.

Real output in the economy may be reduced in still another way by federal debt financing and the ensuing national debt. In the process of creating and servicing the debt, the federal government competes for private saving and, in effect, reduces private saving and private capital formation, that is, the accumulation of real capital assets. The ability of the economy to produce goods and services depends on its stock of capital. A reduced stock of capital—machines, tools, and plants—associated with the national debt, then, lowers the level of national output or income.

Inflationary effects. There are inflationary woes associated with a large national debt. For one thing, government spending financed from debt is likely to be more inflationary than government spending financed from taxes. This point will be covered more carefully in the next section. In addition, a large national debt like ours gives the economy a great deal of liquidity, that is, assets that are near or like money. This liquidity aspect of the national debt means that people will tend to spend at a higher rate than they otherwise would. The national debt, then, may make it more difficult to control inflation because of the liquidity effect.

Summary in regard to national debt problems

There are problems in connection with the national debt. Some of the fears of the public, however, are unfounded. They are often based on an analogy drawn between an individual and the government—an analogy that is often false. Economists, similar to the public, have their worries about the national debt. But economists differ from the public in that their concerns are more related to the economic effects of the national debt on the operation of the economy. The next section, economic analysis of national debt financing, examines these effects more carefully.

ECONOMIC ANALYSIS OF NATIONAL DEBT FINANCING

The following analysis, first, includes a discussion of the different methods of government finance, that is, the different ways in which the federal government can pay for goods and services. Second, the economic effects of government borrowing are presented; and third, the effects of tax and debt financing are compared and analyzed. The analysis draws upon the aggregate demand and supply framework presented in Chapter 13.

Methods of finance

The U.S. government has three primary ways of paying for goods and services. The government can pay for things out of current tax collections, borrow, and create money.

Tax finance. The current income of the federal government is primarily derived from its various taxes, such as income taxes, payroll taxes, and excise taxes. Taxes paid out of private income reduce private consumption and saving and, therefore, reduce private demand for goods and services. The government is said to be running a *balanced budget* when tax collections are equal to government expenditures, a *budget surplus* when tax collections are greater than expenditures, and a *budget deficit* when tax collections are less than government expenditures. The net effect of a balanced budget on aggregate demand tends to be neutral, the net effect of a budget surplus tends to reduce aggregate demand, and the net effect of a budget deficit tends to increase aggregate demand. Figure 16–3 illustrates the net effect of a budget surplus and deficit on the price level and output.

Debt finance. The government incurs debt to finance budget deficits and to pay for goods and services over a period of time. Government debt is incurred by government borrowing, that is, by the government selling securities to private investors who desire to buy them. There are differences between tax and debt financing. People have to pay taxes. People do not have to buy government securities. They do so because government securities are an alternative way of holding interest-yielding assets. Although tax and debt financing both may reduce private consumption and saving, debt financing does not change the total assets of people. It only changes the composition of assets, whereas tax financing reduces the assets of people. Lastly, tax financing is a way to pay for government goods and services today; and, as mentioned above, debt financing is a way to pay over a period of time.

Money creation. The federal government may finance budget deficits and pay for goods and services by creating money. Money may be created by the government printing more money and by the government selling securities to banks, assuming banks have excess cash reserves. This latter way is the modern way to create money or to monetize the debt. Let's illustrate how this is done. Suppose the government runs a $5 billion deficit and covers it by borrowing from

FIGURE 16–3
Net effect of a tax surplus and a budget deficit

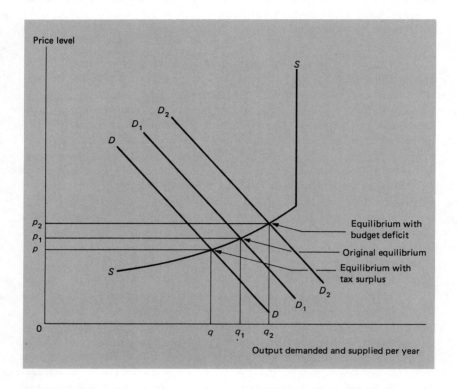

The original equilibrium is at price level p_1 where the output demanded and supplied is q_1. The net effect of a tax surplus is to reduce aggregate demand from D_1D_1 to DD. A tax surplus means that the government is taking more away from the income stream than it is putting into the income stream, thereby causing a reduction in the price level and output. The net effect of a budget deficit is to increase aggregate demand to D_2D_2. A budget deficit means that the government is putting more into than it is taking out of the income stream.

banks. The initial effect of the deficit expenditure is to increase demand deposits and cash reserves of banks by $5 billion. The effect of government borrowing from banks is to reduce cash reserves and to increase government securities held by banks. Then the net effect of the whole fiscal operation is to increase demand deposits or the money supply by $5 billion. A budget deficit of $5 billion has given rise to an increase in the money supply of $5 billion. Thus, in this instance, government debt has been monetized. Is the federal debt always monetized? The answer is no—only in this case when government securities are sold to banks. The money supply is not increased when government borrowing is from nonbank sources such as individuals, businesses, corporations, and so on. Thus, increases in government debt may or may not lead to increases in the money supply. The method of finance will be referred to as money creation when the money supply increases. This terminology stresses the important fact that the debt is monetized.

Economic effects of government debt financing

Although government debt financing may reduce both private consumption and saving, it is likely to have its major impact on private saving. The part of the nation's income that is not consumed is saved. Saving may flow into noninterest-yielding assets such as demand deposits, interest-yielding assets such as private securities and government securities, and real investments. Government securities compete with private securities and all other alternative uses for saving. Thus, when the government borrows, that is, sells securities to individuals, businesses, corporations, and the like, the government is tapping saving and reducing the amount of saving available for private borrowing and investment. Another way of saying this is that government borrowing increases the demand for saving or loanable funds; and, consequently, upward pressures are exerted on the price paid for loanable funds or the rate of interest. This is shown in Figure 16–4. The effect of a higher rate of interest is to discourage private investment. Therefore, increases in government debt may directly reduce private debt and private investment, and indirectly reduce private investment through exerting upward pressures on the rate of interest.

When the government creates money to finance budget deficits, private saving and investment may not be reduced. In this instance, the money supply is increased and the rate of interest may remain unchanged (Figure 16–4). The difficulty here is that, especially at near or full employment, financing the deficit in this way may lead to a demand-pull inflation. The question as to the best way of financing a deficit depends on the state of the economy. Government debt financing is preferable during periods of high production and inflation, and creating money is preferable when the economy is in a deep recession or depression.

Differing effects of tax and debt financing

The differing effects of tax and debt financing may be known by now. However, several important points can still be stressed. Both

FIGURE 16–4
The effect of government borrowing and money creation on the rate
of interest

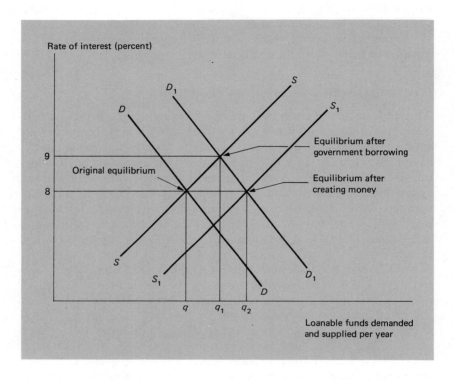

The original equilibrium is at the rate of interest of 8 percent where loanable funds
(saving, etc.) demanded equal loanable funds supplied. Government borrowing
increases the demand for loanable funds from DD to D_1D_1, causing the rate of interest
to rise to 9 percent. Money creation, that is, government borrowing from banks
increases supply to S_1S_1. In this case, the rate of interest may remain at 8 percent as
shown.

tax and debt financing (borrowing from nonbanks) will reduce private demand. Tax financing does it by reducing consumption and
saving and leaving people with fewer assets. Debt financing does it
by reducing primarily saving and increasing the rate of interest.
Which has the greatest downward pull on the economy, tax or debt
financing? Tax financing probably pulls the economy downward the
most, because taxes are a direct leakage from the private income
stream; but both could have a similar downward impact.

Thus, excluding creating money, finance methods have a contractionary impact on the economy and offset the expansionary impact

of government expenditures. Sometimes you may hear people say that government borrowing is inflationary. What they probably mean is that government expenditures may be inflationary and, as compared to tax financing, the net effect of financing budget deficits by incurring debt will tend to be inflationary.

MANAGING A LARGE NATIONAL DEBT

How would you like to be the manager of the national debt? You would be involved in big business. You would have to determine the kinds of government securities to be used and the amounts of each. You would have to determine how they are to be sold and who is likely to buy them. You would be concerned with the economic effects on the securities market of your decisions, and you would desire to coordinate your decision with decisions made in regard to monetary and fiscal policy, which are closely related.

Debt management policy

Debt management policy takes as given the size of the national debt and the cost and availability of money. The size of the national debt is determined by fiscal policy, and the cost and availability of money and credit are in the domain of monetary policy. Debt management policy is essentially concerned with the structural characteristics of the national debt, namely, the types of securities, the ownership pattern, and the maturity distribution of the national debt.

Debt management principles

Stabilization role. Economists differ as to what they believe should be the stabilization role of debt management policy. Some economists argue that debt management policy should be neutral; that is, it should be designed to have no appreciable effect on the economy. Others argue that debt management policy should play a positive role in stabilizing the economy. This would mean, during inflationary periods, that the debt coming due should be funded or refinanced into longer term government securities. The effect of this would be to put upward pressures on the long-term rate of interest and thereby discourage private investment spending. It is the long-term interest rate rather than the short-term rate that is relevant in regard to investment decisions. An alternative to investment is to make loans, especially long-term loans. The long-term rate indicates the cost of acquiring long-term funds for investment.

During recessions and unemployment, the stabilization role of debt management policy would consist of funding the debt coming due into shorter term debt or even money. Since the government's demand for long-term funds would be reduced, this would exert downward pressures on the long-term rate of interest and encourage private investment.

Minimizing interest cost. A principle of debt management often cited is the idea that debt management policy should be designed to minimize the interest cost of the national debt. This would mean, essentially, funding the debt into short-term securities when the long-term rate is high and funding into long-term debt when the long-term rate of interest is low. The difficulty with this idea is that the effects of such a policy would tend to intensify ups and downs in the economy. The long-term rate of interest is usually low during a recession. If the government increased the supply of long-term securities in a recession, this would tend to drive up long-term interest rates and worsen the recession. Thus, minimizing interest cost on the national debt would be desirable only if it can be done without worsening recessionary and/or inflationary forces.

Lengthening the debt. A major problem with the national debt is that it is concentrated at the short end of the market. This means that a high percent of government securities outstanding is in the form of short-term securities such as U.S. Treasury bills that come due within a year. For example, 37.4 percent of marketable securities matured within a year in 1986. The uncertainty and impact on the securities market of the government having to enter the market to fund a huge amount of the existing national debt in this brief time span can be significant. Treasury officials and economists alike agree that the maturity distribution of the national debt should be increased. This would enable the government to better manage and plan its debt management operations and would reduce the frequency and the amount of government securities that would have to be refinanced in a given year. Figure 16–5 shows the impact of refinancing short-term debt into long-term debt on short-term and long-term interest rates.

WHEN SHOULD THE GOVERNMENT BORROW?

The economic effects of government borrowing, and problems associated with a large national debt, have been examined. An important question, however, still remains unanswered. When should the government borrow or, alternatively, when is government borrowing the best or most efficient method of government finance?

FIGURE 16–5
Refinancing short-term government debt into long-term debt

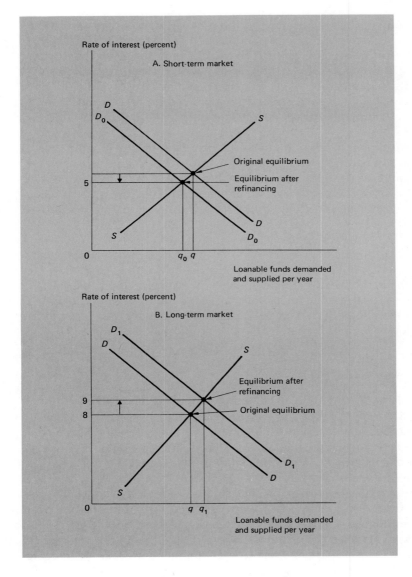

The effect on the rate of interest of refinancing short-term government debt into long-term debt is to put upward pressures on the long-term interest rate and downward pressures on the short-term interest rate. The reason for this is that this debt management operation increases the demand for long-term loans and decreases the demand for short-term loans. Refinancing, that is, paying off long-term government securities, tends to have the opposite effects—decreases the long-term interest rate and increases the short-term rate.

Public investments

Government borrowing may be the efficient way to pay for investment or capital goods. These goods such as bridges, dams, schools, and hospitals provide benefits or real income to society over a period of time. Government borrowing, similar to private borrowing, permits the spreading of the cost of investment goods over a period of time. In this way, costs and benefits can be related over a time span, avoiding the heavy tax claims on private income in a single year.

Government activity of any sort, regardless of how it is financed, should not be undertaken unless it is profitable to do so. In the case of public investments, this means that the present value of the net benefits from the public investment should exceed the present value of the cost of the public investment. After this profitability criterion is met, government borrowing is a legitimate way to distribute the costs of the investment over time.

If government debt is incurred only to pay for profitable public investments, the growth in the national debt would be limited to the growth in public investment goods. Government debt incurred to finance a given public investment project would be paid off over the lifetime of the project. Thus, for the national debt to grow over time, the stock of public investment goods would have to grow.

Economic instability

If the economy operated at full employment without inflation all the time, the only justification for government borrowing would be to finance public investments. However, this is not the case. The economy experiences ups and downs; that is, the economy experiences economic instability. A responsibility of the federal government is to pursue a fiscal policy that tends to stabilize the economy.

The stabilization responsibility of the federal government suggests three fiscal rules to be followed. First, assuming full or near full employment and a stable or near stable price level policy designed to stabilize the economy would dictate a balanced budget. In this way, the impact of fiscal operations on the level of aggregate demand would be largely neutral. Second, under the assumption of very high or full employment and inflation, the appropriate fiscal policy would be a budget surplus. The effect of the tax surplus would be to reduce the level of aggregate demand and, therefore, mitigate the inflation. Third, when the economy experiences low levels of production and employment and a decline in the price level, a budget deficit is the appropriate fiscal policy. The effect of the budget deficit would be to stimulate the economy.

Then, the stabilization responsibility of the federal government justifies government borrowing in times of economic recessions. Even if the government does not consciously plan budget deficits, they would likely occur anyway since tax collections automatically decline during recessions.

Is government debt accumulation necessary during wartime?

A large part of the national debt arose due to government borrowing during wartime. Can this debt increase be defended on economic grounds? The answer is no. During wars, the economy operates at full employment. The economic problem is to transfer resources from private production to war production. This transfer has to be brought about by a decrease in private disposable income and private demand. The best way to do this is through tax financing. Taxes directly reduce private consumption and saving and are the effective way of releasing resources required to pay for the war.

Next to taxation, the best way for the government to finance war expenditures is to borrow from individuals and businesses by paying interest rates high enough to attract saving and reduce consumption. The worst financing alternative during war periods is money creation. This undermines the wage-price control system, which is usually established during major wars, and causes inflation when the war ends.

A budget proposal

A great deal of misunderstanding about budget deficits and the national debt could be clarified by dividing the federal budget into three major accounts—the current account, the investment account, and the stabilization account. The current account would always be kept in balance. This account would include all current costs, including interest costs on the national debt and current revenues exclusive of government borrowing. The investment account would include spending for investment goods and the debt incurred to finance these goods. The stabilization account would include spending programs designed to stabilize the economy and the methods used to finance these programs. The main reason for separating the budget into three major accounts is to make explicit the various responsibilities of government.

The current account recognizes the government's responsibility to manage its current operations based on principles of business and personal finance. Current costs should be met from current revenues. In the case of the government, this means, essentially, that tax revenues should pay for all current or recurrent expenditures such as expenditures for salaries, postal services, recreational services, supplies, interest on the national debt, medical services, welfare services, and so on.

The investment account recognizes that a nonrecurrent expenditure, that is, an investment expenditure, can be financed by government borrowing. This allows for the spreading out of the cost of the investment over a period of time. A $10 billion highway facility could be financed by the government incurring debt. However, the servicing of this debt, and operating and maintaining the highway facility, are current costs and would be paid from tax collections.

The stabilization account recognizes the government's responsibility for economic stabilization. Unemployment represents a waste of human and capital resources. Inflation has undesirable consequences; thus, on the stabilization account, a balanced budget, a tax surplus, or deficit spending would occur, depending upon the state of the economy. The fiscal rules would be (1) a balanced budget when the economy is at full employment without inflation, (2) a budget surplus when the economy is in a serious inflation, and (3) a budget deficit when the economy is in a recession.

With current federal budget procedures, it is difficult to evaluate government activities, since all expenditures are lumped together. Any budget position—a balanced budget, a surplus, or a deficit—is neither good nor bad in and of itself. It would be equally inappropriate for the government to incur debt to finance, say, increases in government employee salaries and not to incur debt to finance a profitable public investment or to promote employment when much unemployment exists.

SUMMARY

Do you now know the answer to the question: Is the national debt bad? You have studied many pages to probe, to understand, and possibly to answer this question. The organization of your answer could be as follows.

The size and growth of the national debt are closely connected to the way wars are financed and the debt incurred during economic recessions. As big as the national debt is, since 1945 it has declined relative to the nation's income and relative to private, state, and local government debt.

The national debt, or the gross federal debt, includes all the securities issued by the federal government. A federal security is a promissory note stating that the U.S. government will pay the owner its face value plus interest over a specified period of time. There are two types of government securities—marketable and nonmarketable. Federal securities are primarily purchased and owned by private investors, although federal securities are held also by government agencies and trust funds and Federal Reserve Banks. Most of the national debt is held by U.S. investors. However, in recent years, foreign investors have increased the amount they own and in fiscal year 1986 held 16.5 percent of the national debt held by private investors.

There are problems associated with a large national debt, but not all the worries of the public are well-founded. Economists are troubled also about a large national debt, especially with regard to the way the national debt may affect the operation of the economy. A large national debt may redistribute income away from low-income groups, reduce national output and the stock of capital, and increase prices.

The economic analysis of national debt financing focused on the three methods of financing—tax finance, debt finance, and money creation—and the effects on aggregate demand of each method of finance. Taxes exert a strong downward pull on aggregate demand by reducing private consumption and saving. Government borrowing from nonbanks tends to reduce aggregate demand by reducing saving and increasing the rate of interest. Government borrowing from banks (money creation) usually monetizes the national debt; that is, it increases the money supply.

Managing a large national debt is no easy task. Debt management policy takes as given the size of the national debt (fiscal policy) and the availability of money and credit (monetary policy), and determines the structural characteristics of the debt—types of securities, ownership pattern, and the maturity distribution of the national debt. Some economists believe that debt management policy should play a positive role with regard to economic stabilization, while some visualize a neutral role. There is general agreement that debt management policy designed to minimize the interest costs on the national debt is not always a desirable policy, and that the maturity structure of the national debt should be lengthened; that is, the national debt should be composed of fewer short-term securities and more long-term securities.

Government borrowing is the appropriate method of financing in two circumstances—to finance profitable public investments and to finance programs designed to stimulate employment. Money creation, that is, government borrowing from banks, is the appropriate method of finance when there is much unemployment and no danger of inflation.

Some of the misunderstanding about budget deficits and the national debt could be lessened by dividing the federal budget into three accounts: the current account, the investment account, and the stabilization account. These accounts recognize the various responsibilities of the government, which are to pay for current expenditures out of tax collections, to pay for investment goods over a period of time, and to prevent both unemployment and inflation. Although not a panacea for government inefficiencies, these accounts would possibly provide a better understanding and a basis for evaluating government deficit spending and the ensuing growth in the national debt.

SUPPLEMENTARY READINGS

Buchanan, James M. *Principles of Public Debt.* Homewood, Ill.: Richard D. Irwin, 1959.

James M. Buchanan disagrees with the conclusion of most economists concerning the primary burden of the federal debt and argues that it is in the future. Pages 48 to 63 are recommended for reading in order to study the argument of Buchanan.

Conference Board, The. *Federal Debt.* New York: The Conference Board, March 1979.

This is a good, brief review of important changes in the federal debt in recent times.

Eckstein, Otto. *Public Finance.* 3rd ed. Englewood Cliffs, N.J.: Prentice-Hall, 1973.

Chapter 7, entitled "The Economics of the Public Debt", covers the growth of the national debt and discusses the burden of the debt.

Mishan, E. J. *21 Popular Economic Fallacies.* 2nd ed. New York: Praeger Publishers, 1973, chapter 5.

One of the 21 popular economic fallacies covered by Mishan is the argument that the primary burden of the national debt is borne by future generations. "First, let us be clear about one thing: that is that the present generation cannot, in any usual sense, borrow from future generations" (p. 61).

Peters, Guy, and Richard Rose. *Can Government Go Bankrupt?* New York: Basic Books, 1978.

Deals with the political consequences of the modern welfare state coping with a large debt.

Rivlin, Alice M. *Economic Choices 1984.* Washington, D.C.: Brookings Institution, 1984.

Chapter 2 discusses the impact of deficits on interest rates.

Glossary

Ability-to-pay principle of taxation. The concept that taxpayers with higher incomes should pay more taxes than those with lower incomes.

Aggregate demand. The total quantities of goods and services demanded per unit of time by the economy at various price levels, other things being equal.

Aggregate demand policies. Policies based on aggregate demand theory. The goal of such policies is to stabilize aggregate demand at high levels of production and employment.

Aggregate supply. The total quantities of goods and services supplied per unit of time in the economy at various price levels, other things being equal.

Aggregate supply policies. Policies based on aggregate supply theory. The goal of such policies is to increase the level of employment through increases in aggregate supply.

Alternative costs. The concept that the cost of an increment in the output of any good or service is measured by the value of the goods and services that must be given up to obtain it.

Backward tax shifting. Shifting the burden of a tax to the owners of resources, usually in the form of lower prices paid for their resources.

Balance of payments. The relationship between a country's total monetary obligations per unit of time to other countries and other countries' obligations to the home country.

Balance of trade. The relationship of the value of a country's imports to the value of its exports of goods and services per unit of time. It is in *deficit* when more is owed for imports than is earned by exports; it is in *surplus* when less is owed for imports than is earned by exports.

Balanced budget. A governmental budget is balanced when its total receipts, mainly taxes, are equal to its total expenditures.

Benefits-received principle of taxation. The concept that taxpayers should pay taxes in accordance with the benefits they receive from the government.

Budget deficit. The situation that exists when a government's total receipts, mainly taxes, are less than its total expenditures.

Budget surplus. The situation that exists when a government's total receipts, mainly taxes, are greater than its total expenditures.

413

Capital resources. The nonhuman resources or ingredients used in production processes. Examples include land, buildings, machinery, tools, and both raw and semifinished materials.

Capital account transactions. International trade transactions that are long term in character, usually investment types of transactions.

Circular flow of production and income. The concept that expenditures of one group are the incomes for others, that in turn spend and provide income for still others.

Collectively consumed goods and services. Goods and services that are consumed by a group or groups as a whole and that yield benefits to the group or groups. No individual can single out and value his or her specific benefits.

Comparable worth. A proposal designed to reduce wage discrimination against females by extending the "equal pay for equal work" principle to require "equal pay for similar work." The similarity or comparability of jobs would be determined by factors such as the skill, effort, and responsibility the job requires.

Comparative advantage. The ability of a country to produce a good or service with a smaller sacrifice of alternative goods and services than can the rest of the trading world.

Comparative disadvantage. The inability of a country to produce a good or service except at greater sacrifice of alternative goods and services than is necessary for the rest of the trading world.

Concentration ratio. A measure of potential monopoly power, defined as the percent of an industry's sales (or assets or output) controlled by the four (or eight) largest firms in the industry.

Consumerism. A movement, or a set of movements, intended to enable consumers to improve their levels of well-being in the economy.

Cost-benefit analysis. Determination of and comparison of the costs and the benefits of an activity to evaluate its economic worth and the extent, if any, to which it should be carried on.

Cost-push inflation. Increases in the average price level initiated by increases in costs of production.

Current account transactions. International trade transactions that are more or less immediate or short term in character.

Current account (budgetary). One of the three major accounts into which a governmental budget can be divided. It represents all current costs, including interest costs on the national debt, and all current revenues exclusive of government borrowing.

Cyclical unemployment. Unemployment caused by economic fluctuations. It results from inadequate levels of aggregate demand.

Dead weight welfare loss due to monopoly. The reduction in social satisfaction, or welfare, due to the tendency of monopolists to restrict output below the socially optimal level.

Debt management policies. Policies to determine the structural characteristics of the national debt, that is, the types of securities, ownership pattern, and maturity distribution of the debt, given the size of the debt and the availability of money and credit.

Demand. The set of quantities of a good or service per unit of time that buyers would be willing to purchase at various alternative prices of the item, other things being equal.

Demand, changes in. Shifts in the entire demand schedule or curve for a good or service, resulting from changes in one or more of the "other things being equal." Should not be confused with a movement along a given demand schedule or curve.

Demand curve facing a firm. A curve showing the quantities per unit of time the firm can sell at alternative price levels, other things being equal.

Demand, law of. The general rule that at lower prices, buyers will purchase larger amounts per unit of time than they will at higher prices, other things being equal; that is, demand curves slope downward to the right.

Demand-pull inflation. Increases in the average price level initiated and continued from increases in aggregate demand.

Developed countries. Countries with relatively higher labor quality, relatively large accumulations of capital, and relatively higher levels of technology, all leading to relatively high living standards.

Diminishing returns. The principle that increments of a variable used with a fixed resource will lead to smaller and smaller increments in product output.

Discount rate. The rate of interest the Federal Reserve banks charge commercial banks when commercial banks borrow from the Fed.

Discrimination, employment. Failure of an employer to hire because of such noneconomic characteristics of potential employees as race or sex.

Discrimination, market. A situation in which the terms on which market transactions are based are not the same for all economic units in the market. Different consumers are charged different prices for identical product units. Employers pay different wage rates for workers with identical productivities.

Discrimination, nonmarket. Social discrimination based on social tastes, attitudes, customs, and laws. Unlike market discrimination, it is difficult to associate monetary costs with nonmarket discrimination.

Discrimination, occupational. Discrimination in the form of concentrations of minority groups in low-paying occupations.

Efficiency. The extraction of the greatest possible value of product output from given inputs of resources.

Elasticity of demand, price. The responsiveness of the quantity demanded of a product to changes in its price. Measured by the percentage change in quantity divided by the percentage change in price.

Elasticity of supply, price. The responsiveness of the quantity offered of a product to changes in its price. Measured by the percentage change in quantity divided by the percentage change in price.

Entry barriers. The various impediments to the entry of new firms into a market, usually classified as (1) private barriers and (2) government barriers.

Equal tax treatment doctrine. The concept that taxpayers in equal economic circumstances should be treated equally; that is, people in identical economic positions should pay the same amounts of taxes.

Equation of exchange. The truism that the money supply (M) times the velocity of circulation (V) equals quantities of goods and services sold in final form (Q) times the average price level (P).

Equimarginal principle. The allocation of spending among different inputs in such a way that the marginal benefits of a dollar spent on any one is the same as for that spent on any other input.

Equity in distribution. The subjective notion of what constitutes fairness in the distribution of income and the output of the economy.

Exchange rates. The costs of units of other countries' currencies in terms of units of the home country's currency.

Explicit costs. Costs of production incurred by the purchase or hire of resources by the producing unit.

Exploitation, consumer. Circumstances in which consumers pay a higher price for a product than its costs of production.

Exploitation, resource owner. Circumstances in which resource owners receive a lower price for a resource than the value of marginal product of the resource.

Exports. Goods and services that economic units in one country sell to other countries.

Externalities. Benefits or costs incurred in the production or consumption of goods and services that do not accrue to the producing or consuming unit, but rather accrue to the remainder of the society.

Fiscal rules. Rules governing taxation and expenditures when the federal government is pursuing stabilization policies. Examples include (1) a balanced budget during periods of full employment and price stability, (2) a budget surplus during periods of inflation, and (3) a budget deficit during periods of recession.

Forward tax shifting. Taxes shifted to consumers in the form of higher product prices.

Free riders. Those who receive social spillover benefits without paying the costs of producing the goods or services that yield them.

Frictional unemployment. Brief periods of unemployment experienced by persons moving between jobs or into the labor market; it is not related to basic aggregate demand or aggregate supply problems.

Full cost pricing. A situation in which the price of a product is equal to its average costs of production.

Government purchases. Government expenditures for currently produced goods and services.

Government transfer payments. Payments made by governments to persons who have made no contributions to current production of goods and services.

Gross federal debt. The total of all outstanding securities of the federal government, including interest and noninterest bearing securities, U.S. and foreign held securities, privately and publicly held securities, and securities held by both central and commercial banks.

Gross national product, current. The value of an economy's annual output of goods and services in final form at current prices.

Gross national product gap. The difference between an economy's potential GNP and its actual GNP.

Gross national product, per capita. Gross national product, either current or real, divided by the economy's population.

Gross national product, potential. The level of real GNP the economy could produce at full employment.

Gross national product, real. Gross national product corrected for changes in the price level relative to a base year price level.

Horizontal equity. The notion that people in the same economic circumstances should receive the same economic treatment.

Human capital. That part of the productive power of human or labor resources resulting from investment in education and training.

Implicit costs. Costs of production incurred by producing a unit for the use of self-owned, self-employed resources.

Imports. Goods and services purchased and brought into a country from abroad.

Incomes policies. Governmental restraints placed on wages and prices intended to reduce cost-push inflation thought to result from the monopolies of labor unions and business firms.

Individually consumed goods and services. Goods and services that benefit directly, and only, those persons who consume them.

Inflation. A rising average price level of goods and services.

Injections. New spending in the circular flow, including new investment, new government expenditures, and new exports.

Investment. The purchase by economic units of such real assets as land, buildings, equipment, machinery, and raw and semifinished materials.

Investment account (budgetary). One of the three major expenditure classifications into which a governmental budget may be divided. It includes spending for investment goods and the debt incurred to finance such spending.

Involuntary unemployment. The situation in which persons qualified for jobs, willing to work, and willing to accept the going wage rate are unable to find jobs. It occurs when the quantity of labor demanded is less than the quantity supplied at going wage rates.

Labor resources. Human resources, all efforts of mind and muscle, that are ingredients in production processes. They range from unskilled common labor to the highest levels of professional skills.

Leakages. Withdrawals from spending in the circular flow, including taxes, savings, and imports.

Lesser developed countries. Countries with relatively low living standards, usually the result of relatively low labor quality, relatively scarce capital, and relatively low levels of technology.

Living standards. The level of economic well-being of a population, usually measured in terms of its per capital real income.

Losses. The difference between a firm's total costs and its total revenues when total revenues are less than total costs, including as a part of total costs returns to investors in the firm sufficient to yield an average return on their investments.

Malthusian theory. The idea originated by Thomas Robert Malthus that a country's population tends to increase in geometric progression while its food supply tends to increase in arithmetic progression, thus holding living standards to a subsistence level.

Marginal benefits. The increase or decrease in the total benefits yielded by an activity from a one-unit change in the amount of the activity carried on.

Marginal costs. The change in total costs resulting from a one-unit change in the output of a good or service.

Marginal revenue. The change in the total revenue of a seller resulting from a one-unit change in the quantity sold of a good or service.

Market. The area within which buyers and sellers of a good or service can interact and engage in exchange.

Market, competitive. A market in which there are many sellers and many buyers of a good or service. No one buyer or seller is large enough to be able to affect the price of the product.

Market, imperfect competition. A market that falls between the limits of competitive on the one hand and monopolistic on the other. It contains elements of both.

Market, monopolistic. A market in which there is a single seller of a good, service, or resource.

Minimum wages. Wage rate floors set for specific occupations or groups of workers by governmental units or by labor unions.

Monetizing the federal debt. Financing deficits or paying off debt with newly created money. The additional money may be created through the sale of government securities to banks or through printing money.

Money creation. The creation of new checking accounts by financial institutions for economic units that borrow from them or that sell them earning assets. Fractional reserves enables such institutions to engage in money creation.

Money multiplier. The maximum multiple over excess reserves by which checking accounts can be expanded, given the required reserve ratio. It is equal to one divided by the required reserve ratio.

Money supply (M). Currency held by the public plus checkable accounts.

Monopoly power. The degree to which sellers can control the supply and hence the price of what they sell.

Near money. Assets that are easily convertible to cash; they are similar to money because they are very liquid.

Nonprice competition. Competition among firms in matters other than product price. It usually takes the forms of (1) advertising and (2) changes in design and quality of the product.

Open market operations. Federal Reserve purchases and sales of government securities for the purpose of increasing or decreasing commercial bank reserves.

Price ceiling. A maximum price set for a product, usually by a governmental unit. Sellers of the product are not permitted to charge higher prices.

Price discrimination. The sale of the same product to different persons or groups of persons at different prices.

Price, equilibrium. The price of a product at which buyers are willing to purchase exactly the quantities per unit of time that sellers want to sell.

Price floor. A minimum price set for a product, usually by a governmental unit or a group of sellers. Sellers are not permitted to sell at lower prices.

Price index numbers. A set of numbers showing price level changes relative to some base year.

Primary burden (of the national debt). The present and future decrease in private production brought about by the national debt.

Production. The process of using technology to combine and transform resources to make goods and services.

Production possibilities curve. A curve showing the maximum production possibilities in a two-product economy, given the economy's resources and its technology.

Profit maximizing output. The output per unit of time at which a firm's total revenue exceeds its total cost by the greatest possible amount. It is the output at which the firm's marginal cost equals its marginal revenue.

Profits. The difference between a firm's total revenue and its total cost when total revenue exceeds total cost, including as a part of total cost returns to investors in the firm sufficient to yield an average rate of return on their investments.

Progressive tax rates. A tax rate schedule that results in an increase in the ratio of tax collections to income as income increases.

Proportional tax rates. A tax rate schedule that results in a constant ratio of tax collections to income as income changes.

Public goods. Goods and services of a collectively consumed nature, usually provided by governmental units.

Public investments. Government spending for capital goods such as roads, bridges, dams, schools, and hospitals.

Quantity theory of money. The theory that changes in the money supply (M) will tend to cause changes in the same direction of total output (Q) and price level (P).

Rationing. The allocation of given supplies of a good, service, or resource among its users.

Recurrent expenditures. Expenditures that the government must make on an on-going basis, for example, salaries, interest on the national debt, postal services, and welfare services. Public investments are excluded.

Relative price. The price of a good or service relative to the prices of all other goods and services.

Relative tax treatment doctrine. The theory that taxpayers in different economic circumstances should pay different amounts of taxes.

Reserve ratio, legal (or required). The ratio of reserves to deposits that banks are required by law to maintain.

Resources. The ingredients that go into the production of goods and services. They consist of labor resources and capital resources.

Secondary repercussions (of the national debt). The income redistribution, output, and inflation effects of the national debt.

Semicollectively consumed goods and services. Goods and services that yield direct benefits to the consumers of them but that also yield social spillover benefits or costs to others.

Shortage. A situation in which buyers of a product want larger quantities per unit of time than sellers will place on the market. It may be caused by the existence of an effective price ceiling.

Social overhead capital. Capital used by the economy as a whole rather than being limited to use by specific firms. Examples include transportation and communications networks as well as energy and power systems.

Spillover benefits, social. Benefits from consumption or production activities that accrue to persons other than those doing the consuming or producing. Examples include the benefits of educational services to those other than the students receiving them. See also, **Externalities.**

Spillover costs, social. Costs of consumption and production imposed on persons or economic units other than those doing the consuming or producing. Examples include pollution of water, land, or the atmosphere. See also, **Externalities.**

Stabilization account (budgetary). One of the three major categories into which a governmental budget may be divided. It includes spending programs designed to stabilize the economy, together with the methods used to finance them.

Structural unemployment. Unemployment caused by a mismatch between the skills (or locations) of job seekers and the requirements (or locations) of available jobs.

Substitution effects. The effects of a price change of a good or service on the quantity purchased of it because of the substitution of relatively lower priced goods for it when its price increases and the substitution of the item for now relatively higher priced other goods when its price decreases.

Supply. The set of quantities of a good or service per unit of time that sellers would be willing to place on the market at various alternative prices of the item, other things being equal.

Supply, changes in. Shifts in the entire supply schedule or curve for a good or service, resulting from changes in one or more of the "other things being equal." They should not be confused with movements along a given supply schedule or curve.

Supply curve of a firm. A curve showing the quantities per unit of time a firm will place on the market at alternative price levels, other things being equal. The concept is valid for a competitive firm only, and coincides with its marginal cost curve.

Surplus. A situation in which sellers of a product place larger quantities per unit of time on the market than buyers will take. It may be caused by the existence of a price floor.

Tastes and preferences. Buyers' psychological desires for goods and services—one of the determinants of demand for any one product. A change in consumers' tastes and preferences for a product will shift the demand curve for it.

Tax efficiency. The extent to which a tax has a neutral impact on resource allocation, and is economical to collect and enforce, thus minimizing the total tax burden.

Tax incidence. The final resting place or burden of any given tax—who actually pays it.

Technology. The know-how and the means and methods available for combining resources to produce goods and services.

Terms of trade. The cost, in terms of the home country's goods and services, of importing a unit of goods or services from other countries.

Transfer payments. Payments made to persons or economic units that are *not* for services currently performed. They do not result in new output but simply transfer purchasing power from some persons or units to others.

Transformation curve. See **Production possibilities curve.**

Unemployment. The number of persons seeking jobs that are not able to find them at current levels of wage rates—a surplus of labor.

Vertical equity. The notion that persons in different economic circumstances should receive different rewards from the economic system.

Wage discrimination. Payment of unequal wage rates to persons with equal values of marginal product.

Wants. The unlimited or insatiable desires of humans that generate economic activity.

INDEX

A

Aaron, Henry J., 389
Abortion
  demand for, 137–39
  economic effects of legalizing, 137–39
  supply of, 137–39
Advertising, deceptive, 192, 194–95
Aggregate demand
  deficiencies in, 322–24
  and employment, 320–24, 326
  and inflation, 353–58
  nature of, 318–19
Aggregate supply
  and inflation, 353–58
  nature of, 319–20
  and unemployment, 320–25, 327–29
Agricultural Act of 1933, 40
Agricultural problems, 37–43
Alport, Geraldine, 188
Alternative-cost principle, 10, 70–72,
    127–28, 154–55
Alvarez, Rudolfo, 305
American Medical Association, 246–47
Antimonopoly policies, 300
Arvey, Richard D., 305

B

Balanced budget proposals, 382–83
Balance of payments, 221, 223–25
Balance of trade, 221, 223–25
Banking system, 343–51
Banks
  balance sheet of, 345
  commercial, 343–44
  Federal Reserve, 348–51
  functions of, 343–44
  lending activities of, 345–48
  reserve ratios of, 345–48
  reserves of, 345–48
Baumol, William J., 164

Beller, Andrea H., 294n
Bergman, Barbara R. 293n
Birth control, 19
Bonello, Frank J., 330
Boskin, Michael J., 389
Bowen, Howard R., 90
Brice, Thomas W., 261
Brown, Charles, 47n
Brown, Peter S., 285
Browning, Edgar, 47n
Brue, Stanley, 21
Buchanan, James M. 412
Budget, federal
  balanced, 382
  current account, 409–10
  deficits, 368, 392–97, 401
  investment account, 409–10
  proposals, 409–10
  stabilization account, 409–10
  surpluses, 391–92, 401
Burrows, James C., 118n

C

Capital account transactions, 220–21
Capital resources
  accumulation of, 13–14, 18–19, 276
  definition of, 7
  distribution of, 276
  pricing of, 274
Carper, Jean, 294n
Carson, Robert, A. 188
Chafetz, Janet S. 305
Chapman, Steven, 43, 61
Chase, Stuart, 196
Circular flow
  of economic activity, 316–18, 322–24
  injections into, 322–24
  leakages from, 322–24
Civil Rights Act of 1964 and 1965, 299
Coal, 98–99, 114–15

Collectively consumed goods and
services
and crime, 129–34
government production of, 130–31,
370–71
nature of, 129
and pollution, 149–50
Colleges and universities
donors to, 74–76
federal grants to, 74–76
private, 75
problems of, 64–66
public, 74–75
state support of, 74–76, 83–85
student support of, 85–86
tuition and fees of, 74–76
Comparable worth, 302–4
Comparative advantage and
disadvantage, 216–17
Competition
individual firm demand under, 172–
74
nature of, 28
price and output under, 172–76
profit maximization under, 172–76
Concentration ratios, 169–70
Consumer problems, 192–95
Consumer Product Safety Commission,
201
Consumers' Research, 197
Consumers' Union, 196–97
Corcoran, Mary, 292n
Cost-benefit analysis
of crime prevention, 131–34
of government expenditure, 369–70
of pollution control, 154–59
Costs
alternative-cost principle, 10, 70–72,
127–28, 154–55
of consumerism, 201–2
of crime, 127–28
of discrimination, 295–97
explicit, 72–73
of health services, 232–35, 254–58
of higher education
explicit, 73–76
implicit, 73–76
implicit, 72
Cowell, F. A., 285
Crandell, Robert W., 223
Crime
causes of, 126
costs of, 127–28
definition of, 124–25
and illegal acts, 124–25
and immorality, 124
against persons, 125

Crime—Cont.
prevention
benefits of, 127–28
"correct" level of, 131–34
costs of, 131–34
nature of, 127–28, 134–36
against property, 125
rate, 125–26
violent, 125
Crude oil; see Petroleum
Currency, 341–43
Current account transactions, 220–21

D

David, Daren, 260
Davis, Karen, 250n, 251n
Dead-weight welfare loss, 179–80
Debt management
lengthening the debt, 406
minimizing interest cost, 406
stabilization, 405–06
Demand
for agricultural products, 38
changes in, 30
of consumers, 29–30, 318, 322–24
definition of, 29–30
for educational services, 64–65
elasticity of, 36–37
for energy, 97–98
for foreign currencies, 219–21
of government, 318–19, 322–24
for health services, 238–42
for housing, 49–51
of investors, 318, 322–24
for labor, 44–46, 273–74, 312–14
law of, 171–72
market, 29–30, 171–72
for natural gas, 54–55
for petroleum, 97–98
Demand deposits
as a component of the money supply,
341–43
control of, 348–51
creation of, 346–48
Demeny, Paul, 17n
Dentzer, Susan, 25n, 61
Department of Energy, 27, 110–11
Depository institutions, 344
Discount rate, 349
Discrimination
alleviation of, 298–302
costs of, 295–97
educational, 298
employment, 292–93
nature of, 280
occupational, 293–94, 301–2
price, 294–95, 300

Discrimination—*Cont.*
  racial, 291–92, 297–98, 301–2
  sex, 291–94, 296–98, 301–4
  social, 297
  sources of, 290–91
  tastes for, 291
  wage, 291–92
Dolan, Edwin G., 61
Domencich, Thomas A., 118n
Douglas, Gordon K. 90
Doyle, Dennis P. 91
Dreifus, Claudia, 205
Duncan, Greg, 269n, 270, 286, 292n
Dworak, Robert J. 389

E

Eckstein, Otto, 412
Economic activity, 6–12
Economic assistance to LDCs, 18–20
Economic efficiency
  and discrimination, 295–97
  and farm programs, 42–43
  and health services, 247–50
  in higher education, 77–83, 87–89
  and inflation, 339–40
  in LDCs, 14–15
  nature of, 9–10
  and pollution, 150–54
  of price mechanism, 115–17
Economic growth
  in developed countries, 12–20
  in LDCs, 12–20
  in United States, 11–12
Education; *see* Higher educational
  services
Educational discrimination, 298, 300–301
Ehrlich, Paul R. 5n, 21
Elasticity of demand
  definition of, 36
  for health services, 238–39
  measurement of, 36–37
  in relation to total receipts, 36–37
Elasticity of supply of physicians'
  services, 243
Emergency Petroleum Allocations Act of
  1973, 107
Employment
  discrimination, 292–93
  minimum wage effects on, 47–48
Energy
  demand for, 97–98, 112
  government policies on, 104–11, 117–
    18
  sources of, 96, 98–104, 114–15
  supply of, 98–104, 112–15
Energy Development Bill, 111

Energy Policy and Conservation Act of
  1975, 107–11
Entry restrictions
  government, 180–82, 185–86
  to health care fields, 246–47
  private, 180–81, 185–86
Environment
  services of, 144–45
  and waste disposal, 145–46
Environmental Protection Agency, 159
Equal Opportunities Act, 301
Equation of Exchange, 352
Equimarginal principle, 134–36
Exchange rates, 218–21, 224–25
Exploitation, 290–91
Exports, 214–17, 220–21, 324
Externalities, 371–73

F

Fair Labor Standards Act of 1938, 26
Farm
  incomes, 37–40
  population, 39–40
  price supports, 26, 40–43
Farm programs
  and economic efficiency, 42–43
  evaluation of, 42–43
  and poverty, 42–43
  storage and loan, 40–43
Feder, Judith, 260
Federal Energy Agency, 108, 110
Federal Energy Regulatory Commission,
  27, 114
Federal finance methods
  debt, 401, 403–5
  money creation, 401–3
  taxes, 401, 403–5
Federal Power Commission, 27, 58–60,
  114
Federal Reserve System
  discount rate control, 349
  functions of, 348–49
  and money supply, 349–51
  open market operations, 349–50
  and required reserve ratio variation,
    349
  structure of, 348–49
Federal securities
  marketable, 395–96
  nonmarketable, 395–96
  ownership of, 396–97
Federal Trade Commission, 192
Federal Trade Commission Act of 1914,
  196
Fiscal policy, 406–7, 410
Food programs, 279
Food supply, pressures on, 6

Foreign exchange markets, 217–21
Fowler, J. M., 119
Fractional reserve banking, 345–46
"Free riders," 130
Free traders, viewpoint of, 212, 222–23
Friedman, Milton, 188, 206
Friedman, Rose, 206
Fuchs, Victor R. 260
Full employment, 311–17
Fusfield, Daniel R., 301n

G

Garfinkel, Irwin 276n, 286
Gilroy, Curtis, 47n
Goldberg, Marilyn P. 293n
Goodman, John C., 61
Government
  borrowing, 406–10
  budget balancing, 382–83
  debt financing
    effects of, 403–5
    methods of, 401–5
  expenditures, 365–73
  purchases, 366–68
  receipts, 368
  regulation, 197–98
  size of, 364–73
  tax financing, 401, 403–5
  transfer payments, 366–68
Gramm-Rudman-Hollings Act, 382–83
Green, Mark J. 167
Gross federal debt, 392–95
Gross national product (GNP)
  actual, 310
  per capita, 11–12
  definition of, 8
  gap, 310
  potential, 310
  real, 11, 326–28
  United States, 11–12, 326–28

H

Haley, Jack, 260
Halsey, Margaret, 289n
Hamblin, Mary, 293n
Harnish, Reno, 118n
Hartman, Heidi I., 305
Hathaway, J. W., 188
Haub, Carl, 19n, 21
Haveman, Robert H. 276n, 286
Health centers, 248–49
Health insurance, national
  alternative proposals for, 253–54
  effects on demand, 241–42, 256
  financing of, 252–53
  nature of, 250–57
Health maintenance organizations, 248, 279

Health services
  costs of, 232–35, 254–58
  demand for, 232–35, 238–42, 254–58
  entry barriers to, 246–47
  funding of, 231–32
  nature of, 231–32
  for the poor, 278–79
  problems of, 237–38
  quality; of, 234
  special characteristics of, 235–37
  spillover benefits of, 236
  supply of 242–45, 254–58
  trends in, 230–37
Heilbroner, Robert L., 226
Helms, Robert B., 58n
Heyne, Paul, 226
Higher educational services
  benefits of, 66–69
  costs of, 69–76
    incidence of, 75–76
    nature of, 72–74
  definition of, 64–67
  demand for, 66–67, 77–83
  direct consumption of, 67–68
  "free" provision of, 83
  human capital, investment in, 67
  incidence of benefits, 68–69
  spillover benefits, social, 68
  supplyof, 77–83
  support of, 65–66
    state, 74–76, 83–85
    student, 74–76, 85–86
Hofler, Richard A. 140
Holihan, John, 260
Hospitals
  costs of, 244–45
  investment in, 245
  supply of, 244–45
  technology in, 245
Housing
  markets, 48–54
  pricing of, 51–53
  and rent controls, 53–54
Human capital, 67, 300–301

I

Illegal activities
  as crime, 124–25
  economic effects of legalizing, 137–39
Immorality and crime, 124
Imperfect competition, 29, 169, 180–83
Imports, 214–17, 220–21
Income
  per capita, 11–12
  distribution of, 186–87, 270–73, 275
  family, determination, 275
  farm, 37–40
  flow of, 316–18, 322–24

Income—*Cont.*
  inequality of, 270–73, 275–77
  and monopoly power, 186–87
  of physicians, 243–44
  redistribution of
    through farm programs, 40–43
    by government, 277–84, 373
    through inflation, 338–39
    through public education, 83–89
  security, 279
  support programs, 277–84
Incomes policy, 357–58
Individually consumed goods and
  services, 128–29
Inflation
  causes of, 351–58
  control of, 353–58
  cost-push, 355–58
  definition of, 334–35
  demand-pull, 353–56
  effects of
    on efficiency, 339
    on health services costs, 233–34
    on income distribution, 338–39
    on output, 340
    on resource allocation, 339
    on wealth, 338–39
  and the energy crisis, 104–11
  measurement of, 335–36
  suppressed, 335
  trends in, 336–37
Inheritance
  of capital resources, 276
  of labor resources, 275
International trade
  capital account transactions, 220–21
  current account transactions, 220–21
  effects on production possibilities,
    213–17
  financing of, 217–21
  gains from, 213–17
  nature of, 212–21
Investment, 318–19, 322–24

J

Jain, Harish C. 305
Job Training Partnership Act, 277–78
Johnson, Conrad, 285
Johnson, William, 47n
Johnston, B. F. 21

K

Kennedy, Edward M. 229n
Kessel, Reuben A. 246n, 247n
Klarman, Herbert E. 236n, 238n, 244n
Kohen, Andrew, 47n
Kozak, Andrew F., 330

L

Labor resources
  definition of, 7
  distribution of, 275–76
  employment of, 44–48
  migration from the farm, 39–40
  pricing of, 44–46
  quality of, 12–13, 18–19, 275–76
LaForce, J. Clayburn, 120
Lazenby, Helen, 232–33
Leftwich, Richard H., 61
Levit, Katherine R., 232–33
Licensing of physicians, 247
Lindsay, Cotton M., 260
Living standards
  measurement of, 10–12
  population pressure on, 6
    in developed countries, 15–19
    in lesser developed countries, 15–20
    in United States, 11–12
Locke, W. H., 360
Lorenz curve, 270–73
Losses, 180–81
Lutterman, Kenneth G. 305

M

MacAvoy, Paul W., 57n
McConnell, Campbell R., 329
McCormick, John, 25n
MacDonald, Maurice, 286
McGowan, Daniel A., 206
McKenzie, Richard B., 140, 164
Magnuson, Warren G., 294n
Malthus, Thomas R., 5–6
Manpower training programs, 277–78
Marginal benefits
  of crime prevention, 132–34
  of pollution control, 156–59
  private, 371–73
  social, 371–73
Marginal costs
  of crime prevention, 132–34
  of firms, 174–76
  of pollution control, 156–63
  private, 371–73
  social, 371–73
Marginal revenue
  of competitive firms, 172–74
  of monopolized firms, 177–78
Marginal revenue productivity, 273–74
Markets
  agricultural, 37–43
  competitive, 28–29
  definition of, 28
  imperfectly competitive, 29, 168–70
  monopolistic, 29, 168–70
Medicaid, 241–42, 278–79

Medical practice, group, 248
Medical schools
  barriers to entry into, 246
  length of program, 249
Medical societies, county, 247
Medicare, 241–42, 278–79
Mellor, J. W., 21
Mermelstein, David, 305
Miller, James C., III, 206
Miller, Roger L., 120, 140, 165, 206,
  291n, 329
Millert, Robert B., 165
Minimum wages, 47–48
Mishan, E. J., 412
Mitchell, Edward J., 112n
Monetary Control Act of 1980, 348–49
Monetary policy, 349–58
Money
  creation of, 343–48, 401–2
  definition of, 341
  functions of, 341
  quantity theory of, 352–53
  supply of, 341–43
Monopoly
  entry restrictions under, 180–81, 185–
    86
  nature of, 29, 168–69
  price and output under, 176–80, 184–
    85
  profit maximization under, 178–80
Monopoly power
  of AMA, 246
  and discrimination, 290–91, 300
  effects of, 176–83, 184–87
  individual firm demand under, 177–
    78
  nature of, 168–70, 181–83
Murphy, Elaine, 19n, 21
Murray, Allen E., 95

N

Nadar, Ralph, 167, 197, 201
National debt
  and bankruptcy, 397
  burden of, 397–98
  definition of, 395
  externally held, 396–97, 399
  financing of, 401–5
  growth of, 391–95
  income redistribution effects of, 399
  inflationary effects of, 400
  internally held, 396–99
  management of, 405–6
  output effects of, 399–400
  ownership of, 396–97
  problems with, 397–400
  in relation to
    GNP, 392–93
    credit market debt, 393–95

National health insurance, 250–57
Natural gas
  markets, 54–60
  production, 114
Natural Gas Policy Act of 1978, 27, 110
Negative income tax
  advantages and disadvantages of, 284
  and income support, 284
  nature of, 283–84
Nonprice competition, 182–83, 186
North, Douglas C., 120, 140, 165, 206,
  291n
Nuclear energy, 115

O

Oates, Wallace E., 164
Occupational discrimination, 293–94,
  301–2
Olsen, Kent, 389
O'Neill, June, 302n
Open market operations, 349–50
Opportunity-cost principle; see
  Alternative-cost principle
Owen, John D., 298n

P

Paramedical personnel, 247
Pasztor, Andy, 165
Pauley, Mark V., 261
Pechman, Joseph A., 252n, 272n, 378,
  379, 389
Pelzman, Sam, 206
Peters, Guy, 412
Petroleum
  allocation of, 107–10, 115–17
  conservation measures, 110–11
  demand for, 97–98
  embargo on, 95–96, 106–7
  imports of, 100–104
  prorationing of, 118
  reserves, 112–14
  shortages of, 95–96
  supplies of, 98–104, 112–14
  U.S. production of, 100–104
Physicians
  incomes of, 243–44
  licensing of, 247
  role in health services, 235
  supply of, 242–43
Pindyck, Robert S., 57n
Pollution
  of air, 146–47
  causes of, 149–50
  control
    through assignment of property
      rights, 163
    benefits of, 155–59
    costs of, 154–59
    by direct means, 159–60

Pollution—*Cont.*
  control—*Cont.*
    by indirect means, 160–63
    of land, 148–49
    nature of, 144–49
    and resource use, 150–54
    of water, 147–48
Population growth
  in developed countries, 15–17
  government policies toward, 18–19
  and health services, 234–35
  in lesser developed countries, 15–17
  positive restraints on, 6
  preventive restraints on, 6
  in United States, 11
Population problems, 5–6
Poverty
  alleviation of, 277–84
  causes of, 12–17, 273–77
  and crime, 126
  and farm problems, 43
  and higher education, 84–85
  incidence of, 267–70
  nature of, 3–6, 266–70
  number of persons in, 267–70
Prell, Michael, 293n
Price
  ceilings
    on natural gas, 27, 57–60
    on petroleum, 104–7, 115–17
    on rents, 27, 53–54
    on shortages, 104–7
  discrimination, 294–95
  equilibrium, 33–36
    above, 34–35
    below, 35–36
  floors
    in agriculture, 26, 40–43
    via storage and loan programs, 40–43
    on wages, 26–27, 47–48
  index numbers
    construction of, 10–11, 335–36
    consumer, 335–37
Product differentiation, 181, 182–83
Production possibilities curve, 8–10, 70–72, 154–55, 213–17, 296–97
Profit maximization
  in competitive markets, 172–78
  in monopolized markets, 176–80
  nature of, 172
Profits, 172–81
Protection
  from cheap foreign goods, 222
  of key industries, 225
  Protectionists, viewpoint of, 211, 222–23
Prostitution, 139
Public assistance, 279–80

Public goods, 130–31, 408
Public investment, 408
Pure Food and Drug Act of 1960, 196
Putallaz, Ann, 360

Q–R

Quantity theory of money, 352–53

Raspberry, William, 363n
Remarque, Erich M., 333n
Rent controls, 27, 53–54
Resources
  allocation of, 38–40, 51–54, 57–60, 77–83, 134–35
  definition of, 7–8
  exhaustible, 145
  pricing of, 273–74
  scarcity of, 7–8
Rivlin, Alice, 412
Robbins, Philip K., 286
Rogers, Harrell R., Jr., 286
Rose, Richard, 412
Russell, Louise B., 261

S

Sales promotion, 181–83
Salkever, David S., 261
Savings, 322–24
Scherer, Frederick M., 184n
Schiller, Bradley R., 330, 360
Schlink, Frederick J., 196
Schultz, Robert S., 21
Seligman, Joel, 167
Semicollectively consumed goods, 129–30
Shapiro, Daniel, 25n
Sharp, Ansel M., 389
Shepherd, William G., 360
Shortages
  causes of, 35–36
  of housing, 53–54
  of natural gas, 58–60
  of petroleum, 95–96, 104–11
Siddayao, Corazon M., 246n, 248n, 249n
Sloan, Peter J., 305
Smith, Adam, 38
Smith, Paula, 209–10
Social discrimination, 297
SOcial service programs, 278
Social spillover
  benefits
    of education, 68–69, 84
    of health services, 236
    of semicollectively consumed goods, 129–30, 271–72
  costs
    of consumerism, 200–201
    of crime, 127

Social spillover—*Cont.*
  cost—*Cont.*
    of semicollectively consumed goods,
      129–30, 271–72
Social security, 278–80
Somers, Herman M. 245, 246n, 248n
Spiegelman, Robert G., 286
Starratt, Patricia E., 59n
Steindl, Frank G., 339n
Stewart, Charles T., 246n, 248n, 249n
Storage and loan program
  costs of, 42–43
  economic effects of, 42–43
  nature of, 40–43
  and surpluses, 42–43
Subsidies, farm
  economic effects of, 42–43
  nature of, 40–41
Supply
  of agricultural products, 38
  changes in, 31, 33
  definition of, 30–31
  of educational services, 77–83
  of foreign currencies, 219–21
  of health services, 242–45, 254–58
  of housing, 51
  individual firm, 175–76
  of labor, 46
  market, 30–33, 176
  of natural gas, 55–56
  of petroleum, 98–104, 112–14
Surpluses
  causes of, 34–35
  of farm products, 42–43
  of labor, 47–48
Swartz, Thomas R., 330

T

Taxes
  ability to pay principle, 374
  benefits received principle, 375
  and collectively consumed goods,
    130–31
  corporation income, 379–81, 384–87
  efficiency of, 375–76
  equity of, 374
  federal, 378–81
  and fiscal policy, 405–6
  and higher education, 83–87
  incidence of, 376–79
  inequities of, 365
  as leakages from the circular flow,
    322–24, 379
  local, 379
  negative income, 282–84
  output, 376–77
  payroll, 379–81
  personal income, 377, 379–81, 384–87

Taxes—*Cont.*
  and pollution control, 160–63
  property, 379–81
  rates of, 379–81, 384
  reform of, 381–87
  sales, 376–77
  sources of, 374–75, 379–81
  state, 378–81
  trends in, 368, 369
  windfall profits, 110
Taylor, Ronald A., 165
Technology, 8, 14
Terkel, Studs, 265n, 309
Terms of trade, 213–16
Thomas, Rich, 25n
Thurow, Lester C., 226, 286, 300n,
  301n, 305
Transfer payments, 366–68
Troy, Frosty, 210n
Tullock, Gordon, 140
Treiman, Donald J, 305

U–V

Unemployment
  causes of, 316–25
  control of, 325–28
  cyclical, 314
  definition of, 311–12
  effects of
    on GNP, 310
    on social relations, 310–11
  frictional, 312–13
  incidence of, 315–16
  involuntary, 312–13
  and minimum wages, 47–48
  rates of, 314–15
  structural, 313–14
Universities; *see* Colleges and
  universities

van der Tak, Jan, 19n, 21
Vanderwaerdt, Lois, 305
Vernier, Paul, 285

W–Z

Wage discrimination, 291–92
Wage rates
  determination of, 46, 273–74
  and unemployment, 46–47, 312
Waldo, Daniel R., 232–33
Wang, Penelope, 25n
Wants, 6–7
Wastes
  biodegradable, 145
  disposal of, 145–49
  from economic activity, 145
  recycling of, 145–46
Weathers, Diane, 25n

Weidenbaum, Murray L., 118n, 201, 206
Weiner, Samuel, 286
Weintraub, Sidney, 357n, 360
Welfare, consumer, 194–95, 198–204
Wentworth, Donald R., 21
White, Ann D., 140
Windfall profits tax, 110
Windham, Douglas M., 91
Wong, S. L., 21

Yandles, Bruce, 206